The Power and Paradox of Physical Attractiveness

The Power and Paradox of Physical Attractiveness

Gordon L. Patzer, Ph.D.

BrownWalker Press
Boca Raton • 2006

The Power and Paradox of Physical Attractiveness

BrownWalker Press
Boca Raton, Florida
USA • 2006

ISBN: 1-58112-443-0 (paperback)
ISBN: 1-58112-444-9 (ebook)

BrownWalker.com

Library of Congress Cataloging-in-Publication Data

Patzer, Gordon L.
  The power and paradox of physical attractiveness / Gordon L. Patzer.
      p. cm.
  Includes bibliographical references and index.
  ISBN 1-58112-443-0 (pbk. : alk. paper)
  1. Interpersonal attraction. I. Title.

HM1151.P38 2006
302'.13--dc22

                    2006008534

Table of Contents

List of Tables

List of Figures

Preface

The Power and Paradox of Physical Attractiveness asserts that physical attractiveness is a phenomenon with far-reaching influences and contradictions. These influences and contradictions transcend surface looks whereupon physical attractiveness concurrently propels and connects to a phenomenal structure of hidden values. The phenomenon driven by physical attractiveness is universal and complex with undisclosed rules, which cause benefit for individuals whose appearance is higher in physical attractiveness and cause detriment for individuals whose appearance is lower in physical attractiveness. This book explores, discovers, and documents the theories, evidence, and circumstances in which physical attractiveness is a remarkable veneer with impacts that go considerably beyond skin-deep.

Physical attractiveness is both a power and a paradox. It triggers, exerts, and controls pervasive effects. These effects impact every individual throughout the person's life—from cradle (Oh, what a cute baby!) to casket (Doesn't he look good?) and everywhere in between. Despite the readily visible exterior of physical attractiveness, people seldom see, rarely recognize, and often deny its effects. Individuals of all ages, males and females, and ultimately entire populations, encounter realities that "beauty is ugly," or, at least, "beauty can be ugly."

The power and paradox of physical attractiveness are surprisingly consistent in every community across the United States and around the world. While many dimensions define appearance, physical attractiveness predominates. All people inherit and alter their physical attractiveness, comprised of a myriad of complex interdependent factors. The collective factors of physical attractiveness elicit or otherwise result in hidden values, orderings, dynamics, and consequences.

Out-of-sight is not out-of-mind for physical attractiveness. With vision more penetrating than generally employed, *The Power and Paradox of Physical Attractiveness* documents that despite professed ideals, people do judge people (as well as books) by their covers. One ramification is that physical attractiveness as part of a person's appearance is a more powerful determinant of a person's fortune and misfortune in life than people admit or realize. No matter the words, thoughts, and ideals proclaimed by overwhelming majorities of people, these same people judge, assume, infer, believe, act, treat, decide, accept, reject, and behave toward or against individuals in patterns consistent with a person's physical attractiveness, their own and that of others.

Physical attractiveness may look skin-deep as a surface aspect of appearance, but looks can be deceiving. Researchers from throughout the world collect empirical data complemented with anecdotal data to probe beyond the surfaces. Through investigations meeting meticulous scientific methodological procedures, acute observations reveal a deeper look at another side of physical attractiveness. It is a side ordered with rules leading to significant benefits and detriments for every person caused by his or her respective level of physical attractiveness.

It is reasonable to identify the mid-1960s as the start of scientific research explicitly investigating physical attractiveness phenomenon. Probing researchers have since discovered a wealth of knowledge, as reported in thousands of directly and indirectly related reports published in scientific journals spanning wide-ranging disciplines. This collective research contains an impressive depth and breadth of investigations, robust research methodologies, and consistent discoveries about physical attractiveness. Continuing growth of this research embraces the previously unforeseen variables studied today and the investigations' robustness.

Pertinent research has grown to comprise robust scientific discovery and dissemination of knowledge about physical attractiveness in the lives of individuals and in the lives of groups of individuals. My perspective for this book has broadened accordingly, encompassing knowledge about new dimensions of physical attractiveness while reasserting the continuous significance of earlier research findings. Nearly thirty-five years ago, I began my investigations with formal scientific research and writings in exploration of hidden values of physical attractiveness. More than twenty years ago, in 1985, I published my first book on the subject, entitled *The Physical Attractiveness Phenomena* (New York: Plenum Press). More than ten years earlier, in 1973, I conducted my first documented scientific research project investigating physical attractiveness phenomenon.[523]

Permit me to mention here with humility, that Elliot Aronson served formally as the editor for my above book. As the publisher stated on the book cover, it was published by Plenum Press within its series titled, "Perspectives in Social Psychology, Edited by Elliot Aronson." Dr. Aronson, who holds his Ph.D. from Stanford University, is the only person ever to whom the American Psychological Association has awarded all three of its highest academic recognitions: distinguished writing, distinguished teaching, and distinguished research. The latter of these awards—Distinguished Scientific Contribution—is the highest recognition awarded to psychologists for a lifetime of research. Moreover, the American Psychological Association recognized Dr. Aronson in 2002 as "among the 100 most eminent psychologists of the 20th Century."[648]

A major reason for me to write this second book is that researchers across the United States and literally around the world have continued to conduct disciplined investigations into this topic. Greater data and findings than ever differentiate between what people know scientifically to be true and what people think, speculate, or hope to be true. Ongoing studies are continuously confirming and expanding earlier conclusions and inferences. Furthermore, populations worldwide, as well as in the United States, provide real-world confirmations to the scientifically collected empirical data. Thoughts and behaviors expressed by these populations match notably the revealing, often discomforting, scientific research discoveries. Applicable manifestations within everyday life, combined with pertinent scientific findings, bring to light ever-expanding significance and understanding of physical attractiveness in the lives of all individuals, regardless where they might live or to where they might move. Accordingly, my anticipation of this book is that another look at earlier discovered premises, from the vantage point of the ensuing research and knowledge, will enhance the context of this scholarship for benefit of researchers and people in their real-world lives.

Chapter 1

Far Beyond First Impressions

For Lucy Grealy [well-educated, successful author of best selling "Autobiography of a Face" who had many friends, family, lovers, and mass media fame], beauty was a fantasy, a private wish fraught with shame. "Truth & Beauty" [a book written by her long-time friend Ann Patchett] provides glimpses of Grealy letting her guard down to obsess with Ann over her desire to be beautiful, but why she was never able to free herself of it remains a mystery.

Chicago Tribune review of book[257, 516] about Lucy Grealy.[577]

Stricken with Ewing's sarcoma at the age of 9, Grealy [who died at age 39] endured years of radiation and chemotherapy followed by a series of reconstructive operations, most of them unsuccessful. Yet it was the anguish of being perceived as ugly, and of feeling ugly, that she identified as the tragedy of her life. ...Grealy came to feel that her suffering as a cancer patient had been minor in comparison.

New York Times review of book[257, 516] about Lucy Grealy, described as a survivor of cancer and recipient of 38 operations.[506]

Beauty [physical attractiveness for men and women, boys and girls] has become what our lives are about, not the clothes, and seasonal fashions, but the rage, grief, a terrible sense of isolation that we get when we don't get back any good feeling from the money and time we invest in appearance. Appearance is everything...

Nancy Friday, Women on Top: How Real Life Has Changed Women's Sexual Fantasies.[227]

INTRODUCTION

Physical attractiveness dominates the plethora of dimensions that define the appearance of a person. It impacts every individual throughout every community, across the United States and around the world. All people inherit and alter their physical attractiveness, and complex interdependent factors, physical and non-physical, determine physical attractiveness. Hidden and not-so-hidden values drive thoughts and actions that, when unchecked, produce significant consequences and realities whereby higher physical attractiveness is overwhelmingly beneficial and lower physical attractiveness is overwhelmingly detrimental.

The first two excerpts above, concerning a well-educated, successful professional with friends, family, lovers, and mass media fame, attest to the depth of physical attractiveness that far exceeds first impressions, while the third excerpt provides a descriptive or explanatory context. Furthermore, while physical attractiveness phenomenon impacts every individual, it does so surprisingly consistently across the United States and around the world, regardless of community size, location, time in history, culture, race, ethnicity, nationality, geographical boundary, demographics, or other composition dimension. Reasonable projection about the future suggests that the physical attractiveness phenomenon will continue within future populations and likely even expand into increasing effects on individuals before birth.

Akin to perspectives about physical attractiveness held by Lucy Grealy, as stated in her 1994 autobiography, are perspectives expressed ten years later in the 2004 autobiography by Hope Donahue.[184] In one of her many pursuits to attain higher physical attractiveness, she visits a cosmetic surgeon promising quick, effortless beauty and thinks to herself, "How can I resist a delicious, illicit offer to become someone I am not? Does he know that, if I could, I would shed my face and body, my very self, on his table as nimbly as a snake sheds its skin, in favor of becoming a beautiful stranger?" Illustrating hidden values of physical attractiveness that extend far below surface appearances, Ms. Donahue, now 37, writes about "a mother increasingly jealous of her daughter's good looks" and a country's widespread support of the values of physical attractiveness translating into a corresponding obsession within herself.

"It is amazing how complete is the delusion that beauty [physical attractiveness] is goodness," expressed in the early 1890s by Russian writer Leo Tolstoy (1828-1910) in *The Kreutzer Sonata*.[457] Certainly, physical attractiveness epitomizes the proverbial eye-of-the storm and, maybe more expressively, it represents the proverbial tip-of-the-iceberg connected to a phenomenon far beyond what meets the eye. Although often unrecognized and frequently denied, physical attractiveness phenomenon, and, therefore, physical attractiveness, is powerful and pervasive. It is comparably consistent for males and females of all ages; it contributes significantly to our truly globalized world as seen readily in one form or another in all cultures and all countries, domestic and international; and it extends from the past, present, and, assuredly, into the future. A reasonable representation of this phenomenon is a circular four-stage process capsulated in the illustration on page 21 (Figure 1-1) of this chapter.

Worldwide today, people appear not to embrace or even to consider the questioning words of Tolstoy in the above paragraph. They instead embrace the words of recognition and encouragement, expressed in the 1600s, attributed to French writer Madame de Sevigne (1626-1696): "There is nothing so lovely as to be beautiful [physically attractive]. Beauty [physical attractiveness] is a gift of God and we should cherish it as such."[454] As history has shown, what determines physical attractiveness changes, flexes, and yields while physical attractiveness phenomenon itself neither changes nor flexes nor yields. Also changing are some historical jokes, adages, and notions that beauty and brains do not accompany each other. In 2005, a United Kingdom newspaper, in the capital of Wales, published an article based on data from *Top Sante* magazine that reported, "More than 50% of women believe improved looks would help them speed up the career ladder. Growing numbers of cosmetically enhanced celebrities appear to be helping undermine the brains-over-beauty battle in the workplace, new research has found."[479]

The Power and Paradox of Physical Attractiveness articulates physical attractiveness phenomenon. It ascertains a phenomenal structure with motivations, processes, and consequences connected to physical attractiveness. Although the surface appearance element of physical attractiveness is easily, readily, and immediately available when we see a person, the considerably greater ingredient of physical attractiveness that people regularly overlook is the conjoined phenomenon that is universally unseen, scarcely challenged, repeatedly denied, rarely spoken, deceptively harmful, and acutely promulgated.

The theory, research data, and knowledge presented in this book document physical attractiveness phenomenon and will lead some to conclude that "beauty is ugly" or, maybe better stated, "beauty can be ugly." Experience shows that these individuals tend to, by and large, agree, accept, identify with, and think of themselves or others they know or have observed whose life experiences are congruent with physical attractiveness phenomenon. People, to whom information in this book is particularly meaningful or signifying, might be saddened, angered, or moved to converse about the topic. They might express opinions, take action, or, at a minimum, have increased awareness, understanding, conscientiousness, and empathy. They, possibly, may become more strategically proactive in their personal and professional lives toward themselves and the people with whom they interact, shun interaction, or even for whom they do and do not cast votes.

Others who read this information might take offense. These individuals might feel and/or express that it overstates physical attractiveness phenomenon because it references an overwhelming preponderance of substantiating documentation and very little accompanying documentation to the contrary. These individuals tend to assert that physical attractiveness is entirely in the proverbial eye of the beholder, followed by citing exceptions to the abundant documentation collected through objective scientific means. First, let me respond, what might feel like overstatement or understatement is not consistent with reality. While this book references scant findings to the contrary, the reality is that such research reported publicly in scientific journals is scant. This situation is probably due in part to a long-standing tradition in which scientific journals infrequently publish research findings that confirm insignificance.

Second, as throughout all other areas of life, exceptions to physical attractiveness phenomenon certainly do occur. Some individuals within the different physical attractiveness levels respond differently and have atypical life experiences than most other people in those groups. These exceptions are analogous to those in literally every group of people identified by scientifically reasonable, descriptive statements in every discipline and for every topic. One example is the medical sciences, where research might show some patients classified within the same group for a type of cancer respond very differently to a particular treatment than most others in that group. Another example is car accidents, where research might demonstrate some drivers of a certain age have very different accident rates than most others in their group. The examples are endless, including the political arena, in which certain groups of people comprising a particular party or cause include some individuals who differ. Still, some other people, on a very personal level, who themselves have life experiences congruent with physical attractiveness phenomenon or have loved ones with such life experiences, take offense, overtly denying the entire physical attractiveness phenomenon.

Third, for those who see the world of physical attractiveness phenomenon different from its reality, "I suggest they get a pair of glasses. You can see the absence of…" equal treatment, equal opportunities, and equal success of people across the United States and around the world for people whose physical attractiveness is unequal—that is, higher or lower in physical attractiveness. The introductory quote in this paragraph is from Gloria Steinem,[661] now more than 70 years of age. Her words were in response to a 2004 *Time* magazine interview question about people who cite exceptions as proof against the group movement message that she helped lead for nearly her entire adult life. That movement and message were to rectify unequal treatments, opportunities, and successes between particular groups of people. Although these words of hers did not refer to physical attractiveness, they did refer to issues concerning different and unequal treatment by individuals and society based on particular different physical appearances, which are issues and dynamics parallel and central to physical attractiveness phenomenon.

PROGRESSION

The Power and Paradox of Physical Attractiveness is another look at physical attractiveness, and it is an advanced step in my lifelong professional career investigating this topic. Investigations of mine have spanned a period of more than thirty years. In 1985, I published my first book in this field: *The Physical Attractiveness Phenomena*[535] and, about ten years earlier, in 1973, I conducted my first documented scientific research project investigating physical attractiveness phenomenon.[523]

Since these 1973 and 1985 milestone dates early in my professional life, much has changed concerning physical attractiveness and physical attractiveness phenomenon, but, at the same time, much also has not changed. Knowledge has grown considerably about physical attractiveness phenomenon, and yet researchers continue actively to conduct research to advance this field of scientific inquiry that began formally in 1965. While visible displays by everyday people concerning the importance of physical attractiveness have grown considerably, less visible values that motivate people have remained constant. Furthermore, throughout all the progression and changes in knowledge provided by researchers and evidenced by actions of everyday people, physical attractiveness phenomenon, itself, has remained the same.

As summarized in the circular four-stage process of physical attractiveness phenomenon (Figure 1-1), physical attractiveness serves as an informational cue from which people infer extensive information, and/or misinformation. The information and inference triggers assumptions, expectations, attitudes, and behaviors, causing pervasive and powerful effects/consequences that are generally beneficial or more favorable for people whose appearance is higher in physical attractiveness and detrimental or less favorable for people whose appearance is lower in physical attractiveness. Chapter 2, specifically the section titled "Circular Four-Stage Process" that begins on page 70, discusses further this conceptualization of physical attractiveness phenomenon.

Figure 1-1. Circular Four-Stage Process of Physical Attractiveness Phenomenon

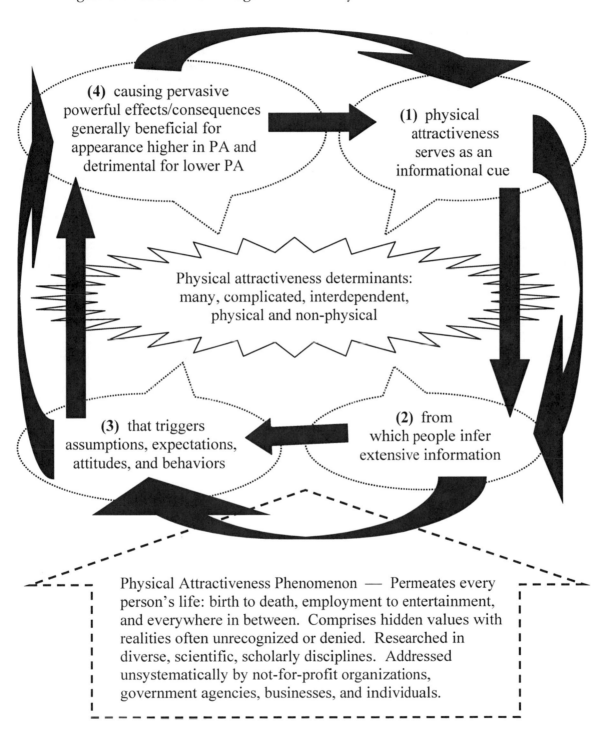

(4) causing pervasive powerful effects/consequences generally beneficial for appearance higher in PA and detrimental for lower PA

(1) physical attractiveness serves as an informational cue

Physical attractiveness determinants: many, complicated, interdependent, physical and non-physical

(3) that triggers assumptions, expectations, attitudes, and behaviors

(2) from which people infer extensive information

Physical Attractiveness Phenomenon — Permeates every person's life: birth to death, employment to entertainment, and everywhere in between. Comprises hidden values with realities often unrecognized or denied. Researched in diverse, scientific, scholarly disciplines. Addressed unsystematically by not-for-profit organizations, government agencies, businesses, and individuals.

Throughout the progression, conflicts or contradictions about physical attractiveness have persisted. People generally express disapproval and even disdain toward those who take innovative steps in pursuit of higher physical attractiveness. These people tend also to speak rather negatively about others of high physical attractiveness and rather positively about others of low physical attractiveness. Conversely, consistent with the adage about actions speaking louder than words, people around the world strongly exhibit thoughts, decisions, and behaviors exemplifying physical attractiveness phenomenon. Individuals have long demonstrated contradiction between their words and actions concerning physical attractiveness. Today's increasing number of people availing themselves to the latest technological advancements in pursuits of greater physical attractiveness amplifies this contradiction of words and actions. As a result, the mass population has elevated physical attractiveness as connected with the appearance phenomenon to center stage importance.

Simply consider the messages of popular mass media—theater, advertising, print, and television. Public demands reflected by viewers and patrons have caused broadcast programs that range from indirect emphasis on physical attractiveness to explicit emphasis. Such broadcasts began to appear everywhere in 2004, including in the next-day conversations among office workers and mall shoppers. They range from *American Idol* in the United States and counterpart programs in other countries, to reality dating-marriage shows such as *The Bachelor* and *Average Joe*, to programs such as *Extreme Makeovers* and *The Swan*. Then, also, there is the annual televised *Victoria's Secret Lingerie Fashion Show*, with no focus other than the high physical attractiveness of their stereotypically beautiful participants. Likewise, mass media programs and magazines of all sorts feature appearance makeover segments focused on physical attractiveness, while cosmetic industries are selling all-time high volumes of products that temporarily enhance physical attractiveness. In addition, medical and dental professions are delivering unprecedented high-demand procedures to alter physical attractiveness permanently.

Akin to the entertainment media, the news media regularly report an increasing number of cosmetic surgeries for males and females of all ages, women who obtain surgery on their normal feet to shorten their toes to fit latest shoe styles, and the soaring popularity of irreversible stomach surgeries to reduce weight for appearance reasons. Despite high death rates associated with surgeries such as obesity stomach surgeries, the number performed continues to increase. A 2005 study by the American Medical Association found associated deaths within one year of surgery to be one in twenty for men (5 percent of men and nearly 3 percent of women) between ages of thirty-five and forty-four, with rates as high as 50 percent for men and 40 percent for women sixty-five to seventy-four years of age.[34, 700] Yet, with more than 150,000 of these surgeries performed in 2005 in the United States, that number is an increase of more than 10 times the number performed seven years earlier, in 1998.[34, 700]

Motivation to lose weight, we would hope, rests on health concerns. However, with the value placed on physical attractiveness, it is not surprising that 60% of Americans would like to lose 20 pounds or more,[491] and weight loss is at the top of annual lists of New Year's resolutions.[395] In the opinion of at least one formerly overweight author, her weight was the reason for her lack of romantic partners, husband, and children.[373] "In the United States, 40% of women and 25% of men are trying to lose weight at any given time, and approximately 45 million people begin a diet each year."[173] Accordingly, amounts spent on weight-loss programs are ever increasing. Data in 2002 from the American Obesity Association showed approximately $30 billion per year spent by people trying to lose weight or prevent weight gain.[23]

People take actions today to enhance their physical attractiveness that in the recent past were unheard of, or at least unspoken of. Consider just one component of appearance, chest-size. Beyond attitudes and intentions that some research might reveal, actual purchases and actions reveal strong pursuits to increase chest-size that are limited neither to females nor to particular ages. The rate of women of all ages securing breast implants has increased steadily and this rate has increased at an accelerated pace during recent years. Citing safety concerns based on statistics that revealed significant health complications when the substance leaked from the implant into the person's body, in 1992 the United States Food and Drug Administration (FDA) imposed a legal ban on silicone breast implants in the United States.[605]

Popularity of breast implants remained strong, and the marketplace turned to saline breast implants as well as other substances, but these substances were less preferred because people considered them cosmetically inferior to silicone. Continuing strong demand for silicone breast implants forced their legalization again in 2003 on a limited basis, followed in 2005 when the FDA gave approval to make silicone breast implants again generally available and legal in the United States.[605] The FDA made their 2005 decision to approve silicone breast implants, based on improved product safety features accompanied by respective safety data from at least two companies (Mentor Corporation and Inamed Corporation) and as advised by surgeons. With breast augmentation surgeries at an all-time high, a market has developed for breast enhancement surgeries as gifts for girlfriends or wives for special milestones in a relationship, for graduating high school students, and even for winning certain radio and television contests. A successful business founded in Vancouver, Canada, sells breast-augmentation gift boxes in four varieties comprised of items to assist post-surgery recovery.[489]

Gifts of cosmetic surgery are growing on all dimensions. A 2004 article in the *Chicago Tribune* about eyelid surgery among Asian Americans cited a family living Los Angeles.[360] The mother, father, and grandmother had emigrated from China and, with great love for the happiness of their American daughter/granddaughter, "offered to get her plastic surgery, specifically, blepharoplasty, for her fourteenth birthday. Commonly known as Asian eyelid surgery, the procedure entails stitching a permanent crease into the eyelid." According to that *Chicago Tribune* article, "the fastest growing type of plastic surgery across the United States for Asians is eyelid surgery and, furthermore, "a rapidly growing number of young girls—both in Asia and the United States—are opting to have the crease surgically added, at a cost starting around $2,000." For parents and children in India, a 2005 newspaper article reported "a major attitudinal change amongst the parents who are themselves keen to rectify flaws and scars that might exist in their children."[688] One parent, Ajay Kumar, when interviewed, stated, "My daughter had a pointed nose so we decided to get a corrective surgery done last month."

Back to the topic of larger chests, males have not stood still in their own pursuits. As well as exercise and, at times, drugs, breast implants to enlarge chest size have entered the radar screen for men, as well as for women. This development for males to enhance their physical attractiveness comes in the form of pectoral muscle implants that augment male chest size.[418] Coinciding with this development is a report published in the late 1990s revealing that during the past 25 years, dissatisfaction with their chests has increased 111% for men (18% to 38%), contrasted with dissatisfaction for women with their breasts that increased 31% (26% to 34%) during the same time.[232]

Efforts among males to increase their physical attractiveness have grown extensively. Adult males have gained a sizable portion of the cosmetic surgeries performed annually, while teenage males have demonstrated a serious motivation to enhance their physical attractiveness, often with dangerous means. A 2004 headline article published by *The Wall Street Journal* read "From Faux Clefts to Implants, [Cosmetic] Procedures for Men Surge; [Despite] The Risks of Nerve Damage."[613] That article reports data from the American Society of Plastic Surgeons, revealing that the number of males receiving cosmetic chin augmentations in 2003 was 600 percent more than 1992 and, in 2003 alone, the number increased 70 percent (to 9,583) from the prior year. Less perilous but equally permanent and nearly equal in popularity for males and females, the incidence of tattoos to enhance appearance has also soared in the United States. The change in frequency has accompanied a change in sizes of tattoos, their designs, their locations on the body, and societal acceptance. In 2004, 10 percent of Americans (one in every 10) bore a tattoo compared to 1 percent of Americans (one in 100) in the 1970s.[359] Reports in 2005 indicate that some major American corporations, notably Ford and Wells Fargo, now have policies "that allow body art as part of their appearance codes."[580] More changes can be expected as younger employees advance into higher level positions, since, as revealed by a Harris Interactive study, the largest segment of the population with tattoos are 25- to 29-year-olds, with 36 percent of these individuals sporting at least one tattoo.[580]

Despite what they proclaim…or hope, actions of people clearly demonstrate their actual non-subscription to adages about beauty being only skin-deep. Their contrary beliefs are evident through their actions that ascribe the negative corollary "ugly as sin" to people whose appearance is lower in physical attractiveness. Based merely on physical attractiveness, people continue to formulate complex notions about an observed person regardless of any available information to the contrary about the person. These notions translate into different verbal expressions and nonverbal behaviors in the form of either positive or negative responses. Nonverbal responses usually include body language communicated through smiles and frowns, unambiguous facial expressions, head movements, and body gestures. These nonverbal factors seem to equate closely with actual social approval and disapproval, acceptance and denial, of a person. Formative experimental research demonstrates that persons of higher physical attractiveness receive significantly greater frequency of positive looks and smiles than do those of lower physical attractiveness.[354] These facial gestures foretell non-visible feelings because more physically attractive evaluators tend to be liked more than their counterparts of lower physical attractiveness by persons being evaluated.[641] Accordingly, people are willing to expend greater effort when requested to perform work by a person of higher physical attractiveness compared to lower.[643] Insight based on data from one research project led the researcher to state:

> …a consistent pattern emerges of the [physically] unattractive person being associated with the negative or undesirable pole of the adjective scales and the

highly [physically] attractive person being judged significantly more positively.[459]

Why is it that when you change the way you look at things, the things change? Knowledge generated by research findings reveals that physical attractiveness plays a dramatic, but largely unexamined and automatic or involuntary, role in an individual's interpersonal interactions, in how others perceive and respond to the individual, and even in the individual's personality development. Generally, the more physically attractive an individual is, the more positively people perceive the person, the more favorably people respond to the person, and the more successful the person's personal and professional lives are presumed to be. Through self-fulfilling prophecy, also known as the Pygmalion Effect, some attributions convert into reality in the lives of people whose appearances differ in terms of higher and lower physical attractiveness. However, self-perception among some beneficiaries of higher physical attractiveness is not always in accord with the view from the outside. Even with perceptions, attributions, and realities in their favor due to their physical attractiveness, some among these beneficiaries continue to endure privately a sense of doubt, inadequacy, or even revulsion over their appearance to extents that affect everyday living and even life itself.

INTERPRETATIONS

Physical attractiveness phenomenon is universal. Therefore, reasons interpreted or offered to explain occurrences manifested in everyday life or identified in scientific research often go to the core of human existence. Among the different cultures between and within countries that translate physical attractiveness phenomenon somewhat distinctively, the similarities are overwhelming. Research projects designed explicitly to compare physical attractiveness phenomenon between countries complement the findings from projects conducted in particular countries that focus on the resident population. The data document that people worldwide favor, and treat accordingly, higher physical attractiveness over lower, and the accompanying phenomenon transcends time, geography, and culture. Findings reported by research projects conducted around the world consistently contribute to the growing, rather virtual, database that allows extrapolation and generalizations that attest to the robustness of physical attractiveness phenomenon.

Data interpretation that offers overarching explanations for physical attractiveness phenomenon relies heavily on the inherent essence of its surface appearance dimension. That essence is its conspicuous tangibility, providing unparalleled visibility and accessibility. Of course, at the same time, parents promulgate physical attractiveness phenomenon to their children in ways intended and not intended. In turn, these children further promulgate the phenomenon to their peers and, eventually, as they age and become parents themselves, to their children. Socialization or indoctrination of children with physical attractiveness phenomenon begins innocently with good, honorable intentions. However, lessons learned or otherwise embraced early about physical attractiveness extend far beyond childhood, as demonstrated lifelong in variant forms. As a result, people of all ages consciously and subconsciously demonstrate their beliefs: positive, favorable, and complimentary to individuals of higher physical attractiveness and quite the opposite toward individuals of lower physical attractiveness.

Few features about a person are as abundantly readily accessible as physical attractiveness, which accounts for a sizable portion of why people consistently use physical attractiveness as an informational cue. Among other comparatively visible features such as a person's race and age, which of course are not always accurately discernable for all individuals, physical attractiveness predominates in informational importance. Race and age demographics might be equally apparent with physical attractiveness, and might have exerted greater influence in times past, but use of physical attractiveness as an informational cue overwhelmingly transcends these demographic categorizations. Regardless of potentially complicating effects due to interdependencies between a person's features, people deem a person's physical attractiveness to be more informative with greater consequences than a person's race or age.

Race

Physical attractiveness permeates most manifestations of social behavior and culture, perhaps as has been the case for millennia and likely even since the appearance of life on earth. Scientific research has documented well this pervasiveness, even though it has specifically addressed physical attractiveness as part of appearance phenomenon for only a relatively short period. Beginning in the 1960s and continuing today, researchers have developed scales and methodologies for measuring physical attractiveness in humans. At times complicating this topic, physical attractiveness as part of appearance phenomenon can be difficult to separate from matters of race. Likewise, fondness and discrimination affected by physical attractiveness can at times be difficult to separate from discrimination aligned with race and ethnicity. Although demographic characteristics can, in some circumstances, confound or complicate research, physical attractiveness still needs research as a separate entity for many reasons. Fundamentally, physical attractiveness as part of appearance phenomenon more often than not transcends all demographic categories (such as race, gender, ethnicity, and age) and underlies extremely important judgments, consequences, and dynamics influencing all aspects of life for all people.

Following the interest, at least the scholarly interest that began in the mid-1960s, researchers in critical mass have conducted investigations about physical attractiveness in terms of what is reasonable to call *physical attractiveness phenomenon*. These research investigations, typically reported as articles in scholarly journals, in total present an impressive depth and breadth of research methodologies with profound consistency of discoveries. People's attitudes, beliefs, and ultimately actions in response to different levels of physical attractiveness range in magnitude from subtle nuances to overt discrimination. Still, most people claim ignorance of, or indifference to, the force of physical attractiveness functioning within most everyday aspects of education, politics, business, law enforcement and legal proceedings, as well as social valuation, cognition, and interaction.

People who prefer to interact with others of the same race illustrate well the transcending power of physical attractiveness. Despite predisposition toward same-race individuals, people increasingly, albeit subtly without overt proclamation, seem to prefer another person of a different race whose appearance is higher in physical attractiveness than a person of their same race whose appearance is low in physical attractiveness. One form of circumstantial data is the increasing number of interracial marriages in the United States. That number has nearly tripled to 1,674,000 interracial marriages with at least one black/African American or white/Caucasian spouse in 2002, up from 651,000 in 1980.[586] Scientific survey data collected by the Gallup Organization provides supporting scientific data, albeit less specific to physical attractiveness.[247] As reported in this 2004 article, "70 percent of whites now say they approve of marriage between whites and blacks, up from just 4 percent in a 1958 Gallup poll," while "80 percent of blacks and 77 percent of Hispanics also say they generally approve of interracial marriages." Also reported, 71% of American adults overall "would not object to a child or grandchild's marrying someone of another race. Perhaps even more remarkable, a large majority of white respondents—66 percent—say they would not object if their child or grandchild chose a black (African American) spouse. African Americans (86 percent) and Hispanics (79 percent) were equally accepting about a child or grandchild's marrying someone of another race."

General understanding of diverse identities has long proliferated, and many scientific disciplines, especially the social sciences, have confronted differences long buried at different levels in culture of the United States, followed by analogous findings in cultures worldwide. The identity of people whose appearance represents diverse levels of physical attractiveness has been long afflicted with general understanding, or misunderstanding, that grossly oversimplified reality, identifying people of higher physical attractiveness as far more valuable and deserving than their counterparts. Despite general understandings, or, rather, misunderstandings that exempted certain demographic categories of people, the scientific endeavors have unveiled findings documenting that physical attractiveness affects males and females of all ages, races, nationalities, religions, and affiliations in similar patterns. Society and individuals bestow rewards associated with social desirability to both genders in rough proportion to one's level of physical attractiveness.[236, 237, 676]

Another dimension to physical attractiveness phenomenon and race is the diminishing resistance among some ethnicities to enhance their physical attractiveness through cosmetic surgery. A cultural concern long held in the United States among African Americans and Asians is that their respective ethnic populations would consider negatively, as in a context of trying to look more Caucasian or white, if they were to choose cosmetic surgeries to their face to increase their physical attractiveness. Changing their eyelids has been a point of cultural resistance for Asians, but nowadays the desire and action are increasingly evident "to give Asian eyes a second eyelid line, making them look rounder and more Western" in the United States among Asian Americans and among Asians in traditionally Asian countries.[405] "A big deterrent to African Americans considering elective surgery [has been the fact that] black skin does scar much more easily than white skin."[609] This deterrent may partially explain why African Americans represent the largest market of beauty products today in the United States, spending more than $20 billion annually. However, "the number of blacks seeking facial or reconstructive surgery more than tripled between 1997 and 2002, reflecting both the growing affluence of African Americans and the subtle easing of some long held cultural taboos against such procedures," as well as reflecting advances in technology and surgeon skills.[609]

Gender

Body dysmorphic disorder (BDD) is a medical ailment believed to inflict males and females about equally.[500] Professionals define BDD as extreme subjective feelings of ugliness regardless of a quite normal appearance, and people with BDD exhibit obsession with one or more facial or body features that may or may not deviate from norms of appearance. Individuals of both genders with these mental distortions seem to think, "I must be perfect, I must be noticed; the only way to feel better is to look better; if I am not the best looking in a social gathering I cannot have a good time; if my body part of concern is not beautiful, then it must be ugly."[500] Correspondingly, BDD aligns closely with differing values imposed through physical attractiveness phenomenon upon and within people of higher and lower physical attractiveness. Few medical practitioners knew of BDD before the early 1990s, but the ailment is neither new nor rare. Even though the diagnostic sourcebook (*Diagnostic and Statistical Manual of Mental Disorders*) for clinicians of psychiatry and psychology did not recognize BDD until its 1987 *DSM-III-R,* it was written about as early as 1891.[476] Professionals estimate body dysmorphic disorder to inflict approximately 1.5 percent of people and actual rates are likely higher due to motivations among those inflicted to keep their ailment secret.

In the relative context that changes are occurring throughout populations toward more equality between the genders, the impact exerted by physical attractiveness in every culture continues to be greater for females than males. One indication that males around the world place greater importance on physical attractiveness of females is a 2002 magazine survey conducted with readers in the United States and the following other countries: Australia, China, Czech Republic, France, Germany, Greece, Hungary, Italy, Netherlands, Russia, Serbia, Slovenia, South Africa, and United Kingdom (UK).[389] Researchers asked respondents, "Who would you most like to sit next to on a long airplane flight?" They placed persons based on physical attractiveness (i.e., supermodels) at the top. Based on these data, physical attractiveness phenomenon seems clearly in charge; in fact, respondents placed people synonymous with high physical attractiveness not just merely at the top but a very large distance from other choices. Even the second preferred choice (country's leader) was approximately one-half the first choice percentage, followed by professional entertainers, financial advisers, religious leaders, and others, as shown in Table 1-1. Percentage of Men in the United States and Fourteen Other Countries Stating Whom They Would Like Most to Sit Beside on a Long Flight.[389]

Table 1-1. Percentage of Men in the United States and Fourteen Other Countries Stating Whom They Would Like Most to Sit Beside on a Long Flight

	Men in the United States	Men in All 15 Surveyed Countries
Supermodel	29	32
Country's Leader	23	16
Comedian	19	20

	Men in the United States	Men in All 15 Surveyed Countries
Stockbroker	10	9
Sports Star	7	12
Pastor/Priest	6	5
Cartoon Character	4	4
Your Boss	2	2

Females are held to higher standards by both genders and are subjected more frequently to negative effects stemming from envy when the "pleasure of regarding beauty turns to resentment."[226] Gender stereotypes persist, with importance ratings different for males and females of all ages. People equate higher physical attractiveness with greater femininity for females and greater masculinity for males.[236] Males continue to place greater emphasis on their mate's physical attractiveness, including mate retention, than do females.[254] Especially in the domain of facial attractiveness, gender difference is well established, with no question that females are "judged by their [physical] attractiveness to a greater extent than are males, and that these judgments have real consequences for them."[317] Also, despite its abstract nature, physical attractiveness of females as opposed to males is more precisely defined or delineated, more well-known, and has higher agreement.[364]

Occasional extreme incidents in all countries indicate the value still placed on physical attractiveness of females by some individuals and the internal character inferred from this informational cue. No less revealing about the value placed on physical attractiveness of females, but certainly substantially more overtly offensive, are the words stated publicly in 2004 by a Florida Circuit Judge, Gene Stephenson, who later apologized. While presiding over a rape case, this judge commented about the accused and the rape victim, "Why would he want to rape her? She doesn't look like a day on the beach."[498]

AGE IN THE TWENTY-FIRST CENTURY

"I'm 19, that's how I keep in shape," responded pop star Avril Lavigne in a 2004 interview discussing how she keeps her exceptional beauty represented by the shape of her body.[54] Age has always wielded a high-ranking role for physical attractiveness phenomenon, but its overt recognition and the explicit pursuit of younger appearances are more intense today than in the past, and likely to be less intense today than tomorrow. One difference is that, although physical attractiveness always has been a significant factor for people of all ages throughout history, it has not been as explicitly important as it is today for younger and older age groups.

Open acknowledgement of the importance of physical attractiveness in our lives has expanded radically and increasingly among both younger ages and older ages. To look more physically attractive, a growing portion of elementary school girls diet, and a substantial number of junior high school boys use illegal body enhancing drugs. In fact, the author of a major national study reported in *Psychology Today* says that dieting is "very common—even among girls as young as 9 years old."[232] The age continuum's other end reveals males in their 50s and 60s obtaining cosmetic surgeries under the premise to compete in the workplace, while women of older ages secure cosmetic surgeries and medical procedures with the idea of transforming the body's outside to match how she feels internally. Between these younger and older age groups, a national survey in 2005 of more than 1,700 people revealed an overall average of 30.9 years of age as when a woman is most physically attractive.[731]

"In youth and beauty wisdom is but rare!" proclaimed English poet Alexander Pope (1688-1744) in *The Odyssey of Homer*.[455] People seem to disregard this message because either they have not heard it, find it to be in error, or value youth and beauty more than wisdom. Values and pursuit of greater physical attractiveness related to youth at the expense of potential perceptions of wisdom is neither new nor limited to any one country. "The fight against old age [to avoid this determinant of physical attractiveness] has long been good business, and it's only getting better. Global retail sales of antiaging skin-care products—up 71% since 2000—are rising faster than any other segment of the skin-care market, according to Euromonitor, a market researcher, hitting $9.9 billion [in 2004]."[707]

As distasteful as it is to some people, an artifact of physical attractiveness phenomenon is that people regularly grant social powers to females based on physical attractiveness characteristics that is, in turn, interrelated strongly with age realities. This practice is just one of many complex double standards of thinking in which long held thoughts and behaviors link aging more negatively with physical attractiveness for women than for men. Some people even argue that perception of a woman's intelligence diminishes in correlation to her degree of beauty. This argument might underlie why "it's hard telling your mother that you don't want to look like her when you're 50," according to a 29-year old female, who after cosmetic surgery, went on to say, "I think my mother resented that and felt hurt, but I had to be honest."[609] If so, in the extreme it might be a kind of infantilism, which, as interpreted by Sigmund Freud, was to deny reality in favor of imagination. This interpretation of Freud's infantilism applied to beauty discrimination might ultimately promulgate a society inclined to view women opposite to the primary fact of physical attractiveness phenomenon. Beauty discrimination referenced in the prior paragraph grants certain social powers to women of greater beauty based on presumptions about greater capabilities. People overwhelmingly equate greater physical attractiveness, in this case greater beauty, with better non-physical traits and skills. The opposite or reverse would equate fewer capabilities, fewer skills, and less desirable adult characteristics for women who possess higher physical attractiveness.

Women who compete in beauty contests, particularly those who win, at times substantiate inverse perceptions held by the public about a woman's abilities and her physical attractiveness. Sometimes people express these perceptions as jokes that a person of high physical attractiveness, or a woman of great beauty, cannot be a person also of high intelligence. Nevertheless, people regularly demonstrate public recognition of the value of physical attractiveness through formal beauty pageants that continue around the world. In the United States, where the number of television viewers of the annual Miss America pageant has decreased significantly since its first annual broadcast in 1960, the pageant has sustained viewers more than forty-five years, a longevity which is without parallel when compared with other network broadcast shows that rarely sustain viewers beyond a few years. Today, approximately ten million people continue to watch the one-evening television broadcast each year for each of the Miss America, Miss USA, and Miss Universe pageants.[170] At least one country, Canada, has tried to eliminate this scenario by canceling all national beauty contests as of 1992, based on the argument they are degrading to women.[121]

Another end of the beauty pageant continuum is the country of West Africa, "where at least in the southern area of the Sahara, the government sponsored [beauty pageant is] the most public of the annual [events]."[358] Unique in rather mainstream pageants around the world, the Sahara contest features male beauty. Also unique among world beauty pageants, China, in 2004, held the first pageant for contestants with cosmetic surgery. This pageant, it is reported, is "part of the country's increasingly fevered pursuit of beauty as the economy soars and people spend more money and time on their looks."[25] One contestant is quoted to say, "Becoming beautiful is everyone's wish," while the Chinese government is credited for recognizing the fast speed at which the cosmetic surgery industry is growing "as patients rush to go under the knife to widen eyes, narrow faces and fill out lips and breasts."[25] Having generated global attention, organizers promoted the event as "part of China's weeklong, first-ever Artificial Beauty Pageant…with the goal to publicize the good side of cosmetic surgery."[377] The Associated Press reported the event as "another sign of China's increasing fixation with beauty as the country grows more prosperous and its people more conscious about looking good at any cost."[26] Organizers stated the pageant had more than ninety applicants from countries outside of China, including female applicants from the United States and Japan. The genesis of the pageant stemmed from an 18-year-old contestant disqualified because of her cosmetic surgery from another Chinese beauty pageant, who sued for emotional damages for that disqualification. One of the female organizers of the new event said, "This contest shows women's strong pursuit of beauty," and "we would like to use it to unveil the mystery of manmade beauty…"[26]

Women's reproductive role has long been a critical component in cultural values of women's physical attractiveness, as revealed in sociobiology studies of natural selection and sexual selection.[317] However, the importance of physical attractiveness seems no longer to diminish with age. Historical anecdotes to the contrary are decreasing rapidly today in a world where perceived age is more important than actual age. Directly challenging formal notions of natural selection, standards of physical attractiveness driven by the appearance phenomenon for much more youthful looking women apply even to women in their forties and fifties. Factors other than evolutionary principles, at least reproductive aspects of evolution, can at times better explain contemporary behaviors. Here, adhering to physical attractiveness phenomenon elevates the value of one's own existence above the evolutionary principle for instinctual promulgation of one's species.

Despite standards for physical attractiveness that are sometimes unrealistic, the appearance phenomenon and physical attractiveness phenomenon compel continuous pursuit of improvements. Pursuit is encouraged by improved cosmetic surgery techniques and technologies, easier access to and greater availability of cosmetic surgeries, shifting acceptance toward cosmetic surgery,[552] and aging public figures who maintain their younger appearance. Although at least one clinical professor of cosmetic surgery asserts that "surgery will never make you look younger, but it can help you look better,"[414] people at disquieting rates pursue both.

Witness the whopping increase of more than 400 percent for Americans who received cosmetic surgeries in 2003 compared to ten years earlier (1.8 million versus 330,000). Among them is the well-known American pop singer Cher. At 60 years of age she possesses an appearance very high in physical attractiveness with features characteristic of much younger ages: lack of wrinkles, free of shrinking lips, void of drooping eyelids, exempt from thinning or graying hair, unfettered from less than bright white teeth, possessing flawless complexion, and liberated from sagging body parts.

No known biological code of nature would equip a woman of that age to possess those age-affiliated looks. Instead, a woman might pursue these younger age characteristics to escalate perception of her sexual capability in hopes of capturing other benefits to satisfy her needs. As put forth in a 2004 *Newsweek* article by a psychology professor at the University of Pennsylvania School of Medicine: "We have evidence showing that whether we like it or not, appearance does matter…and we know that especially among women, we equate beauty with youthfulness."[49] Women's awareness of stereotypically attractive bodies is not limited to song and film stars. Similar wishes and values about physical attractiveness exist among even the most politically powerful and politically correct women. Former American Secretary of State Madeleine Albright, speaking complimentarily, if not enviously, in 2005 about the physical attractiveness of the body possessed by the current, much younger, American Secretary of State Condoleezza Rice, stated, "I think she looks great. And I would give anything to have a figure like hers."[496, 698]

"Trying to present yourself as looking as young as possible might actually make practical sense."[49] Evolutionary theory suggests this pursuit by older persons, not strictly because of reproductive inclinations, as people frequently view Darwin's perspective, but by survival inclinations that are also part of Darwin's perspective.[100] Maslow's Hierarchy of Needs, a more moderate theory described in some detail in the next chapter, offers a potentially more plausible explanation based on physical, security, social, esteem, and self-actualization needs.[433]

Men of ages similar to the pop singer Cher, in their 50s, 60s, or older, might well pursue women whose appearance reflects higher physical attractiveness more consistent with younger ages than with actual chronological age. The motivation for men is not the sexual reproductive capabilities (or lack thereof) of these women. Rather, the likely driver for men is a perception aligned with an extension of physical attractiveness phenomenon. Specifically, the appeal is that the physical attractiveness of these women enhances men's regard for them because of the perceived younger age and equivalent reproductive ability of those ages (even in the context of the men's own naturally diminished reproductive-performance capability). Of course, this, too, explains rather closely the motivations of aging women to pursue enhancement of their physical attractiveness to levels more consistent with younger ages than with their actual chronological age.

Many factors contribute to the dramatic changes concerning aging and physical attractiveness. Particularly in the United States and other western countries, the baby boom effect means the increasing larger population of people entering older life stages, accompanied with stereotypically declining levels of physical attractiveness and potential financial means to counter these declines. The baby boom cited here comprises individuals born between 1945 and 1960, a period spanning approximately 15 years after World War II ended. At the same time, improvements in medical technology for cosmetic surgeries are surging, and societal attitudes toward cosmetic surgery are changing dramatically more favorable.

With people living longer than ever before, they experience a greater decline in their physical attractiveness than ever before. People in the United States today commonly live to their late seventies and eighties, whereas, in 1900, forty-seven years of age was the average lifespan in the United States.[120] All the while, documentation reveals "that men pay more attention to looks than women do [in selecting mates],[99, 250, 330, 331, 332, 675] which has now been shown in many societies," and "the power of female youth in men's [physical] attractiveness judgments…is universal."[695]

MEDICAL PROFESSIONALS AND INDUSTRIES

The medical professions coupled with pharmaceutical companies have developed into a dialectical domain. They openly offer willing patients a popular level of interventions to remedy lower physical attractiveness. Notable among these offerings are cosmetic surgeries, carbohydrate-blocking agents, and diet options to reduce size, ranging from drugs to gastric operations, steroids to increase muscle size, and exercises to enhance appearances—all at the risk of injury and undesired consequences. These professions and companies then stand ready to provide relief for any physiological, psychological, and biological complications that may arise: infections caused by surgery, cancers caused by excessive steroids, bulimia and anorexia caused by eating disorders, depression caused by unfulfilled expectations, and joint replacement caused by excessive exercise.

A purely quantitative interpretation provides reasonable insight about the response by medical professions to this dialectical opposition. On one hand, the substantial amount of empirical study performed by medical specialists involved with cosmetic and reconstructive surgery remains important. On the other hand, these medical communities are performing relatively no parallel study about the after effects of these procedures. This situation persists, despite facts reported by a *USA Today* writer in a 2004 article titled "Beauty products have an ugly side, researchers say," which cited data from a study of 7,500 cosmetic/hygiene products by the Environmental Working Group research organization.[730] That study found "one in three personal-care products has at least one ingredient classified as a possible carcinogen. And one in 100 has ingredients certified by the U. S. government as known or probable causers of cancer." These researchers also surveyed 2,300 people and found, "the average adult each day uses nine such products, containing 126 chemical ingredients. One-quarter of women uses at least 15 products a day." All part of the $5 billion that people in the United States spend each year on cosmetics, toiletries, haircutters, and beauty shops.[122] Statistics from 2004, the most recent available, reveal that "Beauty has grown to be a $32.2 billion industry."[731]

Noninvasive procedures are a further step, but still short of cosmetic surgery. "More than 7.5 million non-invasive procedures were performed in the United States, up 36% from 2000," according to 2004 data from the American Society of Plastic Surgeons.[33] Illustrating the escalating demand for this type of noninvasive pursuit of higher physical attractiveness, U. S. physicians in 2004 performed 2.8 million injections of the wrinkle-smoothing drug

Botox.[656] Similarly, they also performed a 659 percent increase—116,211 in 2003 followed by 882,469 in 2004—of synthetic gel fillers such as Restylane to enhance facial physical attractiveness. "For fans of the fillers, the results are priceless…[according to one 38-year old recipient]. People just say, You look so good."[656]

No helping arm or discipline of science and medicine is addressing the situation. This relative dearth points to an ethical concern, given the comparatively small amount of work performed by medical researchers concerned with the physiological, psychological, and biological implications and complications caused by physical attractiveness phenomenon. Serious, respected institutions offer, and even encourage, procedures and products to enhance physical attractiveness, but neither these institutions nor parallel institutions offer corresponding procedures and products to avoid or resolve complications. If we are to single out one discipline for acknowledgement, social psychology appears to be providing the greatest (and, it is hoped, unifying) mass of substantive evidence about physical attractiveness. The level of empirical research is increasing as researchers and others identify distinct issues. Still, the research is not nearly sufficient for understanding what, when, how, or why physical attractiveness counts so significantly among populations across the United States and around the world.

Historically, overt attempts to enhance a person's physical attractiveness were encouraged for routinely accepted actions but viewed with suspicion for atypical actions. This situation is a dynamic, living continuum, albeit slow to change. Routine, widely accepted and even expected enhancements to physical attractiveness, such as bathing, grooming, and wearing appealing clothing, are at one end. At the other end, non-routine, extremely narrowly accepted, and even publicly rejected, enhancements such as hair transplants, gastric surgeries, liposuction procedures, and various cosmetic surgeries. The former directions continue to receive encouragement and rewards, while suspicions regarding the latter directions are moderating, evolving, or even becoming overtly acceptable today in Asia, Europe, North America, South America, and the United States. An illustration of such overt acceptance is a major newspaper article in England from 2003 that reported "cosmetic surgery patients [are increasingly] going public to show their enhancements… From teenagers to retirees, they show off their new noses, bottoms and breasts, while the surgeons watch the results of their work on display much as designers…"[387]

The physical attractiveness phenomenon captures extensive experiences through which individuals encounter benefits and detriments in proportion to their physical attractiveness. Substantial research has proven many appendages and variations within this phenomenon through which higher physical attractiveness is advantageous to an individual, whereas lower physical attractiveness is disadvantageous. Although first referenced formally in 1972 by research about physical attractiveness and physical attractiveness phenomenon, the notion that "what is beautiful is good" was expressed much earlier in literary fields.[182] Not directly linked to current day expressions and interpretations, this notion was put forth frequently during the romantic period of the arts (roughly the 1800s) when philosophers and poets propounded axioms that "good is beauty, beauty is truth." For example, the writings of Samuel Taylor Coleridge (1772–1834)[593] provide invaluable literary thought about philosophers, critical theorists, and scholars like Immanuel Kant, John Keats, William Wordsworth, F. W. J. Schelling, and A. W. Schlegel. People worldwide still immutably link authenticity, authority, and moral goodness with beauty (i.e., good looks and high physical attractiveness), which is documented with surprising uniformity of data collected by scientific experiments and research. Physical attractiveness ineffably extends far beyond the physical to perceptions expressed in physical attractiveness phenomenon, which, although instantly recognizable, carries unseen or denied values of power, persuasion, and success.

What drives medical professions and industries, and their respective consumers, to pursue greater levels of physical attractiveness? First, physical attractiveness phenomenon occurs worldwide, and people throughout the world clearly place physical attractiveness as a high priority. "If love makes the world go round," then the survey data in a 2004 report (based on marketing research data collected by the Lieberman Research Worldwide corporation from more than 4,000 men and women in 18 countries) confirm that "physical attractiveness also makes the world go round."[132] Among the survey questions was "What attribute is most seductive?" Accompanying choices were fame, looks, money, and power. Table 1-2 shows the percentage of respondents in this survey who rated the respective attribute as most important. These data demonstrate clearly that respondents in every country surveyed, rated physical attractiveness or good looks to be by far the most important quality from the list of looks, money, power, and fame.

Table 1-2. Percentage of Men and Women in Eighteen Countries Rating Specific Attributes as Most Seductive

	Looks	Money	Power	Fame	Not Stated
Australia	69	8	18	4	1
Canada	62	15	12	7	4
Denmark	69	3	14	15	-
Finland	72	4	7	18	1
France	55	15	13	17	-
Germany	64	16	10	10	1
Greece	38	25	24	12	1
Holland	74	9	6	10	1
Hungary	38	21	27	14	1
Italy	40	12	20	23	6
Japan	24	51	10	15	-
Mexico	56	19	19	7	1
Norway	88	6	2	3	1
Portugal	33	23	21	24	1
Spain	23	34	29	16	-
Sweden	73	4	12	12	-
U.K.	58	18	14	1	8

	Looks	Money	Power	Fame	Not Stated
U.S.A.	52	20	14	5	9
Average	55	17	15	12	2

UNDERSTATED UNEASINESS

The road to understanding physical attractiveness phenomenon has held substantial success, but the expedition has been uphill. Resistance exists as a rather understated uneasiness among many people, both inside and outside of scientific research communities. As a topic often resisted in systematic scientific research, physical attractiveness has withstood an almost morphological neglect defined in terms of the study of surface characteristics, rather than structural analysis. It also has withstood what some might label simple, naïve, democratic idealism that creates a reluctance to suggest any form of determinism unrelated to ordinary classifications of opportunity. This state of affairs denotes the resistance to establish a relationship, or to verify unambiguously the long-established relationship, between physical appearance factors and personal characteristics. Although possibly motivated by worthy intentions, a peculiar blindness to appearance exists. The result is a stifling or apparent repression of research into undemocratic assertions that persons who possess higher physical attractiveness are someway better, or in someway experience a better life, compared to persons lower in physical attractiveness.

Prior to the 1960s, research communities did not address physical attractiveness in systematic social science research, at least not beyond individual characteristics such as personality traits as a function of height, weight, hair color, eye colors, and length of nose. Even slower to develop was study pertaining to the potential differences between individuals of lower and higher physical attractiveness. Psychologists Judson Mills and Elliot Aronson, each with his Ph.D. a few years earlier from Stanford University, performed probably the first empirical inquiry into physical attractiveness phenomenon.[464] That study, published in 1965, investigated the relationship between changes in opinion held by a receiver exposed to a persuasive message, as a function of the physical attractiveness of the communicator of that message. As a footnote, it might be worth mentioning, twenty years later, Elliot Aronson served formally as the editor for my first book, published in 1985 within the Plenum Press series titled *Perspectives in Social Psychology, Edited by Elliot Aronson*.

In the late 1960s, as a pioneering researcher in this field, Elliot Aronson offered an explanation about scientists' slow, if not delayed, pursuit of research into physical attractiveness phenomenon. Although he laces his explanation in the context of female-male gender vocabulary usage common at that time, his explanation can be generalized to both males and females as research has since documented the pertinence of physical attractiveness phenomenon to both genders:

> …it is difficult to be certain why the effects of physical beauty [physical attractiveness] have not been studied more systematically. It may be that, at some level, we would hate to find evidence indicating that beautiful women [people] are liked better than homely women [people]—somehow this seems

undemocratic. In a democracy, we like to feel that with hard work and a good deal of motivation, a person can accomplish almost anything. But, alas (most of us believe), hard work cannot make an ugly woman [person] beautiful. Because of this suspicion, perhaps most social psychologists implicitly would prefer to believe that beauty [physical attractiveness] is, indeed, only skin-deep—and avoid the investigation of its social impact for fear that they might learn otherwise.[27]

Since the above statement by Aronson, sentiments and priorities have changed, and research into physical attractiveness phenomenon has become a field of endeavor in its own right. Researchers now regularly perform investigations into this topic within universally accepted standards for both social and biological sciences. This research has confirmed that there are hidden values within the physical attractiveness dimension of appearance. These developments and findings verify or at least corroborate the fear expressed earlier by Aronson that such inquiries might bring to light a truth that people are strongly inclined to keep in the dark.

If, particularly in contemporary times, the human race has evolved by influence of mass communication, then the communications base exhibited from later years in the twentieth century through early years in the twenty-first century has left the human race almost as far behind as Cro-Magnon man. Appearance as a form of communication cannot be overemphasized. Forms of communication (verbal or nonverbal), setting of communication (personal or non-personal), and intent of communication (persuasion, commerce, explanation, courtship, or expression) have all received considerable attention to and recognition of their social value. While the focus of communication has shifted to communicators who are not personally acquainted, still much communication is between persons who are, or have been, visible to each other.

Appearance is a form of communication for which the more rapid the communication, the more set the stereotype must be projected. In the 1980s, my work identified the four common and most important communication interactions in our society as: (a) interpersonal relations with significant others in our lives, (b) business interactions, transactions, and associations of power, (c) commercial marketing communications and advertising, and (d) politicians and political campaigns. These four categories remain critical, and this book reexamines them with new insight that is evolving between personality development, biological health, and personal identity, all as functions of physical attractiveness. When the 1960s brought changes in social examination unparalleled since the Enlightenment and when they asserted ideals of individuality and autonomy, the huge issue of identity within a democratic society presented itself. Identity, both of self and of group, lay at the foundation of whole movements manifest in race, gender, and ethnicity. The "obvious" and "most apparent" cues associated with identification are visual. People seem still to consider these most "obvious" areas to be so self-evident that there is seldom much discussion of them per se; for example, what determines race and what determines sex (now hedged, however, as gender, which is an identity option for some).

Identifying previously unseen "invisible minorities," points to new subtleties of values hidden within appearance and, specifically, physical attractiveness. Physical attractiveness research reveals stereotypes upon which beliefs, attributions, behaviors, and ultimately the entire physical attractiveness phenomenon functions. Often, perceptions and responses gathered in this research reveal another unexpected level of bias or an abundance of further variables that could distort outcome measurements. Since the 1960s, completely new departments in universities have opened in parallel with vastly new areas in law and legislation. Appearance has become a hidden value within many different disciplinary categories, often without comment explicit to physical attractiveness.

Changes in society, particularly advances in technology in the late twentieth and early twenty-first centuries, pose the need for knowledge on new frontiers. Neither universities, science endeavors, nor the arts have thus far kept abreast of physical attractiveness phenomenon as it reaches into the Internet. While many fear the electronic medium for establishing interpersonal relations, proponents state that meeting online yields better results than random meetings. One large service identifying itself as "the fastest growing relationship site on the web" claims their Internet Web dating-matching system "is proven to create deeper, more meaningful relationships designed to last a lifetime."[194] If accurate, an explanation may depend on the lack of a gateway factor served by physical attractiveness that in other settings more readily interferes with individuals of lower physical attractiveness, but others put forth that the feature of a person's physical attractiveness is an even greater gateway restriction factor to achieving meaningful relationships through the Internet. However, future use of knowledge concerning physical attractiveness phenomenon could help promote ways to create more meaningful relationships as well as greater equality in the workplace and throughout society.

Automatization (to make automatic or to turn into an automation) concerning prejudices is a new area of investigation. Experiments are trying to determine whether people someway automatically or involuntarily develop prejudices and if people can rather automatically overcome prejudices that they might hold about certain ethnic, sexual, and racial characteristics. Research suggests that most stereotyping is not volitional or automatic.[165] Cross-race recognition deficit is a visual subcategory in both profiling for African Americans and, in the heightened fear of world terrorism, for white individuals of darker complexion/darker skin tone, who are of either Caucasian ancestry or Hispanic ancestry since "people emphasize visual information specifying race at the expense of individuating information when recognizing cross-race faces."[406]

Youth, the ever-changing wave of the future, have found new ways to participate in physical attractiveness phenomenon. As new generations have done throughout history, youth today have new or different ways that demonstrate the appearance obsession dimension of physical attractiveness phenomenon. Face, body, skin, and adornments have always been central determinants of physical attractiveness. Youth today, as well as some older people not readily identified with the mainstream, have added another definition to these standard determinants. Most recently, new frontiers represented by more advanced, permanent body modifications in the form of body piercing and tattoos continue the "beautiful is good" axiom, much the same way that day-glow hair coloring and shaven heads accomplished a few years earlier. However, even these permanent body modifications are not new, as expressed very well by a *Newsweek* magazine letter to the editor: while some "may find [today's] body modification disturbing, for ages, many peoples of the world have engaged in far more extreme facets of the practice. From tribal tattoos to lip plates, the decision to modify the body in the name of beauty…is…not a recent fad…"[172]

Overt drives to project one's self through one's physical attractiveness seem to have reached unprecedented levels, which may mostly be a reflection of long held wishes now unleashed by technological advances and societal attitude changes. Many people today believe that their physical attractiveness determines their lives, which, while distasteful, is a belief consistent with physical attractiveness phenomenon. At the same time, while people increasingly experience life through the framework of their physical attractiveness, most people are not satisfied with their natural physical attractiveness. People in some instances have accompanied growing evidence of dissatisfaction with their natural physical attractiveness by turning to destructive behaviors, high-risk eating habits, election of risky surgery, and so forth. A dimension often driving these actions is the hope that more physically attractive "face time" can be more profitable in business and politics, and that the fortuitous five minutes of opportunity will provide the introduction needed for success.

These new dimensions have entered into view, and ethics, law, medicine, and commerce—seemingly unchangeable in their orientation—now respond to new trends in the treatment of prejudice. Accordingly, knowledge about physical attractiveness phenomenon has helped contribute to remedies of prejudice. Categories that forestalled growth or development in certain ways had to reinvent themselves. It was no longer acceptable to decide health care based on certain appearance issues, including race, although being overweight still continued to change insurance benefits. However, racial profiling has come under legislation and has addressed moves to end harassment of African Americans for what some activists label DWB (Driving While Black). Sex discrimination, labeled a "glass ceiling" in the workplace, has found EEOC legislation to protect women against unjust acts by management due to gender, but women still earn substantially less than men for equal work. The field of genetics has moved forward to reveal increasing insights about the DNA chain, without revealing what causes racial differences. Sexual minorities have gained significant rights, yet the world still attributes a health epidemic of worldwide proportion mostly to them. Despite great changes, people see homosexual males and females differently from their straight counterparts in even the most progressively thinking countries.

Physical attractiveness actually spans all the appearance designations above, and research demonstrates that appearance can influence any situation, although physical attractiveness of a person can be interdependent with other apparent characteristics. Discrimination based on physical attractiveness can exceed prejudicial discrimination based on differences in gender, race, predominant religion, and even sexual orientation or sexual preference. Regardless of context or age of participants, society tends to view those of higher physical attractiveness as inherently better than those of lower physical attractiveness. This view has produced an environment with serious implications for such far-reaching activities as employment, helping behavior, dating and mating, personality development, achievement, and even election of politicians.

Research has long established the positive relationship between a stimulus person's physical attractiveness and the perception of his/her competency, persuasive ability, and credibility.[535] People judge a person whose looks are higher in physical attractiveness to be more trustworthy, of greater expertise, and more liked than their counterparts whose looks are lower in physical attractiveness. *Science* published research in 2005 investigating the effects of looks specific to political elections, including real-world ramifications to the 2004 American national elections.[703] The research documented that a one-second exposure to a political candidate's photograph creates an enduring impression that often overrides anything the voter hears or sees about the candidate from that moment on, through the casting of ballots. Those researchers found "inferences of competence, based solely on the facial appearance of political candidates and with no prior knowledge about the person, predict the outcomes of elections for the U. S. Congress." Candidates with perceived greater competency based on face appearance factors won their 2004 elections in 72 percent of the U. S. Senate campaigns and 67 percent of the U. S. House of Representatives campaigns. These researchers conclude that despite strategies and assumptions about electorates basing votes on rational, deliberated consideration, considerations based on a person's physical attractiveness clearly contribute and may override all other considerations when casting votes. People perceive a more mature-faced individual, in this case a political candidate, of equal physical attractiveness to a more baby-faced individual to be more competent, intelligent, and better able to provide leadership. A baby-faced adult possesses a more rounded face, larger eyes, smaller nose, higher forehead, and smaller chin.[762]

Differential treatment, in other words, discrimination, occurs throughout life along with different levels of physical attractiveness. A major dissimilarity between discrimination based on physical attractiveness versus sex or race discrimination is that legislation has evolved against the latter, whereas the former is not, yet, legislated against. There is a small movement in that direction with a proposed amendment to existing legislation concerning the Americans with Disabilities Act commonly known as ADA.[323] A major similarity is that sexism and racism have their origins in childhood, as does social stereotyping based on physical attractiveness. The word, further consistent with "ism" words, "lookism" describes this latter stereotyping. Similarly, the negative stereotyping involved with physical attractiveness phenomenon continues to breed into future societies as well within our current society.

The early years of a child do not escape physical attractiveness phenomenon. People introduce infants, literally from birth onward, to the realities aligned with variances of physical attractiveness. Newly born babies in the hospital nursery who are deemed as higher in physical attractiveness, defined at this stage in their life as more cute, are spoken to more, smiled at more, touched more, and held more than those evaluated as lower in physical attractiveness, or less cute.[130, 295, 380]

This early experience imprints the discriminative treatment based on physical attractiveness. It also serves as the beginning of a continuing socialization process for indoctrination and progression of physical attractiveness phenomenon. The most innocent nursery stories involve evil witches who are ugly, whereas the good characters are beautiful. Phrases abound to reinforce ideas that ugly is sin and pretty is virtue, and that ugly ducklings strive to be beautiful royalty. Throughout childhood the individual receives the same social messages delivered both explicitly and implicitly through books, movies, television, and advertising. The messages must have an impact because, by the age of three, children exhibit physical attractiveness phenomenon. Children as young as three years old are more likely to select a photograph of a peer who is of higher physical attractiveness than of lower physical attractiveness.[178] Infants even younger are documented to prefer adults of higher physical attractiveness, as measured by longer time spent looking at faces of higher physical attractiveness compared to lower physical attractiveness.[130]

On another dimension, research increasingly documents that babies are literally born with a preference for higher physical attractiveness. A developmental psychologist provided the latest evidence at the 2004 British Association Festival of Science. Data collected over four years and with more than one hundred newborn babies in England revealed "that babies as young as 5 hours old know a pretty face when they see one."[221] Thus, messages that humans receive about higher and lower physical attractiveness probably merely reinforce and encourage rather than create this preference.

The concepts of physical attractiveness held by these young children are well developed and consistent with the general adult population. Boys and girls at the ages of 3 and 4 equate appearance of elderly ages as lower in physical attractiveness and younger adult ages as higher in physical attractiveness.[187] At ages five and six, children of both sexes even associate negative personality characteristics with those lower in physical attractiveness and positive personalities with those of higher physical attractiveness.[473] Extensive reviews of this research provide support that physical attractiveness phenomenon is just as pervasive and applicable to the lives of infants and children as it is to adults.[295, 380] A disturbing fact of this finding among youth is that these are the formative years, from which time onward encounters with physical attractiveness phenomenon will increase. The experiences will maintain an impact through socialization and throughout the human life cycle—passed and sanctioned from generation to generation.

These three major fundamentals (pervasiveness, subtleness, and socialization) display contradictions that abound with regard to physical attractiveness phenomenon. These contradictions, along with hidden values, are most striking when comparing actions with words. The following quote perhaps explains the reason for the irony involved with physical attractiveness phenomenon:

> It seems somewhat reprehensible to acknowledge publicly that people select friends or employees as much, if not more, for their appearance than their personality traits or skills. It is very much like marrying for money. No one wants to admit how often that occurs. Perhaps we still wish to believe that individual achievement is more important than being born beautiful or handsome.[727]

GOING FORWARD

Research into understanding physical attractiveness phenomenon continues to go forward. One analogy is that the 1960s and 1970s gave birth to these research efforts, while the 1980s and 1990s established this subject matter as an important, robust field of endeavor. Along the way, major changes have occurred: demographics, attitudes, conscientiousness, standards of tolerance, technology accompanying the Internet's birth and proliferation, medical procedures and capabilities, and reverberation of antidiscrimination laws—all of which have created new complexities throughout physical attractiveness phenomenon. While scholarly research abounds in many fields associated with physical attractiveness, the unifying, multidisciplinary, compendious presentation that I undertake is very much absent elsewhere.

It is noteworthy that, despite the attention and research about physical attractiveness generated among scholarly communities as well as among the public, the need to examine and reexamine this subject matter has not decreased but become more compelling. The idea of a person's own value intertwined with his/her physical attractiveness has intensified so significantly that it has become the subject of studies in and of themselves. People who would "obviously" be seen as beneficiaries of dividends of higher physical attractiveness often still see themselves as lacking in appearance, sometimes to the extremes of seeing themselves as approaching grotesque and valueless, which defies explanation in simple social terms and involves complex psychological factors. Self-image has seemingly become more fragile so that an entire nation considers itself largely overweight, regardless of actual size.

What Polly Young-Eisendrath states very well in her 1999 book about the magnitude of appearance problems associated with physical attractiveness for females applies analogously for males:

> Two thirds of all American women, including those who are average size and thin, believe they are overweight. Americans spend an estimated $5 to $7 billion on weight-loss products that are mostly worthless... A recent survey showed that by age thirteen 53% of American girls are unhappy with their bodies, and by age seventeen, 78% are dissatisfied... One large survey showed that 61 percent of college women had some type of eating-related problem... A recent study of 176 women college students showed that those viewing fifty fashion photographs of the "thin ideal" immediately experienced decreased self-esteem and increased self-consciousness, social anxiety, and body dissatisfaction in comparison with those who had not looked at the pictures... Another recent study showed that just thirty minutes of watching TV programs and advertising can alter a young woman's perception of her body![758]

Such studies offer sobering insight into the serious psychological impact of self-perception of one's physical attractiveness. The author of *Appearance Obsession* describes "appearance insecurity" among the many pitfalls of the internalized beauty contest in which women often unwittingly participate.[326] Similarly, the author of *Looking Good* describes a "cult of male body image" where men "fall into the beauty trap so long assumed to be the special burden of women" and that "[t]he traditional image of women as sexual objects has simply been expanded: everyone has become an object to be seen."[418] Such statements emphasize how appearance itself has become a phenomenon, and the need to study physical attractiveness phenomenon is more critical than even previously. It also demonstrates that the field is more complex, diverse, and misunderstood than ever. While the subject matter of physical attractiveness may have been simple and straightforward in earlier years, ignorance is not bliss. The pedestrian axiom that "the more we know, the more we know that we don't know," certainly describes accurately the situation today.

This reverse correlation between knowledge and understanding has many sources, not the least of which is the relatively successful rise in physical attractiveness phenomenon awareness. The public have become informed through ordinary channels that abuses in body or appearance image abound in the mass media with publications including *USA Today, Time Magazine, Smithsonian Magazine, Parents Magazine, U. S. News & World Report*—to name only a sample—publishing informational articles about body image, bulimia and anorexia, obesity, mental disturbances related to body image, etc.

My original assertions that the field of physical attractiveness phenomenon is fragmented remain true today and demand reasserting in the new temporal context. The past twenty years since my first book on this subject have brought up more issues associated with the values of physical attractiveness and, more disturbing, the hidden values. Yet, no formal unified science or other significant undertaking exists to address the phenomenon in totality. Likewise, no other entity exists, institution or umbrella organization, under whose aegis the entire subject falls.

No Age Spared

A Chinese proverb expresses there is only one pretty child in the world and every mother has it. Reality is more intricate, and the younger ages of a person, as well as older ages, do not spare him or her from the impact of physical attractiveness. To begin, specialists, including social scientists, psychologists, surgeons, medical and dental professionals, and others have been customarily, albeit not necessarily explicitly, following indications of physical attractiveness phenomenon in their trade journals and academic publications, many aspects of which have grown into independent fields over the past twenty years. Starting in infancy, hospital protocols exist for infants deemed ugly, born prematurely, or born with superficial defects, and provide special instruction and support for parents of such children. Still, hospitals and others do not offer special support to children whose appearance is average, which is to say, lower than high physical attractiveness. In addition, situations become a social issue for the entire family when parents, who may or may not openly admit that, in their eyes, their child is ugly, or, in less harsh terms, not physically attractive.

Conspicuous childhood disabilities have raised awareness and public consciousness over issues of differences in physical appearances. Diversity training in many areas has bolstered such awareness. Yet, children deemed fat or in other ways physically unattractive still elicit attitudes and influence subsequent discipline. In addition, from among the rather limitless frontiers still calling for researchers to explore, scientists and other professionals need to study the influence on girls when society pays inordinate attention to boys considered bad looking or bad behaving in the classroom. Intertwined here is the idea of being less worthy that probably enters early the life of girls of average physical attractiveness, since the prettiest girls and most bad and physically unattractive boys tend to dominate teachers' time.

Teenagers are deciding major choices concerning appearance, often using drugs ranging from steroids to diuretics in an attempt to build a better shape. Use of diet techniques and drugs by teenagers is prolific, as are cosmetics and minor dermal surgery, such as body piercing and tattoos. Looks dominate teen magazines and day-to-day activities, including media consumption. Self-help experts write especially for teenagers so they can cope with their special problems, including media consumption. One such prominent writer, Sean Covey, advises teenagers to mind their "spiritual diet" by restraining from media use: "Are you feeding your soul nutrients or are you loading it with nuclear waste? …if a one-page ad can sell a bottle of shampoo, don't you think a full-length movie, magazine, or CD can sell a lifestyle?"[146]

Marketers of all sorts use physical attractiveness, also known as looks or good looks, to sell lifestyle to adults as well as to teenagers and younger. Although one would think adults are less impressionable, experiments reveal that such communications affect attitudes approximately equally regardless of maturity. People are either not aware of or are not willing to admit any relationship between a person's physical attractiveness and perceived personal attributes. Experiments continue to prove that, for the most part, people associate persons of higher physical attractiveness with greater excitement, greater emotional stability, and, generally, a more active and exciting social orientation. Their overall impression attributes glamour to attractive individuals and does not expect the same from less attractive people. The experiments demonstrate that "good looking individuals are thought to share many of the characteristics possessed by glamorous people"[50] for whom the range of choices and standards of behavior considerably increase.

Unwittingly as children and teenagers, adults formulate expectations and assumptions based on a person's physical attractiveness, yet firmly believe, or at least proclaim, that physical attractiveness has no significant effect on them. If questioned, they state that, except in their decisions involving relationships, physical attractiveness is superficial and peripheral, and that it does not alter lives. Adults, seemingly as naïve as children, consume cosmetics, clothing, physical alterations, media, and advertising, yet still balk at the admission that a type of discrimination prevails in our culture.

Mass Media Communications

Mass media communications today regularly reinforce, if not lead, the messages central to physical attractiveness phenomenon, such as the concept that higher physical attractiveness is beneficial and lower physical attractiveness is detrimental. A side effect of expanding communications is the multiplicity of new dimensions in appearance. The issues have become more divergent, mutely testified to by the plethora of new publications on eating disorders and, on the other side, of new cosmetic surgeries to counteract overeating. Health issues underlie such articles as "Body dysmorphic disorder: the distress of imagined ugliness," in the *American Journal of Psychiatry*, where the author reports, "Although its concerns might sound trivial, this disorder can lead to social isolation (including being housebound), occupational dysfunction, unnecessary cosmetic surgery, and suicide."[565] Entire journals have emerged, such as *The International Journal of Eating Disorders*, with the aim ultimately to improve and to save lives through increased research and understanding.

Meanwhile, media takes on a second loop of influence when glamour magazines publish details of cosmetic surgeries, surgeons' names, and client lists. Awareness of glamorous resources has increased the market for vanity procedures. Consider, for example, the cosmetic surgery entertainment program—*Nip/Tuck*—broadcast nationally every week during primetime on the FX television network in the United States. As a sign of increasing globalization, now even for physical attractiveness, this television program, already broadcast in other countries, was nominated in 2004 by international correspondents, the Hollywood Foreign Press Association, in the category of "Best Television Series – Drama" for the 61st Annual Golden Globe Awards.[383]

Clearly, messages of good health and appearance have developed deeply conflicting warning signs. The same magazines that publish articles on improving self-esteem and historical references to brave women who changed the human condition vis-à-vis women's rights and honor in society, publish all-but-bare, incredibly underweight, superior toned females in photographs enhanced by thousands of dollars of special effects making them appear real. One cover photo of Michelle Pfeiffer touted that she needs absolutely nothing, yet it was reported that this photo had cost $1,525 to retouch, including "clean up the complexion, soften smile line, trim chin, soften line under earlobe, add hair, add forehead to create better line, and soften neck muscles."[146]

The photographer's studio, the postproduction artist who, pixel-by-pixel, removes every digitized unwanted feature while enhancing wanted features, and the marketing professionals, all add a twist to the meaning of traditionally held truths about perception. Long held truths that seeing is believing and a picture is worth a thousand words, contribute to the hidden values of physical attractiveness phenomenon. These stock phrases relentlessly reinforce a purported truthfulness to the artifice of marketing professionals, their legions, and their counterparts in the ever-optimistic belief that humans successfully discern by sight. Physical attractiveness is such an obvious attribute that its commoditized version in everyday life gives the impression of being natural. Scientific study still seems supererogatory to many—what you see is what you get and all the underlying values should remain exactly where they are—hidden from sight.

Group theorists in today's postmodern world now contend that if enough people believe something, then that something is true. They make this contention regardless of the facts about how people apprehend or interpret material. "Arguably, the single most distinguished and influential social psychologist ever,"[689] Solomon Asch, proved this fact in the 1950s.[30, 31, 32] In carefully controlled laboratory studies utilizing perceptual tasks focusing on the length of lines, he convincingly demonstrated a person would conform to group judgment even though that judgment was clearly in error. Studies conducted in countries literally around the world, as well as with individuals from different cultures in the United States, have reported findings comparable and consistent with Asch.[74] Fifty years later, in 2005, researchers used sophisticated functional MRI (magnetic resonance imaging) scanners to view brain activity during analogous laboratory conformity research.[59] Those data reveal activity in parts of the brain indicating actual cognitive belief change, rather than reflecting a conscious decision to conform to social group pressures. *The New York Times* quotes lead researcher Gregory Berns, a psychiatrist and neuroscientist, as saying, "We like to think that seeing is believing. But the study's findings show that seeing is believing what the group tells you to believe."[69] A Stanford University professor not involved in the research stated, "It's a very important piece of work. It suggests that information from other people may color our perception at a very deep level." Commenting on the research methodology, a Stanford University neuroscientist and acknowledged expert on perception described it as "extremely clever."

Be it postmodern group theorists, twentieth century psychologists, or today's neuroscientists employing the latest technology to achieve real-time views of the brain's workings, all are valuable to advance our understanding of physical attractiveness phenomenon. In fact, nowhere is such knowledge about shared beliefs and values more pertinent than for physical attractiveness phenomenon. People assume physical attractiveness is a vehicle to communicate and reveal truth. Paradoxically, it is, at the same time, a vehicle increasingly created, adjusted, and manipulated to hide and slant values and increase worth. Like game theory, there are critical positions where, if certain strategic actions occur, participants expect some gain. Accordingly, physical attractiveness has evolved into a high stakes arena of life. Miss Universe, Miss America, Miss USA, Mrs. America, and the other pageant/contests across the United States, and even more around the world exhibit values and worth equated with higher and lower levels of physical attractiveness. These formal contests are not unique or separate from lives of non-participants. They represent microcosms that parallel real life each day throughout all populations. Every society bestows dividends to those who naturally possess higher physical attractiveness, or who expend resources to enhance beauty in successful pursuit of ever-greater extremes of physical attractiveness. Exact determinants of what a society deems higher and lower in physical attractiveness vary somewhat, but all societies award benefits to the winners recognized for their higher physical attractiveness, whether it is the rarified world of beauty pageants or the everyday life of ordinary individuals.

Taking Actions

Taking actions to enhance inherited physical attractiveness is not new, nor is it cost free. People of all ages and genders expend their limited time and energy, often at unreal and dangerous levels, in pursuit of unattainable goals of higher physical attractiveness. Some people similarly expend financial resources. Taking actions to increase physical attractiveness ranging from noninvasive creams and injections to invasive surgeries is financially costly "but patients say it is worth it," as reported in a 2004 issue of *Newsweek*.[49] Robin Bothkopf, a 46-year-old real estate investor in Massachusetts, states, "The cost does bother me, and it's a pain to go back every few months. But what's the alternative?"

There is no comparable alternative. Expenditures to enhance physical attractiveness actually translate into financial payoff if higher physical attractiveness is achieved,[540, 541] which might help explain why more than 40% of the more than 8.7 million people who received elective cosmetic surgery in the United States in 2003 financed their pursuits of greater physical attractiveness with loans.[1] Based on a 2005 survey of 1,700 Americans concerning physical attractiveness, *Allure Magazine's* editor in chief concluded, women today "like spending time and money taking care of themselves [to increase their physical attractiveness] because they get back a return on that investment."[261]

The workings of human physical attractiveness (i.e., physical attractiveness phenomenon) prove a history of characteristics and attributed traits that have combined "cheating" with truth. A common principle of beauty, skin tone, for example, has developed surprisingly consistently over time, encompassing enormous geographic and cross-cultural domains.[535] Given the large gaps between cultures and geographies, and the huge disparity between individuals, all immersed in a universe with hidden values ordered by physical attractiveness phenomenon, some "cheating" could be expected in pursuit of greater physical attractiveness.

Skin tone is one dimension important to all cultures, but sometimes with opposite values and definitions. Frequently in current times, Caucasians in the United States seek to darken their skin tone through exposure to natural sunlight, unnatural tanning lights, and topical lotions. Conversely, the author of this book has observed the opposite during his travels in China in 2004 and 2005, Thailand in 2003 and earlier in Hong Kong, Central America, and South America. In these latter countries outside of the United States, women frequently pursue lighter skin tones by taking active steps to avoid exposure to natural sunlight. Accordingly, beauty salons in India in 2005 offer a popular "...service called 'detanning' to lighten a person's skin."[46] Women in Japan currently use whitening cosmetics with chemicals that transform skin color,[263, 374] and Arab women, as they have over centuries, use kohl (wholly imported) to accentuate their eyes.[275] In fact, business news headlines from 2004 in Japan report:[322] "White look [is] back in among Japanese women," "...robust growth in sale of skin-whitening cosmetic products," and "Japan's largest cosmetics firm Shiseido Co. Ltd., famed for its skin-whitening toners and anti-aging creams, is building on women's desire to age beautifully."

Attempting to age beautifully, in other words, attempting to avoid an appearance of aging that might detract from a person's physical attractiveness is not limited to Japan. In the United States in 2004, "Consumers spent $6.4 billion on anti-aging skin products, an increase of 21 percent from the previous year, according to market research firm Packaged Facts."[670] Accordingly, because "[s]ome 78 million baby boomers are approaching retirement age, and many of them have no intention of looking the part...a feeding frenzy [has developed] among doctors and pharmaceutical and cosmetic companies looking to cash in on [the] market..."[670]

There also are optional surgeries. Not just cosmetic reconstruction of eyelids for Asian Americans or rhinoplasty of noses for African Americans, but autologous (in which donor and recipient are the same person) vein collagen transplantation processes to remedy dermal features judged as defects. These defects include natural but unwanted leg or hand veins; botulinum toxin type A injections (brand named, Botox) to correct normal age lines; and elective or optional surgeries to remove results of earlier optional procedures, such as breast implants and tattoos. It took only a few decades to change attitudes toward them. Along the way, dramatic new dimensions, at altitudes never before dreamed, have come to offset actions and aids previously judged as innocent, routine "cheating" of fate, time, or genes.

Demography itself might have predicted a sizable portion of this situation. Changes will be always continuous and one need look no farther than so-called baby boomers (people born between 1946 and 1964, often noted as being born shortly after World War II ended). The 1990s brought the baby boomers into midlife in the United States and in other countries with these particular demographics. This demographic group in the United States comprises about 77 million people, which will continue to affect demand for products, services, and industries associated with physical attractiveness.[391] Shifts in their demands for physical attractiveness will correspond with their shifting ages. Messages currently from this population, of substantial size and financial means, include that physical attractiveness for aging baby boomers is looking healthy and looking younger than their age. Not surprising, reverberating from this population are astronomical increases in health trends and cosmetic surgery for men to look as sharp and competent as possible, as well as for women to possess similar appearances.

Regardless of age category, cultures throughout the United States and the world over still hold a double standard in terms of physical attractiveness. "Working women are judged in a different way than men…they have to keep their appearance up," according to Elliot Jacobs, a plastic surgeon in New York City.[49] Women's successes in the job market have modified their view about enhancing physical attractiveness through cosmetic surgery, which, in earlier times, was a recourse prized by the insecure, but, which is, now an action preferred by those who are or aspire to be successful. In this context, for either a man or a woman who has turned to noninvasive treatments ranging from topical face creams to injections of Botox and Restylane, "you reach a point where you might as well do the [surgical] face-lift. In the end, the only thing that is really going to tighten your skin is to lift it up—and that requires surgery," according to Ramsey Alsarraf, coauthor of the medical textbook *The Aging Face: A Systematic Approach*.[324] Correspondingly, physical attractiveness phenomenon is driving many to heed that advice, as evidenced by 2004 data that "more than 8.7 million cosmetic plastic surgery procedures [were] performed last year, according to the American Society of Plastic Surgeons—an increase of nearly one third."[49]

Self-help studies and support groups, not to mention completely new associations, have emerged. One ramification is that health and identity have become so greatly intertwined that it is sometimes difficult to ferret out physical attractiveness issues from the more traditional medical issues. For example, HMOs (Health Maintenance Organizations), another 1980s creation, routinely set limits on what is medical or medically justified, as opposed to what is optional in terms of apparent cosmetic treatments. The result often produces outcries of individuals determined to secure reimbursed expenditures for enhancing their physical attractiveness. Related reimbursable expenses can represent somewhat unclear distinctions. For example, insurance will routinely reimburse treatment for deformities of the oral region such as the palate, but will not pay for treatment regarding deformities of the teeth. Attempting to keep pace, legislation defines new social policy where state and federal laws regulate certain health care procedures to provide reimbursement for coverage formerly denied on the basis that the procedures were cosmetic. Health care in general has likewise expanded exponentially, becoming a multibillion-dollar industry. The rise of acceptance of cosmetic surgeries, accompanied by increasing social approval, carries substantial economic implications for decisions about insurance reimbursements.

Perhaps the most apparent physical attractiveness trend is again a reverberation of the sixties when, almost overnight, thin became the ultimate goal for women. One consequence has been people, particularly females, who embrace this goal at younger and younger ages. Attempts and ideas about being thin are shown as early as fourth grade, although the author of *Appearance Obsession* states "the correlation between the thin beauty ideal and depression and eating disorders is direct and constant and begins for women in adolescence."[326] The weight loss industry commands more than $5 billion annually, and American society has bowed almost uniformly to an essentially anorexic model. Almost no one rates a female body as too thin, but people routinely judge even average size women as overweight, with more than 10% over ideal weight frequently deemed a health issue. *Exacting Beauty*, a 1999 scholarly book on body image, proves that body image among the overly thin leads to a host of psychological disturbances.[691] The norm today is a mindset goal more akin to appearance achieved through anorexia than appearance achieved through healthy living. This norm increasingly defines higher physical attractiveness, while normal body weight is seen as (hopelessly) diminishing attractiveness, which sets the stage for full-blown eating disorders and health issues—whether anorexia, obesity, or body dysmorphic disorder.

Athleticism is, to many, a euphemism for overindulging their body image affliction to attain greater levels of physical attractiveness rather than greater levels of fitness and health. Health as an appearance indicator has blown completely out of proportion to the human organism, with mesomorphic trends in masculinity appearance subsuming ordinary health concerns, such as procreation. Use of steroids has become much more a part of ordinary society. Steroidal use is among the highest drugs consumed in the country, despite known detrimental side effects. Already in 1990, *Consumer* magazine, published by the United States Food and Drug Administration, reported that American "Teenagers [are] Blasé about Steroid Abuse."[708] Another report that same year by the same publication stated, "Anabolic steroids are not used to build muscle by boys and girls, but they are also used by young men who just want to look better."[708] A 2005 survey of 10,000 teenagers in the United States, conducted by Harvard University, found that 8 percent of girls and 12 percent of boys had used anabolic steroids or other such growth hormones and dietary supplements.[702]

Perceived social and economic benefits of good looks in men became the driving force for completely new types of cosmetic surgery. The author of a book published in 2001 reports that 34% of all male Wall Street brokers have undergone facial surgery, a prodigious number, especially given the overall youthfulness among this field to begin with.[418] Athleticism and health clubs have proliferated under the guise of improved health, but the manifest interest is improved appearance. This same author even states that men have essentially caught up with women; that is, "The traditional image of women as sexual objects has simply been expanded: everyone has become an object to be seen."[418]

Women still are much more likely to vie for the appearance dividend paid by higher physical attractiveness than men are, if beauty contests are an indication. Females, ranging from girls of very young age to young women in their twenties, compete for beauty awards, for which many critics in society believe they pay an enormous personal price throughout their lives. When the stakes are so high, grossly distorted behavior becomes a way of life for millions. Small wonder, then, that eating disorders are likewise inflicting boys. Health concerns and appearance represent competing desires, but have been handed, unsolved, to minors to resolve a great deal by themselves.

The weight loss industry matches mass media when it comes to transmitting messages. Likewise, television programming moves hand-in-hand with advertising, studiously stereotyping by looks, or, more precisely, by physical attractiveness. More than communicated before, the frequency of these varied messages with a common theme about enhancing physical attractiveness has increased exponentially. Whole new fields—ethics in cosmetic surgery, for instance—have arisen alongside the new developments, trying to keep abreast of abuses pertaining to styling one's own physical attractiveness. Similarly, education has acted to assure that perceptions or realities of being overweight do not create the wrong environment for students' progress, with legislation explicitly against bullying and expressly condemning the derision of physical attributes as unacceptable behavior.

SUMMARY

At times, physical attractiveness may be in the eye of the beholder, so to speak, but physical attractiveness phenomenon is never in the eye of the beholder. This distinction contributes to the excitement of research into physical attractiveness phenomenon. Among changing fads and fashions, the larger encompassing and driving principles remain stable, providing higher-level meaning for observations of reality that often challenge logic and common sense, confirm scientific proposals, and, ultimately, reveal hidden values. Experience shows many situations in which physical attractiveness earlier assumed insignificant proves highly significant. Yet many people consistently (and adamantly) report that physical attractiveness is unimportant to how they perceive and respond to others.

Hidden values ordered and controlled by physical attractiveness phenomenon represent the proverbial double-edged sword. Physical attractiveness phenomenon encourages individuals on one hand to enhance their appearances, but pursuit of enhancements, on the other hand, can lead to negative actions and harmful outcomes. A circular four-stage process explains or at least describes physical attractiveness phenomenon: (1) physical attractiveness serves as an informational cue, (2) from which people infer extensive information, (3) that triggers assumptions, expectations, attitudes, and behaviors, and (4) that cause pervasive and powerful effects/consequences. Overwhelmingly, these consequences are more favorable for people who possess appearances of higher physical attractiveness and less favorable for people who possess appearances of lower physical attractiveness.

Each stage of the four-stage circular process depicting physical attractiveness phenomenon is inseparably interdependent with physical attractiveness and the broader concept of appearance. A fundamental of this phenomenon is that the process takes place in an environment that is subtle; people commonly are unaware of it, or unwilling to acknowledge it, to the extent of denying the impact of physical attractiveness on their thoughts and actions. Accordingly, the evidence does not support what people say about the role that physical attractiveness occupies in their thoughts and actions. People do judge others by their physical attractiveness, despite their claims in agreement with the proverbial cliché that people should not judge a book by its cover. Scientific study as well as attentive anecdotal observation provides ready proof that actions do speak louder than words concerning physical attractiveness. Measures conducted by means of scientific research repeatedly show that people severely underrate the influence of physical attractiveness. Many researchers note this contradiction as summarized by one early researcher's statement: "It appears that they are either not fully aware or not fully honest about how important physical attractiveness really is to them."[462]

When confronted about physical attractiveness phenomenon and research into it, people tend to respond in one of three broad ways: One group of people wholeheartedly embrace it, often identifying with the hidden values showing the phenomenon to be far more than meets the eye. A second group of people expresses neutrality, showing neither interest nor disinterest. The third group dislikes the entire idea of physical attractiveness phenomenon and research about it. They tend to be defensive about the topic, express that it is unethical or improper research, refuse to consider overtly the importance and possible influence of physical attractiveness, and attempt to ignore the proven effects of physical attractiveness. Ignorance is not bliss when it comes to physical attractiveness. These latter reactions promote continued unawareness about the person's environment. Be it obliviousness or denial, such a mindset does not cause physical attractiveness phenomenon to disappear, nor does it minimize the impact of physical attractiveness in our lives, our minds, or our interpersonal relations, or in the lives, minds, and interpersonal relations of other individuals.

conferences subject the reports to peer-review screening processes. This screening usually involves blind peer review whereby reviewers are not privy to the names of authors.

Beyond the above community of researchers, and even within this research community, untold numbers of people study physical attractiveness at vastly different levels, intensities, and time spans. At another end of this continuum, people with significantly less official research credentials also study physical attractiveness phenomenon. These people perform significantly less formal studies, but with no less importance. The procedures include personal, largely subjective perceptions by people in everyday life, ranging from a very long timeframe that spans a person's natural life to a brief moment when appearance, particularly physical attractiveness, is unusually significant or outstanding to a person in a positive or negative manner. These latter data, collected through individuals' perceptions in everyday life, are meaningful primarily to the individuals, who likely add the data to an informal database in their minds that contribute in some way to their own perspective about physical attractiveness phenomenon.

This latter form of research, along with all its variations, performed by individuals not holding generally recognized scientific or scholarly credentials represent a form of research best described as ad hoc or personal concern. Generally, individuals conducting these studies do so absent of formal research training and procedures. While these people often find subsequent results to be of great significance to them, these people neither present nor publish their research in scientific forums due mainly to lack of pertinent recognized credibility. Often without distinct starting and ending points, this research varies from imprecise thoughts and observations spread over a lifetime to brief periods when a person finds appearance, particularly physical attractiveness, to be unusually significant in either a positive or a negative manner. Research procedures here frequently consist of highly subjective perceptions by people in everyday life with the subsequent data meaningful mostly only to them, despite the substantial interest that the data sometimes generate among people. These people consciously or subconsciously interpret the data and affix or do not affix the results to an informal database in their minds. Ultimately, the collected data and interpretations contribute in some way to the respective person's perspective about physical attractiveness, but provide little or no additional understanding of physical attractiveness phenomenon to themselves or others.

SCIENTIFIC RESEARCH

Individuals of diverse sorts conduct different types or levels of research in all sciences, yielding findings or conclusions that may vary between times and between studies. It is not usual for scientific research projects to discover data that indicate findings contrary to popular belief concerning many topics in our world, as well as concerning physical attractiveness topics. It also is not usual that greater analysis and alternate interpretation of the same data discover significantly different findings. In 2005, the *Journal of the American Medical Association* published an extensive project conducted by a researcher at the University of Ioannina School of Medicine in Greece to investigate frequency with which later studies disconfirm or contradict findings from earlier studies.[272, 314] That project focused on highly cited medical research studies and discovered that findings from later studies contradicted findings from 32 percent of those medical studies conducted earlier. Composing the 32 percent, findings from the later studies outright contradicted 16 percent of the earlier studies and reported strengths or significance to be substantially less for another 16 percent of the earlier studies.

Mixed directions for research findings are not limited to medical sciences, with equal or greater frequency of diversity of directions possibly expected for research findings in social sciences. The findings in research concerning physical attractiveness phenomenon are not always in the same direction but they have been surprisingly consistent with more convergence than divergence of findings. While research concerning physical attractiveness phenomenon has at times revealed preference for average physical attractiveness, research findings as well as conventional wisdom strongly indicate favor for higher physical attractiveness. When dealing with components of the body, one question becomes what defines greater or lesser appeal and what dimensions about specific body components contribute to raising or lowering an individual's physical attractiveness.

Not unique to physical attractiveness research, data produced by research in all fields frequently, at least initially, suggest apparent straightforward facts. However, data or facts alone do not provide meaningful understanding. They usually require interpretation and context to provide knowledge and understanding. Results from one early research study published in 1980 indicated an aspect of physical attractiveness phenomenon that diverged from cultural stereotype and the larger context provided by collective research findings.[587] Finding from this particular study seemed, at least initially, to diverge from the large majority of findings from physical attractiveness phenomenon research. Data from that 1980 project showed women of moderate physical attractiveness had more opposite-sex dates and more same-sex socializing compared to their counterparts of high physical attractiveness.

The larger context of collective research knowledge about physical attractiveness phenomenon, both then and now, permits at least three explanations for the above data. One explanation for this indicated preference finding is a Matching Hypothesis that motivates people to prefer others whom they judge most similar to themselves in appearance. This reasoning assumes a rather normal or bell-shaped distribution of population and physical attractiveness whereby the majority of persons, i.e., the average person, possesses average physical attractiveness. The two ends of this bell-shaped distribution would then comprise far fewer individuals, respectively possessing lower than average and higher than average physical attractiveness. An alternate explanation regards suitors who consider the probability of success to partner is more likely with others who represent moderate levels of physical attractiveness rather than higher levels. Still another explanation for when moderate physical attractiveness appears preferred over higher levels is that judgments of physical attractiveness as determined by body types may be categorical in a person's mind rather than continuous.[317] With this explanation, people make judgments or decisions about higher and lower physical attractiveness only when confronted with marked deviations from the average that clearly exceeds some perceptual threshold.

LONGITUDINAL EXPEDITION

My study of physical attractiveness combines lifelong and mostly formal research yielding empirical data with less formal research yielding anecdotal data. More than thirty years ago, I conducted my first documented, scientific research investigation into the appearance phenomenon pertaining to physical attractiveness.[523] It was 1973, when scholarly journals had published only a handful of research investigations about physical attractiveness, and my research project was a formal psychology experiment that investigated physical attractiveness in terms of attitudes believed or attributed about people based on their different levels of physical attractiveness.

More than twenty years ago, in 1985, I published my first book about the appearance phenomenon as focused on physical attractiveness.[535]At the time, scholarly journals had published several hundred research investigations about physical attractiveness, and my book was an encyclopedic synthesis of the collective research to provide readers with knowledge gained scientifically about physical attractiveness. My 1985 book was separate from my prior studies about physical attractiveness, but it strongly benefited from the wealth of information and judicious perspective gained during my previous studies. Those studies reflect a career-long, programmatic research agenda to gain and to disseminate knowledge about physical attractiveness. The major research projects required for each of my four formal university degrees also reflect my enthusiasm and steadfast dedication. I focused on further understanding the hidden values of physical attractiveness for each degree's respective culminating research project: Ph.D. dissertation,[528] M.S. thesis,[521] M.B.A. project,[547] and B.A. senior thesis.[523] Similarly, the focus for a large portion of my published scholarly journal articles and professional academic conference research presentations was to further understand the hidden values of physical attractiveness, as well as numerous class term papers.

Four topical categories can describe changes since my experiment conducted in 1973 and my book published in 1985. First, knowledge has advanced considerably about physical attractiveness, particularly physical attractiveness phenomenon. Researchers today actively carry on additional research that continually advances this knowledge. Scholarly journals have now published thousands of pertinent research articles conducted around the world since this field of research began in 1965. These articles collectively reflect an impressive depth and breadth of investigations along with robust research methodologies, all with surprising consistency and corroboration of earlier discoveries about physical attractiveness as a phenomenon. The date of 1965 is reasonable to identify with the start of research about physical attractiveness phenomenon because that year presented the first directly and explicitly related scientific research project.[464] The presentation was a research article subjected to standard scientific research scrutiny and then published by the *Journal of Personality and Social Psychology*. It detailed an experiment about attitude change produced by communicators whose appearance varies by different levels of physical attractiveness.

Second, my own knowledge about physical attractiveness has advanced considerably, and today I actively carry on to continuously advance my knowledge and the knowledge of others. In the process, scholars and researchers in and out of the United States have noted my work formally in more than three hundred published research articles and university textbooks. During these years, I have disseminated knowledge about physical attractiveness, speaking about the topic literally around the world in a variety of forums, as well as publishing articles in scholarly research journals and providing mass media interviews for popular press magazines, newspapers, television, and the Internet. Furthermore, I have created the Appearance Phenomenon Institute (API) for research, advocacy, and assistance. Its mission is threefold: to advance understanding about appearance, to increase awareness of appearance phenomenon, and to improve assistance for people disadvantaged by appearance phenomenon, all particular to physical attractiveness.

As well as directly advancing my knowledge about physical attractiveness phenomenon, I have publicly demonstrated indirect advancements. These include strengthening my professional, technical, and research capabilities, all critically important to scientific fundamentals for interpretation, analysis, screening, and synthesis of research about physical attractiveness. I have published two books that do not deal directly with physical attractiveness but with critical underpinnings for interpreting, analyzing, and qualifying research pertinent to physical attractiveness phenomenon. The second book focused on primary research data and experiment research designs as a research methodology,[525] while the first book focused on secondary research data in the United States and worldwide, including secondary data research procedures as a research methodology.[548]

Third, at the time of my 1985 book, I coined the term Physical Attractiveness Phenomena and titled the book accordingly to communicate that physical attractiveness, with all that it involves, truly meets the dictionary definition of a phenomenon. I chose the plural form of phenomenon to communicate that physical attractiveness, with all that it involves, is far more than one phenomenon. The spheres or realms of physical attractiveness are many, with impact in multifaceted dimensions throughout life. To advance knowledge and understanding of physical attractiveness, I proposed a formal scientific discipline titled Papology ("ology" defined as "the study of," along with "pap" reflecting an acronym through the first letter of each word for Physical Attractiveness Phenomena).

To organize the scattered and fragmented findings pertinent to understanding physical attractiveness phenomena, I reviewed the philosophy and history of sciences in the milieu of physical attractiveness phenomenon research and proposed a formal Physical Attractiveness Phenomena Theory within Papology (see

Figure 2-1. Physical Attractiveness Phenomenon Theory, Six Primary Stages). Now, more than twenty years later that theory proposed then is surprisingly accurate in foretelling today's knowledge about physical attractiveness phenomenon. Through a sequential structure that comprises six elements or stages, the Theory accounts for:

- the consideration that many factors determine physical attractiveness (ascription element),
- the historical recognition of a significant physical attractiveness stereotype (substratum element),
- the extensive consequences associated with physical attractiveness phenomenon (outgrowth element),

- the transmission of physical attractiveness phenomenon between generations (transfer element),
- the gradual shifts that occur for preferred ideals of physical attractiveness (impingement element), and
- the role that society occupies within physical attractiveness phenomenon (collectivism element).

Figure 2-1. Physical Attractiveness Phenomenon Theory, Six Primary Stages

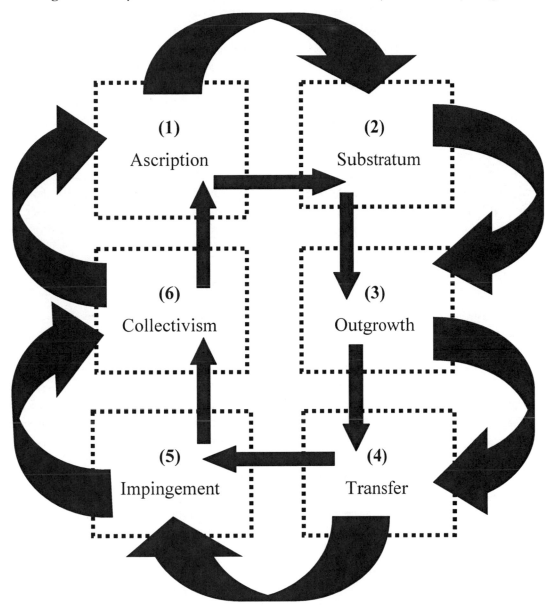

The field of physical attractiveness research has advanced significantly and, in the process, has matured in a manner characteristic of sciences throughout history. From these early labors came today's conceptualizations and designations. Since my first book on this topic, I have now coined the term appearance phenomenon. It is an encompassing term that recognizes physical attractiveness as one part of appearance, albeit a uniquely large and inseparable part. For my 1985 book, I had not yet used the term *appearance phenomenon*, nor had I yet used the term *physical attractiveness phenomenon*. Appearance phenomenon also provides a broad context for understanding and predicting physical attractiveness phenomenon. I have now also adopted the singular form of phenomenon to communicate the entirety of physical attractiveness. In turn, physical attractiveness phenomenon is one part of appearance phenomenon, albeit the predominant part and an integral part.

Fourth, the public has demonstrated increasing interest about physical attractiveness, and that interest today is immense. All the while, the conflict or contradictions about physical attractiveness among people are increasingly great. On one hand, people express disapproval and even disdain about others who pursue and/or in any way openly embrace higher levels of physical attractiveness. On the other hand, the adage that actions speak louder than words is manifest, endemic, and even epidemic across the United States and around the world concerning physical attractiveness. What people say outwardly about the unimportant role that physical attractiveness holds or should hold in our lives is not what the actions of people reveal concerning their actual beliefs or practices about physical attractiveness for themselves or for others.

PRESENT CIRCUMSTANCES

Present circumstances or state of affairs concerning physical attractiveness phenomenon reveal that since my 1973 and 1985 works, one of the most pivotal changes is the considerable progress of related scientific research, both quantity and quality. Since the origin of this research field, researchers have discovered a wealth of knowledge as reported in thousands of directly and indirectly related articles published in scientific journals that span wide-ranging disciplines. The research collection puts forth an impressive depth and breadth of investigations, robust research methodologies, and consistency of discoveries about physical attractiveness and physical attractiveness phenomenon. Pursuit of more knowledge continues today.

Collective knowledge at present documents well that physical attractiveness is a phenomenon profoundly deeper than its tangible surface appearance. Science continues to advance this knowledge with research pertinent to understanding physical attractiveness phenomenon that has expanded beyond its origins in the mid-1960s in social psychology. Social psychology is conceivably the field most central to physical attractiveness, but it is erroneous to suggest one discipline somehow comprises this field's universe. It now finds relevance in scientific disciplines literally from A to Z, anthropology to zoology, as well as throughout the scores of sub-disciplines identified with psychology and sociology. Study of physical attractiveness phenomenon is clearly multidisciplinary with valuable contributions to knowledge about physical attractiveness phenomenon coming from all the formal scientific fields indicated above. Likewise, scientific inquiry and helpful anecdotal annotations come from cosmetic, apparel, and health entities, medical, dental, and legal professions, advertising, marketing, and entertainment industries, as well as government agencies, not-for-profit organizations, and businesses literally of all types.

Interestingly, while knowledge about physical attractiveness and related phenomenon has increased dramatically, public displays of pursuits for higher physical attractiveness also have increased dramatically. Taking note at approximately twenty-year intervals since the mid-1960s, the population at large, as well as the population of related scientific researchers, has demonstrated expanding interest in physical attractiveness and responsiveness to physical attractiveness phenomenon. From mid-1960s to mid-1980s, interest increased substantially within both these populations. During the next twenty-years to midway between 2000 and 2010, interest and actions accelerated immensely, especially in pursuits to enhance a person's physical attractiveness. Through the next twenty-year interval through approximately 2030, high levels of interest in physical attractiveness and corresponding levels of responsiveness to physical attractiveness phenomenon will continue almost certainty.

Throughout all the advances in knowledge provided by researchers and changes evidenced by actions of everyday people, physical attractiveness phenomenon has remained the same. As introduced earlier in the prior chapter concerning the circular four-stage process of physical attractiveness phenomenon (see page 21, Figure 1-1), physical attractiveness continues to serve as an informational cue. From this informational cue, people infer extensive information that triggers assumptions, expectations, attitudes, and behaviors, causing pervasive and powerful effects/consequences that overwhelmingly are more favorable for people whose appearance is of higher physical attractiveness and less favorable for people whose appearance is of lower physical attractiveness.

FOCUS WITH DEFINITIONS

Four interconnected, overlapping constructs define the boundaries and the core or hub of this research into physical attractiveness phenomenon:

- Appearance
- Appearance Phenomenon
- Physical Attractiveness
- Physical Attractiveness Phenomenon

These constructs are fundamental for understanding the effects of appearance and physical attractiveness in the lives of all people; accordingly, this early section in this book provides explicit definitions of each. In research parlance, *concepts*, *factors*, *constructs*, and even *components*, are some interchangeable generic words that reference or describe such entities.

Appearance

Appearance is the way someone or something looks. Due to the appearance phenomenon in which it occurs, appearance can be a blessing or a curse, an asset or a liability, a benefit or detriment. It can grant power or confer weakness. It possesses many dimensions and communicates even more dimensions: physical attractiveness, age, education, ethnicity, gender, race, socioeconomic level, intelligence, fortune-misfortune, health-illness, respect, authority, expertise, liking, sex appeal, suspicion-trust, friend-enemy-terrorist, and so forth.

in New York City. By 1996, it was already broadcasting pictures of desired looks in 68 countries to a measured reach of more than 230 million actual viewers.[723]

Developed

Communications of many varieties contribute to plausible explanations for physical attractiveness phenomenon. Fundamental features of appearance inherent in communication, whether inconspicuous or obvious, possess greater universality and immediacy than other features of communication. These contributions to understanding the hidden values of physical attractiveness rest on learning even socialized undercurrents attributed to appearance, which begins at very young, impressionable ages and continues throughout life. A core consideration of socialization is learning the physical attractiveness stereotype "what is beautiful is good" or, in less common parlance, the stereotype "fine feathers make a fine bird."[390] Although people as a rule deny they embrace the beautiful-good stereotype, the well-known cliché "looks can be deceiving" epitomizes the widely held stereotype that equates higher physical attractiveness with good and lower physical attractiveness with less good or even bad. Unspoken reality seems too often to abide by the West African proverb, "To be ugly is to be unforgiven."[358]

More solid proof reported by scientific research investigating this stereotype documents that people learn the stereotype, or at least subscribe to it, conceivably by instinct, early and robustly, regardless of society, culture, or country. Already in childhood, children demonstrate preference for others whose appearance is higher in physical attractiveness.[137] This childhood preference should be neither alarming nor bewildering. Messages propounding the higher value of higher physical attractiveness besiege children, and the conversely lower value of lower physical attractiveness is equally prominent.

Children

Socialization or indoctrination of children with physical attractiveness phenomenon begins innocently with good, honorable intentions. From shortly after birth, well-meaning parents acculturate children to adhere to the societal norms nearly unanimously mandated for acceptance and success. It begins with unquestionably communicating the importance or requirement for children to look their best when in the company of others. Then there are mass media messages directly delivered to children through targeted television and movies, and indirectly delivered through messages intended primarily for adults via billboards, television, and movies.

Given world realities, there is no acceptable alternative to promulgation of physical attractiveness phenomenon. Good intentions to instill values, actions, and appearances that stress the importance of higher physical attractiveness for success are unavoidable parts of socialization. The best action for people who consciously resist physical attractiveness phenomenon is to be conscientious, moderated, and active in all their communications with their children regarding physical attractiveness.

Parents communicate physical attractiveness phenomenon to their children in ways intended and not intended. Often unintentionally due to lack of active awareness, parents serve as powerful role models through their own behaviors concerning physical attractiveness. These behaviors impress upon their children the different worth for different levels of physical attractiveness. They include preening for work, special occasions, and important company, talking at the dinner table about changing appearances due to stress, work, and obesity, deriding the appearances of coworkers, friends, and enemies, and disciplining their children with vocabulary that equates the lower physical attractiveness (i.e., the word ugly) with undesirable behavior. Rather acute listening will hear adults say "Isn't it terrible little Joey was injured, he is such a cute little boy," unintentionally implying that the injury or illness would not be as terrible if the little boy or girl was less cute, or was maybe ugly.

Another reason that children embrace discriminatory values for people whose appearance is higher and lower in physical attractiveness should unnerve anyone cognizant about the fairy tales read and told by well-meaning parents, workers in day care, and schoolteachers. A 2003 research project studied 168 fairy tales written in the 1800s by Jacob and Wilhelm Grimm.[255] The authors originally wrote these fables to communicate desirable values and behaviors to children in central Europe in the 1800s. Nearly 50% have transcended times, locations, and cultures, reproduced today as children's books and movies with their messages repeated zillions of times to impressionable children in the United States and elsewhere. Well-intentioned people, albeit seriously naive, have woven into our cultural fabric with no end in sight many stories that encourage negative hidden values for physical attractiveness. People now view some stories as esteemed classics, reproduced thus far more than a hundred times in formats that include books, plays, television cartoons, and movies, even though they blatantly promulgate physical attractiveness phenomenon, such as Cinderella, Snow White, and Sleeping Beauty.

This form of communication to children strongly and clearly favors promulgating physical attractiveness phenomenon. Infrequently there is a ray of light to the contrary. Among today's world of fairy tales targeted at young children is *Beauty and the Beast,* in which the female character of higher physical attractiveness comes to love the physically unattractive male character.

These fables, carried forward to contemporary times, overwhelmingly and disproportionately position stereotypically good-looking characters as those who achieve great accomplishments and perform desirable deeds. The messages contained in these stories prescribe determinants of physical attractiveness, equate higher physical attractiveness with good, and equate lower physical attractiveness with bad. Among nearly 50 percent of these fables popular today, 94 percent cite physical attractiveness, nearly 20 percent equate lower physical attractiveness (i.e., ugly) with bad/evil along with punishment for them and not their counterparts of higher physical attractiveness. One fable references physical attractiveness 114 times, with the average fable making 13.6 such references. Two conclusions by the authors of this study: "This trend reinforces the message to children that physical attractiveness is an important asset women should aim to achieve and maintain," and "[f]airy tales, which are still read by millions of American children, say it pays to be pretty."[255]

Adults

Lessons learned early, or otherwise embraced early, about physical attractiveness extend far beyond childhood. Even if not given explicit side-by-side comparisons of individuals higher in physical attractiveness with individuals lower in physical attractiveness, people demonstrate their beliefs to be positive, favorable, and complimentary to individuals of higher physical attractiveness and quite the opposite toward individuals of lower physical attractiveness.

People believe that more physically attractive people possess more socially desirable traits, live better lives, and have more successful marriages and occupations than less physically attractive people.[182] More precisely, people "assume that good looks are instrumental to leading a socially and sexually exciting life."[50] Accordingly, they are perceived to be "more sociable, dominate, sexually warm, mentally healthy, intelligent, and socially skilled."[212] To further support or disconfirm these findings, different researchers conducted a huge separate national survey in the United States.[62] Their findings corroborate other findings about people of all ages believing this stereotype. The research participants invariably expressed a belief that persons of higher physical attractive obtain more happiness, have more sex, and receive greater respect than those of lower physical attractiveness.

The existence of all the beliefs and attributions beneficial toward higher physical attractiveness and detrimental toward lower physical attractiveness presents further explanation for the differential values hidden in dynamics within the appearance phenomenon. These beliefs and attributions, together, also help explain why people pursue higher levels of attractiveness despite the inconvenience, effort, costs, and at times extraordinary and even dangerous means.[70, 572]

UNIVERSAL PHENOMENON, UNIVERSAL VALUES

Physical attractiveness phenomenon transcends time, geography, and culture. Despite intentions to be independent of this phenomenon, the impact of higher and lower physical attractiveness is universal, timeless, and not characteristic of any particular groups of people. Around the world, populations place correspondingly higher values on higher physical attractiveness and lower values placed on lower physical attractiveness.

In 1997, I published the fifth of a series of five annual articles about physical attractiveness phenomenon in the *Journal of Esthetic Dentistry*.[530, 531, 539, 543, 545] Those articles provided me with a uniquely valuable opportunity for feedback from readers around the globe, due to that journal's status as the official publication of the American Academy of Esthetic Dentistry, the European Academy of Esthetic Dentistry, the Japan Academy of Esthetic Dentistry, and the International Federation of Esthetic Dentistry. Each time that journal published another one of my five articles, professionals sent me letters expressing their interests and experiences, and those of patients, confirming physical attractiveness phenomenon as I have written about in this book.

This anecdotal feedback data matches and complements respective separate empirical data. Empirical data and findings reported by scientific research projects conducted around the world consistently contribute to the growing, rather virtual, database that allows extrapolation and generalizations attesting to the robustness of physical attractiveness phenomenon. Stepping back and comparing data from research conducted in particular countries with focus on the resident population reveal the same uniformity as data from research projects conducted explicitly to compare physical attractiveness phenomenon between countries.

One research project comparing populations between countries investigated if physical attractiveness phenomenon exists in the form of excessive concern with physical appearance in China, India, New Zealand, and United States.[192] The subjects comprised equal numbers of males and females who completed questionnaires employing seven-point Likert scales ranging from strongly disagree to strongly agree for a series of statements comprising a vanity scale. This research project published in the *Journal of Consumer Affairs* included five statements (see Table 2-1)[192] to collect data from individuals asked to self-rate the importance of physical attractiveness to them. Six statements (see Table 2-2)[192] were also included to collect data from individuals asked to self-rate their own physical attractiveness.

Table 2-1. Self-Rating of Importance of Physical Attractiveness, Five Scale Statements

The way I look is extremely important to me.

I am very concerned about my appearance.

I would feel embarrassed if I was around people and did not look my best.

Looking my best is worth the effort.

It is important that I always look good.

Table 2-2. Self-Rating of Physical Attractiveness, Six Scale Statements

People notice how attractive I am.

My looks are very appealing to others.

People are envious of my good looks.

I am a very good-looking individual.

My body is sexually appealing.

I have the type of body that people want to look at.

Explicitly comparing multiple countries in the world again corroborates the universality of physical attractiveness phenomenon. "The results of this investigation are conclusive in demonstrating that the vanity scale [assessing physical attractiveness phenomenon] is directly applicable to the four countries examined," stated the study's authors.[192] Results of this 2001 study are consistent with results of a 1995 study conducted by different researchers exploring vanity,[494] which lends credence to the latest researchers' conclusion that a global measure of physical attractiveness "appears to be useful [valid] in both Eastern and Western cultures."

Among the abundance of statistical analyses ranging from simple to sophisticated, mean values (M) for importance of one's own physical attractiveness was statistically the same for people in New Zealand (M = 2.63), United States (M = 2.61), and China (M = 2.52), but mean value was statistically less for India (M = 2.14). Numerous hypotheses might explain this difference for India; however, the most plausible explanation seems to rest not on actual expressed importance but on differences in the social acceptability to acknowledge the importance. The authors attribute this statistical difference for importance of physical attractiveness in India to the lateness of Western mass media's arrival in India. That thought does not adequately account for the expressed ratings of physical attractiveness importance in China. It also does not fully, or maybe not even adequately, account for the critical mass of published physical attractiveness research conducted in India that shows importance of physical attractiveness to be more similar than dissimilar to values prevalent in the United States.

A characteristic of physical attractiveness phenomenon is the conflict within people concerning physical attractiveness, and it is accurate to say that people feel it worldwide. Anecdotally, consider the proverbial wisdom that actions speak louder than words. Propelling this situation is the look of physical attractiveness that people see on the surface of appearance, fused with the hidden values of physical attractiveness phenomenon that impose realities out of sight from most views. This out-of-sight perspective, commonly unseen, unrecognized, or denied, might or might not parallel the level of physical attractiveness seen on the surface. Its assessment, let alone its awareness, is not straightforward.

Accompanying a person's physical attractiveness are long-standing, complex dynamics that readily contrast with goals for social justice, equal opportunity, and other democratic ideals. People frequently tell others, and themselves, that inner qualities are more important than external appearances. The insinuation is that inner and outer qualities are separate. No matter the frequency or source, these words and thoughts pale in comparison to the reality exhibited by actual consequences, as well as actions and efforts expended to enhance physical attractiveness. Throughout society, throughout interactions of all types, and throughout lives of all people, displays at all socio-economic levels contradict the notion that inner qualities are superior. Despite lack of recognition or intensity of distaste, factual importance of external appearances is enormous. In fact, patients who have experienced dramatic cosmetic surgery enhancements to their declining physical attractiveness associated with aging frequently proclaim how much happier they are post-surgery because their external higher physical attractiveness is now in synchronization with their internal feelings.

Research communities around the world encounter topics in which people resist straightforward admission of personal feelings, thoughts, and behaviors. Resistance, conscious or subconscious, most frequently occurs if disclosures differ from standards of societal approval. Problematic disclosures also arise when self-ratings conflict seriously with ratings by others due either to embarrassment or when the respondent genuinely does not know the correct response. While self-completed questionnaires can provide valuable information to some questions, tainted data can result for other questions whereby respondents consciously screen or slant their replies to meet social approval.

Questions to assess thoughts and ratings about one's own physical attractiveness certainly tap such topical areas. In these situations, it is vital to employ procedures beyond self-measures, preferably complementing self-measures with a battery of assessments. Experience shows that research about physical attractiveness benefits immensely from additional methodologies that typically require more time and expense to conduct. For example, experiment research designs that collect data from people providing ratings about others rather than self-ratings have proven vital for accurate knowledge about certain aspects of physical attractiveness phenomenon, particularly questions concerning a person's own physical attractiveness as well as how people behave toward individuals of higher and lower physical attractiveness. In nonprofessionals' terms, an experiment to assess a person's behavior is like a candid camera procedure whereby researchers do not ask a person to state what his/her behavior was or would be in response to a scenario, but instead observe and record the person's natural behavior in a scenario without the person knowing it.

All research methodologies have relative strengths and weaknesses. Research technicalities integral to physical attractiveness research have revealed that unobtrusive measures to collect data about physical attractiveness phenomenon must be the principal research methodologies, with more obtrusive or more obvious measures providing invaluable complementary data. People understate the importance of physical attractiveness, knowingly or unknowingly. One particularly interesting research procedure illustrates well the need to attend to research technicalities. It revealed people underreport the impact on them of another person's physical attractiveness, and there is a definite tendency "to intentionally underreport the impact of physical attractiveness."[265] Researchers asked participants, females in this study, to complete a self-reporting questionnaire concerning dating preferences that included questions about the importance of another person's physical attractiveness.

The design of this research project included a lie detector apparatus while completing questionnaires. While the researchers did not actually operate the lie detector apparatus, when subjects presumed that the researchers had connected them to an operating lie detector machine, these subjects provided significantly different questionnaire answers than when these same individuals presumed they were not connected. The research team concluded their data show people are capable of accurate introspection about the importance of physical attractiveness of another person, even though these people "intentionally underreport the impact of physical attractiveness."[265] Connecting a lie detector to subjects who assumed it to be functioning properly produced more accurate introspective reports than when not connected to such a lie detector. These subjects admitted more extreme influence by physical attractiveness of stimulus persons and endorsed more extreme [lower] dating desirability ratings for physically unattractive men. Likewise, when connected to a lie detector they assumed was functioning, gave ratings that consistently preferred physically attractive men to such an extent that the researchers found physical attractiveness in this study to be the single most influential variable of preferences by subjects for stimulus persons.

CIRCULAR FOUR-STAGE PROCESS

Physical attractiveness phenomenon occurs through a circular four-stage process corroborated by the progression of knowledge based on data collected and analyzed through scientifically sound methodologies. Chapter 1 introduced that process with a diagram depicted on page 21, by Figure 1-1. Circular Four-Stage Process of Physical Attractiveness Phenomenon. This section of chapter 2 now explains more thoroughly, the circular four-stage representation, along with greater description, understanding, and prediction about hidden values of physical attractiveness.

As portrayed, physical attractiveness phenomenon occurs through four stages in a continuous arrangement with each stage flowing from the prior stage into the next stage. This depiction emerges from a macro perspective that extracts the essence of thousands of directly and indirectly related research projects combined with even larger numbers of complementary, more anecdotal, acute observations. These stages collectively represent the promulgation of physical attractiveness phenomenon along with its hidden values through an interconnected continuous relationship of influence and reinforcement.

At the first stage, the appearance dimension of physical attractiveness serves as a multidimensional informational cue. Usually unknowingly and in literally nanoseconds, people comprehend another's physical attractiveness unimpeded by the accompanying determinants that are many and complicated, physical and non-physical, permanent and transitory, and congenital and developmental.

People at the second stage of this process infer extensive information about the observed person (or entity of any sort). Seeing, or even hearing about, the person's physical attractiveness provokes respective out-of-sight cognitive processing accompanying the extensive information inferred.

In the third stage, further cognitive processing triggers or leads to assumptions, expectations, attitudes, and behaviors. Conscious or not conscious of this stage-three cognitive processing, and always regulated by social acceptability, people rarely acknowledge the elaborateness or direction of their thoughts and intentions.

The preceding three stages culminate in powerful effects or consequences at the fourth stage, which, in turn, leads back to reinforce the first-stage informational cue factor. Overwhelmingly, these consequences are more favorable for people whose appearance is higher in physical attractiveness and less favorable for people whose appearance is lower in physical attractiveness.

Despite the visible nature of appearance and physical attractiveness, their respective phenomenon includes the reality of hidden values, often unrecognized, unacknowledged, and denied. Correspondingly, the *Circular Four-Stage Process of Physical Attractiveness Phenomenon* occurs in an environment that is subtle, with people commonly unaware of, or unwilling to acknowledge to the extent of denying, their thoughts, actions, and consequences. Yet, detrimental and beneficial consequences of appearance span a continuum remarkably equal or parallel to points along continuums of lower and higher physical attractiveness.

Critical analysis of the collective published research promotes confidence to conclude that physical attractiveness is a uniquely powerful and complex dimension of appearance. Its impact largely transcends the impact of other appearance factors, most notably race and age demographics, as well as geographical locations and times in history. Without being blind to the double standards that continue around the world for physical attractiveness for males and females, it is accurate to state that physical attractiveness phenomenon also largely transcends the gender demographic.

Even though the world still lives with a double standard that maintains greater importance of physical attractiveness for females than for males, research investigating physical attractiveness phenomenon reveals the importance of physical attractiveness is escalating faster for males of all ages than females, thereby lessening the difference. One research article published in 2002 reported: "[earlier findings] that physical attractiveness was more important in men's perception of women than in women's perceptions of men was not replicated here" in their study.[254] More precisely, a longitudinal research project published in *Psychology Today* measured dissatisfaction with physical appearance in the late 1990s compared to the same measures 25 years earlier.[232] Among the findings was women's dissatisfaction with their overall appearance increased 124% (25% to 56%), and men's dissatisfaction with their overall appearance increased 186% (15% to 43%). While the importance of physical attractiveness for females remains greater than for males, males are catching up with the above change (186% versus 124%) greater for men than for women for dissatisfaction with their overall appearance.

Four summary statements can provide a reasonably comprehensive description of the universe of research findings, regardless of gender or other potentially confounding and influencing variables:

- People whose appearance is higher in physical attractiveness have greater social power than do their counterparts.
- All other things equal, people like individuals of higher physical attractiveness better than individuals of lower physical attractiveness.
- People perceive others whose appearance is higher in physical attractiveness to possess more favorable personal characteristics, including intelligence, personality traits, and success in life.
- People of higher physical attractiveness exert more positive effects on other people and receive more positive responses from others, including influence attempts, work requests, and requests for help, than do people of lower physical attractiveness.

Among the public, physical attractiveness seems largely to exist as an unquestioned substratum of stereotype.[195] More and more people accept the belief that increased physical attractiveness can make their lives better without considering what is wrong with their lives to begin with. This acceptance is blatant worldwide, and comparable even though citizens of different countries vary in how publicly or privately they practice and display it.

People assign a sort of inferred nobility to persons whose appearance is higher in physical attractiveness. They are perceived to have more positive characteristics overall, and are presumed to have happier and more fulfilling lives.[179] Characteristics such as being more intelligent, sensitive, kind, interesting, sociable, and more likely to attend college are associated with higher ranking in physical attractiveness than their counterparts of lower physical attractiveness.[137, 319, 646, 725] Similarly, the less physically attractive a person is, the less the person is liked,[103, 106, 363, 501] the less persuasive the person is,[440, 528] and the less the person is preferred as a working, dating, or marriage partner.[73, 84, 311, 672, 687] Once married, the spouse of higher physical attractiveness is generally more favorable than the spouse of lower physical attractiveness.[283] Spouses of higher physical attractiveness are perceived to be "significantly more poised, interesting, sociable, independent, warm, exciting, and sexually warm than the unattractive spouse."[82]

Empirical evidence pertinent to the above circular four-stage process supports contentions that consequences of higher physical attractiveness are positive, whereas consequences of lower physical attractiveness are negative. A study on the effects of physical attractiveness on impression formation asked male and female participants to indicate their impressions of stimulus persons on seventeen dimensions.[459] This study did not inform participants about the research interest in physical attractiveness. Resulting data revealed that persons of higher physical attractiveness were evaluated as more curious rather than indifferent, complex rather than simple, perceptive rather than insensitive, happy rather than sad, active rather than passive, amiable rather than aloof, humorous rather than serious, pleasure seeking rather than self-controlled, outspoken rather than reserved, and flexible rather than rigid.

THEORETICAL UNDERPINNING

Increasing emphasis on age-related appearances equating with or determining the level of physical attractiveness has accompanied changing times from past to present. In light of increasingly overt actions at present to enhance physical attractiveness, combined with new technological advancements ranging from chemicals to surgeries, the future will see even greater connection between age/aging and physical attractiveness. A double standard continues for gender, but relatively speaking, younger-looking ages equate more than ever with higher physical attractiveness for males as well as females.

Reasons why age or, increasingly, the appearance of age contributes substantially to physical attractiveness surely are due to a combination or nature and nurture. The connection between appearance of age and level of physical attractiveness is partially hardwired inheritance and partially modern-day life, which bombards us with frequent and powerful reinforcing messages. A venerable theory put forth in the early 1950s about human motivation that lends itself well to this aspect of motivation is Maslow's Hierarchy of Needs.[433] The theory has passed tests of time and scrutiny, holding forth in university textbooks in diverse academic areas, scholars in many fields, and executives in for-profit and not-for-profit industries. During its longevity, it has generated reams of discussion, interpretation, application, refinement, and debate. Without detailing the reams of existing deliberation, it seems sufficient here simply to state the essence of Maslow's Hierarchy of Needs Theory. Needs, or, more precisely, the penchant to meet needs, drive human motivation. The needs are hierarchical, with people mostly meeting lower-level needs before pursuing needs at higher levels. These needs align with five ascending levels or categories, commonly conceptualized by interpreters of Maslow's thought to reflect a hierarchical pyramid array as presented in Figure 2-2. Hierarchical Pyramid Depiction of Maslow's Theory of Needs.

Figure 2-2. Hierarchical Pyramid Depiction of Maslow's Theory of Needs

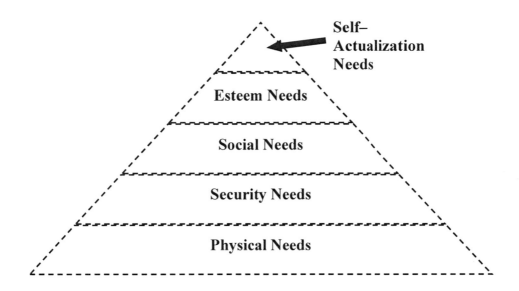

In Maslow's Theory of Needs, the needs lower in the hierarchy most strongly motivate people. With lower level needs sufficiently met, the next higher level of needs then provides the stronger motivation. If a lower level, previously satisfied, becomes no longer sufficiently met, that level then emerges again as the stronger motivation. The most basic physical needs for survival and physiological necessities drive motivations at the bottom of this hierarchical order, including food, water, and shelter. Security needs are the second level moving up this hierarchy. Originally projected as freedom from physical danger, most interpretations now include freedom from financial and employment insecurities. Social needs are the third level up this hierarchy, and pertain to feelings of acceptance by others and belonging to groups. Esteem needs are the fourth level, focused on respect from others, as well as respect for oneself. Power, prestige, and self-confidence often are related concepts. Self-actualization needs are the fifth, and the highest, level in the hierarchy. This highest level of needs, equates with feeling fulfilled such as when idealized self-concept of a person and the person's actual self-concept are the same.

Appearance phenomenon contradictions between older ages and higher physical attractiveness aligned with younger looks is an undeniable new marker. These contradictions are a confluence of living longer, medical advancements, financial prosperity, and changing social mores. Evolutionary biological instincts to reproduce and promulgate one's species seem not to apply. However, evolutionary instincts do explain the pursuit of younger appearance considering the instinct for one's own survival, which then overlaps with

Maslow's Hierarchy of Needs theory noted above. Furthermore, scholars have put forth reasonable propositions that, although people are evolutionarily hardwired for certain biological instincts that emphasize the goal to reproduce, people can be selectively flexible in ranking of goals to pursue. Thus, in this situation, explanation is very much consistent between evolutionary instincts and Maslow's Hierarchy of Needs. A person's motivation to enhance his/her physical attractiveness can be great, even extraordinary, to the extent that the ultimate look is extraordinarily different from traditional age-appearance looks. The key is that increasing a person's physical attractiveness in ways typically aligned with younger ages dramatically increases access to at least the first four of Maslow's five levels of needs (physical, security, social, and esteem) and probably even contributes to the fifth level concerning self-actualization or self-fulfillment.

PROGRESSION OF THE RESEARCH FIELD

Early research into physical attractiveness phenomenon focused most deeply on two dimensions: (1) differential perceptions in conjunction with subsequent differential expectations and treatments, and (2) dynamics of reciprocal interpersonal interactions. That road of research identified a myriad of determinants of physical attractiveness, some physical others non-physical, some compensatory others non-compensatory, and all more complex than initially appeared. Cumulative findings of that research provide the strongest documentation that physical attractiveness of a person's face most represents or determines a person's physical attractiveness, although the determinants of physical attractiveness certainly form a Gestalt defined universally as the total being greater than the sum of the parts.

In the early 1980s, knowledge about physical attractiveness remained scattered and fragmented after two decades of scientific query. Scientific communities still segregated physical attractiveness research into traditional categories of scientific study. My 1985 book[535] combined the newly informed physical attractiveness research into a distinct entity, although not isolated from more global research disciplines. My analyses and discussions examined the relevance of the study of physical attractiveness in applied science and theory. Based on similar utilitarian thought,[24, 333, 584] I knew the need to establish a proper knowledge base in science was inevitable in order for the knowledge to be available and of benefit within the greater society as a whole.

Accordingly, my 1985 book served as a compilation of unexamined substructures of universal beliefs associated with the use of physical attractiveness to inform decision-making on a wide range of activity in modern society. It also served as a compendium of the many aspects of physical attractiveness, and, as such, no other book of its type has superseded it fully. Data from experiments at that time demonstrated that society generally behaves—and bestows rewards accordingly—in rather direct correspondence with the judgment of a person's physical attractiveness.

Broader Research Framework

Physical attractiveness and its surrounding phenomenon exist in the broader framework of appearance and its phenomenon. These concepts and constructs, in turn, exist within broader, often overlapping, frameworks of research principles and issues. Person perception is one broader framework or topical area in which physical attractiveness and appearance represent subordinate or narrower sub-topics. The relationship becomes apparent when we define person perception as the process by which a person perceives and thinks about other persons, their characteristics, their qualities, and their internal traits. This definition has proven reasonable during a span of more than five decades since it was initially put forth.[677]

Person perception includes, but certainly is not limited to, the main part of existing physical attractiveness research. In fact, physical attractiveness research represents only portions of study about appearance, let alone person perception, all which began much earlier and which has taken many forms. Around the start of physical attractiveness research in the mid 1960s, some research provided an important precedent with focus on body deformities.[245] Twenty years later, in 1982, a noteworthy summary of research focusing on body characteristics pertinent to the appearance phenomenon was published.[4] Research investigating negative stigmata represented by body deformities is extremely important as another dimension of physical attractiveness, as well as appearance and appearance phenomenon. Its findings are not fully applicable to the physical attractiveness dimension of appearance, but do make an invaluable contribution to the appearance phenomenon alongside physical attractiveness research. A major distinction is that negative stigmata represented by body deformities account for a very narrow, albeit important, span along the full appearance continuum that ranges from very low to very high levels of physical attractiveness.

In person perception, people draw inferences from observations. In reality, with rare exceptions, a person of perceived higher physical attractiveness reaps greater benefits in all social systems than his or her more average counterpart. A person of low physical attractiveness, on average, reaps the least benefits and actually receives the most punishments within all social systems compared to his or her counterparts of average or higher physical attractiveness.

The importance of physical attractiveness via the appearance phenomenon is timeless. Identified attempts of members of early populations to enhance their appearance confirm the importance of physical attractiveness, as well as its pervasiveness and timelessness. Paraphernalia to increase a person's physical attractiveness is evident in every culture, from the graves of Cro-Magnon man, to the tombs of ancient Egypt, to the caskets of present-day burials. For society and the human race in general, it is dangerously shortsighted to consider research to gain understanding about physical attractiveness as an optional or otherwise needless effort. Charles Darwin, who in 1871 stated, "no excuse is needed for treating this subject [physical attractiveness] in some detail,"[164] expressed early the imperative for scientific research into physical attractiveness. Darwin expanded his statement by quoting German philosopher Arthur Schopenhauer who, speaking about physical attractiveness, wrote:

> ...the final aim of all love intrigues, be they comic or tragic, is really of more importance than all other ends in human life. What it all turns upon is nothing less than the composition of the next generation... It is not the weal

or woe of any one individual, but that of the human race to come, which is here at stake.[164]

The importance of physical attractiveness in society did not begin with Darwin's 1871 articulation about its study. Rather, his statement was a conclusion based on observations that appearance and physical attractiveness have continuously played significant roles throughout the history of humans. Today's mass media coverage of appearance issues leads some to think the attention bestowed upon physical attractiveness is a contemporary occurrence. It is not, by and large.

What has occurred is that contemporary developments in communications technology, combined with competitive business practices to gain audience and customers, have elevated certain appearance phenomenon dimensions. These developments further confirm the significance of physical attractiveness. Anthropological writings document that high value has been associated with physical attractiveness since the beginning of history around the world. Evidence from multiple sources identifies artifacts that reveal attempts to raise physical attractiveness of individuals. Anthropologist Harry Shapiro stated, "...so universal is this urge to improve on nature [i.e., appearance/physical attractiveness] that one is almost tempted to regard it as an instinct."[633]

Questions alluded to in the above quote arise about innate versus environmental origins of physical attractiveness phenomenon. The reality here resembles most areas in our universe, likely a result of nature and nurture, with the extent of each uncertain. The questions can spark interesting deliberation, but this topic is largely not a significant concern for contemporary study of physical attractiveness phenomenon. Nor does modern study explicitly explore when human beings began their concern about physical attractiveness or began such a phenomenon. Scholarly thought expressed in anthropological writings states that "the endeavor to embellish the appearance and personal charms belongs to the most ancient cultural expressions of man."[219]

Scientific disciplines commonly do not have distinct boundaries that clearly separate one discipline from all others. Beyond rather indisputable core topics, disciplines often share interest in some research topics that then blur separating boundaries or edges of disciplines. Physical attractiveness is one such research topic. The most direct research on physical attractiveness as a specific part of appearance phenomenon began in the 1960s in the United States in social psychology. It has grown and expanded dramatically since then. Before then, indirectly related research was conducted in many scientific disciplines, with findings sometimes contributory to today's knowledge and sometimes not. These research projects taken together, and with proper qualified screening, provide knowledge from a rich mosaic of scientific disciplines and projects that ultimately provide understanding about social patterns affected by physical attractiveness. One published study, since invalidated, dates back to 1891.[413] It investigated physical attractiveness in a type of "constitutional psychology" that associated body characteristics with criminal activities. Later studies published in 1925[368] and 1940[635] tried to identify the association of body characteristics with personality traits. Most contributory to physical attractiveness research as it is known today was a project published in 1963[245] that investigated social interactions as a function of body characteristics defined as physical deformities.

Interesting questions pertaining to physical attractiveness are endless. How does physical attractiveness influence person perception? Is treatment of people whose appearance is higher in physical attractiveness always, or in certain situations, different from their counterparts of lower physical attractiveness? When is physical attractiveness an asset and when is it a liability? Do those of different levels of physical attractiveness develop differently psychologically? Are those lower in physical attractiveness physiologically different from those higher in physical attractiveness? Is there a trend in selection, evaluation, and compensation in their careers and jobs for people whose appearance differs in physical attractiveness?

Such questions are of interest to many or should be of interest to many. To a name a few, these include social and biological scientists, government policy makers, physicians of cosmetic and reconstructive surgery, decision makers in advertising and marketing, and the public in general. Despite the interest and the sizable and growing collection of empirical research knowledge, answers to questions have relied more on folklore and conventional wisdom than on scientific evidence about manifestation of physical attractiveness, the appearance phenomenon, and the many pertinent variables. To eradicate harmful consequences among populations in the United States and around the world is a daunting task.

Beyond Usual Boundaries

Researchers continuously advance the boundaries of knowledge about physical attractiveness phenomenon. While people are the scope and focus of this book, mounting knowledge has advanced considerably physical attractiveness phenomenon identified here. It holds applications, analogies, and understanding for nonliving inanimate entities and living nonhuman organisms. In fact, physical attractiveness phenomenon continues to be the same as defined in this book. Regardless of entity or organism, physical attractiveness phenomenon transforms this dimension of appearance into a value that can be a blessing or curse, asset or liability, benefit or detriment. It can make the holder strong or weak, liked or disliked, and desired or undesired. The impact of physical attractiveness phenomenon is pervasive and powerful, while often unrecognized, unknown, or not admitted and denied. It takes place through a circular four-stage process that begins with the use of appearance/physical attractiveness as an informational cue.

Certainly, architects grapple with the topic of appearance and specifically physical attractiveness in the design of buildings, as do city planners, engineers of all sorts, artists of all kinds, and designers of all types. With an eye keenly focused on physical attractiveness, successful designers of nonliving (i.e., inanimate) items and products maintain consciousness that people will use the finished item to perform jobs, to live lives, or, depending on the type of item, to enhance their physical attractiveness. In these situations, the designers are concerned about both the appearance of the nonliving item and its synergistic impact on the appearance of the person associated with these items. This dual appearance consideration confronts all people involved with almost all products directly or indirectly applied or used by people. Clothes designers might first come to mind, but dentists confront analogous dual questions about the appearance of an inanimate item (e.g., shape, color, and look of a tooth cap or porcelain veneer) and its effect on the appearance of the person receiving it.

Non-Living, Inanimate Entities

Whether viewing appearance of others, appearance of ourselves, or appearance of our living and working environments, physical attractiveness phenomenon applies. Higher physical attractiveness is valued more highly than lower physical attractiveness, regardless if a person is interacting with another person, product, or environment. "People work better, feel better, and are more amiable and happier if they experience beautiful shapes and colors in the objects with which they surround themselves…," according to Ellen Key (1849-1926), Swedish reformer and educationalist.[349] A 2004 article published by *BusinessWeek* stated, "Now, Microsoft wants to be known for its aesthetics" to an extent that it raises questions concerning appearance, i.e., physical attractiveness, about their latest product, "Is it a case of design trumping function?" to which the company responds, "We're looking to attract people who appreciate design."[258]

This book focuses on people-to-people relationships driven by physical attractiveness phenomenon, but physical attractiveness phenomenon also drives relationships similarly for people with nonliving, inanimate entities such as commercial products. Consider the 2004 winners at the annual Industrial Design Excellence Awards (IDEA) presented by the Industrial Designers Society of America with global competition judged by an international jury. First, an Asian company won more awards than any United States or European company.[504] Second, winners came from fourteen countries outside the United States:[636] Australia, Britain/United Kingdom, Canada, Denmark, France, Germany, Ireland, Israel, Japan, Korea, Netherlands, New Zealand, Sweden, and Taiwan.

Not all product design efforts focus entirely on the product's physical attractiveness, but there is significant overlap between the two. Repeatedly, people align a product's design with its physical attractiveness despite divergences that can occur between improved aesthetics and improved functionalities. Even though physical attractiveness phenomenon terminology is not common among business magazine analysts, the 2005 cover story in *BusinessWeek* about that year's competition for the above awards stated that "The [product] winners were simple, elegant, and often beautiful."[503] Globally, this year's 2005 awards showed that "Beijing [China] is spending millions of dollars on design, turning out thousands of design graduates each year" and "South Korea, did extremely well again this year. Samsung won three [of these IDEA design awards]" and "has garnered more awards over the past five years than any other company in the world."[503]

Consumer preferences and their marketplace decisions are driving the escalating importance that businesses now place on product design to improve appearance/physical attractiveness as well as functionality. These developments are driving university business schools to infuse their students, future business leaders, with knowledge and skill about product design that includes, ultimately, focus on product physical attractiveness. The August 1, 2005, cover story of *BusinessWeek* titled "Get Creative: How to Build Innovative Companies"[505] includes an article titled "Tomorrow's B-School? It might be a D-School"[448] about the need to teach design school thinking and training to business school students. The latter article discusses actions at major business schools "to inject design thinking into their curricula." Again, while product design and product physical attractiveness are not 100% congruent, product physical attractiveness is an increasingly significant dimension along with product functionality in today's product design. To illustrate one synergy between product physical attractiveness and business, consider the rather mundane, spaghetti, mish-mash of cords in our homes and businesses regularly viewed as a physically unattractive, visual eyesore. An article published in the *Wall Street Journal* verified or at least paralleled the greater value for higher physical attractiveness in business and products as measured by consumer purchases and company sales:

> Aesthetics hasn't always been a priority. Indeed, many wire-management gadgets were originally developed…[with] more concern about price and capacity than aesthetics. But lately, [manufacturers and stores] whose sales have risen 40% a month…, are increasingly designing/selling visually attractive new ways, including new wireless technologies, to hide or eliminate such disarray of wires and cords.[338]

Customers demand the products in which they dress, drive, surround themselves, and even eat to be high in physical attractiveness, or, in more ordinary parlance, to have good looks, to look good, and so forth. Accommodating these demands, businesses create or obtain products to sell that provide customers with greatest satisfaction, being conscious to ensure that potential customers judge their product's design or appearance to reflect higher, rather than lower, physical attractiveness. Consider the following statements identified in Table 2-3 that express well the implications of physical attractiveness phenomenon in their strategies and products. Keep in mind that the following quotes have used the word *design*, which in most instances here is synonymous with the words *appearance* or *physical attractiveness*.

Table 2-3. Statements Indicating Importance of Physical Attractiveness Phenomenon for Products and Business Strategies

Fifteen years ago companies competed on price. Now it's quality. Tomorrow it's design [appearance/physical attractiveness].

Robert Hayes, author, *Strategic [Business] Operations*

At Sony we assume that all products of our competitors have basically the same technology, price, performance, and features. Design [appearance/physical attractiveness] is the only thing that differentiates one product from another in the marketplace.

Norio Ohga, CEO, Sony Corporation

Design [appearance/physical attractiveness] is treated like a religion at BMW.

Tom Peters, author, *In Search of Excellence*

We don't have a good language to talk about this kind of thing. In most people's vocabularies, design [appearance/physical attractiveness] means veneer… But to me, nothing could be further from the meaning of design [appearance/physical attractiveness]. Design [appearance/physical attractiveness] is the fundamental soul of a manmade creation.

Steve Jobs, CEO, Macintosh Computer Corporation

Judging by appearances [level of physical attractiveness] – A University of Michigan study finds that, in the absence of clear financial information, investor decisions are swayed by the aesthetics of financial reports. Plus, the study says, in an effort to buffer themselves from investors' negative reactions, poorly performing companies tend to create more visually compelling reports…

Money magazine, January 2003

The new Beetle fails at most categories. The only thing it doesn't fail in is drop-dead charm [appearance/cuteness/physical attractiveness].

Jerry Hirshberg, Nissan Design International

Object of Desire! Every now and then, a design [appearance/look] comes along that radically changes the way we think about a particular object. Case in point: the iMac. Suddenly, a computer is no longer an anonymous box. It is a sculpture, an object of desire, something that you look at.

Katherine McCoy & Michael McCoy, Illinois Institute of Technology

Design [appearance/physical attractiveness] transforms even the biggest corporations proclaimed Time magazine in an article titled "TARGET--the champion of America's new design democracy," about Target discount mass merchandiser designated "Marketer of the Year 2000" by Advertising Age.

Tom Peters, author, *In Search of Excellence*

Design [appearance/physical attractiveness] is the wellspring of branding. Great design [appearance/looks/physical attractiveness] takes guts and is "soul deep."

Tom Peters, author, *In Search of Excellence*

Physical attractiveness phenomenon permeates the lives of people; therefore, expectedly it concerns the food we eat. Restaurant patrons value food that is better looking, i.e., higher in physical attractiveness. Two dimensions germane to physical attractiveness phenomenon are form/shape and color. These dimensions or determinants of physical attractiveness are also germane to food. According to a 2003 magazine article titled "Culinary Beautification" in the Moscow, Russia, edition of *Where* magazine:[483]

- "Psychologists say we eat first with our eyes. Our mouths water at the sight of a delicious dish."
- "A dish is more attractive when it looks sculptured," states Vladislav Lavrenov, chef at O'Mar Restaurant in Moscow, Russia. That perspective is

shared by Anatoly Galkin, chef at Moskovsky Restaurant in Moscow, who "in his time cooked for President Mikhail Gorbachev and President Boris Yeltsin. When creating a new dish, he [Chef Galkin] first sketches it, just as an artist does in preparing for a large-scale canvas. He knows it's not only the compatibility of ingredients that matters in a dish but the choice of well-matched colors."

- "Connoisseurs can [judge] a dish at a glance—not only by the ingredients but by how it is made to look attractive and how it is presented. Sauces…do not always add beauty to a dish…"

- "Also, many cooks are paying more attention to coloring. It is known that dark shades put off diners, while the bright and pastel attract and stimulate appetite. Salmon filet looks attractive as it is, but if served with slices of asparagus and rings of golden sautéed onion, you have a classic culinary combination of orange and green. The same law of a watering mouth makes the vivid color of undercooked loin a perfect match for the strong green of peas and beans, the white of rice, and the red of sweet peppers."

- "Lately it's become fashionable to use flowers to decorate a dish and stimulate appetite." However, "Twenty years ago a chef at a prestigious American restaurant in California placed an order with farmers to grow flowers for the preparation and decoration of dishes. The farmers thought he was mad. But even a cookbook from the days of ancient Romans mentions violets and roses as ingredients in many dishes and speaks of gladioluses combined with salt and olive oil, while lavender with honey was added to sauces and pastes. …Nowadays orange nasturtium, bright yellow calendula, purple pansies, and, of course, rose petals enjoy well-earned popularity among cooks. …Any cook will tell you that an ordinary stuffed egg is irresistible if you place several bright-colored flowers on the plate. And an unpretentious dessert becomes piquant refreshingly interesting, stimulating, provocative."

Physical attractiveness phenomenon in restaurant food extends well beyond preparations at time of serving or in advance in menu photographs. Diners throughout the decision-production line infer value or goodness of food based on its appearance. Common practice in some Asian countries, as well as occasionally at high-end American restaurants, is for patrons to select a fish from a pool of swimming fish that is then prepared for eating. History has recorded comparable scenarios in which livestock and vegetables before harvest are selected for later preparation and eating, all based on their appearance as defined by the respective criteria for looking good, i.e., high physical attractiveness, for that product category. Of course, ordinary grocery shoppers infer an item's value based on appearance or physical attractiveness each time he or she makes a shopping trip to the produce or meat section of their local grocery store. Actually, this inferred value by means of physical attractiveness phenomenon takes place for each purchase decision throughout the entire grocery store, which is why manufacturers of products throughout the store expend significant efforts and funds for the best looking, most physically attractive packaging.

Living, Non-Human Organisms

How people judge and treat living, nonhuman organisms is a function of physical attractiveness phenomenon. While unpleasant to acknowledge, the physical attractiveness of a potential pet heavily influences adoption likelihood of abandoned cats and dogs at animal shelters. The animal's innate appearance, changes caused by accident or nutrition, and grooming all contribute to determining this physical attractiveness consideration for the potential pet owner.

Physical attractiveness phenomenon involving living, nonhuman organisms is not limited to interactions between humans and animals. To the extent that humans can truly understand nonhuman behavior, empirically based speculation supports the proposition that interaction between nonhuman organisms parallels, more frequently than not, interaction between humans concerning physical attractiveness phenomenon. In fact, in 2003, based on an impressive review of research projects and theoretical interpretations, a group of scholars located in Austria, France, and the United States collectively concluded:

> ...preferences and beauty standards provide evidence for the claim that human beauty and obsession with bodily beauty are mirrored in analogous traits and tendencies throughout the plant and animal kingdoms.[251]

A few examples of physical attractiveness phenomenon among nonhuman organisms include penguins, birds, and scorpion flies.[147]

Female penguins in Antarctica value more highly male suitors with appearance highest in physical attractiveness, as demonstrated by their actions to select mates. A particularly important determinant of physical attractiveness among these penguins is weight, specifically largeness of size or chubbiness. Probably not coincidentally, by selecting the male suitor whose appearance is apparently most physically attractive to the female penguin, the female penguin chooses a mate that can spend several weeks sitting on newly hatched eggs without starving to death. These body characteristics and projected motivations are surprisingly parallel among humans regarding physical attractiveness phenomenon.

The female Gallus gallus (an Asian jungle bird) demonstrate their value for higher physical attractiveness in their apparent preference to select males whose appearance is highest in physical attractiveness as defined by color and intensity of feathers and head combs. Analogous selection criteria are not uncommon among other species of birds. Probably not coincidentally, by preferring to select mates with brightly colored head combs and brightly colored feathers, the female Gallus gallus improves her likelihood of bearing offspring with stronger resistance to disease since these birds lose the luster and color of their head combs and feathers when inflicted with parasites. Again, physical attractiveness phenomenon among humans has many parallels here.

Female scorpion flies exhibit higher value for higher physical attractiveness through their apparent mate-selection preference given to potential mates with the greatest symmetry of wings. Again, probably not coincidentally, by preferring a mate with greater wing symmetry, female scorpions select mates that are most able to kill prey and defend their food source. Early thought regarding physical attractiveness among humans was that the persons judged most highly in physical attractiveness were people with asymmetrical appearances, but later research has shown individuals judged higher in physical attractiveness are those who are more symmetrical than are their counterparts. Interestingly, the scorpion fly exhibits analogous preference and value for this symmetry feature of physical attractiveness phenomenon.

In summary, within the collective research addressing physical attractiveness phenomenon since the mid-1960s, findings support the robustness of this phenomenon. Empirical data corroborate the perspective expressed in 1981 in the scholarly periodical *Science* that higher physical attractiveness is favored even among animals.[98] While such biological, as well as anthropological, issues are interesting, the focus of this book is on physical attractiveness phenomenon in contemporary human society.

INCREASING RELEVANCE

In earlier times, people may have openly considered the study of physical attractiveness phenomenon as less important. The efforts and transitional maturing of this topic area, that identifies hidden values and provides insight confirms increasing relevance. In the 1980s, I began to argue publicly about the relevance and, thus, the need for increasing understanding. The passing years have substantiated this need. Despite increased resources aimed at informing the public, and the fact that the public is more accustomed to many individual aspects relating to the hidden values of physical attractiveness, people do not find themselves more at ease with their bodies, nor have the values been clearly dissociated with physical attractiveness bias. There is, if anything, a profoundly greater awareness that people of lower physical attractiveness will have a harder time succeeding in the current, very competitive environment.

As discussed previously in this chapter, *Psychology Today* published an appearance dissatisfaction index[232] showing that self-judged appearance dissatisfaction with one's appearance has increased dramatically in the twenty-five-year period between 1972 and 1997. Both genders reported increasing dissatisfaction with their overall appearance (see Table 2-4. Appearance Dissatisfaction Expressed by Men and Women: Percentage Comparison Data Collected 25 Years Apart). These increases, which include a 124% increase for females (31 percentage points, 25 to 56) and a 187% increase for males (28 percentage points, 15 to 43), show that approximately one-half of adults report dissatisfaction with their individual overall appearance (females at 56% and males at 43%). Such dissatisfactions breed further afflictions. Somewhat of a footnote to these data is their indication that the abdomen is the number-one cause of dissatisfaction and judgment of lower physical attractiveness for both women and men, providing interesting collaboration with more generalized research knowledge. True to form, these data are consistent in 1997 for women and men, as well as twenty-five years earlier in 1972. Of note, males are catching up with females in terms of physical attractiveness phenomenon; in fact, for women the increase in dissatisfaction is 42% (21 percentage points, 50 to 71) and for men the increase is 75% (27 percentage points, 36 to 63).

Table 2-4. Appearance Dissatisfaction Expressed by Men and Women: Percentage Comparison Data Collected 25 Years Apart

1972			1997	
Women	Men		Women	Men
25	15	Overall Appearance	56	43
48	35	Weight	66	52
13	13	Height	16	16
30	25	Muscle Tone	57	45
26	18	Breasts/Chest	34	38
50	36	Abdomen	71	63
49	12	Hips / Thighs	61	29

SUMMARY

Research professionals and nonprofessionals of a wide array conduct investigations about physical attractiveness and physical attractiveness phenomenon. The professional researchers range along a continuum from one-time inquiries to lifelong inquiries. Regardless of length of inquiry by the researchers, findings contribute to the growing collection of scientifically sound research based on data collected and reported through formal research procedures. However, when confronted about physical attractiveness phenomenon, people respond in one of three broad ways. One group of people heartedly embrace it, often identifying with the hidden values showing the phenomenon to be far more than meets the eye. A second group of people expresses neutrality, showing neither interest nor disinterest. The third group dislikes the entire idea of physical attractiveness phenomenon and research about it. They tend to be defensive about the topic, express that it is unethical or improper research, refuse to consider overtly the importance and possible influence of physical attractiveness, and they attempt to ignore the proven effects of physical attractiveness. These reactions promote continued ignorance about the environment in which the person lives. Such ignorance does not make physical attractiveness phenomenon disappear, nor does such a mindset minimize the impact of physical attractiveness phenomenon in our lives and within our interpersonal relations. Ignorance is not bliss when it comes to physical attractiveness.

Chapter 3

Measurements and Determinants

Beauty as we feel it is something indescribable: What it is or what it means can never be said.
George Santayana (1863-1952), American philosopher, poet, and novelist, born in Spain and lived most of his life in the United States, in his 1936 book, titled *The Sense of Beauty*.[610]

If something exists, it exists in some amount. If it exists in some amount, it can be measured.
Edward Lee Thorndike (1874-1949), American psychologist and educator.[692]

INTRODUCTION

Not considering if the relationship between physical attractiveness and personal attributes is direct or indirect, repulsive or pleasing, denied or acknowledged, rejected or accepted, people (consciously or subconsciously) make robust assumptions about many non-visible characteristics of other people based on the informational cue provided by an individual's physical attractiveness. These attributions translate ultimately into benefits and advantages for people who possess higher physical attractiveness, and detriments and disadvantages for those who do not. Research projects to investigate physical attractiveness phenomenon have accordingly addressed specific determinants of physical attractiveness.

It seems on first appearance that no one can accurately research physical attractiveness phenomenon because physical attractiveness is subjective. It is an esthetic without objective absolute values or measures. While some variables that interest people can be objectively measured (e.g., height, weight, speed of a car, temperature of air, etc.), many variables that interest people cannot be so objectively measured (e.g., love, hate, depression, political goodwill, etc.). For these latter variables, researchers use operational definitions that describe actions or operations to measure the variable of interest. For physical attractiveness, researchers employ "Truth of Consensus" research methodology, whereby others judge the physical attractiveness of a stimulus person without explicit reference to any single determinant, i.e., a Gestalt perspective. If certain features of a person are significant or not significant in determining physical attractiveness, for research purposes it is largely not important or relevant. If a substantial number of judges rate a stimulus person as high or low in physical attractiveness, then for research purposes this person is interpreted (operationally defined) as representative of that respective level of physical attractiveness.

While implicitly acknowledging the structure of determinants of physical attractiveness discussed later in this chapter, research has usually investigated physical attractiveness of the complete person or the complete face/head as opposed to subcomponents. As much as the determinants discussed in the second part of this chapter, as well as the body and face discussed respectively in the following two chapters, contribute to understanding physical attractiveness phenomenon, it is important to keep in mind the bigger picture. The section towards the end of this chapter titled the "Complete Person Research" encapsulates this bigger picture. The bulk of research germane to physical attractiveness phenomenon necessarily employs a Gestalt perspective whereby "the whole is greater than the sum of the parts" to accommodate the vastness and complexity of physical attractiveness and physical attractiveness phenomenon. It is not necessarily simply a person's outstanding nose or skin or any other single part but it is all the parts together that determine a person's physical attractiveness.

An important dimension of this Gestalt perspective is that many determinants of physical attractiveness align closely with a more, rather than less, youthful appearance. In turn, these more youthful appearance factors align closely with levels of estrogen and testosterone exhibited through respective body and face markers that equate with associated face and body features. Recent documentations come from researchers internationally that include the Ludwig-Boltzman-Institute for Urban Ethology in Austria, Université Pierre et Marie Curie, Laboratorie de Parasitologie Evolutive in France, University of New Mexico in United States, Human Cognitive Neuroscience Unit of Northumbria University in United Kingdom, and the Department of Psychology at University of Central Lancashire in United Kingdom.[425, 492, 493, 693, 695, 696]

MEASUREMENTS

The pervasive power wielded by physical attractiveness phenomenon raises questions about what is physical attractiveness, how is it measured, and is it not in the eye of the beholder? Helping to conceal the answers to these questions is the elusiveness of physical attractiveness. One approach to identify the answers, which requires unraveling mysteries fused into physical attractiveness phenomenon, is to identify the determinants of physical attractiveness. On a practical level, answers to these questions provide information valuable for individuals to deal with physical attractiveness in everyday, real-world situations impacted by physical attractiveness phenomenon. Although initially on a less practical or less applied level for individuals, these answers provide valuable information to enlighten scholarly thought and theory for understanding physical attractiveness phenomenon. Of course, at the same time, being able to explain physical attractiveness phenomenon does not mean it will go away or, more importantly, that the ethical dilemmas will go away, even though explanation of physical attractiveness phenomenon might well help to understand it and offer assistance to individuals and populations.

Elusiveness

To say that people cannot describe or measure physical attractiveness attributes even greater power to physical attractiveness than it has already. It is true that physical attractiveness is not as readily or as commonly described and precisely measured as, say, car speed at which we travel or air temperature around us. However, while physical attractiveness is more difficult to describe and to precisely measure, it is not accurate to say that people cannot describe it and measure it, as well as manipulate it, control it, lose it, gain it, decrease it, and increase it. The difference that contributes most to difficulty of describing and measuring physical attractiveness is that neither physical attractiveness overall nor its myriad determinants are necessarily either quantitative or tangible traits, that is, except a few contributing determinants such as weight and height. Therefore, as well as matters of consequence to individuals in everyday life, measurements and determinants of physical attractiveness are matters of consequence for researchers who must identify and manipulate the physical attractiveness variable in order to scientifically study physical attractiveness and physical attractiveness phenomenon. Regardless of obstacles, a judicious perspective to keep in mind is that if something exists, it must exist in some amount, and if something exists in some amount, surely there is some way to measure it.[692]

History

Measurement of physical attractiveness developed slowly because of difficulty encountered when measuring a concept that is rather abstract, often intangible, and much more an esthetic than an absolute. Earliest attempts resembling measurement efforts probably began with a research project published in 1921 by the *Journal of Experimental Psychology*.[560] That research asked subjects to think of their friends who are physically attractive and physically unattractive, and then identify characteristics that made each person representative of their physical attractiveness level. While not particularly valuable for understanding physical attractiveness phenomenon, good grooming emerged from these data as one measure or determinant of higher physical attractiveness.

Good grooming may influence physical attractiveness, but a problem endemic to such research designs is that people are not able to judge physical attractiveness and also to expertly analyze levels of physical attractiveness in a meaningful sense and certainly not through a standard survey research design. Most research endeavors to answer these particular questions about measurements and determinants of physical attractiveness have focused on experiment research designs that control (i.e., manipulate) various subcomponents of a person's appearance and, at times, various subcomponents or dimensions of these subcomponents. These subcomponents include skin (with tone and complexion being subcomponents or dimensions of the skin subcomponent), eyes (with subcomponents or dimensions being size, distance apart, pupil size, eyebrow position, eye contact, and eye gaze), mouth (with subcomponents or dimensions being curvature, teeth, repose and smile, and lip size), facial expression, facial hair, eyeglasses, and so forth.

Investigations focused on components and subcomponents of physical attractiveness can yield interesting findings, but they lack the ability to capture the essence of physical attractiveness required to identify adequate measurements and determinants. The outcome has been an unwritten consensus for a global measure of physical attractiveness to use in the study of physical attractiveness phenomenon, regardless of determinants of physical attractiveness. This measure has turned the abstract, often elusive, concept of physical attractiveness into a powerful research construct.

Eyes of Beholders

Physical attractiveness refers to how pleasing someone or something looks, but not all people define pleasing the same. What one person or one group finds pleasing is, of course, not necessarily the same for all others. Therefore, when speaking about physical attractiveness, people seem to like to recite the age-old adage that beauty is in the eye of the beholder, despite the false suggestion of this cliché. While ratings of physical attractiveness can be subjective and individualistic, even if it is in the eye of the beholder, that fact is largely irrelevant because there is significant agreement among the beholders. Agreement occurs so frequently that it neutralizes and actually negates sentiments that physical attractiveness is so unique that people cannot define, measure, and scientifically study it.

Two quintessential determinants of physical attractiveness known to be pleasing to eyes of beholders around the world are healthier appearance and younger appearance, and thus, both are quintessential motivators for their pursuits. One study reporting the connection of higher physical attractiveness with perception of better health, at least from a genetic quality perspective, found this also to be the case for its subjects in the United States and Austria.[695] Contemporary scientific data increasingly confirm hypotheses that people associate higher physical attractiveness with perception of greater health, which then leads to people placing greater value on correspondingly greater physical attractiveness. This dynamic is not new. Parallel hypotheses and notions whereby perceived physical attractiveness is influenced by perceived health with value assigned accordingly, were indicated in the 1920s[201, 734] and even earlier in the 1800s.[162]

Reality is that a person's physical attractiveness strongly signals corresponding levels of health as well as age. In turn, health and age are integrally interdependent appearance variables that contribute to the determination of a person's physical attractiveness—looks of greater health and younger ages translate into perceptions of higher physical attractiveness. This explains why, on top of the vast array of available cosmetic surgeries, facial treatments, and over-the-counter products, people continue to demand more and more prescription-required pharmaceutical drugs.

The huge and growing demand for surgical and non-surgical means to increase a person's physical attractiveness drives the research and development, marketing, and prescribing of products deemed pertinent. Advanced science is being used increasingly, even combining chemical and electronic technologies to produce new, pricey alternatives to reverse face wrinkles.[175] This context certainly offers understanding for an article published in a 2004 issue of *The Wall Street Journal* that reported:

> The U. S. Food and Drug Administration [FDA] yesterday approved a new facial filler…[called Sculptra in the United States]. The product, first

approved in Europe five years ago to fill creases and wrinkles, is now available in more than thirty countries worldwide.[614]

Use of FDA approved products such as Restylane and Botox for minimally invasive wrinkle treatments is growing dramatically. According to the American Society of Plastic Surgeons, seven million procedures performed in 2003 and described as minimally invasive cosmetic procedures reflected a 43 percent rise from 2002. These usages and numbers will continue their rise given the role of younger appearances, in addition to more healthful appearances, as a huge driver or artifact of physical attractiveness phenomenon. Accordingly, the demand for Sculptra is great because it is "…part of a new class of fillers that are believed to stimulate skin cells to increase skin volume…[which] represents a new and possibly better option…for regaining a youthful volume in large areas of the face such as the cheeks."[614]

Despite conventional wisdom, or more likely wishful thinking to some people, beauty is not in the eye of the beholder…or, if it is, this beholding is not relevant since there is high agreement between beholders about who and what are high and low in physical attractiveness. Physical attractiveness is certainly an esthetic for which there is no absolute gauge, but, maybe surprising, there is convincing agreement about physical attractiveness of males and females of all ages, when rated by males and females of all ages in all cultures and all times. The opening quote to this chapter from George Santayana expresses the intrigue (and frustration) experienced throughout history concerning questions of physical attractiveness characteristics, dimensions, and ultimately determinants. In the 1800s, Charles Darwin wrote that he had observed no universal standard of beauty among people in different parts of the world and further proposed that "each race would [evolve to] possess its own innate ideal standard of beauty."[164] Other scholars and theoreticians before the start of scientific research identified explicitly with study of physical attractiveness phenomenon expressed similar cultural-bound perspective about physical attractiveness.[222]

This view concerning standards or determinants of physical attractiveness may still hold intuitive appeal for some people, but the view is not valid based on both anecdotal and observational data. Furthermore, this view is invalid due to pertinent scientific findings that now document physical attractiveness phenomenon throughout the existence of humans. Very clearly, contemporary times show increasing convergence about physical attractiveness standards/determinants between races and cultures, as well as continuance of the larger physical attractiveness phenomenon between races and cultures throughout history. A reason for diminished plurality among races and cultures about determinants of physical attractiveness is that modern communications technology, combined with widespread acceptance of fashions and lifestyles, is producing what can be recognized as a global village, leading to a universal standard of physical attractiveness.[63] Accordingly, despite the Santayana's notion that beauty is indescribable, people can and do predict with great accuracy the level of physical attractiveness that a person will likely perceive when exposed to another person.

Truth of Consensus

A common mistake by people new to thinking or study about physical attractiveness is the assumption that physical attractiveness is an evaluation unique to each individual and, subsequently, that measuring and determining physical attractiveness are not possible. The error of this assumption stems from ignorance about the high agreement between people regarding who and what are high and low in physical attractiveness. Even though no objective, absolute answer exists as to who is physically attractive or what determines physical attractiveness, people do agree. Contrary to conventional wisdom suggested by the adage that beauty is in the eye of the beholder, research shows that, despite the elusiveness of physical attractiveness, people overwhelming agree in their judgments about the physical attractiveness level of other persons and can distinguish points along a physical attractiveness continuum that are consistent from one time period to another. In turn, the agreement between people about another person's physical attractiveness, descriptively labeled truth of consensus, translates into standards for measurements and determinants along the continuum ranging from low to high physical attractiveness

Truth of consensus is a procedure used in physical attractiveness phenomenon research to measure or determine, in other words to define, a person's physical attractiveness. It requires statistical analysis of mean values of evaluation scores about a stranger's physical attractiveness and variances/standard evaluations of those values. Very importantly, this truth of consensus agreement permits research to establish, manipulate, and study the physical attractiveness variable with scientifically sound validity and reliability, which then permits conclusions based on data that accurately document and contribute to understanding physical attractiveness phenomenon. Truth of consensus embraces the premise that judgments of physical attractiveness are necessarily subjective, and that people form judgments through Gestalt principles of person perception rather than single measures or single determinants. Therefore, for research into physical attractiveness phenomenon, it largely is not critical whether a specific characteristic or the overall appearance is the determinant of physical attractiveness. If a substantial number of judges rate a stimulus person as high or low in physical attractiveness, then, for research purposes, this stimulus person represents that respective level of physical attractiveness, operationally defined.

Process

Asking people to state what determines physical attractiveness has not proved fruitful. Either they do not know, the answer is too difficult, or they are unwilling to express genuine thoughts that do not readily meet social approval. Formal research commonly employs a two-phase procedure with different people participating in each phase. Experimental research projects typically measure physical attractiveness of stimulus persons at a stage separate from the later manipulations to study the physical attractiveness variable. Usually the first phase is a truth of consensus procedure whereby the level of a person's physical attractiveness is established. People not acquainted with the stimulus person(s) typically provide their physical attractiveness ratings through either a forced distribution or a free category rating. Forced distribution procedures ask judges to sort photographs of stimulus persons into a forced normal distribution. Substantially more frequently used, free category rating procedures ask judges to rate stimulus persons along a continuum that ranges from extremely low to extremely high physical attractiveness, very unattractive physically to very attractive physically, or some variation. For example, for infants, the measurement process for physical attractiveness asks judges to rate along a continuum of cuteness.

After a statistically sufficient number of judges give their ratings, values for the mean ratings and the standard deviations are calculated. Judges at this stage of research commonly use a multiple-point scale with 5 to 11 points, starting from low or very low physical attractiveness as noted above to rate stimulus persons. Researchers process these ratings as interval data to calculate the mean value and standard deviation for each stimulus person, selecting stimulus persons with the appropriate mean value and the smallest standard deviation to represent their respective physical attractiveness level. Thorough researchers further scrutinize the ratings with statistical t-tests to ensure significant differences do not exist between scores for stimulus persons intended to represent the same levels of physical attractiveness and do exist between scores for stimulus persons intended to represent different levels of physical attractiveness.

These statistical calculations permit researchers to ascribe operational definitions along a continuum ranging from low to moderate to high physical attractiveness for the stimulus/target persons or their pictures. Researchers base their calculations on respective mean values (i.e., low, moderate, and high ratings) in combination with the smallest variance or smallest standard deviation values. Thus, given the high agreement concerning a person's physical attractiveness witnessed by a truth of consensus, researchers utilize these rated individuals to represent the corresponding levels of physical attractiveness in a wide variety of research settings and procedures to investigate dynamics and consequences for people whose appearance is higher or lower in physical attractiveness. Research projects to identify determinants of physical attractiveness first establish the physical attractiveness level of target persons and then deconstruct the persons to identify differences and similarities in appearances. When patterns emerge in this phase, whereby some levels of physical attractiveness possess certain features significantly more frequently than other levels, it is then valid to conclude which features serve as determinants of physical attractiveness.

To minimize experimental error, researchers present each stimulus an equal number of times within each experimental treatment. Ideally, the research project includes multiple stimulus persons to represent each physical attractiveness level under study to minimize any unique characteristic(s) or unique effect(s) that a specific stimulus person may possess. Despite the potentially misleading impact that a unique stimulus person could have on data, published research rarely reports this precautionary effort, suggesting that a small number of studies use research designs that incorporate multiple stimulus persons for each physical attractiveness level.

Measure Qualification

As an esthetic dimension, people commonly and mistakenly think that, because physical attractiveness is so unique, accurate measurement is not feasible and its determinants unidentifiable. This is partially correct. Accurate self-evaluation of physical attractiveness has proven largely unrealistic. Individuals tend to see themselves "through a dark glass,"[63] producing no statistically significant agreement between self-ratings and ratings by others. In contrast, there is high agreement among physical attractiveness ratings between people, particularly strangers, of other persons.[5] This agreement, demonstrated by high correlation values between judges, exists for same-sex and opposite-sex judges, along with statistical reliability of physical attractiveness evaluations for a person who rates physical attractiveness at one time period and again assigns equivalent ratings later. Inspecting the studies as a whole with thousands of participants, physical attractiveness measures prove extremely worthy and consistent, regardless of the judges' ages, geographic locations, education levels, and socioeconomic classes.

Measure Reliability

A consistent measurement result from independent origins is a goal of measurement reliability in scientific research. The data confirm the truth of consensus procedure yields a research construct that is highly reliable, as well as utilitarian. To the extent that reliability is the same as agreement between measures, physical attractiveness measures are very reliable. Both primary methodologies for assessing reliability—test-retest and multiple procedures— support confirmatory conclusions about the strength of reliability indicated by studies investigating the inter-judge correlations for physical attractiveness measures.[528, 535] Variety and magnitude of demonstrated reliability add credence to the findings. Indeed, in scientific research perspective, the high agreement documents that beauty is not in the eye of the beholder.

Regardless of gender combinations, consistent findings represent significant reliability. Even at the lower end, inter-judge reliabilities range from $r = .49$ to $r = .58$ for both male and female stimulus persons.[725] These statistics are particularly impressive considering the circumstances of this particular study, whereby four raters busily selling tickets interacted only briefly with each person comprising a large number of stimulus persons (752 total, composed of 376 males and 376 females). At the higher end, reported inter-judge reliability ranges from $r = .79$ between two judges,[336] $r = .70$ between more than two judges,[61] $r = .80$ between male and female groups of judges,[486] and $r = .90$ between groups of judges regardless of gender.[486]

Delving deeper into how universal agreement is between judges about another person's physical attractiveness, research documents comparably high inter-judge agreement between judges from different countries. Data collected for males (92 in total) in Austria and the United States revealed very high agreement when judging facial physical attractiveness of females.[695] While subjects in Austria were homogeneous in culture, subjects in the United States self-reported to be Oriental/Asian American, Hispanic, American Indian, and Caucasian. Self-reported ages of these subjects ranged from nineteen to fifty-five. Regardless of these differences in cultures and subcultures, the commonly used Pearson Product Moment statistical test identified significantly high agreement (i.e., statistical correlation) between ratings of the physical attractiveness of stimulus persons, $r = .81$ among the judges. When judging physical attractiveness of the front of a stimulus person's body with the face masked, agreement of physical attractiveness ratings was $r = .89$ for subjects from these two countries. Judging the back of stimulus persons produced an equally high agreement of $r = .92$ between subjects in Austria and United States.

Measure Validity

A measurement that actually measures what it intends or portends to measure is a goal of measure validity in scientific research. Two major dimensions of validity are internal and external. Internal validity focuses on strict controls to assure that resulting data are due to manipulation of the experimental variable. Generally, experiment designs provide good internal validity at the expense of external validity. External validity focuses on realism of the experiment, which regards how well findings generalize to broader populations beyond the data of a particular research project. The collective physical attractiveness phenomenon research provides assurance for internal validity and external validity. The findings about physical attractiveness phenomenon from laboratory experiments have involved solid internal validity, which permits conclusions that physical attractiveness has caused the resulting variances. Similarly, the findings from field experiments that show solid external validity have verified findings of internally valid experiments.

Measure validity has additional dimensions in the form of convergent validity and discriminant validity. Although seldom reported in individual research projects, the collective physical attractiveness phenomenon research performs well in these regards. When explicitly performed and reported, both primary methodologies for assessing validity—multi-method matrix and test-retest procedures—support confirmatory conclusions about the strength of convergent and discriminant validity within physical attractiveness phenomenon research.[528, 535]

Efforts that have explored convergent validity and discriminant validity in physical attractiveness phenomenon research have assessed whether subjects, including comparison of subjects in the United States and South Africa, have found that people hold different meanings for concepts such as sexiness/sex appeal and physical attractiveness/good looks.[474, 475, 528, 535] However, with this particular set of concepts, despite a priori assumptions of differences, data do not permit such definitive conclusions about discriminant validity for sexiness (at least not with a modified version of Sigmund Freud's definition[225] emphasizing sexual or erotic arousal due to appearance) and an original definition of physical attractiveness emphasizing pleasing looks.[528] The correlations based on this exploratory attempt did not yield evidence in favor of discriminant validity for the physical attractiveness construct. In fact, concepts or traits of physical attractiveness and sexiness proved statistically similar and interdependent (as might be expected intuitively).

Self-Measures versus Measures by Others

Familiarity significantly affects physical attractiveness, familiarity with the person and with the person's appearance. Research conducted in Ireland in 2004 among raters not personally acquainted with the stimulus persons, shows that increasing the number of times these raters see stimulus persons/photos increases familiarity with the visual stimuli and, in turn, increases the ratings of the stimulus persons, which, of course, is the person's physical attractiveness.[562]

Other research conducted in 2001 reported comparable findings. Single exposure, regardless of minimal length of time, influences physical attractiveness ratings of a person's face.[590] Similarly, raters who recognize faces when presented photos of stimulus persons systematically assign higher physical attractiveness to these faces than to faces unfamiliar to them.[310] Much earlier research in the late-1980s[76] and late-1960s[761] revealed equally interesting findings about familiarity effects, providing more basic or general knowledge about human perception workings. Those two earlier studies found that people judge even nonhuman, nonliving objects higher in physical attractiveness when the objects are familiar versus unfamiliar.

Research published in 2003 conducted by researchers in New Zealand and Australia pursued further the question about physical attractiveness ratings given to nonhuman, nonliving entities.[267] They used birds, fish, and automobiles for stimulus materials and found raters' familiarity with the stimuli favorably influenced physical attractiveness ratings. The averageness of stimuli also increased subjects' ratings of physical attractiveness for birds and fish, but not for automobiles, which the researchers hypothesized "may reflect a preference for features signaling genetic quality in living organizations."

Moving along the familiarity continuum from only visual familiarity to personal familiarity unrelated to visual appearance, research data show that personal familiarity of stimulus persons significantly affects (ratings of) his/her physical attractiveness. Personal familiarity is greatest for the knowledge or familiarity that a person has concerning him or her, followed to varying lesser extents by others in their lives ranging from persons met a few minutes earlier to lifelong friends and family members. Common categories of familiarity utilized in physical attractiveness research are self-ratings or one's self and other-ratings of complete strangers. Individuals in between vary in degrees of familiarity from casual or infrequent acquaintances to spouses. All three broad categories yield different ratings and, because physical attractiveness is an esthetic without absolute metrics, the category of others rating complete strangers provides the most accurate data and certainly the most frequently used measures. Complicating considerations in this research can align with spouse and potential spouse dynamics, as well as the standard research assumption that raters are heterosexuals. Furthermore, regardless of sexual orientations, raters might harbor interests in or attractions to potential dating-mating stimulus persons even though not currently acquainted.[250, 578]

Self-Measures

Self-judgments consistently prove the least accurate measures. In addition, males are consistently and substantially less accurate compared to females (with the males, unlike females, rating their physical attractiveness substantially higher than reality). Verification that self-measures are poor measures is not difficult to find, with the correlations between self-rating and impartial judges reported from $r = .37$[6] down to $r = .17$.[672] These low correlations associated with self-measures of physical attractiveness translate into people not seeing themselves as others see them; in fact, self-ratings are consistently overestimated, whereas underestimation is extremely infrequent, and females are more accurate in their self-ratings of physical attractiveness than are their male counterparts.[40, 581]

Research using police cadets as subjects (37 in total, ranging in age from 20 to 56 years old) found self-ratings of a person's physical attractiveness and ratings by others to be not statistically significant, i.e., to be very dissimilar.[188] People might expect this contradiction for an often non-objective characteristic like physical attractiveness because a similar pattern emerges for characteristics that are more objective. For example, the Health and Human Services Department of the United States federal government found in 2005 that 30 percent of Americans see themselves as overweight or obese, but the actual objective number is 64 percent.[701]

More extensive than the above, a doctoral dissertation disguised as a study investigating self-concept asked subjects to rate themselves as to how others would judge their overall physical attractiveness on a 10-point scale, with 1 being extremely unattractive, 5 being attractive, and 10 being extremely attractive.[40] Ratings by others yielded inter-judge reliability of $r = .89$ for the entire sample. Separated by sex, inter-judge reliability for the female subjects was $r = .89$ and for the male subjects it was $r = .87$. Separated by physical attractiveness level, the inter-judge reliabilities for low, average, and high physical attractiveness were $r = .81$, $r = .76$, and $r = .77$, respectively. Compared to the high inter-judge reliabilities, the correlations between self-ratings and ratings by others were very low at $r = .22$.

The dissertation concluded that self-ratings of physical attractiveness were dramatically inaccurate and were most frequently in the direction of overestimation as opposed to underestimation.[40] In probing the data, overestimation varied according to the person's physical attractiveness. Those of higher physical attractiveness tended to be more accurate, whereas those of average and lower levels tended to be more inaccurate. Males and females high in physical attractiveness tended not to give self-ratings significantly higher than the judges did, but both males and females of low or average physical attractiveness gave significantly higher self-ratings than the judges afforded them. Furthermore, male subjects exhibited greater discrepancy between ratings by self and ratings by others than did the female subjects.

To explain the greater accuracy found among females compared to males, the researcher put forth that females throughout their lives receive more frequent feedback than do males. With this feedback, females learn to adjust their self-ratings to coincide with this information, thereby reducing overestimation of their own physical attractiveness relative to their males counterparts.[40] Steady lifetime feedback to females may also offer partial explanation for results of a 2005 study asking 3,200 women around the world to describe their looks, to which only 2 percent evaluated themselves as beautiful.[79]

In 2005, *Developmental Psychology* published a strong methodological research project that shed light on one more dimension of self-ratings, particularly by females.[720] The research acknowledged that as many as one in three girls growing up in the United States experiences child sexual abuse, which lowers women's self-ratings about worth, body image, and self-esteem in adulthood. That research extended this knowledge into a question asking if child sexual abuse also lowered self-ratings about physical attractiveness by these women in adulthood. The subjects, 623 demographically diverse women, were between 18 and 50 years of age from Missouri and New Mexico, composed as follows: 40% European Americans, 27% African Americans, 21% Latin American, 4% Asian American European, 4% Native American, and 4% designated other or bi-racial. On a five-point interval scale, participants retrospectively self-rated personal qualities of "looks," "kindness," "intelligence, and "talent" during elementary school years and teenage years. Included in the myriad of measures, the participants indicated through well-accepted assessment procedures any child sexual abuse experienced before 14 years of age. Child sexual abuse (CSA) uniquely affected self-rating of physical attractiveness. The researchers concluded, "[W]e predicted that CSA may negatively influence girls' and women's self-evaluation, especially as related to traits that are linked to men's mate choices—in particular, physical attractiveness." While the researchers responsibly caution about their self-report and retrospective procedures, their resulting data found "CSA was associated with lower self-evaluated looks [physical attractiveness] in childhood and during the teenage years but was not related to self-evaluated kindness, intelligence, or talent."

Measures by Others

Measures of physical attractiveness by others regard two distinctly different types of judges: (a) acquaintances of the stimulus persons, and (b) strangers who neither know nor have ever seen the stimulus persons. While measures of physical attractiveness by others differ dramatically from self-measures, those measures by others discussed in the immediate prior section regarded strangers who do not know and have never seen the stimulus persons. Within the first type, acquaintances vary along a continuum of little to great familiarity, and measures of physical attractiveness vary somewhat accordingly. In all cases, because no absolute measure of physical attractiveness exists, the judgment by strangers is logically the true measure. It is then reasonable to assume that judgments by strangers yield an objective, impartial measure and certainly the best measure for researchers investigating physical attractiveness phenomenon.

A hierarchal order emerges when reviewing data for three types of physical attractiveness measures: (a) self-evaluations, (b) evaluations by acquaintances, expressly spouses, and (c) evaluations by others, expressly strangers. The order of physical attractiveness ratings for the same stimulus persons, array highest to lowest from spouse, self, and stranger.[486, 487] Presumably, judges of a person's physical attractiveness, to whom a stimulus person is a stranger, are impartial, objective, and thus most accurate. Factually, the others/strangers category of judges rate physical attractiveness lowest, with higher ratings by self-evaluations, surpassed with the highest ratings by spouses.

An interesting unanswered question regards the direction or sequence tied to the high ratings by a person's spouse. One answer might be that a long-term spousal commitment leads to increased perception of the person's physical attractiveness. This could be due to familiarity, which causes greater liking, which in turn causes increased favorable evaluations of physical attractiveness. Alternatively, perhaps an internal strategy reduces cognitive dissonance (likened to buyer's remorse) by justifying the decision with an unjustly high perception of the person's physical attractiveness. Another answer might be that people have uniquely shaped brain receptors that cause them to perceive another person's particular physical attractiveness unjustly higher than other people with differently shaped brain receptors, all then leading to resultant long-term spousal commitment.

Assuming impartial judges present the most correct physical attractiveness rating, it is then accurate to state that most individuals overrate their own physical attractiveness.

Furthermore, individuals overrate their spouse's physical attractiveness even more. These findings, of course, contradict popular notions that people see their physical attractiveness at levels less than reality. Research for a doctoral dissertation found stable and replicable patterns when it explored these rating differences.[732] Subjects (88 in total) were married couples (40 husbands and 40 wives) and strangers (4 males and 4 females) asked to rate physical attractiveness using a 10-point scale with endpoints labeled as very unattractive or very attractive. Measures by others (i.e., the strangers, assumed impartial judges) showed mean values for the husband and the wife for each couple were similar with no statistically significant difference in physical attractiveness. As presented in Table 3-1, this doctoral dissertation research revealed that the lowest rating of physical attractiveness was from the strangers and the highest was from the spouse, regardless whether the rating was a wife evaluating a husband or a husband evaluating a wife. These data also offer support to the proposition that people really do overrate their own physical attractiveness, while males overrate their own physical attractiveness more than females overrate theirs.

Table 3-1. Mean Values for Physical Attractiveness Ratings Comparing Three Types of Measures/Ratings: Strangers, Self, and Spouse

Type of Raters	Husband's Physical Attractiveness	Wife's Physical Attractiveness
Strangers (Impartial Judges)	3.6	3.6
Self	5.4	5.1
Spouse (Wife/Husband)	7.2	6.5

DETERMINANTS

Measures, or ratings, of physical attractiveness identify rather definitive levels of physical attractiveness, whereas research into physical attractiveness phenomenon identifies less definitively the determinants that underlie the broader measures, or ratings, of physical attractiveness. Regardless, research has identified myriad determinants within physical attractiveness phenomenon that underlie a person's physical attractiveness. The structure of determinants align with permanent components visible on a person's body and face along with a multitude of other components, subcomponents, characteristics, and types all captured later in this chapter within Figure 3-1. Determinants of Physical Attractiveness, Characteristics (page 102). Research conducted explicitly and in some instances less explicitly, to identify determinants of physical attractiveness, identifies determinants that make tangible the general descriptors of "Characteristics" for the determinants. These, for example, include the listings later in this chapter in Table 3-2. Determinants of Physical Attractiveness, Representative Sampling Overview of a Person in Total (see page 104) and Table 3-3. Determinants of Physical Attractiveness, Representative Sampling of Body Components of a Person (see page 105).

Still additional determinants, or, at times better-termed sub-determinants, contribute to and detract from a person's physical attractiveness. Some factors are characteristics of the stimulus person, whereas some are characteristics of the judge. Characteristics of judges documented through scientific research include the judges' own physical attractiveness,[680] their self-esteem,[248] internal arousal based on heart-rate information,[747] and even heart-rate information that is bogus.[346] Research with miscellaneous characteristics possessed by stimulus persons has produced statistically significant data about the stimulus person's voice,[71, 512] first name,[234] and eye features, such as gaze,[230, 357] pupil size,[96, 293] and movement.[246]

Permanency, Impermanency

Physical attractiveness is the impetus, the engine, the heart of physical attractiveness phenomenon. Accordingly, an illustration of physical attractiveness phenomenon depicts physical attractiveness at command center, affecting all other entities and factors surrounding it (see Figure 1-1 on page 21 in chapter 1). Physical attractiveness, like its larger, all-encompassing phenomenon, is far more than meets the eye, and like its phenomenon holds hidden values. To understand the dynamics and consequences of physical attractiveness phenomenon, it is important to understand the underlying determinants of physical attractiveness.

The structure of determinants of physical attractiveness rests on dimensions of permanency and impermanency. This structure is a stable fundamental of physical attractiveness phenomenon constructed overwhelmingly with permanent components supplemented by comparably minute, impermanent fashions. Regardless if particular determinants of physical attractiveness are physical aspects of a person, non-physical aspects of a person, physical aspects separate from a person, or non-physical aspects separate from a person, these comparably permanent aspects do not vary by culture, time, or geography. In contrast, the standards, or what might be called fashions or fads, that accompany the permanent components often change or vary between cultures, times, and geography.

The Power and Paradox of Physical Attractiveness puts forth that physical attractiveness phenomenon is consistent throughout history and among people of all cultures. The overwhelming portion of its focus is on the permanent or ongoing aspects of physical attractiveness, while recognizing that some permanent aspects have impermanent or temporary characteristics. Within the consistent dynamics, power, pervasiveness, and consequences of physical attractiveness phenomenon, styles, fashions, and fads describing many comparably permanent determinants change and vary. While the fundamental values that include dynamics and determinants are consistent over time and between all people, the specific design of determinants varies between times and between people. However, particular fashions or styles (such as with clothes, hair, jewelry, cars, etc.) are, in themselves, of minor or peripheral pertinence to physical attractiveness phenomenon put forth by *The Power and Paradox of Physical Attractiveness.*

The permanency of physical attractiveness phenomenon is the consistencies of hidden values along with the dynamics that lead to different consequences, which for people of higher physical attractiveness are generally beneficial and for people of lower physical attractiveness are generally detrimental. It states that dimensions or components that determine physical attractiveness are similarly consistent across time, geography, and culture. The permanency of physical attractiveness phenomenon does not conflict with the impermanent characteristics under its umbrella that follow fashions and fads. Furthermore, while physical attractiveness phenomenon as put forth by this book most importantly identifies permanent hidden values, it also takes into account comparably minor changes constantly occurring in fashions and fads associated with more permanent components and dimensions.

Physical attractiveness may at times be in the eye of the beholder, so to speak, but physical attractiveness phenomenon is never in the eye of the beholder. While particular changes in fashions and styles affect physical attractiveness, the role of fashions and styles as determinants of physical attractiveness do not change within physical attractiveness phenomenon. People have always followed what is in vogue in pursuit of greater physical attractiveness. For impermanent determinants of physical attractiveness such as clothes and other adornments, this following and pursuit represent rather continuously transitory trends. Nowadays, analogous to following what is in vogue that use to apply only to impermanent determinants, also applies to permanent determinants such as face and body components in pursuit of greater physical attractiveness. While following and pursuing these latter trends are continuous and analogous, the changes achieved are substantially less transitory for permanent than for impermanent determinants.

Staying in vogue has dissimilarities as well as similarities for impermanent and permanent determinants of physical attractiveness. A major difference is the newness of following trends for permanent determinants in pursuit of greater physical attractiveness, made possible recently due to technology advances and societal attitude changes toward cosmetic surgery. A second major difference is the longer time cycles required between changes to permanent determinants and impermanent determinants. Clearly, the effort, cost, and time necessary to undergo cosmetic surgery in pursuit of greater physical attractiveness, by changing a face feature to a certain look that is in vogue, is hugely greater than to change a piece of clothing or hairstyle to be more fashionable in pursuit of greater physical attractiveness. Although many people in absolute number make changes to permanent determinants in their pursuits of greater physical attractiveness, the number relative to those who make changes to impermanent determinants is of course tremendously far smaller.

A permanent determinant of physical attractiveness influenced by physical attractiveness phenomenon is a person's lips. Lips are consistently an important body or face component that affects physical attractiveness for all people, but the dimensions of lips judged most physically attractive vary in style and even fashion. An interesting feature of lips is their complexity within physical attractiveness phenomenon. While lips are a permanent determinant of physical attractiveness, changes throughout history in related style preferences contribute an impermanent dimension in terms of fashion changes for lipstick shine, color, gloss, and so forth. Lips as a permanent determinant of physical attractiveness vary in preferred size, shape, and fullness between cultures and times.

While lips of a person are a permanent determinant of physical attractiveness, consider, for a moment, their size dimension. People today as well as people throughout history have placed different value on the size of lips, primarily the size of lips for women. In the extreme, there are today some cultures in parts of the world that have long-valued large lips as a determinant of higher physical attractiveness, to an extent that others consider extreme since the most desirable large size hinders ability for those individuals to eat properly. Nowhere near that extreme, in the United States and many other parts of the world, a definite shift in preference in the later part of the twentieth century moved from smaller, thinner lips for females to larger, fuller lips. More specifically, it was not long ago in the United States when smaller or thinner lips among Caucasians were valued more highly than today when larger or fuller lips are valued more highly as determinants of higher physical attractiveness. Accordingly, with contemporary advances in cosmetic surgeries and product injections, women in contemporary times choose increasingly to make their lips fuller and larger in pursuit of higher levels of physical attractiveness, whereas women in earlier generations valued less large and less full lips as determinants of higher physical attractiveness.

Lips of a person as determinants of physical attractiveness are not alone to possess both permanent and impermanent dimensions. Another determinant with permanent and impermanent dimensions is body piercings.[161] Body piercings are permanent but the frequency with which people follow the trend or fashion have undergone changes relatively recently, is characteristic of impermanent determinants.

Regardless of their permanency and impermanency dimensions, body piercings represent physical attractiveness phenomenon well in terms of pursuits by people to increase their physical attractiveness at costs and actions that others might consider extreme. In response to an article published by a national news magazine in 2004,[161] a middle age woman writes about another woman, "some of these piercings have to hurt like hell" and then, in a derogatory tone asks, "Is this how the Gen-whatevers define beauty?"[233] Despite the implication of being new or unusual, people throughout human existence, while regularly changing definitions of determinants, have always modified their bodies beyond temporary changes achieved with clothes, jewelry, and cosmetics in pursuit of higher physical attractiveness. Even in this case, a 25-year-old woman replied, "I have this piercing because I like the way it looks, much as I suspect [the woman above] enjoys the way her earrings look…noting that the holes in her ears were likely made by a piercing…" accompanied by at least some pain.[233] Regardless the pain or results achieved, typical pierced earlobes and more unusual body piercings both represent an important aspect of physical attractiveness phenomenon, which is the fact that people take actions along a continuum in pursuit of higher levels of physical attractiveness that others might consider extreme.

While determinants within physical attractiveness phenomenon remain consistent, definition of particular determinants varies substantially. One culture defined by any number of labels might value earlobe piercings only, and another might value multiple ear, face, and tongue piercings together, one might value short hair and another long hair, thin lips and another group valuing fuller lips. Most every determinant of physical attractiveness (weight, skin tone, clothes, teeth, and so on) is analogous with the determinant consistently influential and pursued with corresponding preferential-detrimental treatment by society and individuals in society, with the form, fashion, or style of these same determinants varying between people with changes in time.

Characteristics

Physical attractiveness as a field presents experimental science with the difficulty of developing a reliable construct for measuring it and, thus, identifying its determinants. This situation is not unique and is, in fact, analogous to research efforts to identify and classify determinants of biological diseases. For physical attractiveness, while each determinant and each category of determinants contributes to and subtracts from a person's physical attractiveness, the determinants are often interdependent. The result is that physical attractiveness is ultimately, usually, a Gestalt, whereby the whole is greater than the sum of the parts.

Biological sciences often provide useful observations comparing humans and animals. In physical attractiveness, gender characteristics tend to be reverse for humans and animals. Unlike the animal kingdom where males often possess more features of greater physical attractiveness than females, in humans, the females possess features more valued for physical attractiveness. For women, a constellation of factors often equated with age and health generally describes their physical attractiveness.[101, 317] For men, the concerns have long been more concentrated on appearances of physical fitness and body shape. In fact, in 1940 American "manly" physiques were divided into standard classifications of "endomorph" (large/overweight compared to average, sometimes accompanied by muscular build), "mesomorph" (average/medium), and "ectomorph" (small/thin compared to average) replete with personality traits assigned to each body type.[418] Still, in 1964, one scholarly book author wrote that our society knows less about the physical attractiveness variable pertaining to people than it does for fish.[300] Here, Figure 3-1 provides a description of characteristics of determinants of physical attractiveness: many and complicated, unequal and shifting appeal, physical and non-physical, compensatory and non-compensatory, enduring and transient, influencers that are dynamic and many, and Gestalt in which the whole is greater than the sum of the parts.

Figure 3-1. Determinants of Physical Attractiveness, Characteristics

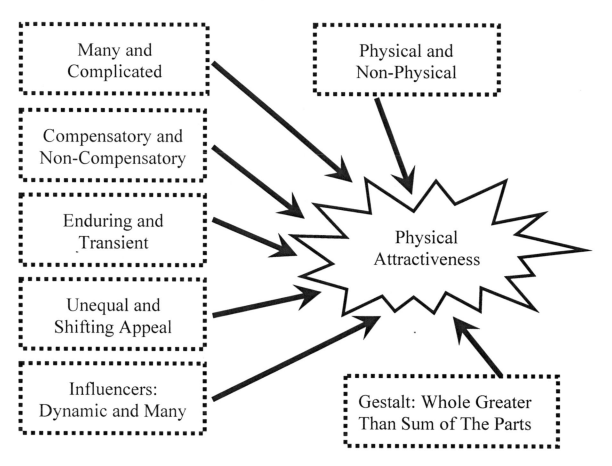

Determining physical attractiveness is complicated. It extends well beyond basic pedestrian thoughts that a very few, easily identified, features of the face or body determine physical attractiveness. Those basic pedestrian thoughts typically suggest constant tangible dimensions for each of the few determining features. Greater thought and analysis reveals that determining physical attractiveness is a complex situation with complicated determinants that are many in number. Unequal and shifting appeals of individual determinants influenced by different situations and different persons contribute to complexities of determining physical attractiveness.

Compensatory and non-compensatory relationships further complicate goals to identify physical attractiveness determinants. Compensatory relationships occur when determinants exist interdependently whereby a favorable or unfavorable component offsets the favorableness or unfavorableness of another component. Particularly appealing features of a person such as attractive eyes, nose, or mouth can at times balance, or compensate, unappealing features such as unattractive eyes, nose or mouth. The reverse occurs in which a particularly unattractive or unappealing feature balances and in this case diminishes the attractiveness of other features, ultimately decreasing a person's overall physical attractiveness.

Non-compensatory relationships occur when a particularly favorable or unfavorable feature affects a person's physical attractiveness independently, or rather singularly, as if viewed in isolation. Depending on the component and the people involved, a particularly appealing component is non-compensatory when it does not balance or in this case increase the appeal of a particularly unappealing component. Very attractive eyes or nose, for example, might be non-compensatory for other very unattractive features of the person's face or body. These very attractive features will not balance or not raise the physical attractiveness of other less appealing features and ultimately will not contribute favorably to determining overall physical attractiveness. Likewise, determinants in a non-compensatory relationship mean that an unattractive, unappealing feature of a person will not reduce the attractiveness or appeal of another feature and will not lessen the overall physical attractiveness of the person who possesses other more physically attractive features.

Some determinants are enduring and others are transient. However, the distinction between enduring and transient is not set in stone. What was earlier enduring, or permanent, as well as earlier transient, or temporary, is no longer necessarily the case. For example, some people have surgery to alter the shape of their noses, while other people choose to make permanent their eye shadow cosmetics. Tangential to enduring-transient descriptions of physical attractiveness determinants is the above discussion about consistently important basic components—hair, body shape, lips, teeth, and so on. In contrast, design or fashion of these basic components is transient, varying between and within countries, cultures, and times. The appeal of certain hairstyles, body shapes and builds, prominence or fullness of lips, shade of teeth, body adornments like clothes and jewelry, and so forth, all change and vary.

Listing the many determinants of physical attractiveness grows more complex when people realize that both physical and non-physical factors contribute to a person's physical attractiveness. Determinants of a person's appearance are complicated in part because there are so many determinants of a person's physical attractiveness. The number is largely due to the sizeable number of dimensions that compose the physical exterior of a person, combined with the non-physical aspects of a person that also affect perception of a person's physical dimensions. In other words, physical attractiveness is determined both by visual physical components and by non-visual non-physical aspects. A long list of non-physical aspects of an observed person such as reputation, career and occupation, education, speech and voice, odor, finances, attitude, environment, friends and mates, and much more can significantly influence observers of a person's physical attractiveness. At the same time, sometimes independently and sometimes interdependently, the visible physical components of a person's body and face influence physical attractiveness.

Above all else, influencers of physical attractiveness determinants are dynamic and many. These influencers are outside potential control that a person might exert concerning his or her physical attractiveness. They include nearly endless qualities of technology, ethics, religion, societal norms, social pressures, and financial resources, as well as an individual's own judgment and motivation. All these influencers assist to define actions and alterations acceptable for a person's physical attractiveness overall, as well as for particular determinants. Practically all these influencers encompass continually evolving and complex considerations to where now, people increasingly embrace the abilities and actions to alter a person's appearance, let alone gender, before birth. The cover story of a 2004 issue of *Newsweek* magazine provides an example as its title headline states, "Parents Now Have the Power to Choose the Sex of Their Children. But as Technology Answers Prayers, It also Raises Some Troubling Questions."[337] The article goes on to discuss:

> While the [high-technology] advances have received kudos from grateful families, they also raise loaded ethical questions about whether science is finally crossing a line that should be crossed. If couples can request a baby boy or girl, what's next on the slippery slope of modern reproductive medicine? Eye color? Height? Intelligence?[337]

Within this context, Table 3-2 and Table 3-3 list a reasonably representative sampling of explicit determinants of a person's physical attractiveness for both males and females.

Table 3-2. Determinants of Physical Attractiveness, Representative Sampling Overview of a Person in Total

Individual Person in Total
Physical aspects of a person
Body with its many components (detailed in following table)
Face with its many components (detailed in following chapter)
Non-physical aspects of a person including personality, body language, voice such as tone, pitch, speed, and accent, and speech such as grammar and pronunciation
Body odor such as cleanliness, soap fragrances, pheromones
Physical aspects separate from a person such as adornments (e.g., clothes and jewelry) and accouterments (e.g., residence and car)
Environment such as location and setting
Physical attractiveness of colleagues, friends, spouses, and spousal partners
Non-physical aspects separate from a person including status, credentials, and reputation
Observer's own characteristics separate from the person judged, such as the observer's own psychology, biology, reference point/level for physical attractiveness, life experiences, relation to or familiarity with stimulus person, stimulus person's resemblance to observer, etc.

Table 3-3. Determinants of Physical Attractiveness, Representative Sampling Overview of Body Components of a Person

Body Components
Static or relatively static such as torso, extremities, and height
Dynamic such as body language, personal space, appearances related to aging, accidents, fitness and muscle tone, weight gain, weight loss, etc.
Adornments such as jewelry and cosmetics
Procedures including routine hygiene
Symmetry, profile, and height
Shoulders: breadth, shape
Chest: males and females
Figure: symmetry, proportion
Posterior / buttocks: shape, size, firmness
Weight and weight distribution
Muscles, muscle tone
Stomach: size, shape
Arms: symmetry, length, size, proportionality to body
Hands: symmetry, size, skin
Fingers: symmetry, length, skin, nails, cuticles
Legs: symmetry, length, size, proportionality to body
Face, both as a body component and as a separate entity itself

Separate from Person Judged

Table 3-2 above lists determinants of a person's physical attractiveness that include factors that are separate from the physical components or physical features of the person. In addition to a person's tangible body components and tangible face components in determining his or her physical attractiveness, there are physical aspects and non-physical aspects separate from the person that affect his or her physical attractiveness. Research documentation shows, for example, that physical attractiveness of colleagues, friends, and spousal partners contributes to determining a person's physical attractiveness. Non-physical aspects separate from the person but which contribute as physical attractiveness determinants are an observer's own characteristics such as psychology, biology, reference point/level for physical attractiveness, life experiences, relation to/familiarity with stimulus person, stimulus person's resemblance to observer, and so on.

The determinants of a person's physical attractiveness, apart from that person's own appearance, include the physical attractiveness of associates. Scientific research about physical attractiveness phenomenon provides underlying and explanatory data for such mass media proclamations as "hanging with [beautiful actress] Angelina Jolie established [physically unattractive actor] Billy Bob Thornton's desirability, and made him more attractive to other women."[745] At least one research project has discovered that one determinant of physical attractiveness for females is the physical attractiveness of their male significant other.[669] Subjects (30 males and 30 females) were presented with a female stimulus person photographed with a male stimulus person of either high or low physical attractiveness, then later evaluated the female. Research manipulations included eight bipolar adjective scales for the subjects to rate the female stimulus person within each experimental treatment condition. Significant main effects for physical attractiveness but not for gender of judges surfaced in the statistical analysis. These data showed positive consequences for females partnered with a male of high physical attractiveness and negative consequences for females associated with a male of low physical attractiveness. In other words, as well as evaluating females more positively on all scales, the subjects also rated the females' own physical attractiveness higher when paired with a male of high physical attractiveness. No significant interactions occurred between gender and physical attractiveness manipulations, which is to say that the pattern of a female's physical attractiveness ratings varied with the higher or lower physical attractiveness of male partners.

Variables within both male and female observers themselves cause and/or align with how they determine or rank physical attractiveness of other persons. One research project investigating cross-cultural values found males of lower socioeconomic levels consistently place higher value of beauty on higher levels of female body weight or fat than males of higher socioeconomic levels.[154] Another study about self-ratings of physical attractiveness revealed adult women who have experienced sexual abuse as a child, compared to those who have not had this experience, rate their physical attractiveness lower in retrospect to when they were elementary and high school ages.[720]

Research about ratings of physical attractiveness of children by adults is quite consistent pertaining to resemblance. Overwhelmingly, men and women rate physical attractiveness of children higher when the child more closely resembles the rater. In one study published in 2004, this effect was by and large the same for both men and women when the child's photo was morphed to be closer in resemblance to the rater.[171] In another study, also published in 2004, which included functional magnetic resonance imaging (fMRI) of the raters' brains and brain functions, this effect was greater for adult males than for adult women.[570] Explanation hypothesized for this difference between men and women is "that human males may use and favor facial resemblance as a paternity cue" more than women do.

Within observers themselves, stage of menstrual cycle contributes as a determinant of how people judge the physical attractiveness of another person. A very thorough, scientifically solid experiment used subjects (42 females, 18 to 35 years of age, 40 in the United States and 2 in Vienna, Austria) whom the researchers first qualified as heterosexual, not currently pregnant or breastfeeding a child, and not currently taking any steroid medications or birth control pills.[328] Each subject completed a personal history form with questions asking "exact date of her last menses (first day of bleeding), the typical length of her menstrual cycle, regularity of her cycle, her age, her prior hormone use, and her pregnancy history."[328] The researchers combined this information with findings from other researchers concerning menstrual cycles. With this combined information, the researchers then used the number of days before and after each subject's ovulation to determine the menstrual state of subjects when each subject participated in the rating of physical attractiveness of the experiment's stimulus persons. The subjects were accordingly categorized at the time of participation in the physical attractiveness rating task as either high conception risk (defined as being within nine days before ovulation) or low conception risk (defined as anytime outside the nine days time definition for high conception risk). A Quick Time movie using Adobe Premier that allowed careful systematic modification, morphing, and presentation of faces along an appearance continuum from extreme male to extreme female presented the stimulus persons to the subjects.

In preparing the stimulus materials, photographs of 16 Caucasian males 18 to 26 years of age and 16 Caucasian females 18 to 30 years of age were manipulated, modified, and morphed. Researchers then presented subjects with stimulus materials comprised of 15 faces. At the conclusion of the entire, extensive, meticulously conducted research project and data analysis, the researchers stated, "the results are interpreted as support for a hormonal theory of facial [physical] attractiveness whereby perceived beauty depends on an interaction between displayed hormone markers and the hormonal state of the viewer."[328] More specifically, data from this research project supports strongly the hypothesis that people change their judgment about physical attractiveness as a function of hormonal changes within the observers, in this case based on data from female judges aligned with their menstrual cycle. These researchers go on to explain their data argues clearly that changes in physical attractiveness judgments align convincingly with complex hormonal forces within observers, and not with any sort of general mood changes within the observers. Judgments of physical attractiveness by females changed only for male stimulus person with faces of stereotypically high physical attractiveness. The females' judgments did not change for any faces of female stimulus persons.

Other research provides similar findings. Data reveal that females exhibit a statistically significant pattern of judging physical attractiveness of males as higher or lower in conjunction with stage of menstrual cycle.[557] Female subjects categorized as high conception risk (defined as anytime within nine days before ovulation) rated more masculine/less feminized male faces higher in physical attractiveness, whereas the low conception risk subjects (defined as anytime other than within nine days stated for the high conception risk group) rated less masculine/more feminized males faces higher in physical attractiveness. Data from a follow-up study generated equivalent findings from subjects (139 females responding to a magazine survey) who express greater preference, during high conception phases of menstrual cycle than during low conception phases, for more masculine/less feminine faces of males.[557] Explanations for these findings emphasize they "signal adaptive inherited genetic characteristics, such as immunocompetence."[328]

Hierarchical Ordering, Body and Face

Dimensions of body and face do not contribute equally to physical attractiveness. Their contributions reflect a two-level, sequential, hierarchical system. On the first level are such encompassing components as the face and the body. On the second level are subcomponents such as the face's nose and mouth and the body's stomach and build. Attempts to construct a hierarchy of importance for determinants of physical attractiveness are difficult for at least three reasons. First, facial components, defined within the category of all body components, interact with many components. Second, research is difficult to compare because investigated variables, or components, differ between studies. Third, individual studies sometimes treat both macro components or features (such as a face's appearance and profile or a body's appearance and profile) and micro components or features (such as a face's lips and eyes or a body's arms and legs) as equivalent and/or interchangeable. Despite these complexities and limitations, the research reveals serious attempts to identify relative contributions of individual components that determine physical attractiveness.

The variables are complex, variations in methodologies make it difficult to compare pertinent research precisely, and identification of an exclusive hierarchy is not practical. This difficulty is due primarily to the wide range of dimensions studied in each effort. Three pertinent research projects conducted in the 1950s span the number of investigated dimensions or determinants, ranging from a low end extreme of one dimension[468] to a high end extreme of forty-six determinants,[628] and, between these two extremes, involving twelve determinants.[334] In the mid-1970s, ten years after research into physical attractiveness phenomenon began explicitly, individual research projects investigated twenty and twenty-five determinants.[60, 422]

Body dimensions contribute to the evaluation of physical attractiveness. One study collected data over a five-year period from about 600 people equally divided male and female.[93] Participants described their level of physical attractiveness using body dimensions they deemed significant contributors. Analysis of these data in light of related research identified a collection of forty-four body dimensions, or determinants, of physical attractiveness. These data supported the research project's hypothesis that both sexes agree on ideal traits for both males and females; providing further evidence that beauty, or physical attractiveness, is not an assessment unique to any one observer. However, forty-four body dimensions proved unnecessarily numerous because only six contributed substantially.

Regardless of stimulus persons' sex or judges' sex, the same six features accounted for about 75 percent of the variance in the physical attractiveness evaluations. One feature alone accounted for about 50 percent of total variance for all sex dyad combinations. By far, the most important body component in determining physical attractiveness was the face. The data revealed a slight difference in rankings about male and female stimulus persons. For male stimulus persons, regardless of judges' sex, face was first (accounting for about 50 percent of the variance) and weight/weight distribution was second (accounting for about 10 percent of the variance). For female stimulus persons, regardless of judges' sex, weight/weight distribution was first (accounting for about 50 percent of the variance) and face was second (accounting for about 10 percent of the variance).

Similarities in judgment by both sexes are greater than the dissimilarities. Males and females agree strongly on the relative importance of body components as determinants of physical attractiveness. Strong agreement also exists about corresponding rankings for an individual's own physical attractiveness, even though men tend to overrate significantly their own physical attractiveness compared to self-ratings by women. This latter agreement between judgments of oneself and judgments by others is likely due to the interactive nature of attitude, self-image, and self-perception formation.

Using different methodologies in pursuit of the same goal, two studies found insignificant differences for importance of specific determinants among males and females. Both studies dissected overall (i.e., Gestalt) ratings of physical attractiveness into minute details through either a self-evaluation methodology[123] or evaluations by evaluations by others.[93] The studies used multidimensional scales and factor analysis to identify components of physical attractiveness. Table 3-4 presents the determinants in rank order. Unlike data from other research projects documenting that self-evaluations of overall physical attractiveness do not match a person's physical attractiveness judged by others, the data in this table reveals that evaluations by others, regardless of gender combinations, produced judgments very similar to self-evaluations for importance of components of physical attractiveness.

Table 3-4. Determinants Cited Most Significant for Physical Attractiveness, Late-1970s/Early-1980s

Females Judged by Self	Females Judged by Females	Females Judged by Males	Rank	Males Judged by Self	Males Judged by Males	Males Judged by Females
Weight	Weight	Weight	#1	Face	Face	Face, Face Features
Face	Face	Face	#2	Legs	Weight	Weight
Height	Complexion	Height	#3	Weight	Legs	Hair
Legs	Legs, Height	Hands	#4	Torso	Shoulders, Arms	Body Profile
Extremities	Hands	Figure	#5	Voice, Hair	Complexion, Hands	Shoulders, Arms
No Mention	Face Profile	Teeth	#6	Height	Hair, Head	Height, Voice

Besides dimensions of body and face not contributing equally as determinants of physical attractiveness (as noted above at the opening of this section), body and face do not necessarily generate equal benefits and detriments in response to a person's physical attractiveness. A 2005 study conducted in Australia by four researchers at the University of Western Australia investigated if individuals of higher physical attractiveness have greater mating success.[591] Subjects (746 total with 345 males and 401 females) ranged from 17 to 51 years of age. The researchers concluded, "Facial [physical] attractiveness correlated with the number of short-term, but not long-term sexual partners for males and with the number of long-term, but not short-term, sexual partners and age of first sex, for females. Body [physical] attractiveness also correlated significantly with the number of short-term, but not long-term sexual partners for males... Body [physical] attractiveness did not correlate with any sexual behavior variable for females."

COMPLETE PERSON RESEARCH

The best description of what determines a particular person's physical attractiveness is the complete person and not any certain parts or components. A research project published in 1974 expressed well the continuing approach of most studies of physical attractiveness phenomenon, as well as the perspective of most people in their everyday interpersonal interactions:

> ...if a significant number of judges designate a person as physically attractive, then that person is defined as physically attractive. Whether it was the dimple on the chin which the judges are responding to, whether more redheads than brunettes are classified as attractive, is not typically a matter of concern.[63]

Ultimately, the research shows that determinants of a person's physical attractiveness are a Gestalt whereby the whole is greater than the sum of the parts. From both research perspectives and practicality perspectives for everyday perception of physical attractiveness, a simplifying strategy such as the Gestalt orientation is a necessity for cognitive processing in this area. Therefore, most physical attractiveness research uses manipulations consistent with a Gestalt view of measurements and determinants. The determinants, relationships, and values that lie beneath physical attractiveness are too numerous and complex to do otherwise. Correspondingly, methodologies involving truth of consensus procedures detailed in this chapter have proven to be enduring and robust because they align closely with the Gestalt quality of physical attractiveness. Not emphasizing every individual factor that determines physical attractiveness undoubtedly represents a simplifying strategy used by researchers as well as by people in their everyday interpersonal interactions. Entirely too many potential determinants influence physical attractiveness, further complicated by the more overarching characteristics and types, to do otherwise.

SUMMARY

Physical attractiveness is at the center of physical attractiveness phenomenon. It is therefore important to understand physical attractiveness, including its hidden values, to understand the broader dynamics and consequences of physical attractiveness phenomenon. To measure physical attractiveness, Gestalt perspectives implemented in research through truth of consensus procedures have worked well to study physical attractiveness phenomenon. Gestalt perspectives also serve people well in everyday interpersonal interactions. Measuring physical attractiveness and identifying its determinants entail all the components and dimensions of a person in total. Setting the context in which specific tangible features function, a good structure to understand physical attractiveness is to be cognizant that its determinants and dimensions are:

- Many and Complicated
- Shifting and Unequal in Importance
- Physical and Non-Physical
- Compensatory and Non-compensatory
- Enduring and Transient
- Influencers: Dynamic and Many
- Gestalt: Whole Greater Than Sum of The Parts

Furthermore, while each determinant and dimension contributes to and subtracts from physical attractiveness, a person's physical attractiveness is ultimately a Gestalt whereby the whole is greater than the sum of the parts. However, insofar as discrete tangible and intangible components exert a role in helping to determine the whole, along with adornments such as clothes and cosmetics, perceptual distortions such as reputations and accomplishments, and even environmental factors, it is valuable to identify disparate components of physical attractiveness.

Researchers can identify many factors that contribute to physical attractiveness, and they can identify that the significance of factors varies. But definitive, hierarchical ordering of body factors that consistently or universally contribute to physical attractiveness is nearly impossible beyond saying the broad component of face wields a higher rank ordering than the broad component of body. While the impact of higher and lower physical attractiveness determined by a person's face and body is clear, the rank order of even these two broad determinants of physical attractiveness is not clear. A 2005 survey of 1,500 girls between the ages of 13 and 18 asked participants if it is more important to have a pretty face or a good body. Alyssa Tani, age 13, gave a typical response when she said, "They go hand in hand. If you have a pretty face and a good body, you have more of a chance of having more friends, boyfriends and just being more happy and satisfied with yourself."[2]

Chapter 4

Body Parts

[A]s time wore on even I had to admit I had a sexy body…and even though these new dresses hid none of my curves, I believed they hid my fear of being ugly. I thought I could use my body to distract people from my face. It made me feel worthy.(pp. 207-208)

Written by Lucy Grealy at age 31
in her widely praised autobiography, *Autobiography of a Face*.[257]

INTRODUCTION

A person's body, male and female, contributes vividly to his or her physical attractiveness, and is integral to the attendant dynamics and consequences of physical attractiveness phenomenon. Data from the *Female Body Survey of Great Britain 2005* found that among those respondents:

> The majority (95 percent) said they felt unhappy about their body on a daily basis [and] 51 percent thought their careers would progress faster if they had a better body and were more [physically] attractive. But it is not just men who are pushing women to extreme measures—78 percent said that other women were more critical of their weight and shape than men. The survey found that if they had a better body, 65 percent of women would change their lifestyle, 46 percent would change their career and 12 percent of them would change their partner. Women were also [fearful] of looking old, with 58 percent jealous of women their own age who looked younger.[479]

Lauren Libbert, editor of *Top Sante*, the magazine that conducted this research project, stated in 2005:

> Women today are judged on [the look of] their body more than any other time in history. They are constantly faced with body perfection…and they see good-looking women seemingly achieving more than just [intelligent] ones. No wonder more and more ordinary women now see cosmetic surgery as the key to changing their lives—be it their career, partner or general lifestyle.[479]

When speaking about specific tangible features that determine a person's physical attractiveness and which evoke the physical attractiveness phenomenon, body is second only to face. A person's body, as the quoted excerpt above testifies, can be a very substantial compensating factor in raising or lowering a person's physical attractiveness in the person's own mind and in the minds of others. Determinants of a person's physical attractiveness include all the components or subcomponents of the body. Within the Gestalt context of physical attractiveness, the body is a principal determinant that contributes significantly in the form of components and dimensions of physical attractiveness. Accordingly, the body as one determinant or a collection of determinants composing a person's physical attractiveness has received attention from philosophers, artists, scholars, and many others, from ancient times through modern times.

Scientific research attempts have advanced understanding about the complexities of factors possessed by the body as they make relative contributions to determining physical attractiveness. This research shows that constructing a hierarchy of importance for body components is no less difficult than constructing a hierarchy of importance for physical attractiveness overall or, for that matter, for face components. Body factors in physical attractiveness phenomenon are complex because the body constitutes many components, dimensions, and influencers that are compensatory and non-compensatory, enduring and transient, and dynamic and static. Furthermore, additional physical and non-physical considerations, including the face both independent of body and interdependent with body, all increase complexity inherent with a person's body within physical attractiveness phenomenon.

If the body is evaluated as three major components—face view, body front-view with no view of face, and body back-view—research documents that comparable to physical attractiveness overall, judgments of physical attractiveness represented by a person's body is largely the same among beholders. A study with subjects representing cross-cultural dimensions of ages, ethnicities, and countries found statistically high agreement regardless of culture and subculture differences.[695] Analyzing data about judged physical attractiveness separately for front of a stimulus person's body with face blanked out and back of a stimulus person's body found agreement of physical attractiveness ratings was $r = .89$ among judges for front and $r = .92$ for back. These subjects were males (92 in total) in Austria and United States ranging in self-reported age from 19 to 55. The Austrian subjects were homogeneous in ethnicity while the ethnicity of the subjects was diverse in the United States, self-reported to be Oriental/Asian American, Hispanic, American Indian, and Caucasian. Underscoring that "beauty is *not* in the eye of the beholder," data analyses found statistically significant levels of agreement between Austrian subjects and diverse American subjects for the ratios of ratings for all combinations of face, body front, and body back of stimulus persons. For these details, see Table 4-1 on the next page that presents Pearson Product Moment correlation value (r) in each cell for the agreement of data between judges and the probability (p) due to chance of the respective correlation value.

Table 4-1. Agreement of Ratings from Cross-Cultural Judges Concerning Physical Attractiveness of Face, Front of Body, and Back of Body of Stimulus Persons

	Judges in Austria	Judges in United States
Face and Front of Body	r = .29; p = .0022	r = .25, p = .009
Face and Back of Body	r = .30, p = .0015	r = .31, p = .0013
Body Front and Body Back	r = .31 p < .00005	r = .67, p < .00005

COMPONENT DIMENSIONS

The role of body as a component or determinant of physical attractiveness is a very distant second to the face, but, like the face, the body is a component composed of many subcomponents or dimensions. To increase understanding of the role of body within physical attractiveness, research has gone beyond an importance hierarchy into the realm of dimensions of each component. These efforts acknowledge the impossibility to identify and qualify unequivocally all the relevant subcomponents. One approach used by researchers to overcome this obstacle uses drawings rather than live stimulus persons or photographs of persons. The necessary trade-off in this methodology is less realism for greater experimental control. To further increase procedural controls in order to gain greater research validity, the drawings of stimulus persons have presented bodies with faces obscured.

One subset of research about body components and physical attractiveness relates most directly to the relationship of body components and personality. For example, one early research project investigated perspectives and preferences of males by using silhouettes of nude females.[737] Manipulations of stimulus persons concentrated on size and shape of breasts, buttocks, legs, and overall shape. After subjects indicated their preferences, researchers administered a battery of personality inventories to assess differences among subjects who preferred certain dimensions. Another study with the same basic methodology but directly investigating physical attractiveness expanded the stimulus persons to include both males and females.[52] Profile silhouettes again manipulated size and shape of chest, buttocks, and legs. Male and female stimulus persons with large buttocks received the most negative evaluations. Male stimulus persons received highest physical attractive ratings when presented with moderate chest size, moderate-sized legs, and small buttocks. Male stimulus persons with large chests described as "Atlas-type" received least favorable ratings for their physical attractiveness.

Research conducted in England examined the relationship between body type and assumed qualities.[664] Stimulus materials were photographs of females with faces masked. The body component studied was overall body build, soma-typed as endomorph (large/overweight compared to average, sometimes accompanied by muscular build), mesomorph (average/medium), or ectomorph (small/thin compared to average). The subjects were 25 males (average age of 25.1 years) and 25 females (average age of 23.8 years). Each subject received a package of three stimulus persons representing each of the three soma types, and was asked to rank the stimulus persons from "most suiting" to "least suiting" on each of 15 concepts. Results were quite neutral for mesomorphs, positive for endomorphs, and negative for ectomorphs. Endomorphs were ranked as liked best, most likely to be successful, and most likely to be a leader, whereas the ectomorph was judged as liked least, most likely to be homosexual, and most likely to be alcoholic. These data did not yield a sex difference for any soma types or measured concepts.

While body component preferences research permits indirect inference about physical attractiveness, other research directly addressing the relationship between body component dimensions and physical attractiveness permits direct inference. One study used detailed, front-view drawings in a stated attempt to maximize realism.[302] Special production procedures permitted extreme care in drawing the figures to comply with standard anthropometric mean values for dimensions and proportions. Eleven female drawings presented manipulations of (a) full figures with standard hip and waist, (b) standard waist with four different hip widths, (c) standard hip with four different waist widths, (d) narrower waist and hip combination, and (e) wider waist and hip combination. Eleven male drawings presented manipulations of (a) four shoulder widths, (b) two waist widths, and (c) two hip widths. All 22 figures obscured facial features. The researchers presented these stimulus materials to male and female subjects (131 males and 229 females), asking them "to rate drawings of male and female figures for attractiveness."[302] Ratings used a 9-point labeled scale.

A variety of statistical analyses performed on collected data revealed several distinct relationships between ratings of physical attractiveness and component dimensions. Statistically significant main effects revealed differences for sex of stimulus persons, but not for sex of judges. For male stimulus persons, greater shoulder width and ratio of shoulder width to waist width exerts positive influence in determining ratings of higher physical attractiveness. In addition, the researcher stated that slenderness and waist size of the male body influence physical attractiveness positively, while hip width does not.

For female stimulus persons, less waist width and less hip width exert positive influence in determining ratings of higher physical attractiveness. Although decreasing waist width produced higher ratings of physical attractiveness, lessening hip width did so only to a certain level. After a certain threshold, too small a hip width resulted in lower ratings of physical attractiveness than a slightly larger width. Within the range manipulated, physical attractiveness ratings increased as slenderness increased. Contrary to popular belief, greater curvedness of the female stimulus person was associated with lower ratings of physical attractiveness. The definition of curvedness used in this study was the ratio of hip width to waist width.

Cross-cultural research has investigated the question of body components among people in the United States and Israel. Cards showing carefully drawn male figures without detailed faces were presented to university students at Boston University (30 males and 57 females) and at Tel-Aviv University (45 males and 45 females).[239] An artist drew all figures with a goal to create identical front and side views. Thirty-two male figures presented body manipulations described as either somatic or postural. Three somatic body components involved two values each: (a) shape, Atlas or pillar; (b) neck, thick or thin; and (c) abdomen, presence or absence of protruding abdomen. Two postural body components also involved two values each: (a) head, held up or bent forward; and (b) shoulders, held straight back or slouched forward. An experimenter the same sex as the respective subjects gave instructions to rank order each figure as higher or lower in physical attractiveness.

A thorough series of analyses of variance tests performed on the data showed no significant effects due to cross-cultural differences of subjects. Differences of gender showed some differences in response to the stimulus persons, while extensive interactions occurred among practically all combinations of manipulated variables: abdomen, shoulder, neck, head, and body shape. Although the many interactions make summary statements difficult, the abdomen revealed a consistently powerful impact. Subjects reliably evaluated physical attractiveness lower for stimulus persons with a protruding abdomen compared to persons without a protruding abdomen. In all the experimental treatment conditions, this effect of protruding stomach was strongest, with greatest impact, on the male stimulus persons.

Shared perspectives rather than cross-cultural differences seem to take the proverbial driver's seat for much in the domain of physical attractiveness phenomenon. Data collected in 15 countries through an international survey in 2002 even confirmed the above perspective surrounding a person's stomach identified 20 years earlier.[389] This latter research, conducted by *Men's Health* magazine, asked readers, which body part "would you like to be perfect?" Overwhelmingly, inside and outside the United States, the surveyed men ranked their stomach/abdominals at the top of the list with the next item a very distant second (Table 4-2).[389] Notably, the data revealed the appearance factor of stomach/abdominal ranked incredibly higher than the health/comfort factor of back, as well as greatly higher than pectoral muscles, legs, bicep muscles, and buttocks.

Table 4-2. Percentage of Men in the United States and Fourteen Other Countries Stating Their Body Part They Would Like Most to Be Perfect

	Men in United States	Men in All 15 Surveyed Countries
Stomach/Abdominals	73	69
Pectorals	11	13
Legs	5	6
Biceps	5	4
Buttocks	4	45
Back	2	4

BODY SIZE, BODY BUILD

Huge amounts of medical literature and psychological literature discuss body size and physique. These discussions emphasize overweight physiques, which beginning in about 2003 literally exploded in popular media in the form of frequency of news articles about alarming rates of people who are overweight and obese in the United States and Europe. These publications focus on relationships between overweight, physical health, and mental health.

The psychological publications also deal with interpersonal consequences of being overweight, which routinely is a stigma within our society despite its greater than ever commonness. A survey of 4,000 overweight women performed in 2005 by a London based magazine found "only 1 percent of women like their bodies and 83 percent are consumed by a deep self-loathing."[229] It further reported, 70 percent encountered negative comments regularly about their size, 80 percent felt inadequate due to size, 91 percent were depressed by their size, and 94 percent felt their size caused them to be treated like second-class citizens. Supporting data from the *Female Body Survey of Great Britain 2005* found, "Just one in 100 overweight women in Scotland is happy with their size (UK average four percent)."[479]

Males and females hold distinct preferences about physical attractiveness for body type for stimulus persons of same sex and opposite sex. Overwhelmingly, the favored physique is average or moderate body size and body build with equally overwhelming dislike of overweight and obese physiques and mild disfavor for thin or underweight physiques.[397, 401, 625, 657, 658, 737] Children hold body size preferences similar to those held by adults. Children of all ages, even as young as five years old, exhibit the same liking pattern as adults for mesomorphic (average/medium), ectomorphic (small/thin compared to average), and endomorphic (large/overweight compared to average, sometimes accompanied by muscular build) physiques. When children are asked which body type they prefer in response to stimulus persons (presented in photographs, line drawings, or descriptions), girls occasionally select ectomorph,[657, 658] endomorph is practically never selected, and mesomorph is practically always chosen.[80, 397, 401, 404]

Body-specific stigma pertaining to weight or non-weight considerations is mostly outside the scope of this book about physical attractiveness phenomenon. However, as a starting point for interested readers, an admirably exhaustive review published in 1982 by Gerald R. Adams, discusses well the issues of stereotyping pertinent to physical attractiveness phenomenon and body stigma separate from being overweight.[4]

ADORNMENTS, APPENDAGES

A person's body as well as his/her face is a major determinant of physical attractiveness, while adornments and appendages can further enhance or lessen physical attractiveness. Like other determinants of physical attractiveness, adornments and appendages span overlapping continuums between endpoints ranging from permanency to impermanency, inanimate to animate, minor to major, common to rare, and so forth. These adornments and appendages can apply to either the body or face and include cosmetics, clothing, jewelry, fragrances, body tattoos, permanent impregnated face make-up, natural perspiration odor, products to counter natural perspiration odor, voice pitch and tone, and even first names given at birth. Despite prominence of these variables, formal scientific research has not given them particularly notable attention with regard to physical attractiveness phenomenon. However, private interests within each industry have probably amassed their own empirical and anecdotal data about the relationship between physical attractiveness and body adornments. Unlike scientific research published in scholarly journals, research conducted for private interests (in other words, for benefit of commerce) normally remains restricted proprietary information not disseminated for public or widespread knowledge.

People's desire to increase physical attractiveness certainly drives the demand for embellishments affected by adornments and appendages. For example, pheromones—chemicals produced and secreted by animals known to attract other same-species animals—have generated interest, recent folklore, and sales of accordingly formulated men's colognes involving human pheromones and their influence on attraction between people and, perhaps, even judgment of another person's physical attractiveness. Some research has explored specific human body chemicals such as androstenol to understand the impact on perceptions of physical attractiveness,[68] but at this time scientifically collected data do not yet bear out speculation about significance of human pheromones within attraction between people. In fact, the article mentioned in the prior sentence expressed its findings rather explicitly in its title: "Androstenol as a Human Pheromone: No Effect on Perceived Physical Attractiveness" as published by the prestigious journal *Behavior and Neural Biology.*

Data collected through scientific research procedures as early as the 1950s[305] as well as 20 years later in the 1970s[502] have documented that cosmetics[110, 249] and clothes influence perceptions of personality and appearance. While physical attractiveness phenomenon is more concerned about clothes overall than about particular trends and fashions, research in physical attractiveness phenomenon does investigate why people wear certain styles and what impressions are spawned by certain styles.[186, 270, 271, 439] Some pertinent preceding scientific research that helped establish physical attractiveness phenomenon dealt more explicitly with physical attractiveness of females than males, due in large part to the era when those earlier scholarly explorations were conducted. These include a 1945 publication by Columbia University in New York City titled *Clothing and Appearance, Their Psychological Implications for Teenage Girls*[644] and a book published in 1941 in London titled *Why Women Wear Clothes.*[155] While these titles might suggest a certain gender orientation characteristic of common vocabulary usages in the 1940s in the United States, fundamental considerations from these books are analogously applicable to boys and men.

Clothes, cosmetics, jewelry, and fragrances, as well as the rather endless list of other varied adornments and appendages used to embellish a person's body and face undoubtedly all exert an influence on the physical attractiveness of an individual. Accordingly, these adornments and appendages are all-important factors within physical attractiveness phenomenon and, thus, to all people, regardless if they do or do not use them. Beyond this mention, this current book does not give further details for research projects, as well as anecdotal thoughts and views, on these determinants and categories of determinants of physical attractiveness because those respective investigations and perspectives are generally outside the primary focus of this book.

HEIGHT

Bigger bodies and bigger body parts may not necessarily always be better. Tall height contributes positively to higher physical attractiveness unless the height is unusually lofty. Taller height favorably influences perceptions of physical attractiveness, especially for males, with preference for both male and female stimulus persons judged most favorable for average or, more accurately, slightly taller than average. That is, after a certain level of height, the body component of height that is too tall exerts a negative influence upon physical attractiveness as judged by the person herself or himself and as judged by others.

Height plays a serious role as a body component within physical attractiveness phenomenon with shorter and taller heights typically associated correspondingly with lower and higher physical attractiveness. Despite occasional divergences where extreme tallness is a detriment, shorter than average males of all ages seem most negatively affected by this body component while taller than average males are most positively affected through an unchallenged discrimination based on height. A best-selling book published in 2005—*Blink, The Power of Thinking Without Thinking,* by Malcolm Gladwell—includes data from a survey of about one-half of all CEOs (Chief Executive Officers) of the Fortune 500 companies.[240] The average adult American man is 5'9" tall, but the average CEO is about three inches taller at about 6 feet. Less than 4 percent of adult American men are at least 6'2" tall, but 30 percent of the CEOs are 6'2" or taller, with 58 percent at least 6 feet tall.

John Kenneth Galbraith, a highly esteemed economist who stood 6' 8" tall, expressed well the bias in favor of tallness when quoted in the *Christian Science Monitor* as saying that height is one of society's "most blatant and forgiven prejudices."[713] A scholarly presentation at an annual meeting of the American Sociological Association declared the same sentiment as it stated: "American society is a society with a heightist premise: To be tall is to be good and to be short is to be stigmatized."[424]

While taller height is more physically attractive, the bias and stigma expressed in the prior paragraph are particularly negative against shorter heights. Compared to shortness of height, average height individuals fare relatively well in physical attractiveness phenomenon. As a body component of physical attractiveness, height contributes to determining physical attractiveness and at the same time receives benefits and detriments rather directly in its own right. Generally, individuals of taller heights receive more positive attributions than received by individuals of average and shorter heights. Furthermore, individuals of shorter heights receive more negative attributions than individuals receive who are average in height and taller. One study found that males of average height (defined in this study as 5'9–5'11") are perceived as more socially attractive than exceptionally taller men over 6'2" and exceptionally shorter men under 5'7",[256] but height is a body component involving high interaction with other physical and non-physical attributes.[317]

Like non-physical factors that influence perceptions of physical attractiveness, non-height factors influence perceptions of height. This influence on physical attractiveness might be less surprising given the subjective nature of physical attractiveness, whereas height at its core is a strictly objective measure. Even though height can be measured objectively, research shows the perceived height of a person increases as the person's status increases[744] and as social distance increases.[365] Associated dynamics link height to gender, with greater importance placed on the height of males than on the height of females. Research reveals that estimates of height correlate positively with perceptions of male stimulus persons' physical attractiveness, social attractiveness, professional status, personal adjustment, athletic orientation, and masculinity, with no such corresponding correlations for females. The research project reporting these findings used two methods of assessment—trait ratings and percentage estimates—to investigate stereotypes of males and females based on height.[318]

Subjects (237 in total) evaluated stimulus persons (males and females) of short, tall, and average height on seven characteristics: social attractiveness, professional status, personal adjustment, athletic orientation, masculinity, femininity, and physical attractiveness. The data collected showed shortness to be a greater liability for males than tallness was an asset, and a greater liability for males than females, although shortness emerged also as a liability for females.

Height by itself is important in physical attractiveness phenomenon. Height is also important as one very visible body component of physical attractiveness. Desires to alter and accentuate the body component of height are analogous to desires to enhance its larger context of physical attractiveness. Their similarities extend beyond visual appearance. Like overall physical attractiveness, physical height of an individual is not a neutral characteristic in our society. Its effects are subtle and pervasive, with implications ranging from friendly social interactions to employment decisions. Assigning or aligning greater value or authority to a person can adjust that person's height or perception thereof, which, for practical purposes, is one-and-the-same since perception of reality is by and large more important in this area than actual reality. Accordingly, because taller height is more valued than shorter height, understanding these dynamics contributes to understanding values hidden within physical attractiveness phenomenon.

Status

Early perceptual distortion research explored the effect of academic status on height and found a significant relationship between a person's status and perception of his/her height. Nursing students asked to estimate heights of people with whom they interacted—the school's assistant director, an instructor, the class president, and a specific fellow student—overestimated heights of school administrators and underestimated heights of fellow students.[160]

Another set of students at a university in Australia served as research subjects to test a hypothesis that increases in academic status raise perceived height.[744] The research project presented the same male stimulus person to five groups of undergraduate students. After the stimulus person left the room, the course instructor asked the students to estimate the person's height to the nearest half inch. The introductions were identical for all five groups except for systematic changes of the same stimulus person's academic status, described always as from the Cambridge University psychology department, but either as a student, graduate assistant, lecturer, senior lecturer, or professor. The course director, known to all the students, also asked them to estimate his own height. Results convincingly supported the research hypothesis that increasing academic status causes perceived height to increase. Height ratings of the course director were not significantly different between groups, but results showed the stimulus person's mean estimated height directly related to his academic status.

An early investigation conducted in 1974 focused on perceived physical attractiveness as a dependent variable with gender and status as manipulated or controlled independent variables.[403] The procedure introduced a male or female stimulus person to ten different undergraduate classes as either Tony Smith or Toni Smith, respectively. Both these stimulus persons were 22 years old, white, average height, weight, and physique for their age, and not known by any subjects. The male wore a jacket, tie, and slacks, and the female wore a dress of comparable style. Separate judges earlier rated their appearance as average—neither high nor low—in physical attractiveness.

All ten groups of subjects (184 females and 117 males) were in similar rooms, given identical procedures, and introduced to the experimenter by their instructor as someone who wanted a few minutes of class time. The experimenter passed out data sheets, face down, informing the subjects that the experimenter wanted them to meet someone before explaining these sheets of paper. The experimenter then asked the stimulus person to enter the room, at which time he or she did so and remained standing at the front of the room for fifteen seconds before leaving. The stimulus person, introduced as an undergraduate student, a graduate student, a recent master's degree graduate, a Ph.D. candidate, or a recent Ph.D. graduate, at all times maintaining the same behavior, position, and distance from the subjects. After the stimulus person left the room, subjects were then told that this was a study on perceptual memory and that they were to rate anonymously the stimulus person with respect to several characteristics.

All groups of subjects received identical procedures and information, except for the status manipulations that varied academic standing designations. Statistical analysis of the data showed a significant relationship between status and perceived height but no statistically significant main effect between these differing levels of academic status manipulations, gender, and perceived physical attractiveness. For physical attractiveness, the analysis did show statistically significant interaction with lower status levels. At lower levels of status, female subjects rated female stimulus persons higher in physical attractiveness than they rated the male stimulus persons, whereas at higher levels of status they rated male stimulus persons more physically attractive than the female counterparts. While the meaning of data for height and status in this study is clear, the meaning for physical attractiveness and status in this study is not clear. Particularly for physical attractiveness, interpreting this study's data is difficult and tenuous at best because of its mixed results and deviation from the larger collection of pertinent research findings. These data seem also confounded in a manner consistent with a generally common bias at the time of the study, in the 1970s, when professional-career achievement was associated to be more important for males than females.

Prejudice

All cultures have a subtle and even not-so-subtle predisposition against shorter people in favor of taller people, especially for males. A common response from listeners of radio talk shows on which I have spoken about physical attractiveness phenomenon inevitably includes calls from shorter-than-average males expressing unhappiness and frustration about their first-hand experiences. "Short People," a one-time best-selling pop song, even signaled societal acceptability of bias against shorter people with exaggerated lyrics that claimed "short people got [sic] no reason to live."[495]

Whether American press shapes or reflects society, it plays a notable role in attitudes about height. A content analysis performed outside of exacting scientific procedure investigated whether the press deals with individuals differently as a function of their height.[350] Results of this content analysis documented that descriptive writings by the press predominantly treat males and females most favorably when they are taller as opposed to shorter. Words that people use to describe taller men are often *tall, handsome,* and *athletic,* whereas the words often used to describe shorter men are *small, pallid,* and *bland.* Words commonly used for taller women are *tall, lithe,* and *supple,* whereas words referencing shorter women are *short, wiry,* and *frenetic.* A lengthy listing of vocabulary usages in our society points out rather convincingly that negative words are associated commonly with shorter people and positive words with taller people, including such references to shorter women as *cute* and *perky* but never as *elegant.*[350]

The value of height as a body component of physical attractiveness phenomenon is not new. References to this value occur throughout history and throughout cultures. Scientific comment about these height references arose in 1927 as epitomized by a prominent sociologist, who after analyzing many cultures determined the "correlation of tall stature with the upper social classes and low stature with the low social classes which exists in present civilized societies has also existed in the past and in the most different societies."[652] Wall paintings in ancient Egypt reflected status by height with the more important the person the taller the figure. Anthropologists find prehistoric tombs that have individual skeletons of taller height in elegant crypts but multiple skeletons of shorter height in common graves. Just as discriminatory are linguistic patterns that echo the social messages of height preference. We respect people who "stand tall" or who possess "stature," but we lower our expectations for the "midget-minded" or those with "Napoleon complexes" and castigate negative actions with promulgating biases about "stooping really low" or "belittling."

Adjustments

Shorter people and their significant others frequently wish to transform shorter heights to taller heights. Despite the lack of a transforming miracle formula, people act on these wishes from time to time. Options for tangible adjustments of height range from long-known physical devices to modern-day pharmaceutical drugs that promote growth, and, now, pioneering surgical procedures to lengthen leg bones. Options for adjustments not based on tangible means range from alignment with credentials or qualifications of higher regard to distorting perception through hair and clothing styles.

Desire and actions to be taller rather than shorter is no doubt a ratio of a million to one and span centuries. The motivations for such hopes range from increasing social ease to qualifying for occupations with height requirements. Today, human growth hormone (hGH) is available for children of nonessential levels of need and interested persons can even purchased it on the Internet. (As a footnote here, human growth hormone is fast becoming the newest anti-aging hormone treatment for adults). Professionals have progressively utilized many ingenious interventions and accommodations more safely and inexpensively than hGH. To increase height, women often prefer higher heels or thicker soles and men sometimes resort to the infamous risers placed within their shoes adjacent to the heel. In addition, the apparel, cosmetic, and coiffeur industries all have their own prescriptions to alter perceived height.

Techniques directed toward modifying perceived height are not mere folly. Generic perception research offers scientific studies that document adjustment of perception of objective tangible entities, even those with standard measures such as speed or height, versus more esthetic entities such as pleasure or physical attractiveness. Research in the 1940s and 1950s established that people estimate the size of coins as larger than same-sized non-monetary discs,[89] and they overestimate the size of cards in relation to the monetary values assigned to each.[191] Magicians no doubt rely on a host of perception adjusting principals and procedures throughout their magical shows, some of which rely on internal subjective factors in the form of personal motivations and values applicable to produce perceptual accentuations of a stimulus person's physical height. To a degree, clichés about "in the eye of beholder" and "a face only a mother could love" offer anecdotal support of adjustment techniques for height, even if limited to adjusting only perception.

Perceptions, Attributions, Political Examples

Height is relative, and like many facets in life, perception is more important than reality. Statistically, the average adult American male is 5'9" tall (five feet nine inches) and the average adult American female is 5'4" tall (five feet four inches). A mere two- or three-inch difference separates individuals considered short or tall in the United States and many other countries around the world. Males of 5'8" are short whereas men of 6'1" are tall. Perception of height is often more truthful to people than actual reality. Like perceptual distortions that occur for inanimate objects when assigned differing values, perceptions, and attributions about the height of people function similarly.

People perceive taller people as more physically attractive, especially males whose height is a greater determinant of physical attractiveness than females. In politics, at least for elected officials, it is reasonable to say that height and physical attractiveness are critical strategic factors, albeit factors not publicly admitted by politicians and campaign managers. One particularly notable pertinent political contest was the 1960 presidential campaign in the United States. Readily acknowledged as the candidate with substantially higher physical attractiveness, John F. Kennedy won the election over challenger Richard M. Nixon. While Kennedy's height at 6' placed him marginally taller than Nixon at 5'11½", in the appearance arena, Kennedy's physical attractiveness far exceeded Nixon's physical attractiveness. While one may hope that a candidate's physical attractiveness is not sufficient to decide an election, there is no doubt that it is a significant contributing factor. In fact, according to an article in the *San Francisco Chronicle*, "Some historians have blithely suggested that John F. Kennedy won the presidency because female voters swooned over his looks."[264]

People perceive individuals that are more important, or more valuable, as taller. They attribute the desirable body component of greater height to more important people, who are accordingly more valued. Conversely, people perceive taller people as more important (i.e., more valuable). This two-direction perception concerning height is analogous to the larger mass of physical attractiveness research identifying circumstances in which what is beautiful is good, and in the other direction, research also identifies circumstances in which what is good is also beautiful.[341] In American politics, the electorate more often than not elects the taller of the final two or three candidates. No voter would proudly confess that a political candidate's height swayed his or her vote, rather than issues, records, and stances. Yet, the proportion of candidates elected over long periods that are taller rather than shorter is too great to be coincidental. Explanation might begin with height as a body component in determining physical attractiveness, possibly combined with voters who lack thorough knowledge about issues and candidates and, instead, vote their visceral feel. In these cases, the more physically attractive candidates might be more persuasive about leadership qualities, trustworthiness, expertise, liking, and so forth, which all reflect standard benefits for people of higher physical attractiveness within physical attractiveness phenomenon.

Demonstrated election actions in favor of higher physical attractiveness via taller height are not an isolated instance in political contests. More than 100 years of elected officials bear witness to what seems more than coincidental and which is very understandable in light of physical attractiveness phenomenon. In fact, the taller of the two final candidates won ten of the past twelve United States presidential elections (more than 80 percent), that is, until 2000 when Al Gore Jr., at 6'1", lost to George W. Bush at 5'11". However, even that election was, by popular vote, in favor of the taller candidate with 543,895 more votes, overridden by the electoral college system used in American presidential elections. Consistent with presidential elections, tabulation of the 1990 United States Senate political campaigns revealed the taller candidates won twenty-four of the thirty-one elections (more than 75 percent).[436]

Whatever the arguable subjective circumstances, the objective fact is that the 2000 United States presidential election produced the first president in two decades in the United States with a height under 6'.[436] The 2004 United States presidential election process added more evidence against people with shorter height compared to taller height. During advanced stages of the primaries running up to the 2004 presidential election, the Democratic political party had a field of about ten major contenders. Media pictures of candidates together showed John F. Kerry, at 6'4", always towering physically far above every one of his Democratic Party competitors. Despite early disfavor among voters, consistent or expected according to this dimension and other dimensions of physical attractiveness phenomenon, sure enough, Kerry emerged from the crowd as the elected representative of the Democratic political party to challenge the incumbent president, George W. Bush. Standing next to his competitors, the impression was certainly the proverbial head-and-shoulders above the others in appearance and physical attractiveness, leading to corresponding beliefs of ability and leadership. Standing next to his competitors, the impression of candidate Kerry was strongly the proverbial head-and-shoulders above the others in appearance and physical attractiveness, leading to corresponding beliefs of ability and leadership.

The height of the Democratic political party representative, John Kerry at 6'4", in the 2004 American presidential election, was a dramatic contrast to the Democratic political party representative, who ran sixteen years earlier in the 1988 American presidential campaign, Michael Dukakis, who stood 5'8½". Consistent with this aspect of physical attractiveness phenomenon, candidate Dukakis, who lost the election, suffered greatly "in the editorial cartoons and late-night comic monologues, for being a half-foot shorter than the eventual winner, George H. W. Bush."[436] Many factors surely contributed to the loss by Dukakis in that election campaign, but political pundits still allude to his small physical size especially compared to his Republican political party opponent, George H. W. Bush. Even today, a turning point often cited about that political campaign is a television commercial in which Dukakis looked awkwardly small as he peered out of a huge army tank that dramatically visualized his actual small body size and short height. To dramatize the height difference in that presidential campaign, one political observer "recalled a 1988 presidential debate when the senior Bush [George H. W. Bush at 6'2"] greeted Massachusetts Gov. Michael Dukakis with an exaggerated long handshake—a move he said was orchestrated by Bush's campaign manager to reaffirm the fact that Bush was taller."[706]

Height can drive perceived competence and importance in political campaigns, while perceived importance and competence can drive perception of height. Perceptions of height of important people are routinely taller than they are in reality. College students who were asked to compare former President Jimmy Carter's height one year after he entered office, to that of former President Richard Nixon who had left the office in public disgrace, perceived Carter as the taller.[350] In reality, Nixon was two inches taller than Carter was, but a whopping 66 percent of those surveyed perceived Carter as the taller of the two men. President Nixon stood 5'11½" and Carter stood 5'9".[738] When former President Lyndon Johnson no longer held his highly elected position, he, too, seems to have given up his taller height when he lost his public stature. On his first return to Washington, DC, after leaving office, Johnson's height was commented upon by one long-time observer who stated he looked "less tall" than in the past.[350]

On the other side, taller people become important people more readily than shorter people do. *USA Today* published an article reviewing the two major party candidates—George W. Bush and John F. Kerry—leading up to the 2004 United States presidential election that focused on the heights of past presidential election winners and their challengers. "Since advent of the television age, taller candidates for president have almost always won the elections. And it has been more than a century since a shorter-than-average man was elected to the White House."[513] Consider Ronald W. Reagan who, at 6'1", was elected president of the United States in 1980 versus his major opponent, Jimmy Carter, at 5'9½" and elected again in 1984 versus his major opponent, Walter F. Mondale, at 5'11".

In the world of politics, Gray Davis at 6',[482] was well into his second term as the elected governor of the state of California when he was unseated in 2003 by Arnold Schwarzenegger at 6'2". While a two-inch difference in height is distinguishable, the electorate if surveyed would likely estimate the height difference to be much greater. The reason based on physical attractiveness phenomenon is the expectation that the electorate would perceive a much greater height difference amplified in this case by Schwarzenegger's movie stardom. This effect is further intensified because of the person's other designations of importance indicated by his numerous world bodybuilding championship titles related to unusually large developed muscle size. Additionally, the first United States president, George Washington, began his first of two terms in 1789 and was 6'1½" in height, while the tallest of all American presidents is also likely the most universally respected: Abraham Lincoln with a height of 6'4".[738]

Preferences for Height

People prefer taller people, but in some situations also prefer people of similar height to themselves. An expression of this preference is the amount of physical distance maintained by individuals as a function of height. Subjects asked to move toward stimulus persons of different heights (in a research project in which height is not known to be of interest to the subjects), remained twice as far from the 6' 3" stimulus person than the 5' 4" counterpart.[280] These research findings about personal distance may explain why friends tend to be similar heights more than chance would direct. Measuring heights of individuals for 514 friendship dyads, data revealed height differentials between the individuals to average 2.76 inches, which is significantly less than chance pairing.[58] An unrelated doctoral dissertation conducted at Temple University offers an explanation for these interpersonal interactions based on height, suggesting that being with others of dissimilar height causes doubts about oneself, whereas being with others of similar height promotes positive feelings about oneself.[571] These studies together suggest an approach-avoidance circumstance based on height itself, or as a body component determining physical attractiveness. Either way, it influences the acquaintance process and ultimately the development of friendships.

The impacts of height extend beyond nonromantic interpersonal interactions into romantic involvements and these influences follow physical attractiveness phenomenon. Height by itself or as a body component that contributes to determining physical attractiveness translates into benefits for those taller and detriments for those shorter. Statistical analysis after self-reported data of heights from male subjects (72 college students) exposed a significant correlation between the height of a male and physical attractiveness of his romantic partner.[213] In compliance with scientific research methodology, ratings of independent, impartial judges established the level of physical attractiveness of each subject and each subject's girlfriend. Males with romantic partners more physically attractive than themselves averaged 2.6 inches more height than males who had romantic partners less physically attractive than themselves.

Differing heights translate into likely unequal attention and certainly unequal service provided by strangers in favor of taller heights. A form of real-world research conducted by a newspaper's staff found people of taller heights were served before their shorter counterparts.[350] Two newspaper reporters working undercover sought help from various people who normally service the public. The two reporters, with heights of 6'2" for one and 5'6" for the other, simultaneously, in as identical a manner and appearance as possible, asked for service. In every test situation, the taller individual received help first. In later debriefing with the service providers, a car rental clerk stated the tallness of the one customer was a motivating force to speak with him first. A restaurant waiter expressed that she never thought about it, but she now thinks she must be serving taller customers first all the time. While caution is appropriate for interpreting the findings of this experiment conducted outside of formal scientific procedures, the results are still valuable as part of a much larger mass of similar research findings collected through a growing robustness of methodologies.

Preferences for people of taller heights carry real-life consequences that include differences in incomes and career successes. An extensive analysis of research data through formal meta-analysis research in 2004[335] "found that taller people generally tend to receive higher evaluations and be paid more even when the job involved has nothing to do with height."[513] The first author of that research reported, "Taller people are seen as more authoritative and as stronger leaders," speculating, "That could be a remnant of human evolution, when the species' survival in the jungle or on the plains depended on strength and power." More concretely, that research found physical height relates significantly with self-esteem, leader emergence, and performance. It found these relationships more strongly related to success for males than females; which is consistent with other physical attractiveness phenomenon data that reveal height is a determinant of physical attractiveness, and it is more so a determinant for males than females. This meta-analysis research project, based on data from 8,590 people, discovered "that height is positively related to income after controlling for sex, age, and weight." The authors conclude in their abstract, "Overall, this article presents the most comprehensive analysis of the relationship of height to workplace success to date, and the results suggest that tall individuals have advantages in several important aspects of their lives and organizational lives."[335]

FEMALE BREASTS

Bigger is better is a popular notion worldwide for a number of body components. It certainly is a popular notion for female bust size. Males and females of all ages around the world communicate recurring interest about women's busts. The interests range from shape to size, from type and design of undergarments to no undergarments, from surgical enhancement for cosmetic purposes to surgical removal for purposes of illness and disease. "People want to be able to stand under the Christmas tree with their new car, new living-room cabinet and new breasts," the president of the German Association for Aesthetic Plastic Surgery is quoted to have said in 2004 pertaining to the demand for cosmetic procedures leading up the end-of-year holidays.[497]

A Birmingham, England, newspaper article reported in 2005 that,[66] "breast enlargement still remains the most popular cosmetic procedure in the UK, according to surgeons. It accounted for 35 percent of all the procedures undertaken" in 2004 at one of the largest medical groups. In India, where the number has doubled between 2003 and 2005, Dr. Manoj Kumar, a senior consultant, reports the number of breast enlargement surgeries "is expected to grow phenomenally in the next few years."[688] That article goes on to state, "one of the commonly cited reasons for this changing trend [in India] is the mass media-driven body-consciousness among today's youth." A scholarly, American, longitudinal study found that during a twenty-five-year period, breast dissatisfaction among women increased 31 percent, or eight percentage points, to 34 percent of adults in 1997 from 26 percent in 1972.[232] Underlying these percentage increases are, one can speculate, increased concerns among younger girls on one end of the age continuum and increased numbers of concerned baby boomers whose naturally aging figures are unwelcome signs in a society that values bust shapes and sizes more characteristic of younger women.

Exceptions to the rule exist. The human race is too numerous and diverse to expect otherwise, but conventional wisdom that bigger is better is unrelenting for this body component of women. Individuals seemingly not affected negatively in this area even possess the experiences and mindset in favor of larger breasts. Actor Goldie Hawn stated in a 2005

CBS Television Network news interview, "I was very flat in high school. It caused me always to sit on the sidelines at dances. It is a wonder I didn't grow up with a terrible self-esteem."[123] Internationally famous as a singer and successful for many accomplishments and recognitions, Dusty Springfield, who died at age 59, said she "never shook off the feeling of being a fat, ugly kid."[235]

Actual decisions and actions by women of all ages and all positions in life provide objective evidence about the driving power translating from admiration and pursuit of larger breasts regardless of financial or physical costs. In 2004, speaking about her decision not to have her breast implants removed, pop singer Lil' Kim stated, "Sometimes [they] hurt my back. But I have too much fun with them."[615] *The Wall Street Journal* cites a 20-year old college student in 2005 who "after four years of experimentation [with non-surgical pursuits] has spent almost $1,000 and countless hours on a quest to increase her bust size."[129] Like many other people, she has yet to see the desired results but continues to consume pills as an alternative to surgery and injections in her pursuits of increased physical attractiveness through larger bust sizes and improvements to other determinants of physical attractiveness. Related, a professor at Georgetown University in Washington DC who has conducted research on bust-enhancing products says, "There is no published evidence that these products work. There is certainly no evidence that long-term use is safe."[129]

A 37-year-old woman described in a 2004 *Chicago Tribune* newspaper article illustrates another scenario common to physical attractiveness phenomenon and female bust size. Several months after breast augmentation surgery, she stated, "I didn't go obscenely huge, but clothes fit better and I am not as insecure."[386] This woman's decision made and her action taken in pursuit of higher physical attractiveness comes after she had adamantly:

> …always said she would *never* get breast implants. She thought it was ridiculous. She was confident about how she looked for years. Then the media monster claimed her…sexy advertisements, actors and models spilling out of their dresses, the television makeover shows that routinely produce Barbie doll look-alikes took their toll. Surgery just seemed to be the easy solution. She got breast implants in April [2004].[386]

Right or wrong, resistant or compliant, actions shaped by media or actions reflected by media, driven by anxiety or otherwise driven, great and growing numbers of women pursue higher levels of physical attractiveness by choosing to increase breast size and shape through surgery as well as other means. Based on data from the *Female Body Survey of Great Britain 2005*, commissioned by *Top Sante* magazine, a Glasgow, Scotland newspaper reported, "35 per cent [of the women surveyed, expressed] bigger breasts helped a woman's career."[159] Physical attractiveness phenomenon research documents well that this body component is more multidimensional than popular notions put forth. Yet, as in many dimensions of life, perceptions are frequently more important than reality, and cultural stereotypes rather universally put forth that larger bust size contributes inordinately to determining physical attractiveness. Of course, all judgments of a person's physical attractiveness are a Gestalt whereby some factors compensate for others.

A scholarly study to investigate internal qualities associated with bust size conducted a series of four experiments assessing first impressions of females as a function of bust size.[356]

In the first experiment, before evaluating a variety of characteristics pertaining to the stimulus persons, subjects (135 males and 135 females) read written descriptions about female stimulus persons that included subtly suggested small, medium, or large bust sizes. Resulting data agreed with other research that paired subjects of both sexes with silhouette figures representing female stimulus persons. A golden mean emerged in that too small or too large was not as favorable as moderate bust size. Stimulus persons rated highest in personal appeal and liking were those with medium bust sizes as compared to either small or large sizes.

Three other experiments in this series employed photographs. To minimize effects due to potential extraneous variables, the photography manipulated bust size in a manner to permit the same stimulus person in each experimental treatment condition for small, medium, and large sizes. After viewing the photographs, subjects (147 males and 141 females) evaluated the stimulus person. Data analysis revealed no significant differences for liking or personal appeal evaluations according to bust size. The researchers attributed this lack of significance to the likelihood that subjects considered more information than bust size when viewing photographs of stimulus persons. Postulation is that physical attractiveness of the person's face took precedence over less prominent features visible in the photographs, which then overrode potential effects of bust size due to the less than primary focus afforded in these photographs. Other evaluated traits were positive for the experimental treatment conditions with small bust size and negative for large bust sizes. Subjects perceived the stimulus person in the experimental condition presenting small bust sizes as most intelligent, competent, modest, and moral. They perceived those stimulus persons with large bust sizes as relatively unintelligent, incompetent, immodest, and immoral.

Different types of research methodologies yield the same lack of proven statistical significance for the importance of female bust in determining physical attractiveness. Factor analysis of body component data summarized in Table 4-3 below presents the resulting factors for body components with the respective values of factor analysis loadings in parenthesis.[93] Results from the statistical analyses of these data indicated that neither male nor female judges considered the female bust to be important enough to yield very high loadings on any factors:

- Female bust size for female judges did not produce any significant factor analysis loading values. For male judges, female bust size produced a significant loading factor value of .58 on a fifth highest factor that explained 3.4 percent of total variance.
- Male chest size produced statistically significant values for female and male judges. Data from female judges for male chest size produced a significant loading factor value of .72 on a fifth factor that explained 4.2 percent of total variance. For male judges, male chest size of stimulus persons produced a significant loading factor value of .74 on a fourth highest factor that explained 5.8 percent total variance.

Table 4-3. Factor Analysis Results for Importance of Body Components Using Others-Evaluation Data for Male and Female Gender Dyads

Male Judges		Female Judges	
Judged Males	Judged Females	Judged Males	Judged Females
Factor 2 (7.6% total variance)	*Factor 1 (52.4% total variance)*	*Factor 1 (45.7% total variance)*	*Factor 1 (67.2% total variance)*
Weight Distribution (.92)	Waist (.95)	Hands (.69)	Weight (.94)
Weight (.89)	Weight (.93)	Foot Size (.67)	Waist (.89)
Trunk (.87)	Body Build (.91)	*Factor 2 (14.2% total variance)*	Body Build (.88)
Overall Body Appearance (.84)	Back (.90)	Overall Body Appearance (.97)	Overall Body Appearance (.88)
Waist (.81)	Hips (.88)	Weight Distribution (.96)	Weight Distribution (.87)
Body Build (.76)	Buttocks (.88)	Thighs (.96)	Hips (.84)
Buttocks (.75)	Weight Distribution (.87)	Trunk (.96)	Buttocks (.83)
Back (.65)	Overall Body Appearance (.85)	Weight (.95)	Trunk (.79)
Thighs (.60)	Trunk (.81)	*Factor 4 (4.5% total variance)*	Arms (.77)
Factor 3 (6.5% total variance)	Thighs (.80)	Waist (.76)	Thighs (.76)
Calves (.87)	*Factor 3 (5.9% total variance)*	Buttocks (.75)	*Factor 4 (5.2% total variance)*
Leg Length (.73)	Height (.65)	Body Build (.68)	Leg Shape (.76)
Knees (.71)	Leg Length (.65)	Neck (.60)	Calves (.73)
Leg Shape (.69)	Knees (.60)	Back (.60)	Ankles (.67)
Ankles (.65)	*Factor 4 (4.3% total variance)*	*Factor 5 (4.2% total variance)*	Knees (.64)
Thighs (.51)	Fingers (.81)	Biceps (.76)	Foot Size (.55)
Factor 4 (5.8% total variance)	Nails (.68)	Chest Size (.72)	Height (.51)
Biceps (.86)	Hands (.49)	Shoulder Width (.70)	Leg Length (.50)
Shoulder Width (.74)	*Factor 5 (3.4% total variance)*	Arms (.60)	*Factor 5 (4.0% total variance)*

| Male Judges | | Female Judges | |
Judged Males	Judged Females	Judged Males	Judged Females
Chest Size (.74)	Bust Size (.58)	*Factor 6 (3.6% total variance)*	Nails (.67)
Wrists (.73)	Posture (.54)	Leg Length (.73)	Fingers (.66)
Arms (.63)	Ankles (.53)	Height (.67)	Hands (.57)
	Calves (.51)		

One qualification of the data presented in Table 4-3 above is that less-than-extreme bust sizes presented in this study rated quite favorable on the respective physical attractiveness scale. Therefore, if presence of extremes leads to greater awareness, the lack of extremes may explain the lack of indicated importance. Regardless of qualifiers, the lack of importance is congruent with other research showing bust size is not as important in determining physical attractiveness as popular thought maintains.[64, 302, 303, 423] Unless breast size is unusually small or large, research supports hypotheses that it is not a significant determinant of physical attractiveness despite conventional wisdom to the contrary, which is predictable as a corollary tendency of choice toward average.[317] Another research project found physical attractiveness ratings to be negatively correlated with bust size but qualified the accuracy of their findings, concluding the data obtained did not differentiate between substantial weight and large bust size since the two varied together in the research stimuli.[695]

Data less objective than collected through scholarly research sheds light, at least anecdotally, that the reality for many women is that bust size is less important that popular stereotypes attest. Cindy Jackson, an internationally recognized expert on cosmetic surgery with real-world personal experience with smaller, then larger, then smaller bust size, provides another perspective beyond notions that bigger is better, especially when surgical implants achieve the bigger. In her autobiography, published in 2002, she expresses that it is most important that bust size matches the woman's psychological self-view and matches her other body components. After having her breast enlargement implants removed, she writes from her home in London, "…I had realized they didn't really suit me. I'm not a busty, blousy sort of person and, frankly, I was a little embarrassed by them. But now that I had a less voluminous chest [after removal of the breast implants] it made my hips seem pear shaped…"[316]

Despite arguments put forth to the contrary, real-world actions overwhelming coincide with preferential notions expressing that bigger is better for women's breasts. Women are accordingly motivated. Current numbers of women obtaining breast augmentation surgery are substantial, with upcoming generations showing even more rather than less tendency to increase their breast sizes because of physical attractiveness phenomenon. Consider that breast implant surgeries for girls age 18 and younger nearly tripled in one year from 2002 to 2003. Among this age group, 11,326 breast implant surgeries were performed in the United States in 2003 and in 2002 the number was 3,872 according to data from the American Society for Aesthetic Plastic Surgery.[749] Which generation, the girls or the adults or both, drives these thoughts and actions is not clear, since, according to one cosmetic surgeon, "There is a trend in which parents are giving implants as a gift, including as a graduation present." The co-chair of the American Society for Aesthetic Plastic Surgery's breast surgery committee goes on to say that "there's no advertising for implants targeting that age group, but the images are all around them" and "well-endowed teen idols…as well as reality-TV shows…have made some girls dislike their own bodies."[407]

Strong desires for larger breasts lead to motivations that lead to decisions and actions. Data from the American Society of Plastic Surgeons show that nearly eight times more women (252,915) obtained breast augmentation surgery during 2003 than in 1992 (32,607) when the FDA banned silicone implants in the United States.[640] Women obtaining breast implants state they think clothes look better on women with larger busts, and although they express feeling good about themselves pre-surgery, they believe post-surgery they will look, think, act, and feel better. Friends provide ready evidence of the before and after improvements. Further encouraging and reinforcing these decisions and actions, 94 percent of those who receive breast augmentation surgery say they would recommend it to friends or family members, according to scholarly research published in 2003.[176]

Some women seek subtle changes to their bust size with intent to be noticed mostly only by the person herself, while some women seek the opposite for obvious notice mostly by everyone. Bust shape is nearly as vital as bust size to women seeking breast implants, and at least three segments compose the breast implant population—women who never had the size desired, women who once had the size and shape desired, and women who want poster-size, head-turning large. It is reasonable to project substantial increases for breast implant surgeries in the coming years driven by physical attractiveness phenomenon at a time in society when increasing numbers of individuals are passing from younger life stages characteristic of greater physical attractiveness. Particularly motivating for this group of women is their interest to reverse the lessening effects on their physical attractiveness due to aging and child rearing that have reduced and re-shaped their breasts from earlier stages of life. Accompanying their increased awareness of changes in physical attractiveness associated with normal aging, these women also are entering life stages marked by increase financial means that further encourage thoughts about cosmetic surgeries to resize and re-shape their breasts.

Like so much of physical attractiveness phenomenon, it is difficult to obtain truly accurate data about this body component in relation to physical attractiveness. Appropriate scientific research methodologies are essential to conduct research to understand behaviors concerning this facet of physical attractiveness phenomenon because people tend to state socially acceptable responses regardless of accuracy of those responses. The *Journal of Women's Health* published a 2003 study that found the primary reason for breast augmentation surgery was because those women are dissatisfied internally with their breasts rather than because of external pressure from romantic partners or sociocultural standards about physical attractiveness.[176] Based on survey responses from twenty-five women interested in breast augmentation surgery and thirty similar women who were not interested, the number one reason identified as expressed by 91 percent of the research participants, is for the woman to look better in her own eyes when without clothes.

Although women regularly state their breast augmentation surgeries are for themselves, no one makes decisions in a societal vacuum. Few people in any society are without influences from significant others in their lives or from the world in which they live.

The *Los Angeles Times* quotes clinical psychologist Rita Freedman on this precise topic:[595] "Nobody does this just for themselves. The decision that seems to be your own is a product of what you've learned from the culture." Furthermore, according to the *Los Angeles Times*, "[S]he suggests that societal pressure to look good has overtaken concerns about safety," which is a primary principle of physical attractiveness phenomenon overall, as well as specific to breast implants. Similarly, the editor in chief of *Allure Magazine*, Linda Wells, in interpretation of data from the 2005 Allure State of Beauty National Study that surveyed more than 1,700 Americans concluded, "I see that women are taking care of themselves for themselves, but there's that underlying sense of, What do men think of all this?"[261]

Whatever or whoever the drivers, influencers, and deciders, "more women than ever are paying the price—and taking the risk—to have perkier or bigger breasts" according to a 2005 article published in the *Los Angeles Times*.[595] That article reports cosmetic surgeons who say, "[M]ost women have concluded that the benefits outweigh the risks. Women will have no qualms about choosing the cosmetically superior silicone implants for augmentation should the FDA lift the moratorium. More than 90 percent of women in Europe, where both silicone and saline are available, choose silicone."

Further verifications about the importance of this body component within physical attractiveness phenomenon are the immense efforts and expenditures worldwide that focus on bras since their invention up to the present and for sure into the future. Despite a long history of designing and re-redesigning brassieres, the purchases, pursuits, and, even rather frequent, mass media news reports, of new, improved bras intended to produce greater physical attractiveness, as well as greater comfort, never ceases. For example, the *Chicago Tribune* newspaper reported in 2005 that in the United States:

> Big-name manufactures have deployed teams of scientists and designers, sometimes trailed by patent lawyers, to re-engineer the brassiere. At stake is nearly $5 billion a year that women spend on bras. [Related] Marshal Cohen, chief analyst at NPD Group, a marketing information company said, …bra sales grew strongly in 2004, up 8 percent [because] many women went out of their way to update their intimate wardrobe so they could be seen in public.[631]

FACE AS BODY COMPONENT

Research that explores rather precise individual determinants of physical attractiveness often considers a person's full body and, in the process, considers the face as one component of the body. Males and females asked to self-evaluate the importance of their body parts in determining their physical attractiveness place the face near the top of respective lists, as do males and females asked to evaluate other males and females in determining physical attractiveness.[93, 423] While the two research projects representing these two methodologies (self-evaluation and evaluation by others) explored somewhat different body components that reduce exact comparison of findings, both projects employed multidimensional scales to collect data and factor analysis to analyze their data.

Additional factor analysis tests to analyze components further, specific to the face, were used in the research project that employed the evaluation by others method (see Table

4-5. Determinants of Physical Attractiveness: Rankings of Relative Importance of Body Components, page 139).[93] These data warranted these additional statistical analyses because the research that focused on approximately twenty body components consistently identified face as the number one or number two component of the body for all male and female gender dyads. Before discussing Table 4-5 that deals with components and subcomponents of the body, Table 4-4 deals with components and subcomponents of the face, which this same research project also investigated.[93] Specifically, Table 4-4 (titled, Factor Analysis Results for Importance of Face Components using Others-Evaluation Data for Male and Female Gender Dyads) presents results from the factor analysis statistical tests focusing on subcomponents of the face, arranged sequentially from factor analysis factors that account for larger variance in the data followed by factors accounting for smaller variance. As well as listing the resulting factor analysis factors for face components, this table presents the respective values of the factor analysis loadings in parenthesis. Immediately preceding Table 4-4, results from these analyses specific to subcomponents of the face are summarized in narrative form in the following four bulleted paragraphs arranged according to the four gender dyads (males judging males, females judging males, males judging females, and females judging females):

- Males judging Males (face components) – Males judging males produced six factors that accounted for 77.1 percent of the total variance. Of these six factors, three included face components. Factor 1, labeled face, accounts for 49 percent of the total variance. The highest factor loadings reported were overall facial appearance (.78), smile (.69), face (.66), eyes (.63), teeth (.59), and nose (.58). Factor 5 accounted for 4.5 percent with facial complexion (.74) being the only facial component. Factor 6 accounted for 3.7 percent and included hair (.77), head shape (.53), face (.47), and hair color (.47).

- Females judging Males (face components) – Females judging male stimulus persons produced six factors that accounted for 78.1 percent of the total variance. Of these six factors, four included some components of the face. Factor 1, labeled face and features, accounts for 45.7 percent of the total variance. The relevant face components were nose (.79), lips (.78), skin texture (.77), facial complexion (.75), profile (.68), smile (.66), forehead (.59), and chin (.56). Factor 2, with 14.2 percent, included only two face components, face (.96) and overall facial appearance (.93). Factor 3, with 5.9 percent, included hair (.81), hair color (.75), and head shape (.52). Factor 4, with 4.5 percent, included only teeth (.63) as a component of the face.

- Males judging Females (face components) – The factors for the female stimulus persons were not identical but sufficiently similar for the author to call them "remarkably similar."[93] Males judging females produced six factors that accounted for 79.4 percent of the total variance. Of these six factors, two involved components of the face. Factor 2, labeled face accounted for 10.9 percent of the variance. This face factor included overall facial appearance (.82), forehead (.81), lips (.78), face (.77), facial complexion (.76), nose (.72), head shape (.71), smile (.68), chin (.67), eyes (.67), skin texture (.66), and teeth (.66). Factor 6, with only 2.5 percent, had teeth (.56) as the only loading.

- Females judging Females (face components) – The sex dyad of female judges and female stimulus persons accounted for 76.2 percent of the total variance with six factors. Of these six factors, three involved components of the face. Factor 2, with 8.5 percent, was labeled face and included teeth (.76), smile (.75), lips (.73), eyes (.63), face (.60), forehead (.56), and overall facial appearance (.50), Factor 3, with 5.8 percent, included facial complexion (.84), skin texture (.83), and face (.52). Factor 6, with 3.6 percent, consisted of nose (.66), profile (.47), and chin (.47).

Table 4-4. Factor Analysis Results for Importance of Face Components using Others-Evaluation Data for Male and Female Gender Dyads

Male Judges		Female Judges	
Judged Males	Judged Females	Judged Males	Judged Females
Factor 1 (49.0% total variance)	Factor 2 (10.9% total variance)	Factor 1 (45.7% total variance)	Factor 2 (8.5% total variance)
Overall Facial Appearance (.78)	Overall Facial Appearance (.82)	Nose (.79)	Teeth (.76)
Smile (.69)	Forehead (.81)	Lips (.78)	Smile (.75)
Face (.66)	Lips (.78)	Skin Texture (.77)	Lips (.73)
Eyes (.63)	Face (.77)	Facial Com-plexion (.75)	Eyes (.63)
Teeth (.59)	Facial Com-plexion (.76)	Profile (.68)	Face (.60)
Nose (.58)	Nose (.72)	Smile (.66)	Forehead (.56)
Factor 5 (4.5% total variance)	Head Shape (.71)	Forehead (.59)	Overall Facial Appearance (.50)
Facial Complexion (.74)	Smile (.68)	Chin (.56)	Factor 3 (5.8% total variance)
Factor 6 (3.7% total variance)	Chin (.67)	Factor 2 (14.2% total variance)	Facial Complexion (.84)
Hair (.77)	Eyes (.67)	Face (.96)	Skin Texture (.83)
Head Shape (.53)	Skin Texture (.66)	Overall Facial Appearance (.93)	Face (.52)

Male Judges		Female Judges	
Judged Males	Judged Females	Judged Males	Judged Females
Face (.47)	Teeth (.66)	*Factor 3 (5.9% total variance)*	*Factor 6 (3.6% total variance)*
Hair Color (.47)	*Factor 6 (2.5% total variance)*	Hair (.81)	Nose (.66)
	Teeth (.56)	Hair Color (.75)	Profile (.47)
		Head Shape (.52)	Chin (.47)
		Factor 4 (4.5% total variance)	
		Teeth (.63)	

HIERARCHY OF IMPORTANCE

Collective research efforts about the body's role in determining physical attractiveness are analogous to collective research about the face's role. Researchers and other scholars have made substantial efforts to identify the hidden hierarchy of importance for components and subcomponents for both the body and face that serve as determinants of physical attractiveness. One distinction, however, is that much more research investigates the face and physical attractiveness phenomenon than the body and physical attractiveness phenomenon. The proportional importance of these two variables to determine physical attractiveness justifies this difference in amounts of corresponding research.

Enthusiasts for knowledge about the hierarchical importance for body parts must be realistic. The task is extremely difficult, far beyond what initially might seem plausible. Data from the *Female Body Survey of Great Britain 2005* revealed that "women in Scotland are particularly unhappy with their legs (85 percent, UK average 78 percent), followed by their feet, hands, face, and hair. Only 2 percent [of respondents] felt happy about their body."[479] Furthermore, "the survey revealed that the parts of the body that caused the most unhappiness included the hips, thighs, stomach, and breasts." However, this research project did not attempt to identify a hierarchy of importance for the different body components, which is not the same as noting more simply the differences in the percents of respondents who expressed unhappiness with different body components.

Once scientific research would accurately identify a rank order of body components (e.g., height, weight, legs, arms, hands, fingers, head, shoulders, buttocks, neck, posture, skin, face, and so forth), then the relative importance of dimensions and sub-dimensions of each component would need identification. Some dimensions for some body components might be possible to identify in a meaningfully manner because they are more tangible and measurable than others (e.g., fat/heavy, average, skinny/thin for weight, and short and tall for height). Other dimensions pose greater difficulty, such as proportion of legs and arms versus body; length of fingers; texture and tone of skin; size and shape of head, shoulders, buttocks, and so forth. Adding to this complexity, each body component and each component's dimensions function independently and interdependently. For additional discussion of complexities concerning a hierarchy of importance for body parts, refer back to the entire chapter 3 concerning measurements and determinants of physical attractiveness and refer forward to chapter 4 concerning face values. Within chapter 3, refer especially to Figure 3-1. Determinants of Physical Attractiveness, Characteristics (page 102), Table 3-2. Determinants of Physical Attractiveness, Representative Sampling Overview of a Person in Total (page 104), and Table 3-3. Determinants of Physical Attractiveness, Representative Sampling Overview of Body Components of a Person (page 105).

Attempting to identify a rank order of body components or determinants specific to a person's physical attractiveness carries all the overarching perils discussed in the next chapter with regard to the hierarchical importance for components specific to face. Those perils include the discussion in that chapter section pertaining to the 2005 survey of more than 1,700 individuals concerning relative importance of noticing women's eyes versus women's breasts when first meeting.[731] People seeking a hierarchy of importance for body components need to remain cognizant about the Gestalt nature of physical attractiveness, the fact that many determinants and dynamics identify a person's physical attractiveness, and the strong tendency for people to give only socially acceptable answers when asked about physical attractiveness.

Within the above precautionary sentiments in mind, it is reasonable to summarize that data collection with methodologies employing self-evaluations and evaluations by others produce comparable findings at a level of fundamentals. While different body components vary in their importance for determining physical attractiveness, there is not yet agreement for the actual hierarchy or precise ranking of importance of specific body components. It is pertinent to note here that the quantity of self-evaluation research is much greater than the quantity of evaluations by others to assess importance of body components as determinants for overall physical attractiveness.[64, 399, 400, 421, 597] However, this methodology carries limitations due to the high inter-correlation values between components and their dimensions that make it difficult to separate the importance of each.

Among research projects that focus on body components with findings pertinent to identifying a hierarchy of importance, one project used a methodology that permits direct comparison of data based on evaluations by others and data based on self-evaluations.[93] As shown in Table 4-5, when identifying factors important to judging physical attractiveness, rather than who or what is physically attractive, other evaluation ratings and self-evaluation ratings were consistent in this study, particularly for factors at the top of the hierarchy. Regardless whether data were collected through evaluation by others or by self-evaluation, and regardless of gender dyad (males judging males, males judging females, females judging males, and females judging females), face and weight emerged at the top of the hierarchy with nearly always first or second place rankings. Beyond this first tier of face and weight for the hierarchy of importance, no pattern emerged between these data collected by self-evaluations and evaluations by others.

Table 4-5. Determinants of Physical Attractiveness: Rankings of Relative Importance of Body Components

Self-evaluation Method		Rank	Others Evaluation Method			
			Male Judges		Female Judges	
Males	Females		Judged Males	Judged Females	Judged Males	Judged Females
Face	Weight	#1	Face	Weight	Face	Weight
Legs	Face	#2	Weight	Face	Weight	Face
Weight	Height	#3	Legs	Height	Hair	Complexion
Torso	Legs	#4	Shoulders Arms	Hands	Body Profile	Legs Height
Voice Hair	Extremities	#5	Complexion Hands	Figure	Shoulders Arms	Hands
Height	(none)	#6	Hair Head	Teeth	Height Voice	Face Profile

SUMMARY

Physical attractiveness is at the center of physical attractiveness phenomenon. A primary question that follows, then, is what determines physical attractiveness? Determinants of physical attractiveness include all the components and dimensions of a person in total, and the body certainly holds a primary role second only to face. The body in its entirety contributes as a determinant of a person's physical attractiveness. This constitutes the body as a whole, also known as a Gestalt, along with its many components or subcomponents. Consistent with the configuration of physical attractiveness determinants, determinants specific to the body are many and complicated, shifting and unequal in importance, physical and non-physical, interdependent or compensatory and non-compensatory, enduring and transient, and influencers are dynamic and many. All the time, while each component and dimension, physical and non-physical, contributes to and subtracts from a person's physical attractiveness, physical attractiveness is ultimately a Gestalt whereby the whole is greater than the sum of the parts.

Chapter 5

Face Values

Whatever sense of inner worth I developed was eroded by the knowledge that I could only compensate for, but never overcome, the obstacle of my face.(pp. 205-206)

It was true I hated it [my face] and saw it as the cause of my isolation, but I interpreted it as some kind of lesson... [asking myself] what was there to learn from a face as ugly as mine? I undertook to see my face as an opportunity to find something that had not yet been revealed. Perhaps my face was a gift to be used toward understanding and enlightenment. This was all noble enough, but by equating my face with ugliness, in believing that without it I would never experience the deep, bottomless grief I called ugliness, I separated myself even further from other people, who I thought never experienced grief of this depth.(p. 180)

Lucy Grealy, 31, from her *Autobiography of a Face*.[257]

INTRODUCTION

A person's face is omnipotent in physical attractiveness phenomenon. "The face plays a crucial role in animal and human social cognition and behavior," begins a report by researchers at the Human Cognitive Neuroscience Unit of Northumbria University in United Kingdom, the Ludwig-Boltzman-Institute for Urban Ethology in Austria, and the Department of Psychology at University of Central Lancashire in United Kingdom.[492] It certainly is all-important in determining a person's physical attractiveness, both in the perception of an individual himself/herself and in his or her perception by others. As illustrated well in the excerpted testimony opening this chapter, people not only attempt cosmetic ploys on components of the face to distract observers from one or more components that may be lower than others in physical attractiveness, but also attempt ploys of the total person, using the body to distract observers from a less physically attractive face. All the while, as illustrated in the remarks quoted above, the level of physical attractiveness of a person's face not only overpowers the body's level of physical attractiveness but also exerts determining power for self-worth.

A person's face contributes values to physical attractiveness phenomenon that are without equal. Physical attractiveness is the impetus, the engine, and the heart of physical attractiveness phenomenon. A person's body and body components make major contributions to a person's physical attractiveness, but the engine, the heart of physical attractiveness, is the person's face along with its many components and dimensions. Accordingly, the face, rightfully so, is the most frequently used visual component or stimulus in research about physical attractiveness. It is surely the determinant of physical attractiveness used most frequently by people in all cultures to judge a person's physical attractiveness, and is, thus, likely the paramount dimension of a person that drives the informational cue aspect of physical attractiveness phenomenon. The face indicates and represents the level of physical attractiveness, and ultimately *is* the physical attractiveness of a person, moderated from time to time by a person's body when exceptionally contrasting. Accordingly, with rare exceptions, the face has been the primary and, more often than not, the only determinant of physical attractiveness or lack thereof in research into physical attractiveness phenomenon.

As well as the determinant of physical attractiveness used most frequently in all cultures to judge a person's physical attractiveness, judgment of what are and are not faces of higher and lower physical attractiveness is amazingly the same in all cultures. Maybe most illustrative, "Show an insular European two African faces, and the one the European picks as more attractive is also the one an African person would pick, and vice versa."[221] Except in the case of cross-race recognition deficit, whereby individuals have difficulty recognizing individual members of a race different from their own, the face is the most enduring and informative feature about physical attractiveness.[406] "The face is a focus of much attention when it comes to physical attractiveness, because this body part/person part represents the person's identity and is most exposed to public view. Thus, whether a person is in general considered beautiful or not depends much on facial beauty."[166] Accordingly, consumers spend billions of dollars annually in the United States and other countries to enhance the face through actions ranging from applications of cosmetics to removal of hair to reconstructive surgeries to, increasingly popular, pharmaceutical drug injections to eliminate face wrinkles and creases. Outcomes from these efforts and expenditures cannot obliterate the face, but only alter it. Even the aging process does not transform the face beyond recognition.

While the face receives abundant attention in research and everyday living, surprising varieties of writings discuss the face as a physically limiting-enabling condition. Abraham Lincoln, for example, once stated in a speech that based on the appearance (i.e., physical attractiveness) of his face, no one ever expected him to be president.[604] Mr. Lincoln lived from 1809-1865 and died by assassination while serving as president of the United States. He was clearly cognizant of physical attractiveness phenomenon albeit not then known by that label. He also proclaimed, "The Lord prefers common-looking people. That is why he makes so many of them."[453] Mr. Lincoln's statements about his face and physical attractiveness as an informational cue, in his case as a limiting rather than enabling informational cue, strikingly reflect the power of physical attractiveness phenomenon even then and in that setting, yet still for a person of such strong historical significance. It is in such sundry musings about physical attractiveness of one's face that the assumptions of observers can be determined to provide substantial and wide-ranging in everyday applications.

HISTORY

Use of the face as an indicator of non-facial or non-surface qualities began long ago, continues today, and will sustain its prominence far into the future. Unlike most other body parts, all people show their faces and all people expect to see a person's face, with rare exception. All religions seem to have or have had some special consideration about the face, particularly the faces of women. Portions of people who practice the Muslin religion require the faces of women to be unseen in public. This concealment ranges from requiring women to cover surrounding areas of their faces with a scarf to near complete or even complete coverage with an Islamic veil or chador from head to foot. A traditional Afghan version of this face cover is the cloth veil, or burqa, with a mesh that also covers the women's eyes. Less concealing and more common is the hijab, which is a traditional Muslim veil worn by conservative Islamic women to cover their hair.

Unlike other body parts, both static and dynamic components compose every person's face. Long-standing interest in dynamic components of the face is well documented and well presented in a 1973 book, *Darwin and Facial Expression*,[198] which draws upon dynamic face components put forth in the 1872 book by Charles Darwin, *The Expression of the Emotions in Man and Animals*.[163] These books are interesting treatises about facial expressions across species, as well as across people, with categories identified for facial expressions in nonhuman primates, infants and children, and dissimilar human populations. Another treatise dedicated to the face is an equally interesting look into its interpersonal, sociological dimensions in a book published in 1988 titled *The Social Psychology of Facial Appearance*.[95] Attempts at humor directed at the face pose another sociological artifact. These range from commonly voiced clichés such as "a person with a face that only a mother could love" to repugnant jokes such as a men willing to have relations with a woman whose face is low in physical attractiveness if she has a body of high physical attractiveness as long as her face is covered with a paper bag.

People throughout history have attributed personal traits based on physical attractiveness by way of face components and physical head components adjacent to the face, often to extreme extents. Beliefs as late as 1870 advocated evaluation of components of a person's face to identify criminal nature. As advanced by Italian physician Cesare Lombroso, head components could differentiate even the type of crimes a person would commit or had committed.[413] The overconfident "science" of phrenology that developed under the assumption that skull or head components coincide with personal traits[409] lost credibility quickly as an infallible straightforward instrument to identify criminals based on static (i.e., inherited) head or face components. However, fifty years later, German psychiatrist Ernst Kretschmer's belief that the face represents the entire person supported Lombroso with statements that "the face is a visiting card of the individual's general constitution,"[368] which is consistent with a statement attributed to Aristotle that "personal beauty is a greater recommendation than any letter of reference."

Moving to the face from the head, physiognomy developed. Now discredited as a pseudoscience, physiognomy put forth that a person's appearance, primarily the face, tells the personality and character of a person. According to the online *Wikipedia Encyclopedia*:

> Notions of the relationship between an individual's outward appearance and inner character are as old as time, and are occasionally reflected in early Greek poetry. The first indications of a developed theory appear in fifth century Athens. By the fourth century, the philosopher Aristotle makes frequent reference to theories of the sort, and also to some sort of literature.[741]

Wikipedia Encyclopedia goes on to state:

> Up until the time of English King Henry VIII, [physiognomy's] validity was so widely assumed that it was taught in universities and was an everyday concept that had developed. The principal promoter of physiognomy in modern times was the Swiss pastor Johann Kaspar Lavater (1741–1801)... Lavater's essays upon physiognomy were first published in German in 1772 and gained great popularity. His essays upon physiognomy were translated into French, and English, and were highly influential.[741]

Although certainly not government sanctioned or scientifically hypothesized as a predictor or telltale sign of criminal actions, static face components continue today to serve as a broadly used gauge for comprehensive knowledge assumed about a person. While not openly confessed, people the world over presume the face as a determinant of physical attractiveness to be an accurate indicator of specific personal attributes. Indubitably, dynamic features of a person's face, commonly referred to as facial expressions, do very often accurately communicate the full range of underlying emotions. Despite the ability of some to display a so-called poker face that eliminates telltale communications, personal bodyguards, general law enforcement personnel, military officers in war zones, and security workers assigned to airports undergo explicit training to scrutinize faces in the crowd. This training emerges from proven evidence that, for many, the face is a valid window through which to observe impending danger. Pertinent as determinants of physical attractiveness, early research investigated components of the face such as eyebrows,[342] facial expression,[163, 216, 484] eye contact,[206] pupil size,[292] body language,[210] and even personal space.[651] Researchers have more recently evaluated cognitive values to substantiate judgments about facial expression.[205] A need expected to expand into the future is to examine interactions within more holistic contexts.

FUTURE

These research findings have become largely proverbial "common knowledge," with the effect that researchers employ the knowledge as a resource in their scientific hypotheses. This speaks very strongly to reliability of the research, some of which is necessary to reassert in this book because it epitomizes current research, is integral to physical attractiveness phenomenon, and will provide the springboard for research in the future. Without repeated attention to knowledge about physical attractiveness phenomenon, many boundaries advanced through accomplished research might slip back into former positions in which physical attractiveness was a completely unexamined substratum in society. If the earlier research fades from consciousness, the reasons for the hypotheses that drive other research will become more difficult to understand. One hope is that this repeating will add fuel to scholarly attention for physical attractiveness as a broad human phenomenon.

The face will not diminish in importance anytime in the future with respect to physical attractiveness phenomenon nor in any other of its current respects. Information provided by the face, real or assumed, combined with physical attractiveness phenomenon is simply, overwhelmingly too strong. The face and its components have already grown into new areas of value in the past few years. They now occupy new, prominent roles in attempts to counter terrorists' attacks and to identify criminals of all sorts. Increased emphasis is certain for the application of eye measures in the form of iris readings to establish identification needed for security, such as ATM banking transactions and entry into security-sensitive locations. These locations include airports, airlines, likely other forms of transportation in the future, and a long list of buildings, as well as countries concerned about entry controls for international travelers.

Advancing technology and increasing threats to security combine to amplify the value and attention paid to a person's face. An article published in 2004 in an international newspaper[285] reported "the years since September 11, 2001 have seen a steady convergence in one area of endeavour: biometrics"—the ability to measure, store, and use information about a person's unique physical characteristics to identify individuals. While fingerprints, voice patterns, palm prints, ear shapes, and even body odor are parts of biometrics, the greatest interest now is for face recognition camera technology and even iris scanning technology. Current state-of-the-art technology places iris recognition at accuracy rates "just tenths of one percent short of perfection." [285] Lower accuracy for fingerprint systems is "occurring in a few percent of the cases," and "rates for facial recognition systems show up markedly lower, failing in more than 10 percent of cases." Despite accuracy differences with today's technologies, face recognition is preferred over fingerprint scans and iris scans for future uses. Among the strengths and weaknesses, face recognition technologies offer less intrusiveness and more expediency, and procedures for processing authenticated photographs are currently commonly accepted practices.

More germane to physical attractiveness phenomenon, "face time" is the most valuable opportunity for ambitious people. Personal dating advertisements with photographs of the face are eight times more likely to receive responses on the electronic dating and matching services that the same advertisements with no face photograph, according to that industry's spokespersons. Futuristic literature once predicted that facial expression will be so important and correspondingly accurate that the wrong appearance (i.e., "facecrime") would result in punishment,[510] and, indeed, looks can be limiting. Documentation in other popular media supports observations that increasingly "it's who you look like, not who you are."

Face physical attractiveness, mass media, and technology form a remarkable threesome. Critics of mass media frequently propose it to be responsible for significant portions of physical attractiveness phenomenon. Television technology has certainly advanced standards and thus popularity of television programs. With huge consequences at stake, television technology has facilitated rising standards for physical attractiveness to largely unattainable, idealized levels seemingly possessed by admired on-screen models. Accordingly, critics often accuse mass media for anxiety and excessive pursuits to increase one's physical attractiveness, placing special emphasis on television as a driving cause. At the same time, the television technology that conveys idealized appearance is making others anxious that it will soon make those unrealistic ideals more realistic. Men and women admired for their higher physical attractiveness on television, and those people who surround them, fear that spreading popularity of HDTV (high definition television) will increasingly reveal that a person on the television screen with previously unattainable beauty actually possesses less beauty than historically has met the viewers' eyes through less sharp television technology.[133]

UNIQUENESS

The face is unique. It possesses unique importance in ours lives due in part to its exceptional and largely unrecognized intricacy and complexity. One stream of research complementary to physical attractiveness phenomenon is neuroscience research targeted toward the role of face perceptions in human cognitive processing. Findings from those endeavors offer collaboration, justification, and, ultimately, validation for the face in judgments about physical attractiveness and the prominence of a person's face in investigating physical attractiveness phenomenon. The root of this sort of validation is the demonstrated broad range of cognitive processing levels that accompany judgments of appearance based on the face.

Exceedingly intricate research to investigate cognitive processing of the human mind has used the face, specifically a continuum of morphed faces, as a stimulus variable.[51] These research results find that faces produce higher levels of cognitive processing. With the continuum of faces employed in such research projects, categorical perception occurs wherein the human mind differentiates most accurately between faces of different categories versus faces within a similar category. Other equally intricate neuroscience research investigating cognitive processing of the human mind has used the face as a stimulus variable because of its unique complexity that forces the human mind to cognitively process coarse and fine scales of information in order to perceive a face.[244]

Neuroscience research and cognitive neuroscience research pertinent to physical attractiveness phenomenon offer clear confirmation that the face is unlike any other appearance feature or even any other visual stimulus. The research noted above is largely outside the scope of physical attractiveness phenomenon as discussed in this book. However, it is worthwhile to observe that a portion of research conducted in the neurosciences pertains directly to the face, as expressed in the sample of titles of research articles published in respective journals identified in Table 5-1.

Table 5-1. Neuroscience and Cognitive Neuroscience Research Pertinent to the Face, Titles of Illustrative Articles and Journals

Title of Published Article	Journal	Year
How Does the Brain Process Upright and Inverted Faces?	*Behavioral and Cognitive Neuroscience Reviews*[766]	2002
Is Sex Categorization from Faces Really Parallel to Face Recognition?	*Visual Cognition*[764]	2002
How Does the Brain Discriminate Familiar and Unfamiliar Faces?	*Journal of Cognitive Neuroscience*[768]	2001
The Distributed Human Neural System for Face Perception	*Trends in Cognitive Science*[288]	2000

Title of Published Article	Journal	Year
Right N170 Modulation in a Face Discrimination Task	*Psychophysiology*[107]	2000
Hemispheric Asymmetries for Whole-Based and Part-Based Face Processing in the Fusiform Gyrus	*Journal of Cognitive Neuroscience*[765]	2000
The N170 Occipito-Temporal Component Is Delayed and Enhanced to Inverted Faces But Not to Inverted Objects: An Electrophysiological Account of Face-Specific Processes in the Human Brain	*Neuroreport*[767]	2000
Neurophysiological Correlates of Face Sex Processing in Humans	*European Journal of Neuroscience*[481]	2000
Recognition and Sex Categorisation of Adults' and Children's Faces	*Journal of Experimental Child Psychology*[742]	2000
Asymmetric Dependencies in Perceiving Identity and Emotion: Experiments with Morphed Faces	*Perception and Psychophysics*[624]	1999
Effect of Familiarity on the Processing of Human Faces	*Neuroimage*[189]	1999
A Neuromodulatory Role for the Human Amygdale in Processing Emotional Facial Expressions	*Brain*[763]	1998
The Fusiform Face Area: A Module in Human Extrastriate Cortex Specialized for Face Perception	*Journal of Neuroscience*[340]	1997
Encoding Activity and Face Recognition	*Memory*[140]	1997
Understanding Face Recognition	*British Journal of Psychology*[88]	1986
A Case of Prosopagnosia with some Preserved Covert Remembrance of Familiar Faces	*Brain and Cognition*[91]	1983

FACE-SPECIFIC RESEARCH

Research into physical attractiveness phenomenon might take new directions in the future, albeit unlikely, but research performed up to now and into the foreseeable future focuses greatly on the face. While physical attractiveness research involves many variables (e.g., body types, perceptual distortions, and associations), visual presentation of the face is overwhelmingly the most frequently manipulated stimulus to investigate physical attractiveness phenomenon. Furthermore, consistent with overall physical attractiveness, scientific research about the face centers not so much on separate components and detailed dimensions of various components, but on the face in its entirety, which is consistent with how people generally think about physical attractiveness and the face. When exceptions to this Gestalt approach occur, they are more so for physical attractiveness of women than for men.

Research specific to the face involves many variables (e.g., nose, eyes, complexion, eyeglasses, face and head hair, and even head shape), but the overall face is practically always the manipulated stimulus in research; as well as it is in reality of everyday living. The overall face is most informing about physical attractiveness, but the overall face is the composite of a large number of components. Accompanying these components are many subcomponents and dimensions of each component, with each contributing in some manner as a determinant of physical attractiveness of the overall face. Furthermore, variable circumstances affect observing a person's face, ranging from illumination conditions, to angle of viewing, to facial expression.[478]

Facial expression is certainly an important topic for face physical attractiveness and physical attractiveness phenomenon. While facial expressions extend far beyond physical attractiveness (and beyond the scope of this book on physical attractiveness phenomenon) into communication realms of joy, pain, sorrow, and so forth, such peripheral information provides valuable supplemental understanding of physical attractiveness phenomenon. An example is a research project that investigated the relationship between face physical attractiveness and the ability to send nonverbal signs of emotion.[384] To limit factors extraneous to the research focus, judges evaluated videotapes of sixty stimulus persons expressing emotions via facial expression. Results revealed that people on the receiving end of facial expressions evaluated them more accurately when transmitted by people with faces of higher physical attractiveness compared to counterparts of lower physical attractiveness.

The many components, dimensions, complexities, and intricacies of the face make it unfathomable to give meaningful research attention to each. While there are certainly compensatory and non-compensatory dynamics, the Gestalt of the face, akin to the Gestalt of body and person, is most meaningful for physical attractiveness phenomenon. Within that context, attempts to identify the differential values of face components that determine physical attractiveness are not new. When investigating the value and order of independent components that determine physical attractiveness of a face, research has ranged from philosophical, literary, and artistic views to scientifically conducted surveys, observations, and experiments.

Beyond Adults

Hidden values of the face and its physical attractiveness are not necessarily consequences of socialized cognitions or learned responses. The face as a powerful stimulus extends beyond adults to children and infants. Implications include potential predispositions for child abuse scenarios as well as different behaviors toward children during their early formative years based on faces that represent different levels of physical attractiveness. Ultimately, these data may hold implications for eliciting and inhibiting aggression related to abused children.

Infants Reacting to Adults

A review of relevant research literature discloses that the unique impact of the face exists already in early infancy.[301] Infants three and four months old give greater attention and fixate longer on faces than other similar non-face stimuli,[362] and this pattern is shown with infants as young as four days.[209] Moreover, even younger, a developmental psychologist at Exeter University reported in 2004 at the British Association Festival of Science, research findings that "babies as young as 5 hours old know a pretty face when they see one."[221] That research, conducted over a four-year period, showed photos of adults of varying levels of physical attractiveness to more than 100 newborns. "Invariably, the infants spent more time looking at the [physically] attractive face."

Research such as the above shows that cultural socialization does not explain why infants prefer adults of higher physical attractiveness. Compatible with the above findings, research conducted by psychologists at the University of Texas in Austin found infants prefer faces of higher physical attractiveness for both male and female stimulus persons, regardless of the stimulus groups' age and race categories.[304] When presented the stimulus materials, infant subjects reacted with favor to faces of higher physical attractiveness and with disfavor to faces of lower physical attractiveness. These researchers conclude that while infants and children responses are consistent with physical attractiveness phenomenon in favor of higher physical attractiveness, it is not until about three years of age that children "express the full-blown version of the stereotype that beauty is good."

Eyes exert a particularly profound role in the early impact. During the first two months, infants do not smile in response to a real face that has the eyes hidden, but they do smile in response to a face mask with eyes only represented by dots.[17, 653] By the age of four weeks, infants begin to establish actual eye contact. Scrutiny of infants indicated that they scan a face until they locate the eyes, at which time the infant exhibits a substantial change in focus.[746] As infants grow older, the face components necessary to hold their interest require more than just the eyes. During maturation, the attention capability of infants increases and, correspondingly, more parts of the face are needed and cognitively processed before responses are elicited from the infant.[78]

Adults Reacting to Infants

While the face is instrumental in eliciting responses from infants, the face of infants and children is instrumental in eliciting responses from adults. Such responses from adults to faces of infants and children supports a hypothesis put forth in 1943[415] about specific characteristics of infants eliciting specific caretaking behaviors in adults. The question about what determines or defines physical attractiveness of infants is thus central to this dimension of physical attractiveness phenomenon. Accordingly, research has found adults respond more favorably to head shapes that are more infantile than adult in terms of forehead height and forehead curvature.[308]

Work to identify face components of infants defined as higher or lower in physical attractiveness focuses on definitions of more or less cute at such early ages of their lives. One research project investigated 14 different face components for infants at ages of 3 months, 5 months, 7 months, 11 months, and 13 months.[297] It concluded that large forehead, large eyes, large pupils, and short and narrow features determined physical attractiveness, in other words cuteness, at this age for infants. One study focusing on pupil size of the eyes of infants asked supermarket shoppers to indicate the most physically attractive/most cute infants based on photographs.[352] These research participants did not know the photographs pictured the same infant but with different pupil sizes. Results showed that people selected infants with more prominent pupils as the infants most cute.

Other research has explored the eyes of infants in greater detail with variations in eye height, eye width, eye height and width, iris size, and vertical variations in the eye position.[662] While experimental confounding can occur due to other face components such as chin, nose, and forehead size, adults did assign different levels of physical attractiveness/cuteness with differences in the eye variations. Adults gave higher physical attractiveness ratings to those infants with most "babyish" characteristics, regardless of judges' sex. Specifically, infants assigned higher ratings of physical attractiveness possessed:

- large eyes as opposed to small,
- less eye width as opposed to greater eye width,
- higher eye height as opposed to lower eye height, and
- moderate to large iris size as opposed to smaller iris size.

Face components of infants judged higher in physical attractiveness included those who possessed small chins and large foreheads as opposed to large chins and small foreheads. The data revealed no significant differences in responses to any features as a function of judges' experience with children, social class, religion, or gender.

Recognition and Memory

Research methodologies based on cognitive aspects of recognition and memory document differences concerning reliability of physical attractiveness ratings, as well as research directly investigating face memory as a function of physical attractiveness of a person's face. The explanation of such data may exist in published literature not related directly to physical attractiveness research but with cognitive processes used with different strategies for facial memory.[441, 515] Pertinent documentations and explanations reside in research literature about differences concerning eyewitnesses in criminal identifications for accuracy of memory of male and female eyewitnesses,[756] older and younger ages of eyewitnesses,[751, 753, 757] and effects of time delay on eyewitnesses between exposure and recognition attempt.[754] Research findings document further differences for effects of physical attractiveness, saliency of components or features, and liking of the stimulus person's face.[752]

Sex of Face

The reliability of physical attractiveness ratings as a measure of face recognition and memory varies by gender of the face. Physical attractiveness ratings of female faces are more consistent in test-retest situations than corresponding ratings of male faces.[348] This inconsistency over time is in contrast to high agreement of physical attractiveness ratings between male and female judges. The fact that both male and female judges look at, focus on, remember, and recognize female faces significantly more than male faces may explain this difference.[345]

Sex of Judge

Recognition and memory of faces also varies with gender of judges. Research shows that, overall, women recognize and remember faces better than do men.[755] Female faces make this difference especially pronounced. A review of research revealed results that were not unanimous but which generally found female judges to be better at facial recognition and memory than male judges.[443] This difference aligned with sex of judge appears to be a same-sex effect with the difference particularly great for female judges, as shown in a substantial review of facial memory and sex differences[442] and as later found in a research project employing five experiments.[443]

Time Span

A significant relationship exists between face physical attractiveness, memory of faces, and length of time between exposure and recognition. When researchers in one project asked subjects who did not anticipate their task, to recognize faces seen immediately before, faces of higher physical attractiveness were most memorable.[152] In a two-hour time span, the faces of lower and higher physical attractiveness were recognized and remembered better than those of moderate levels.[220] This latter study involved 24 subjects (12 males and 12 females) asked to rate physical attractiveness of 35 photographed stimulus persons. The procedure to assess subjects' recognition ability involved researchers presenting subjects with the 35 photographs rated earlier and now randomly mixed with 10 previously unseen photographs.

Another study using three time intervals found greater recognition and memory for the faces at the ends of the physical attractiveness continuum as opposed to the middle.[637] Researchers presented slides of 27 female faces to 36 subjects (18 males and 18 females) followed by recognition tests of these faces presented immediately after the presentation, six days later, and thirty-five days later. Recognition scores decreased significantly more for lapsed time intervals for faces of moderate physical attractiveness than for the faces of either high or low physical attractiveness. One study has reported different findings, with data suggesting faces higher in physical attractiveness are more difficult to remember. However, that study qualified its findings by stating "it is unclear why" these results contrasted with other research and offered explanation that "caution must be exercised in interpreting correlational data" in light of this study's lack of an experimental research methodology.[410]

Determinants

Many components with many dimensions determine physical attractiveness of a person's face. These components concerning the face share the same broad overarching characteristics of determinants cited earlier for a person's physical attractiveness (see Figure 3-1. Determinants of Physical Attractiveness, Characteristics, page 100). These characteristics are Many and Complicated, Unequal and Shifting Appeal, Physical and Non-Physical, Compensatory and Non-compensatory, Enduring and Transient, Influencers that are Dynamic and Many, and Gestalt in which the Whole Is Greater Than Sum of the Parts. Beyond the more broad characteristics of physical attractiveness of a person, face physical attractiveness has its own additional characteristics particular to the face as detailed below in Table 5-2.

Table 5-2. Determinants of Physical Attractiveness, Representative Sampling Overview of Face Components of a Person

Face Components
Macro components (proportionality, delicacy-coarseness, size, shape, etc.)
Micro components (eyes, nose, mouth, skin, complexion, lips, etc.)
Static, relatively (nose, eyes, mouth, shape, etc.)
Dynamic, slow change and rapid change
Slow change (facial hair, head hair, blemishes, age indications, etc.)
Rapid change (facial expressions, smiles and frowns, open-closed eyes, eye contact, tears, pupil size, open-closed mouth, etc.)
Routinely always visible (nose, eyes, mouth, skin, etc.)
Routinely intermittently visible (e.g., teeth, tongue, eyes, etc.)
Adjacent proximity (head, hair, ears, neck)
Adornments and procedures (routine hygiene, cosmetics, jewelry, etc.)
Symmetry and Profile
Skin Complexion (color, tone, smoothness, tightness, stiffness, tautness, etc.)
Eyes (shape, size, location, distance between each, color, lashes, brows, lids, etc.)
Routinely Intermittently Visible and Not Visible (Eyes: iris, pupil, color, symmetry; Teeth, etc.)

So-called permanent static components of the face such as lips, nose, chin, skin, and so on are not necessarily permanent or static. People as well as nature routinely alter what might initially seem to be permanent static components. These alterations are temporary through use of cosmetics, but also permanent through natural aging, accidents, illnesses, and elective cosmetic surgeries. A reasonable categorization begins with natural changes that a person does not have choice about, which may be temporary or permanent as presented in Table 5-3 titled Permanent Static Components of the Face, Natural Changes. People may influence these natural changes through more and less cautionary lifestyles but ultimately, of course, these changes come without choice and frequently align with accidents, diseases, and routine aging throughout a person's lifetime.

Table 5-3. Permanent Static Components of the Face, Natural Changes
Natural Changes Without Choice: Temporary
Illnesses, diseases, and accidents with temporary effects while healing, such as acne, pimples, herpes (mouth), weight gain and loss (face), and strokes with temporary facial muscle effects. Also, hair growth on the head, face, and upper lip.
Natural Changes Without Choice: Permanent
Aging, illnesses, diseases, and accidents with permanent effects, such as wrinkles, acne scars, car accidents, knife/cutting crimes, head hair graying and loss, and muscular dystrophies with permanent facial muscle effects.

Following the natural changes categorization, a second category is then unnatural changes that a person has choice about as Table 5-4 presents. Somewhat analogous to natural changes, unnatural changes may be temporary or permanent. Temporary changes range from direct adjustments where a person changes a specific particular feature such as through application of cosmetics and jewelry, to indirect changes by such as adjusting a hairstyle to place more or less emphasis on the shape or size of another component such as nose or chin. Face components that change unnaturally include routine changes with temporary effects achieved through customary hygiene practices, eyeglasses to aid sight, application of familiar cosmetics, and wearing of jewelry. Within the categorization of unnatural changes are non-routine changes aligned most frequently with permanent effects. These include cosmetic surgeries of all types, ranging from tattoos and permanently embedded cosmetic colors to medical surgery that changes components of the face generally considered static such as the nose, firmness of the skin, eyelids, and so on. Of course, there are components in the unnatural categorization that can be either temporary, as when people choose to have substances injected into the face to enlarge lips and remove wrinkles. These components can be relatively permanent, as when people choose to have cosmetic surgery performed for a face-lift to remove wrinkles or choose to embed tangible materials surgically into the lips to enlarge them.

Table 5-4. Permanent Static Components of the Face, Unnatural Changes

Unnatural Changes With Choice: Temporary
Cosmetics, hair cutting and shaving, jewelry, eyeglasses, hair coloring and ornaments, head and face clothing, dentistry and dental products for teeth whitening, and customary hygiene.
Unnatural Changes With Choice: Permanent
Cosmetic surgeries (eye lids, nose, lips, face skin tightness, etc.); permanently embedded cosmetics (eye shadow, lip hair coloring); esthetic dentistry such as teeth crowns, bonding, and veneers; tattoos, and body/face piercing.

Macro Face Components

The face comprises macro and micro components. Micro components are the generally tangible, or distinct, components routinely noticed about a person's face: nose, lips, complexion, eyes, and so forth. Macro components, or features, are generally less tangible and generally less distinct unless the magnitudes are unusual: proportions, coarseness and delicacy, and so forth. Integral to this dimension of the face is its age, or more accurately, its apparent age. A face, particularly a female face, that looks younger than its actual age is liked more and judged more physically attractive by males, as has been identified in at least five populations.[331] This relationship is particularly strong when the female face but not the male face possesses features more juvenile in age characteristically represented by smaller lower jaw, smaller nose, and larger lips, as evidenced when professional models are compared to females in the general population.[331] These considerations relate to "facial markers" indicative of evolutionary aspects of reproductive ability suggested by visual physical characteristics normally aligned with estrogen and testosterone levels, such as ability to produce offspring for females and ability to provide and protect for males.

Proportions

Conventional wisdom has long argued in favor of an average-looking face that is not perfectly shaped and not perfectly balanced; however, social scientists have firmly established that faces seen as most physically attractive are those with greatest symmetry.[231, 252, 425, 470, 617, 694] A notable research project conducted in Germany measured symmetry and asymmetry of faces of stimulus persons and separately asked subjects to rate physical attractiveness of each stimulus person based on the person's face.[253] The data revealed stimulus persons/faces with greater symmetry received higher ratings of physical attractiveness compared to less symmetry by male and female judges. One study that investigated perceived facial physical attractiveness, left-right symmetry, and health concluded: "In both animals and humans, the natural subtle asymmetry of the human face may be relatively unimportant for judgment of facial [physical] attractiveness."[760]

Despite earlier thoughts, symmetry of the face is more valuable than asymmetry. Attempts to identify the value of face components and dimensions leading to symmetry rather than asymmetry are not limited to social scientists. Long ago, philosophers, writers, and artists quite frequently offered definitions and descriptions about determinants of physical attractiveness of the face. Their descriptions have sometimes stood tests of time and scientific research, with significant accord between early ponderings and much later discoveries by social science researchers. Earliest recorded work sought to objectify face beauty/physical attractiveness in terms of mathematical formulas ranging from "golden proportions" put forth by ay ancient Greeks as explained by Plato, to "preoccupation with facial proportions" exhibited in analyses of drawings by Leonardo da Vinci.[409] Ancient Greeks believed the most physically attractive face depended on harmony, symmetry, and balance, with length composed of equal thirds. Later, during medieval times, people thought the most physically attractive face was composed of sevenths. Table 5-5 presents examples of such proportional formulae.

Table 5-5. Face Physical Attractiveness as a Function of Early Mathematical Proportions

Three Equal Distances (ancient Greece)	Seven Equal Distances (Middle Ages)
Hairline down to eye brow: 1/3 of face	Forehead: 2/7's of face
Eye brow down to mouth: 1/3 of face	Nose: 2/7's of face
Mouth down to tip of chin: 1/3 of face	Nose to bottom of mouth: 1/7 of face
Face width: 2/3's of face height	Mouth to start of chin: 1/7 of face
	Eyes (each eye): 1/5 of face width
	Eyes separation — 1/5 of face with space between eyes width of each eye
	Face width: twice the nose length

Delicate and Coarse Structure

The English language lacks robust words to describe the structure of face components, but the adjectives of delicate and coarse serve to communicate this topic reasonably well. Data from formal scientific research and from regimented anecdotal observation indicate components of the face with delicate structure to be associated with higher physical attractiveness more so than components with coarser structure. Delicate components tend to be thinner, lighter, or less strong in structure compared to coarse components that are thicker, heavier, or stronger in structure. Like much of physical attractiveness phenomenon, ratings favoring certain structure types of face components operate within quite narrow ranges of space along a continuum, in this case along a delicate-coarse continuum. While preference clearly favors the structure of face components to be more delicate rather than coarser, exceeding thresholds judged either delicate or not adequately coarse then breaks this pattern of preference for physical attractiveness.

To explore this aspect of physical attractiveness phenomenon, research to understand face components in terms of determining high and low physical attractiveness includes unstructured and structured methodologies akin to formal projective techniques practiced in psychoanalytic therapies. One unstructured technique required subjects to create face components without aid of tangible stimuli, instructing them to draw a person of high or low physical attractiveness.[438, 663] Alternatively, a structured technique asked research subjects to comment on levels of physical attractiveness with aid of tangible face components as stimuli.[721] Both these unstructured and structured methodologies found that people judge more delicate faces and face components as more physically attractive than faces and face components with more coarse structure.

The above rating patterns in preference for delicacy of face components were consistent regardless of the subject's race. Conclusions based on findings such as from the above research projects are relevant to the somewhat common, sometimes controversial, perspective that people perceive African Americans that possess more "white physical features" to be higher in physical attractiveness. Even though vast changes have occurred in race relations, racial identities, and racial pride, these specific facial preferences concerning delicateness of components identified in research conducted in substantially earlier times in the United States continue to be pertinent today regarding physical attractiveness phenomenon. Despite resistance to acknowledge these dynamics, popular culture or general mass media can be found to parallel the above scholarly research findings. A 1988 movie written and directed by Spike Lee, titled *School Daze*, is particularly pertinent to this discussion.[392] Characters in that movie vividly portray differential favor given by African Americans toward other African Americans based on lightness and darkness of skin color. Research, statements, and material of this sort can create discomfort and even rancor about assertions of racism.

More recently, analogous deliberations have arisen concurrent with the growing popularity for particular types of cosmetic surgeries elected by people of Asian heritage and African American heritage. In pursuit of increased physical attractiveness, these surgeries alter inherited face components toward the direction or dimensions of face components more typically inherited by people of Caucasian heritage. A front-page article, about high demand for cosmetic surgery by Asians in and around South Korea, in a 2005 issue of *The Wall Street Journal* describes one 25-year old woman, "who flew more than 1,000 miles to a clinic [in Korea] for operations to raise the bridge of her nose, make her eyes appear larger and sharpen her chin."[208] That article goes on to report:

> …women from around the region—and some men, too—are flocking to Seoul to have their faces remolded. …what appeals to many about Korean looks are exactly those features that make them look more Western. In

physical terms, the Korean ideal is a relatively small, oval face with a high-bridged nose and large eyes with Western-style eyelids.[208]

Whatever the arguments and perspectives, the pattern of more favorable preferences and behaviors toward people with more delicate structure of components of the face occurs regardless of race, culture, and geographical location. It is similar regardless whether the judgments of physical attractiveness represent individuals between races or within races, non-white and white. While the extent of preferred delicateness and coarseness for face structure is relative somewhat between and within groups of people defined by numerous demographic variables, the pattern is surprisingly robust with consistency for people within and across cultures and subcultures. An explanation for this consistency around the world regards the global community that exists for physical attractiveness and physical attractiveness phenomenon, facilitated immensely by influential, readily available, mass media and other communication technologies.

Tangential Face Components

Some components of a person embraced by physical attractiveness phenomenon are nearly as visible as the face and influence perception of it but are located only in close proximity or tangential to the face. These components are between the categorizations of macro and micro face components, aligning more closely to the latter (micro) than the former (macro). Head shape, head hair, hair ornaments and procedures, and jewelry and procedures to augment appearance of ears and necks are all influential tangible determinants of physical attractiveness located tangentially to the face. Other components located in closer proximity to the face but still tangential in location are visible as part of the face at intermittent times. Products and surgeries target features beneath the surface to enhance the component itself. These procedures include dental work and surgery to correct a gummy smile or to enhance the face by altering underlying shapes as when a patient opts to have a recessed jaw extended or an overextended jaw/chin moved back with surgery. Considerations tangential to the face that influence physical attractiveness include actions and products foreign or unnatural to the face. These are frequently impermanent ornamentations with both fully cosmetic and partially functional aspects: earrings, eyeglasses, eye shadow, contact lenses, and so on. Age and complexion are still other considerations tangential to the face.

Head Shape

The chapter on primitive facial elaborations in the aforementioned book titled *The Human Face*[409] documents early practices to artificially shape (in effect to deform) the skull to increase physical attractiveness. At least partially pertinent to this early practice is a contemporary research project that investigated the relationship between head shape and perceptions of physical attractiveness.[22] A series of three experiments employed morphological changes of head shape characteristic of stages in a child's development. Researchers used drawings of infants' heads as stimulus materials to manipulate the physical attractiveness aspect of appearance, defined as cuteness at the age of infants. Research subjects judged physical attractiveness (i.e., defined as cuteness at the infant stage) to decrease as the head shape changed through its normal early developmental periods.

Age

Age is not strictly a face characteristic, but appearance of face, as well as appearance of body, is typically an important determinant of physical attractiveness. Even though it is a rather tangible, intangible feature of a person, age as a determinant of physical attractiveness works its influence through the face and body. People certainly judge physical attractiveness of others differently when the face or body presents older or younger ages. Appearances with older faces and older bodies equate with lower physical attractiveness. Researchers manipulated photographs of males and females, in age categories of either 31- to 38-years-old or 14- to 16-years-old, to investigate face age as a determinant of physical attractiveness.[364] Sixty subjects first sorted these stimulus persons according to physical attractiveness, and second, according to age. As perceived age increased, perceived physical attractiveness decreased. More recently, a study conducted in 2002 verified that perceived physical attractiveness holds a prominent role in many stereotypes and certainly within age-related stereotypes.[254] Accordingly, this study, using stimulus materials composed of digitized images, found significant correlation between physical attractiveness and age, with younger ages judged higher in physical attractiveness and older ages judged lower in physical attractiveness.

Complexion

Skin complexion involves the appearance of a person's entire body, but the face conveys this component most prominently. Accordingly, research indicates that face complexion is an ingredient of physical attractiveness, although there are differences between males and females. Darker complexions align more often with higher physical attractiveness for males, while the inverse is true for females, regardless of race or ethnicity. One scientific investigation used more than 1,000 Caucasians (approximately 500 males and 500 females) to study complexion preference in general and between sexes.[215] Females expressed significantly greater preference for men with dark eyes, dark hair, and dark complexion, whereas the males expressed significantly greater preference for females with light eyes, light hair, and light complexion. These early researchers also stated that both white and black people hold these complexion preferences. As noted above, despite changes in societal attitudes over the years about racial differences and identities, and despite sometimes rather adamant denials, the patterns of preference for lighter and darker complexions continue today. Likewise, investigations conducted in the early stages of research specific to physical attractiveness phenomenon found that variations in preferred complexion color might occur across cultures and countries with preference generally toward whiter or lighter color and tones. In Japan, light skin color is preferred for both sexes, and Japanese females especially prefer males with light-colored skin.[309] Accordingly, as noted previously, people in Japan today continue to use whitening cosmetics that transform skin color.[263, 322, 374]

Beards

Head hair and face hair are congenital parts of people that certainly influence physical attractiveness. People judge the physical attractiveness of both the appearance of head and face hair in isolation and as an adornment to the face. However, the huge variety of head and face hair makes it extremely difficult to make scientifically definitive conclusions in terms of physical attractiveness phenomenon. It still is reasonable to conclude that, while appearance of head hair and face hair in the form of beards and moustaches varies greatly, statistical averages found in scholarly research show that face hair contributes to lower physical attractiveness more often than to higher physical attractiveness. Of course, the collective multitude of hairstyles along with nearly innumerable combinations and variations with other components of a particular person, make it difficult to conclude definitively that face hair has a constant significant effect on one's physical attractiveness.[214, 223, 344]

Eyeglasses

Additions to the face that are not congenital parts of people also affect physical attractiveness. Investigated accessories include eyeglasses. While styles of eyeglasses vary greatly with corresponding variation in determining physical attractiveness, statistical averages found in scholarly research show that eyeglasses contribute to lower physical attractiveness more often than to higher physical attractiveness.[63, 682, 684, 686] This connection between wearing eyeglasses and lower physical attractiveness is revealed both for observers of others who wear eyeglasses and on self-ratings of those who wear eyeglasses. However, because the styles of this tangential face component vary greatly, especially as styles interact with other determinants of a particular person's physical attractiveness, it is difficult to conclude definitively at this time that eyeglasses have a constant, significant directional effect on one's physical attractiveness. Some very early research found detrimental effects for personality[426] as well as physical attractiveness, while other much earlier research found favorable effects from eyeglasses upon perceived intelligence.[90, 697]

Micro Face Components

Micro face components are generally tangible, noticed routinely, and are aspects of a person's appearance normally considered parts of the face (e.g., nose, mouth, and eyes). Unlike the mathematical formulae about proportions employed by early artists and philosophers that differ greatly from the judgmental perspective of today's social scientists and average pedestrians, there is substantially greater agreement between then and now about so-called micro face components. For example, *The Human Face* is a comprehensive book that reports high concordance for physical attractiveness between ancient and modern times and in contemporary times between persons of different countries.[409]

The author of *The Human Face* notes that the ideal physical attractiveness for a female during medieval times may be summarized as described by Curry.[409] Similarly, he notes two more modern-day surveys conducted in the United States and one conducted in England that report findings compatible with notions during medieval times. Researcher Richard W.

Brislin has studied cultures worldwide spanning decades during his career and holds an authoritative perspective about the influence of culture on behavior.[83] Among his work is a research project conducted in North America in which he concluded that, based on the high agreement he found among people, calculation of a "beauty score" is possible for every face.[148] Table 5-6 presents a comparison as much as possible between these notions and findings about the face as discussed in *The Human Face*.[409]

Table 5-6. Descriptions of Face Components of Higher Physical Attractiveness, Research in 1970s and Prose in Medieval Times

| | Two Studies Conducted in the 1970s Focusing on Face Components of Males and Females[409] | | | Medieval Times Prose[409] |
	Males	Females	Females	Females
Cheeks	No mention	No mention	No mention	Lily white, rose pink
Cheek Bones	No mention	Not protruding and not large	High	No mention
Complexion	No mention	Clear	No mention	Lily-white or rose pink, soft
Ears	No mention	Not protruding and small lobes	No mention	Small
Eyes	No mention	Large and blue	Large, far spaced apart	Sparkling bright and light blue
Eyebrows	Bushy	Fine	No mention	Fine or removed
Fingers	No mention	No mention	No mention	White, long, slender
Hair	No mention	Straight	No mention	Blonde, golden
Lashes	No mention	Long	Long	No mention
Lips	No mention	Fine	Gentle, not too thick	No mention
Mouth	No mention	No mention	Medium to small	Small
Nose	Roman	Straight diamond-shaped	Small, slim	Small

| | Two Studies Conducted in the 1970s Focusing on Face Components of Males and Females[409] | | | Medieval Times Prose[409] |
	Males	Females	Females	Females
Proportion	Good ratio of central area to total face area, mouth width greater than cheek width, forehead height greater than chin height	Good ratio of central area to total face area, mouth width greater than cheek width, forehead height greater than chin height	No mention	No mention
Shape	Square	Oval	No mention	No mention
Skin	No mention	No mention	Clear, smooth	Soft as silk
Teeth	No mention	No mention	No mention	White

Viewer's Biology

Primary determinants of physical attractiveness of a person's face are facial components and dimensions. However, variables not part of the face or any part of the stimulus person contribute to determining physical attractiveness of that person's face. An experiment in 2001, that was conducted exceptionally well, discovered the viewer's own biology contributes to ratings of physical attractiveness of another person's face, which in this research was the menstrual cycle of females.[328] (Chapter 3 details this study's procedure, beginning on page 105 within the Determinants section in the "Separate from Person Judged" subsection.) Researchers presented subjects (42 females, 18- to 35-years of age, 40 in the United States and 2 in Vienna, Austria) with male and female stimulus persons (16 male Caucasians 18- to 26-years of age and 16 female Caucasians 18- to 30-years of age). Modified photographs presented subjects with fifteen faces of stimulus materials as identified below in Table 5-7, as published in 2001 in *Evolution and Human Behavior*.[328]

Table 5-7. Faces of Morphed Stimulus Persons to Investigate Hormonal Theory of Physical Attractiveness

Male Stimulus Faces	Female Stimulus Faces
Average male face	Average female face
Attractive male face	Attractive female face
Dominant-looking male face	Dominant-looking female face
Healthy-looking male face	Healthy-looking female face

Male Stimulus Faces	Female Stimulus Faces
Masculine-looking male face	Feminine-looking female face
Intelligent-looking male face	Intelligent-looking female face
Good-father male face	Good-mother female face
Androgynous face	

Analysis of these data led the researchers to conclude "support for a hormonal theory of facial [physical] attractiveness whereby perceived beauty depends on an interaction between displayed hormone markers and the hormonal state of the viewer."[328] Their data support strongly the hypothesis that people change their judgments about physical attractiveness as a function of hormonal changes within the viewers, which in this case aligned with menstrual cycle of females interacting with/judging males. There results are consistent with similar findings of other research that reveals females exhibit a statistically significant pattern of judging physical attractiveness of males as higher or lower in rhythm with stage of menstrual cycle.[557] Typically, during high conception phases of their menstrual cycle rather than during low conception phases, female subjects express greater preference for more masculine/less feminine faces of males.[557]

In the 2001 experiment cited above concerning stage of menstrual cycle of female subjects, the numerous specific findings revealed and pertinent for this book about physical attractiveness phenomenon include:[328]

- Females exhibit preference with higher ratings of physical attractiveness for a more masculine male face during the high conception phase of their menstrual cycles compared to the low conception phase. In other words, during their low conception phase, females selected an attractive male face that was less masculine than they selected during the high conception phase of their menstrual cycles.

- Among all the male and female variations presented and preferences data collected, the preferences expressed by subjects (females) for an attractive male face is the only preference that changed significantly along with change in conception phase of their menstrual cycles.

- Size of shift associated with menstrual cycle stages that revealed preference between more and less masculine male faces varied considerably in association with measures revealing substantially different personalities of subjects. Subjects assessed as non-androgynous women displayed a significantly larger shift in rating of male stimulus persons between their high conception and low conception phases than did the women assessed as androgynous women.

- Overall, the male stimulus person's face judged high in physical attractiveness was also more masculine than the average male face and, except for the healthy male face, was significantly different from all other faces.

- Factor analysis (Principal Components Analysis) revealed an upper threshold for masculinity appearance of male faces. For example, one statistically significant factor revealed factor loadings of physically attractive, sexually exciting, masculine, healthy, and protective, compared with another statistically significant factor that contained factor loadings of threatening, volatile, controlling, manipulative, coercive, selfish, dominant, and impulsive.

- Overall, the female stimulus person's face judged high in physical attractiveness was also more feminine than the average female face and, except for the feminine female face, was significantly different from all other faces.

- Plotting of males' faces concerning desirability for a short-term mate or a long-term mate (with third-order polynomial curves fitted to the mean ratings of males' faces) revealed increases in desirability for both types of mates with appearance of increasing masculinity; it reaches a maximum value, and then declines in desirability as the masculinity appearance increases farther. However, among this general pattern, the subjects (women) who demonstrated the greatest shift in rating of more masculine male faces during the high conception phase of their menstrual cycles also expressed higher rating of more masculine male faces as short-term mates.

In turn, the researchers conclude:[328]

- In agreement with prior studies, the current results support the conclusion that women prefer male faces that are more masculine than an average male face. That is, the [physically] attractive male face possesses more extreme testosterone markers, such as a longer, broader, lower jaw and more pronounced brow ridges and cheekbones than the average male face. These same hormone markers are also associated with good health...

- Clearly, the women in this study viewed pronounced testosterone facial markers [beyond a certain moderate level] to be associated with dominance, unfriendliness, and a host of negative traits (threatening, volatile, controlling, manipulative, coercive, and selfish)...

- The changes in females' preferences over their menstrual phase provide additional support for an adaptive model of aesthetic preference. First, of all the preferences examined, only the [physically] attractive male face varied as a function of menstrual phase. Second, this shift in preference occurred under very specific circumstances: during the nine days prior to ovulation, when conception risk is highest...[in other words,] the menstrual phase when there is a unique hormonal mix—high estrogen levels accompanied by low progesterone levels. Third, the overall shift in preference was very specific; a more masculine male face was preferred when conception risk was high…these observations are strong evidence for adaptive design. It appears that a female's estrogen/progesterone ratio may be a significant factor in attraction to the testosterone markers on a male's face. This suggests that the neural mechanism responsible for generating such positive feelings is sensitive to these circulating hormone levels. The observation that the preference change is restricted to the time of high conception risk indicates that the "healthy male" preference may involve genetic factors…from this perspective, the positive feelings evoked by testosterone markers [on a male's face] are a fitness-enhancing adaptation [for females judges].

Findings compatible to the research above were published in 2003, concluding that appearance of physical attractiveness of male faces yields higher ratings of attraction/liking than appearance of masculinity or dominance.[492] This study, conducted by a team of four researchers in the United Kingdom and Austria, directed their attention on markers in the male face associated with testosterone and estrogen. Stimulus persons (males) and subjects/judges (females) were young adults at the same university but unknown and unseen by each other outside the experiment. To ensure accuracy of data, separate raters at a different but local university conducted ratings of the stimulus persons' face appearances for levels of physical attractiveness, masculinity, and dominance. The primary objective of this research was to determine if the preference for male faces with an appearance of higher masculinity, as suggested in other research, was actually due to the appearance of intricately interrelated physical attractiveness, masculinity, or dominance when all three occur simultaneously.

RESEARCH METHODOLOGY

Face components do not contribute equally to determining physical attractiveness. There is a hierarchy with some components of greater importance than other components. Exact ordering of face components/features in determining physical attractiveness is interesting to ponder, difficult to achieve, and largely of little merit for understanding the larger physical attractiveness phenomenon. Obstacles to identify an exact ordering of face components begin with the Gestalt character of a person's physical attractiveness, followed by the inability to compare research projects with divergent methodologies exploring unlike face components. Within this qualifying context, research has provided insights into the importance of individual face components as determinants of physical attractiveness.

Common survey research methodologies are largely incapable of penetrating physical attractiveness phenomenon. People either do not recognize, know, or admit their thoughts about physical attractiveness overall, and survey questions specifically about face components yield no better answers. Data collected through a survey research design relying on self-completed questionnaires can usually benefit from either conducting an additional less obvious/obtrusive measurement procedure as a form of validity test, or by substituting altogether a less obvious procedure. Therefore, in addition to analyzing or, in effect deconstructing faces judged overall high or low in physical attractiveness, research has employed procedures focusing on measures of attention of subjects and memory of subjects regarding particular face components.

A reasonable hypothesis, or belief, is that observers' attention to individual face components reflects relative importance in determining physical attractiveness in the observers' mind. To determine importance under this assumption, one study chose to scrutinize subjects' viewing rather than query research participants about ordering importance of face components.[750] An apparatus known as a pupilometer recorded eye movements as each research participant observed a photograph of a person's face. This research found that when people encounter a stimulus person's face, the stimulus person's eyes and mouth receive greatest attention. When presented with a face stimulus, people scan it in its totality and then return repeatedly to focus on the eyes and mouth.

Two investigations focused their research procedure on the reasonable belief that observers' memory about individual face components reflects relative importance of particular determinants of physical attractiveness. The first project used recall measures about individual components of a stimulus person's face.[169] The researchers presented subjects with a photograph of a stimulus person's face, removed it from their presence, made changes, and then presented it again, asking subjects to indicate their recognition of new facial components. Based on this research procedure, results found the mouth and eyes were the most important face component in determining physical attractiveness. A second study focusing on memory and recognition tests supported the relative importance of mouth and eyes.[627]

HIERARCHY OF IMPORTANCE

Pulling together research findings, analyzing procedures of investigations, extrapolating meanings, and acknowledging topical complexities, a reasonable view emerges about the comparative importance of components that compose a face. Keep in mind the Gestalt nature of physical attractiveness, the myriad of related determinants and dynamics identified earlier in this chapter, and the difficulty inherent in a person truly knowing himself/herself the importance of face components as they judge themselves and others. In addition, people have a strong tendency to avoid identification with socially unacceptable or undesirable perspectives by stating only socially acceptable answers in all situations and especially when asked about physical attractiveness.

Correct research methodology is critical to collect data to understand physical attractiveness phenomenon. Consider the merit of conclusions based on data collected in 2005 through a large survey of more than 1,700 individuals.[731] Those researchers concluded: "With results surprising to both men and women…The Eyes Have It" in answer to what women think men notice first when meeting a woman and what men actually notice first or, probably more accurately in this situation, what men actually *say* they notice first. The data show that women (who most people think know best given their lifetime experiences of meeting men) say "her breasts" in answer to the question "What does she think [men] notice first about a woman." Men in this survey (31%) say a woman's eyes are at the top of items that they notice first and "only 13% put breasts at the top of their list." Within the above context, as best can be deciphered from pertinent scientific research, the hierarchal order of importance of face components in determining physical attractiveness regardless of gender can be ranked as:

#1 – Eyes (without eyeglasses)
#2 – Mouth
#3 – Hair
#4 – Nose

A battery of research procedures is best for providing confidence about investigative findings such as the comparative importance hierarchy of face components. Research findings are most dependable when multiple research projects and procedures, and ideally multiple researchers, all identify the same findings. As well as multiple methods and multiple projects, a research goal should be convergent validity (where, basically, similar procedures yield similar results) and divergent validity (where, basically, dissimilar procedures yield dissimilar results). Although confirming data from more investigations and more investigators are preferred, multiple methodologies pertinent to collect data do support the above listing: (1) self-ratings,[682] (2) ratings of dissected photographs by independent judges,[683] and (3) ratings of intact photographs by independent judges.[681] Furthermore, a scientifically credible scholarly journal published the articles that reported these findings. The above three research methodologies are not directly comparable in terms of components investigated, but together they provide convergent findings. As presented below in Table 5-8, the relative rankings based on statistical correlation values (r) are the same for mouth, eyes, hair, and nose, regardless that the exact statistical correlation values differ.

Table 5-8. Numerical Ranking of Relative Importance of Face Components Using Three Different Research Methodologies

	Rank Order	Ratings by Self Method	Ratings by Others Method	
			Dissected Photos	Intact Photos
Eyes	#1	r = .51	r = .44	r = .68
Mouth	#2	r = .54	r = .53	r = .72
Hair	#3	r = .49	r = .34	not assessed
Nose	#4	r = .47	r = .31	r = .61

The three studies summarized in Table 5-8, together offer valuable perspective to the understanding of relative importance for four primary face components—eyes, mouth, hair, and nose—more so than does any one study in isolation. Even with these very similar research projects, attempting to draw conclusions by comparing findings across multiple projects is complicated because of small but important procedural differences. In this current situation, two of the three studies assessed hair but not the third study.

The first two articles[682, 683] allow direct comparison of facial components and show corroborative rankings investigated from two different perspectives. Both studies measured importance by correlating the ratings of specific facial components with ratings of overall facial physical attractiveness. The self-ratings came from 45 females and the ratings by others involving dissected photographs that isolated face components came from 25 males and 25 females. The third article,[681] with intact photographs, collected data by presenting photographs of stimulus persons to 25 male and 25 female subjects. These subjects used a 10-point scale to rate seven specific face components as well as overall physical attractiveness for each stimulus person. Comparable to the results with the previous two studies, the ordering was first mouth (r = .72), followed by eyes (r = .68), and nose (r = .61). It omitted hair while including additional face components with results showing facial expression (r = .76), which is actually a combination of mouth and eyes, mouth (r = .72); eyebrows and complexion tied in correlation values (r = .69); eyes (r = .68); chin (r = .64); and nose (r = .61).

A potential complication in these data about the rank order of eyes as a determinant of physical attractiveness is due to combined data based on some stimulus persons who wore eyeglasses and some who did not. One of the researchers initially concluded that despite supremacy assumed about the eyes component of a person's face as a physical attractiveness determinant, eyes actually hold a position secondary to the mouth in determining physical attractiveness. However, eyeglasses confound such research-based conclusions. On further analysis of the data, that researcher qualified this statement by suggesting the research showed the eyes to be the most important component unless altered by eyeglasses. The mouth component of a person's face ranked higher than eyes only when eyeglasses accompanied a person's eyes. Whatever future research may clarify, it is reasonable at this time to conclude that eyes are one of the top few face components, if not the top face component, of greatest importance as a determinant of physical attractiveness, with mouth a close second to eyes.

NARRATIVE DESCRIPTIONS

Beyond the numerical ranking of face components discussed up to this point in this chapter, contemporary research findings that withstand passage of time identify descriptive characteristics of these components. Despite conventional wisdom expressed in clichés that beauty is in the eye of the beholder, agreement is robust about both comparative rankings and narrative descriptions of the respective components in the rankings. Table 5-9 below summarizes these descriptions from two research methodologies employed to investigate the same face components.[721] This table provides descriptions for only the face components rated to be of greatest importance to these respective judges and their stimulus persons.

Table 5-9. Narrative Descriptors of Face Components Rated Most Important to Determine Physical Attractiveness, Female Judges

	Rating Methodology		Comparison Methodology	
	Caucasian Judges: Male Stimuli	Caucasian Judges: Female Stimuli	Asian Judges: Female Stimuli	Caucasian Judges: Female Stimuli
Hair Texture	(not rated)	(not rated)	Straight	Frizzy
Hair Color	Brown: Dark or Light	(not rated)	Black, Dark Brown	(not rated)
Face Shape	Squarish	Heart, Pear	(not rated)	(not rated)
Nose Profile	Roman	Pug	(not rated)	Roman
Nose Width	(not rated)	Narrow	Medium	Narrow
Mouth	(not rated)	Full Lips	(not rated)	(not rated)
Skin Tone	Tan	Fair, Rose	Fair	(not rated)

The first methodology, summarized in Table 5-9, designated rating methodology, attempted to arrive at definitions of physical attractiveness for male and female stimulus persons by asking 40 white females to use a 6-point importance scale to rate the following narrative descriptions for the respective face components:

- Hair texture: straight, wavy, kinky, frizzy
- Hair color: black, dark brown, light brown, blonde
- Face shape: heart, oval, pear, squarish
- Nose profile: pug, hawk, Roman
- Nose width: wide, medium, narrow
- Mouth: full lips, average lips, thin lips
- Skin tone: fair, rose, tan, light brown, chocolate

The second methodology compared the ratings of face components of American judges with those of Asian judges. Subjects were 10 Asian females and 20 Caucasian females, all American born. The stimulus persons were female and subjects used the same scales as employed in the first methodology. The characteristics that the judges rated highest in physical attractiveness (i.e., most important) are listed above in Table 5-9 within the columns designated comparison methodology.

SUMMARY

Physical attractiveness is at the center of physical attractiveness phenomenon, and a person's face is at the center of what determines physical attractiveness. As with the previous chapter focusing body components, this chapter, with its focus on face components, provides important insight into understanding physical attractiveness, including its hidden values along with the broader dynamics and consequences of physical attractiveness phenomenon. Determinants of physical attractiveness include all the components and dimensions of a person in total; however, when speaking about specific tangible features that determine a person's physical attractiveness, the face and its components are first in importance, followed closely by body and its components.

The values that a person's face contributes to physical attractiveness phenomenon are without equal. While determinants of physical attractiveness include all the components and dimensions—physical and non-physical—of a person in total, when speaking about specific tangible features that determine a person's physical attractiveness, the face and its components are first in importance. As always, it is important to keep in mind that each determinant and dimension of the face is important by itself, while also being part of a person's physical attractiveness, which ultimately is a Gestalt wherein the whole is greater than the sum of the parts. Consistent with the structure of physical attractiveness determinants, determinants specific to the face are: many and complicated, shifting and unequal in importance, physical and non-physical, interdependent or compensatory and non-compensatory, and enduring and transient. Influencers are dynamic and many.

The face holds special significance in physical attractiveness and physical attractiveness phenomenon research, but it is only one part (albeit very important and large) of a person. As always, while each feature and dimension indicated as a determining characteristic contributes to and subtracts from a person's physical attractiveness, it is important to keep in mind that a person's physical attractiveness is ultimately a Gestalt, whereby the whole is greater than the sum of the parts.

Chapter 6

Interactions: Strangers and Friends

Unlike those whose appealing looks entreat the world to cosset [protect/care for] them, not once in my life had I ever felt safe. Prettier girls reaped all the rewards in life, whereas I had to live like a pauper. Others were offered a helping hand when they needed it, but not me. Because of my appearance [of lower physical attractiveness], everyone assumed that I could look after myself.

Cindy Jackson, writing at age 47,
in her autobiography published in
England titled *Living Doll*.[316, p. 135]

Beauty can be as isolating as genius, or deformity. I have always been aware of a relationship between madness and beauty.

Attributed to U. S. fashion and portrait
photographer Richard Avedon (1923-2004).[449]

INTRODUCTION

Observations of reality, first-hand experiences, and scientific research data all confirm the impact articulated by *The Power and Paradox of Physical Attractiveness*. These observations and data also confirm that feelings, desires, and drives such as expressed in the above opening quotes are actually rational aspirations throughout the world where physical attractiveness phenomenon wields consistent, powerful, and pervasive effects. These effects occur mostly unknowingly, unrecognized, or recognized but denied for those interpersonal interactions in everyone's lives with strangers, friends, and with individuals in hope of long-term committed spousal relationships. As the opening quotes attest, lack of high physical attractiveness can isolate a person from meaningful interactions, and paradoxically, high physical attractiveness can be isolating to some.

Thresholds no doubt function whereby individuals possessing relatively high physical attractiveness access benefits or privileges provided by society and by persons in the society that are not available to individuals of lower physical attractiveness. Individuals of average or moderate physical attractiveness, as well as those of lower physical attractiveness, experience lives accordingly with fewer benefits and more detriments than do their counterparts of higher physical attractiveness. A person whose physical attractiveness is significantly greater than some very high upper threshold probably does live with some detriments that include feeling isolated. Adding to these complexities are individuals of higher physical attractiveness who appear to attempt to be politically correct concerning their physical attractiveness. Their credibility is surely questionable when their actions contradict their words and their words contradict the obvious benefits their physical attractiveness has brought and bought for them. While physically attractive people frequently downplay the corresponding benefits in their lives because they possess an appearance of truly superior physical attractiveness, and while they may encounter unrelated trials and tribulations common to all people, it is not believable that their physical attractiveness has not provided values that they desire. Consider the very physically attractive, highly talented, actor Halle Berry who recently stated, "Being thought of as a beautiful woman has spared me nothing in life. No heartache. No trouble. Beauty is essentially meaningless."[133]

Despite rare, contrarian, self-serving proclamations by some movie stars judged to possess exceptionally high physical attractiveness, people the world over would prefer to have higher rather than lower physical attractiveness. Admittedly, it is a preference not readily voiced in the schizophrenic context exhibited by populations that value different levels of physical attractiveness differently, but more often than not, populations either fail to recognize it and/or deny it. Nevertheless, evidence underscores that higher external physical attractiveness causes or at least equates with favorable internal psychological qualities. Lower external physical attractiveness has the converse cause, or association. To some, this information is new. Consider researchers for the 2005 *Allure State of Beauty National Study* that surveyed more than 1,700 Americans and concluded, "…among the most surprising statistics from the study is that enhancing their [physical] appearance fuels women's confidence."[731] Data from that 2005 survey showed "Ninety-four percent [of the respondents] agree that the more beautiful they feel, the more confident they are." The two factors are interrelated intricately as signaled by the high portion of respondents, 94 percent, who "say that when they feel more confident, they take more time to look good."

COGNITIVE CONTEXT

The first quote at the opening of this chapter offers precious firsthand anecdotal corroboration for corresponding objective data, while the second quote suggests a dimension of physical attractiveness phenomenon mostly void of such targeted scientific research data. Clearly, repeatedly, and consistently research data reveal the worlds are much different for those born with an appearance of lower or higher physical attractiveness. From literally birth (and increasingly into the future, maybe even before birth) through death, physical attractiveness phenomenon translates into more favorable interpersonal interactions for those higher in physical attractiveness and less favorable interpersonal interactions for those lower in physical attractiveness.

Beauty is in the eye of the beholder, according to an age-old cliché. Similar clichés urge everyone not to judge a book, let alone a person, by its cover, or appearance. Despite best intentions and despite professed ideals, realities show that actions do speak louder than words. People do judge other people and interact correspondingly with them based on the level of physical attractiveness possessed by these other people. Underlying these judgments and interpersonal interactions are often irrational values that beholders of a person's physical attractiveness ascribe to the person observed, along with intertwining intrinsic and extrinsic features. These values may not issue from an objective judgment or may rely purely on a superficial inference.

Science has engaged itself in understanding what ideas and constructs in the perceiver's view direct physical attractiveness judgments that drive behaviors toward and interactions with others as a function of physical attractiveness. Current research knowledge indicates that physical attractiveness judgments are a kind of shortcut for establishing value in a visually saturated environment. One study investigated the relationship between physical attractiveness and the need for cognition in which people have different levels of propensities to engage in and to enjoy cognitive activity.[559] This study hypothesized that individuals who possess lower need for cognitive activity assume that people of higher, compared to lower, physical attractiveness have social/interpersonal characteristics that are more favorable. That study based its hypothesis in part on earlier research that showed persuasive efforts have greater influence within these individuals than within people with higher need for cognitive activity. Subjects of low and high need for cognitive activity made bipolar assignments for a list of seventeen personality traits to male and female stimulus persons (exhibited by photographs) of different levels of physical attractiveness. All subjects attributed more socially/interpersonally valuable characteristics to the stimulus persons of higher physical attractiveness, with a difference in magnitude of attributions supporting the study's hypothesis.

Physical attractiveness as a set of perceptional cues most certainly ensues similar to known functions in other cognitive evaluations. For example, the purest and most beautiful tones are the result of the most symmetrical acoustical signals, essentially pure sine waves, within an average range of perception, such as well-trained human voices or songbirds. Analogously, beauty may be the simplest, most symmetrical distribution of features within some range of shapes. In this context of thought, since simplicity creates cognitive shortcuts, a person of higher physical attractiveness is easier and more pleasant to recognize due to straightness of the lines that profile and form his or her appearance.

Cognitive proceedings that surround physical attractiveness align readily with notions that genetic constitution hardwires physical attractiveness phenomenon into the perceptual apparatus of people. Authors and researchers especially with psychobiological perspectives conjecture that natural selection functions in our deepest understanding of beauty. A derivative supported by research data is that our collective appreciation of physical attractiveness can accordingly be described in terms of maximum fertility cues, according to one contemporary prominent researcher using computer-enhanced imagery.[327]

Of course, "optimum" most likely supplants "maximum" due to a point of diminishing return. Natural differences between the sexes, believed driven by notions of mating health, are not absolute values as demonstrated by a man's large jaw or a woman's large eyes. Correlations between mating choice and certain physical attributes commonly do not exist too far outside the range of average to retain their appeal value. Too large a jaw for males or hydroencephalic eyes for males deviate too far from average to be perceived as beautiful, claim the authors of a research project published in 1990 titled "Attractive Faces Are Only Average."[378] However, ten years later, a scholarly article states the prior researchers are "simply wrong."[396] The more recent data collected by later researchers (particularly Victor

Johnston, who has a long-term commitment to this topic area of research) identifies, explains, and argues convincingly that the image processing procedures used by the earlier researchers were flawed and that average faces are not the most physically attractive.[327]

CONTEMPORANEOUS ASSOCIATION

Physical attractiveness of a person is determined more in context rather than in isolation. Perhaps the most common context is that of association or even co-association with other individuals seen in comparison or in contrast. Physical attractiveness evaluations vary in relation to an observer's earlier and concurrent exposures to physical attractiveness of other persons. This dynamic is not unlike reference point dynamics researched in other disciplines, such as marketing in areas of price sticker shock or product-line pricing practices commonly used in restaurants and all sorts of consumer products and services. Everyday, real-world life bears out the solid empirical research data, particularly about determinants of physical attractiveness that are associated respectively with persons of higher or lower physical attractiveness. A recent Associated Press newspaper article about intimate relations off-screen between movie stars reported "hanging with Angelina Jolie established Billy Bob Thornton's desirability, and made him more attractive to other women."[745]

Earlier Context Exposure

A series of three studies performed to explore the affect on an individual's perceived physical attractiveness, based on the observers' prior exposure to the physical attractiveness of others involved subjects (227 males) within both a naturalistic field setting study and a controlled laboratory experiment.[345] The field experiment asked subjects (81 males) without advance notice, who were watching a popular television show with female actors of high physical attractiveness, to rate physical attractiveness of a female stimulus person. Photographs showed stimulus persons, whom judges had rated earlier to possess a moderate level of physical attractiveness. Subjects watching the female actors of high physical attractiveness in this naturalistic setting rated the stimulus persons significantly lower in physical attractiveness by contrast with a comparable control group who were not watching similar programming.

The second and third studies consisted of controlled laboratory experiments with 146 different subjects. An experimental group viewed a videotape of female stimulus persons of high physical attractiveness, while a control group did not view such a videotape. After an equal length of time lapsed for both groups, researchers asked the subjects to evaluate physical attractiveness of a previously unseen stimulus person. As in the field experiment above, data from this laboratory experiment produced evidence of the same pattern, whereby judges rated stimulus persons lower in physical attractiveness after first observing stimulus persons of high physical attractiveness.

Concurrent Context Exposure

Two separate studies determined equivalent context effects. While concurrently viewing "context persons" of either high or low physical attractiveness, subjects (140 total) rated physical attractiveness of stimulus persons (photographs of females) of interest to researchers.[447] These subjects rated stimulus persons of moderate physical attractiveness to be higher in physical attractiveness when in an environment containing persons of lower physical attractiveness. Similarly, stimulus persons of moderate physical attractiveness received ratings lower in physical attractiveness from subjects in the context of an environment of persons of higher physical attractiveness. Another experiment using three treatment-presentation conditions—successive viewing of stimulus persons and context persons, concurrent viewing of stimulus persons and context persons, and isolated viewing of stimulus persons—reported the same context effects as above with the greatest differences in physical attractiveness ratings reported for the concurrent viewing condition.[674]

Recurring Context Exposures

Recurring exposures to people of higher physical attractiveness produce disorders related to appearance such as eating disorders, according to evidence put forth by some researchers.[326] The risk arises from accumulated dissatisfaction as a function of repeated or sustained exposure to excessive concerns about self-rating one's physical attractiveness in the context of appearances, often unattainable by anyone in reality, promulgated in media. Women in the United States, for example, are generally dissatisfied with their body images as a composite.[320] Similarly, men in the United States are also dissatisfied with their body images, albeit to a lesser extent.[232] A series of articles in *Newsweek* magazine dedicated to men's health reports that most men are satisfied with their appearances; but in the same article the depth of male insecurity, including the inability to admit any deficiency including illness, is well documented.[148, 361, 576] That inability is summarized well in the title of one of the articles, "Mind of a Man: Stop Pretending Nothing's Wrong [with Your Health]. "[463]

If this picture is correct, it tells once again that male preferences dominate culture in the United States, let alone in more obviously male-centric countries around the world. The importance of physical attractiveness of females remains greater than the importance of physical attractiveness of males due to the options still available more commonly to women. However, the change in men using elective cosmetic surgery and pursuing other appearance enhancements is larger than the rise in use of these and analogous enhancements by women. Popular media as well as scientific research, rather routinely now, report yearly jumps in interest and actions among males to increase their own physical attractiveness. When reports provide objective numbers, females remain ahead of males but with greater annual increases by males for improving one's own physical attractiveness. The difference is narrowing with males possibly catching up to females and even surpassing them in the future if the rates of changes continue as they have the past few years.[232] At the same time, the importance placed on physical attractiveness of women is diminishing, albeit ever so slowly, in some respects as well.

Pertinent empirical research conducted in locations around the world reveals that personal dissatisfaction with appearance is worldwide. Given the common influence of media images and their power to reposition the ideals of beauty worldwide as well as in the United States, individuals who frequently subject themselves to mass media engage in progressive reevaluations of themselves. The result, some contend, are destabilized evaluations that contribute to health problems. Even still, while the correlation between negative self- and other-judgments in comparison with media images is constant, defining media relevance for setting a personal standard is scant in the scientific research literature. In most countries, it is rather uncomplicated to understand how the marketing principles involved in a single commercial can influence the viewer to respond favorably to the image created of a better lifestyle, complete with better looks, which can be compounded through exposure to ordinary programming.[146] Accordingly, there are general thoughts that might be considered conventional wisdom that people should avoid physical attractiveness messages put forth through mass media in order to retain good self-image about their appearance and, subsequently, their physical and mental health.

Pollution

The media may cause motivating but unattainable norms that people accept for their desired physical attractiveness, but the values exceed the limits of that context. Other circumstances include factors that pollute our environment and that are external to the individual. These factors can create a significant shift in a person's physical attractiveness as perceived by others. In a polluted atmosphere, strangers demonstrate judgments of greater physical attractiveness and, correspondingly, greater liking for another as compared to a clean environment.[603] Adverse environmental conditions can also promote the opposite effect where judgments of physical attractiveness are decreased and, accordingly, liking of individuals is decreased by heat,[53, 260] crowding,[204, 224] and noise.[94]

Music

Music is a common factor in life, in one form or another throughout history as well as now during contemporary times. While music is sometimes a focal point of our attention, more often it is a less noticed part of our environment. This common feature of our environment apparently affects an individual's physical attractiveness. An experiment designed to test the effect of background music on physical attractiveness used stimulus persons either high or low in physical attractiveness (males portrayed in photographs).[437] The background music was rock music (described as positive-affect evoking), avant-garde music (described as negative-affect evoking), or an experimental treatment of no background music. In addition to consistently preferential evaluation of stimulus persons of high physical attractiveness, the differences in music produced variations of physical attractiveness ratings. The music condition described as evoking positive affect resulted in the highest ratings of physical attractiveness for the stimulus persons.

Time

Threatened behaviors and possessions become more valuable.[736] Decreasing time available to make a decision can induce this threat experience and as time available to make a decision decreases, differences in the values of alternatives become less distinct.[411] Integrating these findings of threat, value, and time, there emerges a relationship between physical attractiveness and time pressures. One study tested a related hypothesis that physical attractiveness of an opposite-sex stimulus person would increase as the time available to interact with the person decreased.[556]

A field study collected data at three different locations to identify, if any, the effect of decreasing decision time on perceptions of physical attractiveness. Same-sex interviewers questioned subjects (52 male and 51 female customers at 3 bars) at three-and-one-half hours, two hours, and one-half hour before each bar's closing time. All interviews included evaluations of physical attractiveness of opposite-sex customers. The closing times produced divergent physical attractiveness ratings for both genders with no statistically significant differences between males and females. The authors concluded that ratings of physical attractiveness did increase as time available to make a decision to interact decreased. Results from this scholarly research testing a rather implied theory from a popular song originally performed by Mickey Gilley titled "They All Get Prettier at Closing Time"[238] offers notions relatable to evolutionary theory pertinent to physical attractiveness phenomenon and to individuals as they socialize in recreational settings and as they age.

A recent study conducted in a laboratory setting by researchers at two universities in Scotland explored another dimension common to bar settings, moderate amounts of alcohol consumption.[329] The researchers conclude that findings from that research raise health issues involving physical attractiveness phenomenon concerning increased likelihood of risky sex. Through three scientifically conducted experiments, researchers asked male and female subjects to rate faces of males and females unfamiliar to them and, as a control variable, to rate physical attractiveness of human non-face objects (in this case, wrist watches). Male and female subjects who had consumed moderate amounts of alcohol revealed a significant "alcohol consumption enhancement effect" but only for the ratings of physical attractiveness of opposite-sex faces. Neither same-sex ratings of faces nor ratings of the physical attractiveness of non-face objects produced data indicating this effect.

The journal of *Experimental and Clinical Psychopharmacology* published a research article in 2005 that went beyond the more sociological-psychological considerations of the research discussed immediately above.[372] Conducted in the United States, the research found males to have significantly greater sexual interest and intentions regarding female stimulus persons of higher physical attractiveness. Unlike findings of other research projects,[16] the level of physical attractiveness of female stimulus person in this study was not significantly related to the sexual risks perceived by these male subjects. Two substantial methodological differences in this study compared to the study immediately above were manipulation of level of alcohol consumption and focus of dependent measures. The study above simply questioned subjects about amount of alcohol consumed before arriving at the experiment, while this study gave each person a Breathalyzer test upon arriving.

These latter researchers selected only heterosexual male subjects with zero percent of alcohol indicated in their systems, and then asked each to drink various amounts of alcohol under close watch of the researchers. Dependent measures did not assess subsequent impact on physical attractiveness ratings. These measures instead assessed and found no significant differences due to different levels of moderate alcohol consumption. In other words, it appeared that sexual interests and perception of risks held by the male subjects in regard to the female stimulus persons of higher and lower physical attractiveness, remained the same after moderate alcohol consumption as before that consumption.

PEOPLE IN OUR LIVES

Interpersonal interactions are an important part of every person's life. Interactions with people in our lives and the context of these connections are all-important parts of every person's life. Certainly, what people believe and expect about another person—intentionally or unintentionally, consciously or subconsciously—influences the bidirectional links between the person and the people in the person's life. The state of affairs is a context significantly more favorable for those higher in physical attractiveness.

Assumptions, Expectations, Attributions

Results from an impression formation study conducted in 1970 have laid a foundation for investigation of expectations, assumptions and behaviors based on physical attractiveness.[459] History has shown this often-cited research project to be a seminal study in pursuits to explore and understand physical attractiveness phenomenon. Subjects (males and females) expressed their impressions about stimulus persons (males and females) unknown to the subjects for numerous nonappearance characteristics. Without explicit regard to physical attractiveness of stimulus persons, subjects judged those higher in physical attractiveness more favorably at statistically significant levels than those lower in physical attractiveness. The results of a later national survey in the United States found that people believed the same directional favor in terms of happiness, sex lives, and receiving respect.[64] Table 6-1 lists these disparate impressions.

Table 6-1. Impressions About Persons of Higher and Lower Physical Attractiveness Without Attention to Person's Physical Attractiveness

Persons of Higher Physical Attractiveness		Persons of Lower Physical Attractiveness
Curious	rather than	Indifferent
Complex	rather than	Simple
Perceptive	rather than	Insensitive
Happy	rather than	Sad
Active	rather than	Passive

Persons of Higher Physical Attractiveness		Persons of Lower Physical Attractiveness
Amiable	rather than	Aloof
Humorous	rather than	Serious
Pleasure-seeking	rather than	Self-controlled
Outspoken	rather than	Reserved
Flexible	rather than	Rigid
More happy	rather than	Less happy
Better sex lives	rather than	Less good sex lives
Receive more respect	rather than	Receive less respect

Wishful dreaming or hopeful thinking, correct or incorrect, people do associate physical attractiveness with glamour.[50] Subjects (332 in total) participated in three experiments designed to identify attributes that differentiate individuals of lower and higher physical attractiveness. Factor analysis of the data revealed a glamour effect. When placed into an experimental research design, regardless of what they might openly admit, people exhibit strong assumptions about personal characteristics and qualities based on physical attractiveness. These assumptions and attributions are potent, with definite advantages assumed and attributed for those whose appearances are higher in physical attractiveness and definite disadvantages for their counterparts of lower physical attractiveness. These effects of physical attractiveness on people are either truly unrecognized or consciously denied, as exhibited by people who express strong opinion consistent with socially approved perspectives that they, themselves, are not influenced by another person's physical attractiveness. The contradiction between admitted, or acknowledged, stance versus dissimilar actions highlights the need for research projects based on experimental designs to secure accurate data, or even unobtrusive research observations, rather than survey-interview techniques that work very well for other research topics in many other fields.

Personality

Personality and character can overshadow physical attractiveness or, actually, change physical attractiveness. In other words, ascribed personality and ascribed character can distort perceived physical attractiveness. One study reversed relationship between physical attractiveness and perceptions of personality to assess the impact of personality on physical attractiveness.[262] To achieve this turnaround, stimulus persons (females, photographs) rated earlier as high, low, or moderate in physical attractiveness, were paired later with either a favorable, unfavorable, or neutral personality description. After presented with the stimulus persons, subjects (69 males and 56 females) rated physical attractiveness of the stimulus persons (females). For each level of physical attractiveness, persons paired with a favorable personality description received higher ratings of physical attractiveness than their earlier independent ratings that involved no personality descriptions. Data revealed this pattern for all three levels of experimental conditions for personality attributions.

The impact of character upon perceived physical attractiveness involved manipulation of sex-role orientation for both subjects and stimulus persons.[81] Using the Bem Sex-Role Inventory, subjects (43 males and 60 females) were classified as either sex-typed or androgynous. Stimulus persons (males and females, photographs) were correspondingly attributed the character of either a feminine female, masculine male, or an androgynous person. After subjects viewed two opposite-sex stimulus persons (one sex-typed and one androgynous), they expressed their likings and their ratings of physical attractiveness for each. While this experimental character manipulation did not affect the liking expressed by male judges for female stimulus persons, female judges, regardless of their own sex-role orientation, liked significantly better the androgynous male stimulus persons. Likewise, regardless of gender of judges or stimulus persons, judges gave increased ratings of the stimulus persons' physical attractiveness when sex-type attributions were either feminine female or masculine male compared to androgynous.

Attitude

Similarity and type are two categories of attitudes that shape perceived physical attractiveness. For the first category, similarity of attitudes, research has manipulated both quantity and quality, and a rather huge amount of research exists pertaining to attitude similarity and attitude liking.[527, 532, 534] One study directly related to attitude similarity and evaluations of physical attractiveness asked subjects (67 in total) ranging in age from 19 to 50 years to rate physical attractiveness of stimulus persons (represented by photographs).[325] Experimental treatments assigned stimulus persons to conditions of either support or nonsupport for political candidates in a recent national election. Persons rated highest in physical attractiveness were those supposedly aligned with the same political attitude as the subjects. Congruent research findings consist of causal data showing positive impact of physical attractiveness on perceived attitude similarity[313, 431, 620] and correlation data showing positive relationship between perceived physical attractiveness and perceived attitude similarity.[37, 67, 118]

The second category, type of attitude, has received relatively little research attention in terms of studying relationships between variety of attitudes and perceived physical attractiveness. One study involved attitudes pertaining to feminism.[42] Subjects (76 in total) were males with earlier measured attitudes toward females indicating if they either supported or did not support feminism. Stimulus persons (females represented by photographs) were attributed attitude statements that reflected either a feminist or a non-feminist orientation. After presented with the stimulus materials, subjects used an 8-point scale to rate physical attractiveness of the stimulus persons. Subjects identified earlier with pro-feminist attitudes rated stimulus persons higher in physical attractiveness when identified as pro-feminist compared to non-feminist. In turn, subjects identified earlier with non-feminist attitudes rated stimulus persons higher in physical attractiveness when identified with non-feminist orientation.

Another study involving types of attitudes manipulated sexual attitudes of stimulus persons and measured sexual attitudes of subjects.[521] Two experiments tested two main hypotheses while using male and female stimulus persons (represented by photographs). The first hypothesis proposed that sexual attitudes of a subject affect attributions of sexual attitudes to stimulus persons when the only available information is the stimulus person's physical attractiveness. The second hypothesis proposed that presumed sexual attitudes of stimulus persons affect ratings of a stimulus person's physical attractiveness when the only information available is his or her appearance and sexual attitudes. Both experiments employed female subjects, 30 in the first experiment and 38 in the second experiment:

- In the first experiment, independent variables were blocking variables for level of physical attractiveness of stimulus persons and sexual attitudes of subjects. Dependent variables were subjects' ratings of stimulus persons' physical attractiveness and subjects' attributed sexual attitudes.

- In the second experiment, independent variables included (1) each stimulus person's physical attractiveness, controlled or manipulated by the researcher as assessed independently earlier by different subjects and (2) each stimulus person's sexual attitudes through respective attributions by the researcher. This experiment manipulated three levels of physical attractiveness (low, moderate, and high) for the stimulus persons and four levels of sexual attitudes (conservative, moderate, liberal, and unknown) for the stimulus persons. Dependent variables were physical attractiveness ratings expressed by subjects for stimulus persons who varied systematically in terms of physical attractiveness and their randomly paired sexual attitudes.

Results from the first experiment were significant for the relationship between sexual attitudes of subjects and the attribution of sexual attitudes to stimulus persons. Particularly notable was that all subjects seemed to value liberal sexual attitudes the least, and then accordingly attributed these attitudes to stimulus persons of lowest physical attractiveness. Also particularly notable, all subjects identified their sexual attitudes most closely with the most physically attractive stimulus persons. These and other significant effects revealed in the data from the first experiment included:

- Stimulus persons of lower physical attractiveness were attributed liberal sexual attitudes most frequently, regardless of subject's own indicated attitudes.

- Stimulus persons of higher physical attractiveness were attributed moderate sexual attitudes by subjects indicating liberal sexual attitudes, whereas subjects indicating conservative sexual attitudes attributed conservative sexual attitudes to stimulus persons of higher physical attractiveness.

- Stimulus persons of moderate physical attractiveness were attributed sexual attitudes similar to the subjects' own attitudes.

- Stimulus persons were most frequently attributed/assumed attitudes similar to the attitudes of subjects, that is, subjects indicating liberal sexual attitudes attributed liberal sexual attitudes whereas subjects indicating conservative sexual attitudes attributed conservative sexual attitudes.

The second experiment revealed significance for both main and interaction effects, which translated into a general conclusion that the additional information of a stimulus person's sexual attitude does influence perceptions of his or her physical attractiveness. Significant effects revealed in the data from this second experiment included these observations:

- Lack of information is important in determining perceived physical attractiveness. Subjects with information about a stimulus person's sexual attitudes demonstrate the influence of such information when they subsequently rate physical attractiveness of that person differently than from subjects without this information. Subjects with knowledge of a stimulus person's sexual attitudes demonstrated this difference in their rating of physical attractiveness of that person differently from subjects without this information. When judging physical attractiveness of stimulus persons, subjects gave the highest ratings to those whose sexual attitudes were unknown. An explanation suggests that subjects may formulate their own ideals of a stranger's sexual attitudes in a situation of no such information. With this assumed ideal sexual attitude of a stimulus person, subjects then accordingly raise their perceptions and ratings of the person's physical attractiveness.

- Perceived physical attractiveness is not independent or absolute. Non-physical factors can influence physical attractiveness, which in this experiment were sexual attitudes attributed to stimulus persons. Subjects with different sexual attitude information about a stimulus person rate differently the physical attractiveness of that person. Interaction effects revealed in the statistical analyses showed overall patterns of similarity or assumed similarity of sexual attitudes between stimulus persons and judges to cause the highest ratings of physical attractiveness, regardless of actual types of sexual attitudes.

Strangers

Strangers are part of every person's life. A particularly vital and frequent facet of strangers in every country and culture is helping behavior. Strangers frequently seek help, and strangers frequently provide help, which includes routine and mundane help as well as serious and sometimes vital help that is largely unpredictable and can touch any person's life at any time. Help can range from everyday assistance in stores while shopping, on streets asking directions, in workplaces with favors small and large, to incidents of illness, accidents, and crimes with need for emergency assistance. Two parties—help seekers and help givers, ranging from volunteer amateurs to paid professionals—are the nucleus of helping behavior. Characteristics of these two parties can either facilitate or impede the execution of a helping behavior episode, small or large. While the following text categorizes discussion between help seekers and help givers, the distinction is difficult since the two are interdependent with help providers an integral part of discussion about help seekers.

Seekers of Help

Regardless whether an individual is in control of his or her circumstance needing help, differences due to physical attractiveness are the same. If the predicament is a controllable form, as when a person commits a crime or an uncontrollable predicament caused simply by bad luck over which the person has no control, physical attractiveness of the person seeking help influences treatment by potential and actual help givers. When people low in physical attractiveness experience some sort of unfortunate predicament over which they have no control, they receive less sympathy and less help than do people higher in physical attractiveness.[634]

When people of differing levels of physical attractiveness find themselves in circumstances for which they need help, all ultimately tend to receive some, albeit different quality, forms of help. People higher in physical attractiveness more often than not receive a greater quantity and quality of help than those lower in physical attractiveness. In the same circumstance of needing help, scientific research[480] and acute observations of more anecdotal data[567] confirm that persons of higher physical attractiveness more frequently receive actual tangible help (i.e., higher quality assistance). Data show that a person of lower physical attractiveness in the same circumstance will receive lower-quality assistance, either because it is too brief or perhaps because it is limited to directions about where to receive assistance rather than actually taking the person to the point of assistance.

Bystanders react differently when an emergency involves a person lower, rather than higher, in physical attractiveness.[569] An early research project providing these data conducted a field experiment in which the independent variables manipulated by the researchers were physical attractiveness of individuals needing help (i.e., stimulus persons) and personal costs to the help givers or potential help givers for helping. Subjects were New York City subway passengers ranging in age from six years to seventy-two years. The procedure (conducted 166 times over many different times of day and night) was a male stimulus person falling in a subway car, either in the middle of a subway run (i.e., low helper cost) or at the end of a subway run (i.e., high helper cost). Dependent variables were whether bystanders offered help and, if so, the speed with which they offered help, measured for 166 data-collection episodes. Although time of day for the data collection, defined as low and high helper cost in this research project, did not yield different results, the experimental treatment conditions in which the stimulus persons were higher in physical attractiveness produced significantly more help and faster help.

Self-Disclosure

Helping behavior received by a stimulus person interacts between the person's physical attractiveness and the person's level of self-disclosure. In a field experiment, stimulus persons (females) of different levels of physical attractiveness asked subjects (216 males) for directions.[277] Researchers manipulated the level of physical attractiveness of the stimulus person by varying facial characteristics with differences in hair and cosmetics, and body characteristics with differences in clothing. Results revealed more time spent helping stimulus persons higher in physical attractiveness compared to stimulus persons lower in physical attractiveness. Self-disclosure (i.e., giving name as opposed to not giving name) showed no significant main effects, but an interaction occurred in which the greatest amount of help (i.e., giving directions) was given by subjects when asked by stimulus persons of higher physical attractiveness who self-disclosed as opposed to these same stimulus persons who did not self-disclose. These data might suggest that, apart from self-disclosure's enhancement of helping behavior, it might also enhance perceived physical attractiveness.

Complementing the finding above that persons higher in physical attractiveness receive more help when they self-disclose, another study found that persons lower in physical attractiveness who self-disclose receive less help than those at this lower level of physical attractiveness who do not self-disclose.[743] Persons receiving the least help are those lower in physical attractiveness who self-disclose. In light of physical attractiveness phenomenon, the help provider seems willing to help persons lower in physical attractiveness but, at the same time, wants to keep their distance by not becoming more involved with the person than necessary. This research investigation manipulated self-disclosure through two different tasks. A stimulus person (female) with either high or low physical attractiveness approached subjects (males) for help. One task asked subjects (30 males) for directions, and the other task asked subjects (40 males) to mail a letter. Regardless of task, stimulus persons of higher physical attractiveness who self-disclosed received significantly more help.

A later study that expanded the methodology of earlier work employed five experiments with subjects (540 total) in a variety of experimental treatments.[355] Research manipulations included male and female stimulus persons, either low or high in physical attractiveness, three levels of self-disclosure, and several topics of self-disclosure. Data revealed that for self-disclosing conditions, subjects evaluated female stimulus persons more favorably with the highest level of disclosure than those with low or moderate levels of disclosure, especially when the topic dealt with sexual attitudes or parental suicide. When the topic dealt with aggressive feelings of competitiveness, the female stimulus persons of highest self-disclosure were less preferred than those females of moderate self-disclosure. For the male stimulus persons, the results were quite different. Subjects rated male stimulus persons least preferred when they exhibited high self-disclosure. Among all the complexities inherent in the data from these five experiments, some summary findings do emerge explicitly to physical attractiveness. Regardless of gender, subjects evaluated less favorably the stimulus persons who self-disclosed and were of lower physical attractiveness than the stimulus persons who self-disclosed and were of high physical attractiveness. Again, in this research as with other research, data indicate that people will provide reasonable evaluation and help to people with lower physical attractiveness needing help, but the evaluation and help are reduced when the help giver is not able to maintain certain involvement and interaction distances from the help seeker.

Gender Impartial

Males and females do more when directly requested, or even when not requested, by people of higher physical attractiveness compared to lower physical attractiveness. In turn, the helping behavior offered by males and females is affected more-or-less equally. One study asked subjects (20 males and 20 females) to evaluate participants in a videotaped debate, as a disguise to the study's purpose to investigate interpersonal attraction, physical attractiveness, and help volunteering dynamics.[465] The presumed debaters were either low or high in physical attractiveness and displayed behavior described as either nice or obnoxious. After viewing the videotape, stimulus persons (females) of either high or low physical attractiveness asked the audience for volunteers to help with a task. Stimulus persons of higher physical attractiveness obtained volunteers significantly more readily than did their counterparts of lower physical attractiveness, regardless of the subject's gender.

Givers of help, regardless of gender dyads, demonstrate increased helping behavior based on a stimulus person's higher physical attractiveness even in the absence of interaction or personal contact. In response to a stamped letter left in a telephone booth, without meeting or seeing the person, male stimulus persons of higher physical attractiveness received more help than their counterparts of lower physical attractiveness, with the same pattern regardless of the subject's sex.[56] Accompanying the "forgotten lost" letter was a message that stated urgency for its delivery, along with an application that included a photograph of the supposed applicant. Data revealed that when the application letter contained a photograph of a person of higher physical attractiveness, the finder of the letter was significantly more likely to mail it.

Moving from total detachment to at least a distant glimpse, a research project placed stimulus persons in a distress situation, specifically a lady in a stalled car on a highway.[35] To exert greatest research control, this field experiment used the same stimulus person (female) in both the conditions of lower and higher physical attractiveness by manipulating the person's appearance accordingly. Initial contact was limited to a brief distant glimpse as the subjects traveled past the stimulus person at highway speeds. Females in the higher physical attractiveness condition resulted in more male motorists stopping and offering help than in the condition of lower physical attractiveness. This outcome was probably predictable according to some dimensions of general conventional wisdom, but that does not make these data any less disconcerting about human thoughts and actions as well as any less confirming about physical attractiveness phenomenon in the lives of all people.

Need Severity

Severity of need or emergency interacts with help seeker's physical attractiveness.[733] A field experiment design approached subjects (60 males) for help as they walked past a building. The person seeking help was female of either low or high physical attractiveness, and appeared in either low or high need of help manipulated by severity of emergency. The stimulus person claimed a rat had bitten her, and as she spoke, she visually displayed her hand wrapped in either a clean handkerchief (low need for help condition) or a bloodstained handkerchief (high need for help condition). The amount of help provided to the person in need was the dependent variable, defined in terms of amounts of money donated. The severity manipulation resulted in more help for the high emergency condition (bloodstained handkerchief) than in the low emergency condition (clean handkerchief). An interaction resulted between manipulations of physical attractiveness and level of severity, in which physical attractiveness did not affect amount of help in conditions of low severity emergency. However, the physical attractiveness of the stimulus person did significantly affect helping behavior in conditions of high severity of emergency. Collapsing or disregarding severity levels for a moment, when stimulus persons were high in physical attractiveness, money donated was greater across the board than when stimulus persons were low in physical attractiveness.

Givers of Help

The previous section discussed research about the affect of physical attractiveness on the public's offer to help a person in need. Turning around the situation poses the question: Does a helper's physical attractiveness enhance or inhibit people who are seeking help in need of assistance? Two plausible competing hypotheses, each with reasonable probability, follow.

First, if physical attractiveness phenomenon applies in this situation, one can reasonably hypothesize that persons in need of help will ask first or more readily, the potential help givers with higher physical attractiveness for assistance rather than help givers of lower physical attractiveness. An explanation for why this hypothesis might bear out is because, throughout physical attractiveness phenomenon, robust data document higher physical attractiveness to represent greater value, kindness, and knowledge in observers' perspectives compared to lower physical attractiveness.

Second, an alternate hypothesis, if physical attractiveness phenomenon applies in this situation, is that persons in need of help will ask first or more readily the potential help givers with lower physical attractiveness. An explanation for why this hypothesis might bear out is because, consistent with data about physical attractiveness phenomenon, higher physical attractiveness represents greater value than lower physical attractiveness, which may communicate a greater social distance between average help seekers and help providers. Therefore, the seeker in this circumstance may assume a probable chance of greater rejection when asking for help from potential help givers of higher physical attractiveness, and would therefore ask first or more readily the potential help givers of lower physical attractiveness.

Physical attractiveness proves pertinent for help providers as well as help seekers. While the level of physical attractiveness, as discussed above, affects the quantity and quality of help received by help seekers, the level of physical attractiveness also affects help givers.[667] To test the effect of physical attractiveness upon help givers, an experiment presented subjects (80 in total) with two stimulus persons of either high or low physical attractiveness.

A pattern based on three relevant findings emerged from among the data. First, subjects (help seekers) sought less help from providers with high physical attractiveness compared to those with low physical attractiveness. Second, fewer subjects approached providers who were of higher physical attractiveness. Third, subjects communicated quicker and with less hesitancy when the help providers were of lower physical attractiveness compared to their counterparts. Subjects (help seekers) provided possible explanation for these differences when, upon post-interview, they reported feelings of greater uneasiness and discomfort in the presence of help providers of higher physical attractiveness. Speculation for the unease and discomfort could relate to embarrassment or anxiety not to show weaknesses and problems to someone thought to be more competent or in some other way superior. These subjects might have felt it easier to be themselves, needs and all, with help givers lower in physical attractiveness than higher. The authors conclude that, "While a 'what is beautiful is good' stereotype may in fact exist, it also appears that under certain circumstances 'what is beautiful is correct' stereotype may also exist."[667]

Friends

An article published in 1937 in the *American Sociological Review* referred to external rewards to be associated with, or even just seen with, physically attractive people.[724] Now, scores of years later, researchers increasingly identify and document these benefits, producing evidence of physical attractiveness phenomenon that people often would rather not acknowledge, not admit, and ultimately would rather deny. Despite wishful thoughts that physical attractiveness of other people in our lives is irrelevant, research reveals that one determinant of a person's own physical attractiveness is the physical attractiveness of those with whom he or she associates. Regardless of the type of interpersonal relationship or gender of the individuals, an association effect within physical attractiveness phenomenon contributes to a person's own physical attractiveness. Mere association with a person of lower physical attractiveness produces a negative social reaction,[642] whereas association with a person of higher physical attractiveness results in positive social reaction in the form of increased perceived social status.[43]

Inductive Reasoning

Be they strangers, friends, or just potential friends, we, consciously or subconsciously, value people in alignment with their physical attractiveness. As discomforting as the thought may be, people value more physically attractive surroundings, and friends are part of every person's surroundings. The less-than-explicit process that people go through in forming friends, at least concerning physical attractiveness phenomenon, represents inductive reasoning procedures.

Observe elementary school friendships, primary school friendships, and secondary school friendships, and there emerges rather discomforting patterns indicating more similarity than dissimilarity of physical attractiveness among friends. With exceptions, individuals of higher physical attractiveness form friendships with people of like levels of physical attractiveness. We all can certainly remember our sometimes-cruel school days of when the least popular, least valued kids were those also judged as least physically attractive. There might be a moderating effect in adulthood friendships, but the pattern remains prominent. People prefer to be friends with others who their community like more, value more, and, not coincidentally, are more physically attractive, compared to others who the community might like less, value less, and, not coincidentally, be less physically attractive.

In the process of forming friendships, we begin the process with inferences, at levels that reflect a combination of consciousness and subconsciousness, about another person through the informational cue dimension of physical attractiveness phenomenon. Many considerations contribute to the value of a potential friend. Intricately interwoven into substantial portions of these considerations is physical attractiveness. In these situations, an accurate alternative label for the informational cue with which we use physical attractiveness is inductive informational cues. Through rather classic inductive reasoning, we move from small to large, rather than deductive reasoning in which a person moves from large to small. Based on the smallest amount of information gleaned initially when first seeing a person, people infer substantially greater and expansive information, rather than withholding inference and judgment about a person until seeing much more about the person.

Inferences prove to be universal geographically regarding a person based on judgment of his or her physical attractiveness. In a most basic application of physical attractiveness phenomenon, in many cultures, the eyes are traditionally the gateway to the soul and symmetry between the eyes is particularly important. Folklore holds that a straight disposition of the eyes may signal that the person is not "crooked," along with an abundance of linguistic elements centering on this connection. As unpleasant as it might be to some people in some countries and cultures, people in more locations around the world, rather than fewer locations, readily assume or at least readily acknowledge the assumption that physical attractiveness is both a used and a useful informational cue. People in locations, countries, and cultures of the world, that overtly deny or downplay this use do so often on a base of noble ideals. Common to those ideals is the perspective that it is not good to judge others by appearances and especially not by the physical attractiveness dimension of a person's appearances. Despite such ideals expressed, actual words and behaviors of those expressing them appear to be only marginally less in unison with physical attractiveness phenomenon than the words and behaviors of people in other countries and cultures who are more overt in these matters.

No one can argue credibly that physical attractiveness phenomenon is not substantial in the United States. A glimpse at scholarly research findings pertinent to interactions between strangers and between friends underscores the existence of physical attractiveness phenomenon beyond the United States. A review of three Russian studies on person perception concludes that before beginning relationships, physical attractiveness serves as an informational cue among the Russian population from which personal qualities are inferred.[514] A study in France with French boys as subjects (5 to 10 years old, 64 in total) yielded similar results and confirmed the reality of the informational cue for physical appearance/physical attractiveness.[143] Youths lower in physical attractiveness, defined here primarily as a function of dress, were attributed more negative acts and more socially unacceptable behaviors, whereas their counterparts were attributed more positive acts and more socially acceptable behaviors. Likewise, researchers found confirmatory data in a study performed in Germany where expectations of another person differed according to physical attractiveness defined by facial skin appearance,[77] and a study conducted in India found women of higher physical attractiveness were perceived as more likely to hold more favorable attitudes toward feminist causes.[15]

Only Friends

People might expect physical attractiveness to be pertinent to interpersonal interactions of intimate or romantic types, but it proves also surprisingly pertinent to interpersonal interactions of friends (i.e., non-intimate interactions). Furthermore, since the quantity of most every person's interpersonal interactions includes a far greater number of relationships that are only friends, compared to spousal and other equivalent relationships, the quality of influences in this realm of physical attractiveness phenomenon takes on meaning accordingly. Like interpersonal interactions by strangers discussed above as a function of physical attractiveness, physical attractiveness of friends is analogous. The reality is that the role of physical attractiveness in determining nonromantic friendships is no less prominent than in romantic attraction, with the effects reported for both same-sex and opposite-sex friendships.

Documentation through data collected by scientific efforts is not new regarding liking among friends as an effect of physical attractiveness. As early as 1921, a study published by the *Journal of Experimental Psychology* reported significant correlation between liking and physical attractiveness.[560] Nearly fifty years later and with a much more stringent research design, an experiment investigating the effect of physical attractiveness found physical attractiveness to be the most influential variable in determining non-intimate attraction between strangers.[92] Of course, attraction between strangers is most always a necessary stage that must occur at some point between two individuals if a friendship is ever to exist between them. After nearly another fifteen years, another examination of a host of physical and non-physical characteristics concluded that physical features "are the best predictors of the attraction response."[420] A long list of additional studies have found data supporting equivalent positive relationships between physical attractiveness and interpersonal attraction.[3, 87, 141, 153, 274, 279, 363, 367, 596, 672]

At least two studies have reported findings that physical attractiveness is of lesser importance than non-physical attractiveness considerations in non-intimate friendships.[655, 718] Even though these findings cannot be disregarded, scrutiny of measures assessed (i.e., methodologies employed) is very important in instances when findings from one research project differs significantly from a large body of research findings. For example, different data can result from measures that employ gradients of disliking to liking versus a scale ranging from weak to strong. An early project, presented as a conference research paper, used a continuum ranging from disliking to liking, rather than a continuum from weak to strong liking.[424] Subjects (80 males and 80 females) presented with stimulus persons (via videotaped interview) who were either high or low in physical attractiveness and who either exhibited behavior described as pleasant or unpleasant, later indicated their liking or disliking for the stimulus persons. Data revealed an interaction between physical attractiveness and type of behavior. When the behavior was unpleasant, subjects disliked the stimulus persons in both conditions of physical attractiveness, but in the pleasant behavior condition, subjects disliked only the stimulus persons of lower physical attractiveness while expressing liking for the stimulus persons of higher physical attractiveness.

Positive effects of higher physical attractiveness on non-intimate fondness in friends-only relationships have been widely demonstrated since early physical attractiveness phenomenon research. Documented situations include (a) face-to-face interactions inside and outside of laboratories, (b) photographs in diverse circumstances, and (c) varying lengths of exposure between persons. The collected data have provided consistent results ranging from methodologies for simple exposure to photographs to periods of prolonged interaction among participants to varying lengths of exposure time to the other persons of research interest.[104] Research into nonromantic interpersonal attraction has often dealt with initial encounters, which is appropriate for research questions about potential interest in forming friends-only relationships. A variation in research methodology has involved investigating initial meetings that have the possible intent of leading to additional interactions beyond nonromantic friendship.[105]

Still another variation in these research questions concerns the effects of physical attractiveness in non-intimate friendships when the people are no longer strangers. Again, respective research shows that even after people interact person to person, the influence of physical attractiveness phenomenon persists. This persistence is not only important during the initial phases of interaction, but maintains its influence with accumulated interaction time and additional information about the persons.[104, 353] One study with children as subjects found that physical attractiveness of individuals was strongly and positively related to friendship choices following two weeks of intense social interaction.[353] Instead of a single interaction, other research into the relationship between physical attractiveness and liking has varied the number of interactions and frequency of exposure to be either 1, 2, 5, 10, or 25 times.[564] These respective data revealed that the greater the exposure frequency, the greater the magnitude of liking, and that the stimulus persons of higher physical attractiveness were liked better regardless of exposure frequency.

PERSUASIVE COMMUNICATION

Communication is the sustenance of every interaction discussed in this chapter between strangers and friends, and as discussed in the next chapter between dates and mates. Not just any communication but, more precisely, persuasive communication is the lifeblood of interactions ranging from relatively minor requests with minor ramifications to major requests with major ramifications. In addition to friends in our lives, strangers and loved ones try regularly to convince us about their ideas and wishes, some big, some small. Businesses advertise their products and services, not-for-profit organizations ask for financial donations, politicians campaign for election votes, trial lawyers advocate for clients, drivers whose cars are stopped for speeding plead leniency with arresting police, religious leaders preach to their congregations, children argue with parents for favors, government agencies send public service announcements, and so forth.

Strategic use of physical attractiveness phenomenon to persuade people carries ethical dilemmas and social responsibilities. I have discussed ethics and social responsibility, implicitly and explicitly, in many forums about the marketing techniques executed by businesses[18, 518, 529] and not-for-profit organizations[553] in the United States [168, 551] and other countries.[582, 583] More relevant to this book, I have discussed ethics and social responsibility directly as they concern using and exploiting physical attractiveness phenomenon for marketing strategy,[519, 524] as well as the focused applications used in political campaigns.[546]

Underneath the ethical and responsibility ideals, we know that people who are most effective at persuading others will reap benefits that people less effective at persuading will not. In turn, greater understanding about persuasive communication is likely to yield greater effectiveness in our attempts to persuade others and in our effectiveness to resist persuasion by others. Like most things in our lives, it is not one single factor or component but multiple components that determine the effectiveness of persuasive communication. In addition, as documented throughout this book, physical attractiveness, specifically physical attractiveness of the communicator, contributes to effectiveness or ineffectiveness of persuasive communication.

With hopes that entities whose sole purpose of existence balances on persuasive communication effectiveness and would therefore eagerly provide funds to gain greater related understanding, in the late 1970s I contacted the three largest American television networks (ABC, CBS, and NBC). I asked them for funding to help me conduct research into the relationship between a communicator's physical attractiveness and the effectiveness of persuasive communication. The Director of Corporate Projects at ABC television network headquarters responded with thoughts of personal curiosity. This television network executive posed the question, "Should a government, a corporation, or other institution consider physical attractiveness factors in determining who should present a message?" Furthermore, he pondered, "If the president of the United States should ask the vice-president, press secretary, a spouse, or some other person, depending on their physical attractiveness, to announce and garner support for a new program?" This executive posed still another question: "To gain attention and convince consumers, should the major automobile makers use different persons with different levels of physical attractiveness to announce a new car model and to announce a major recall of a particular car model?"

When seen together, these questions from the television network executive exposed the nexus between politics and commercial address, and deserved more than anecdotal observation. I then designed experiments that studied these issues as a central topic and in a manner normally required by scientific research standards and journals. It is critical in my opinion to convey to the public at large, as well as to the scientific world, knowledge in this area that helps understand the linkage or impact of the communicator's physical attractiveness upon persuasive communication effectiveness.

Need

To prosper, let alone to survive, individuals as well as organizations can improve immensely with improved understanding of the communication that flows from them to their others. Although the types of communication and delivery medium vary, substantial amounts of communication from all types of organizations and individuals are persuasive communications delivered by a communicator. Regardless of whether persuasive communication is obvious commercial advertising, noncommercial public service announcements, or personal appeals from individuals, the sender's intent is for the receiver(s)/audience to acquire that message. In other words, a primary concern is always, or should always be, to achieve persuasive communication effectiveness.

An antecedent to achieving persuasive communication effectiveness is the need to realize the environment in which an individual lives, especially in the case of both for-profit and not-for-profit organizations attempting to persuade. These organizations need to keep aware that persuasion is a process of stages, starting with the individual's comprehension of the persuasive communication, and before that, the communication must get and hold the individual's attention. Complicating a successful movement through these stages is the fact that information overload is the norm for people today. Individuals in today's society are literally drowning in a sea of information via persuasive communication attempts that bid for their attention. A consequence is that much communication becomes excessive information never noticed, attended to, or perceived, let alone comprehended en route to even having a chance to achieve the communication's goal of persuasion.

Such selective perception continues to increase in importance as the amount of excessive information continues to increase. Practitioners of persuasive communication must appreciate at least the rudiments of neurological processes explained in the early 1970s that include the human brain's ability to work as a filtration system.[509] This filtration system permits a person only to observe, perceive, and encode limited amounts of information into the mind. Persuasive communication practitioners can increase their effectiveness by keeping cognizant of the need, even in the most basic conceptualization of the brain's processing, to permeate each individual's perceptual filters. For example, *cognitive economics* is a term coined in 1979 to explain the fact that: "People are flooded by information which must somehow be reduced and simplified to allow efficient processing and to avoid an otherwise overwhelming overload."[466]

Primary Components

Who says what to whom through what channels and with what effects is a long held view about communication.[385] Stated differently, the communication process is an interaction of four major components[202]—source, message, medium, and receiver—and scientific research has long ago documented that each component affects persuasive communication effectiveness between individuals and between organizations and individuals.[440]

Without going outside the scope of physical attractiveness phenomenon into details more central to communication process and theory, a fundamental at least to note here is that, generally, the more credible the source/communicator is perceived to be, the greater the influence of the delivered persuasive communication.[134, 306, 307] Researchers define source/communicator credibility a number of ways. Three most common definitions, or dimensions, are source expertise, source trustworthiness, and liking of the source.[85, 103, 461, 544] Five formal theories detailed in my 1985 book predict and explain the relationship between the physical attractiveness of a source/communicator and the impact on credibility of the source/communicator. Those theories also predict and explain, ultimately, the impact that physical attractiveness of communicators has on effectiveness of persuasive communication:[535] attribution theory, learning theory, distraction theory, consistency theory, and selected parts of information processing theory about the human brain.

Also pertinent is the AIDA (attention, interest, desire, and action) model of advertising effectiveness whereby people move through a hierarchy of stages, from unawareness, to awareness, to liking, to preference, to the decision, action, and behavior.[517] My own published research of primary data has shown three appearance factors other than physical attractiveness documented to gain attention in a cluttered information overload environment: gender,[536] sexiness,[520] and nudity/partial nudity.[522] Indirectly related, I have conducted and published research revealing that the length of communication can also determine its effectiveness of penetrating perceptual filters erected by the human brain.[533] However, all these data suggest the impact of those appearance variables might not be as effective or robust, beyond the early stages of the AIDA model of advertisement effectiveness, as physical attractiveness.[542]

In one of my own experiments to collect primary data, I employed 542 subjects to investigate the relationship between the communicator's physical attractiveness and persuasive communication effectiveness.[528] The research was a three-factor factorial experiment with multiple values for each factor, specifically a 2 x 2 x 4 factorial design. Three interdependent variables were gender of communicators (male, female), gender of receivers (male, female), and physical attractiveness of communicators (no information, low, moderate, high). Dependent variables were a lengthy list of measures to assess perceptions of communicators (including trustworthiness, expertise, and liking as elements of source credibility) and effectiveness of persuasive communication. These latter measures included belief and recall of statements and resulting affective, cognitive, and conative attitude components.

Overall, results of this experiment revealed that a communicator's physical attractiveness might efficiently pierce the perceptual screens inherent in the human mind. With the exception of insignificant impact on recall of details due to the physical attractiveness manipulation in this experiment, the most significant and pertinent findings for this book are the consistently strong monotonic positive relationship discovered between communicator physical attractiveness and key indicators of persuasive communication effectiveness. As Figure 6-1 illustrates with primary data, higher communicator physical attractiveness caused greater communicator credibility (i.e., higher levels of perceived trustworthiness, expertise, and liking), regardless of communicator gender and/or receiver gender. Similarly, as Figure 6-2 illustrates with primary data, higher communicator physical attractiveness caused corresponding greater belief of persuasive communication and significantly more favorable effect on receivers' attitudes in terms of affective, cognitive, and conative attitude components.

Figure 6-1. Persuasive Communication Effectiveness: Communicator Credibility Elements as a Function of Physical Attractiveness

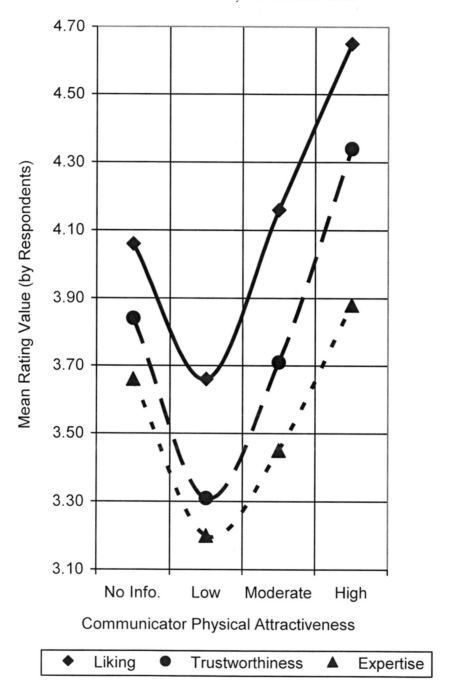

Figure 6-2. Persuasive Communication Effectiveness: Belief and Tri-Component Attitude Elements as a Function of Physical Attractiveness

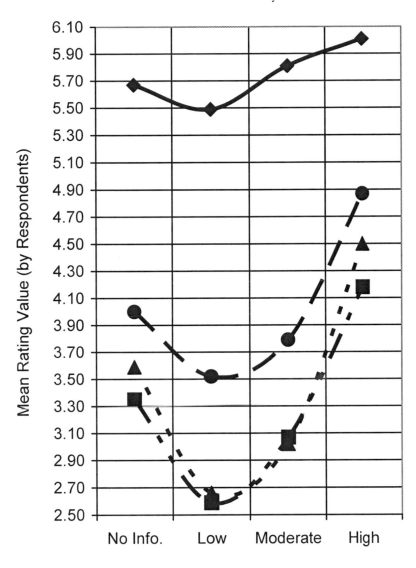

SUMMARY

Successful, fulfilling, meaningful interpersonal interactions depend on many factors, of which physical attractiveness is only one, albeit an extremely important one. While a litany of factors spanning the fields of psychology, sociology, and other disciplines influence interpersonal interactions between strangers, acquaintances, and friends, physical attractiveness is a key factor that is influential in interpersonal interactions of all types with people of all types. These types, of course, also include persuasive communication efforts, whether from friends and colleagues or for-profit and not-for-profit organizations attempting to persuade people to buy their product, vote for their election, donate money, purchase their cosmetic surgery, sign up for their military service, and so on. This influence, as distasteful as it might be to some people, means that physical attractiveness phenomenon is firmly in place, with interpersonal interaction consequences generally beneficial for people whose appearances are higher in physical attractiveness and interpersonal interaction consequences generally detrimental, or certainly less beneficial, for people whose appearances are lower in physical attractiveness.

Chapter 7

Meeting-Dating-Mating

In the wake of my recurring disappointment I'd often chide myself for thinking I'd ever be beautiful enough, good enough, or worthy enough of someone else's love, let alone my own. Who cared if I loved my own face if no one else was going to? When I walked down a street or hallway, sometimes men would whistle at me from a distance, call me Baby, yell out and ask me my name. I was thin, had a good figure, and my long blond hair, when I bothered to brush it, was pretty. I would walk as fast as possible, my head bent down, but sometimes they'd catch up with me, or I'd be forced to pass by them. Their comments would stop instantly when they saw my face, their sudden silence potent and damning. (pp. 187-188)

The major reason I was still a virgin when I graduated from college was obviously the lack of genuine opportunities combined with my crippling lack of self-esteem, but I persisted in seeing it as proof that I had lost out on the world of love only because of my looks. (pp. 206 207)

Written by Lucy Grealy at age 31 in her classic,
widely praised autobiography, *Autobiography of a Face*.[257]

INTRODUCTION

Interest in another person for a long-term, committed relationship that is beyond platonic friendship and leads to spousal partnership almost always precedes eventual mating. Regardless how humans define this interest, process, or culmination, it retains critical importance because it ultimately constitutes the perpetuation of the human. No amount of disparagement can undercut the relevance of long-term, committed spouses and equivalent partners for the human race in general and for the success of individuals in particular.

Attraction that may or may not lead to a relationship of spousal partners (which is the term used in this book to describe spouses and equivalent partners) remains complex and continues to elude thorough understanding. We do know that among the variables involved in these attractions, interpersonal interactions, and subsequent bonding of individuals, much revolves around physical attractiveness of individuals. Research documents strongly that physical attractiveness exerts its impact at every stage: from interest, attraction, courting/dating and agreement for faithfulness, to publicly recognized commitment. Publicly recognized commitment takes the form of long-standing, worldwide traditions of marriages, civil unions, and cohabitations in which physical attractiveness phenomenon proves analogously influential regardless of gender dyads. Complementing the empirical data, Lucy Grealy's autobiographical perspective cited above at the opening of this chapter underscores vividly how a person's physical attractiveness, in this case represented by low physical attractiveness of a person's face, qualifies and screens out potential meetings—let alone opportunities—that might lead to relationships of love and sexuality.

Existing physical attractiveness phenomenon research explicit to meeting-dating-mating interactions has rarely focused on sexual orientation but has ostensibly assumed heterosexual individuals. However, in light of the robust quality and quantity of research documenting physical attractiveness phenomenon, it is reasonable to extrapolate that the findings presented in this chapter and book are overwhelmingly the same pattern for individuals, couples, and groups, regardless of sexual orientations. Nothing in the scientific research findings to date suggests otherwise, while much in the less empirical data collected through acute observations suggest the same physical attractiveness phenomenon patterns within, across, and between individuals regardless of sexual orientations. Clearly, the collective research evidence justifies projection that physical attractiveness phenomenon transcends differences in sexual orientations, as it does for differences in geography, time, culture, race, age, social class, and so forth. Of course, an important frontier today is research that would explicitly investigate questions about physical attractiveness phenomenon explicit to meeting, dating, and mating among people spanning the complete length of sexual-orientation continuums.

UNIVERSAL EXCHANGE CURRENCY

A person's physical attractiveness is an important currency of exchange in interpersonal interactions of all types, ranging from volunteer help to paid employment to platonic friends to spouses and equivalent life partners. Not unlike some advertising slogans about certain credit cards recognized worldwide, people around the world recognize physical attractiveness as an accepted, valid, form of currency connected with mate and partner selection. This exchange medium is noteworthy for its universal acceptance around the world in all types of political environments. However, it is equally noteworthy for how substantially what people proclaim or admit contradicts with what they actually do in this regard. As with much of physical attractiveness phenomenon, the value of physical attractiveness as an exchange currency is commonly unrecognized and even denied, at least overtly. Despite such lack of acknowledgement, the reality is abundantly evident, readily observed, and documented throughout populations irrespective of ethnicity, gender, sexual orientations, geography, socioeconomics, or political philosophy.

In the realm of interpersonal interactions particular to spouses and equivalent partners, the role of physical attractiveness phenomenon is parallel. One might idealistically envision that although physical attractiveness phenomenon influences interpersonal interactions between strangers and maybe even platonic friends, people surely look beyond physical attractiveness when searching for and committing to a long-term spousal partner relationship. Even though people undoubtedly look for characteristics in addition to physical attractiveness of spousal partners, physical attractiveness is a barrier beyond which people must first be able to see. Second, physical attractiveness serves as a window with a screen through which people must look and which continuously affects much of what they later see, experience, and feel.

One unwritten rule, practiced throughout committed, long-term spousal partners in loving relationships beyond platonic friendships is that people trade, or exchange, their physical attractiveness for a mate's resources. With emphasis on the other person's financial, social, and status resources, exceptions rarely exist even though moderations occur. Although research discussed later in this chapter documents that same-sex spousal partners exhibit the same pattern concerning physical attractiveness as opposite-sex spousal partners, the overwhelming majority of research has investigated male and female spousal partners. This research orientation is not surprising given historical traditions and perspectives worldwide as practiced overtly for couples. Scientific research and anecdotal observation yield compatible results. While the fact discomforts many people, evidence documents that at every stage of spousal partner relationships, females customarily and effectually trade their physical attractiveness for a spousal partner's financial, social, and status resources. In turn, males exchange their financial, social, and status resources for a mate's physical attractiveness. Higher physical attractiveness essentially and rather directly yields a mate of greater financial, social, and status resources. On the other side, greater financial, social, and status resources rather directly yield a mate with greater physical attractiveness. This exchange of physical attractiveness as a valuable exchange currency is real for both females and males who enter the mating realm of human life, regardless whether their sexual orientation is heterosexual, homosexual, or some combination.

Equality of Genders

In the United States, as well as in many other countries, the role and status of women are changing in the direction of greater equality. Accordingly, differences between the genders are lessening in the realm of physical attractiveness phenomenon. Physical attractiveness for females of all ages has been of far greater importance throughout history than for males. Even though this pattern of great importance continues today, males of all ages in recent years have exhibited greater changes in concern with their own physical attractiveness compared to the changes women have exhibited in concern with their own physical attractiveness. These differential changes are particularly evident in the United States, Western Europe, certain Asian countries, and parts of South America. At the same time, in countries in other parts of the world, some movement away from extremes has occurred in the value that males and females place on physical attractiveness of mates and potential mates.

Will the role of males' own physical attractiveness some day match that of females (or even surpass females as exhibited in many animal populations where the importance of male beauty seems to exceed that of female beauty)? Future equality of males and females concerning physical attractiveness might be reasonable to conjecture from other areas of life. For example, *BusinessWeek* magazine reported in 2004 that a new study by a highly respected organization called the Committee of 200 observes women progressing slowly but steadily toward equal influence in corporate America.[299] Looking at an index of ten benchmarks—business ownership, wage parity, salaries, MBA program enrollments, access to venture capital, and so on—that committee's study "concludes that the earliest females [in the United States] can achieve equal influence is 2019." Accordingly, it seems reasonable to deduce, especially based on differential rates of increased concern about one's own physical attractiveness in recent years, that by approximately that same date, physical attractiveness phenomenon will equally apply to males and females.

An exceptional study, notable for its longitudinal perspective, collected data over a time span of more than fifty years in geographically diverse locations to assess preferences for a marriage partner.[102] That study, published in 2001, offers an invaluable cultural, evolutionary perspective built on data collected to assess mate preferences over an extended time. The data collection began in 1939 with 628 subjects and continued in subsequent years as follows: 1956 with 120 subjects, 1967 with 566 subjects, 1977 with 316 subjects, 1984/1985 with 1,496 subjects, and 1996 with 607 subjects. During these fifty-seven years of data collection, the basic exchange relationship has remained intact: females bring physical attractiveness to the mate-search-negotiation process and males bring financial resources to the mate-search-negotiation process. Within that context, however, documented changes among both males and females both include an increasing value placed on a mate's physical attractiveness as well as a mate's finances. This increase has been a greater change for the importance that males place on the financial resources of mates/potential mates, even though the relative importance of financial resources continues to be greater for females in consideration of mates/potential mates. Other changes during these more than fifty years of data collection include a somewhat decreased value among males for a partner's domestic interests and abilities, along with a somewhat increased importance by both genders for a mate's mutual love.

Finances, Status, Physical Attractiveness

As previously stated, in the arena of spousal partners, the most important assets for a man are his wealth, status, and potential status. For a woman the most important asset is her physical attractiveness, which interweaves with her age or appearance of age. Research early in the study of physical attractiveness phenomenon, in the late 1960s, established intelligence likely to be the most important determinant of occupational mobility for men,[199] but for women, research showed intelligence to be less important than physical attractiveness.[200] That era of research also confirmed that the more a man's social status exceeds that of his wife's, the more likely the appearance of his wife is exceptionally high in physical attractiveness.[200] The research found that a woman's physical attractiveness in high school remained positively correlated even twenty years later with the status of whom she marries.

Be it a high school reunion, college reunion, or most any type of reunion after an extended period, our own physical attractiveness or that of others is a concern or at least a primary topic of interest.[619] Some potential attendees whose physical attractiveness has changed unacceptably in their eyes will forego these events, yet similar others will take special measures to prepare for their attending. In a 2005 survey regarding high school reunions, 70 percent of respondents admitted to having changed their appearance to look better before attending their class reunion.[351] In this same survey, 55.6 percent of the research participants expressed intentions to increase their physical attractiveness before attending a class reunion and, "It is not just women; in fact, more men than women responded that they worked out to get in shape before a reunion" for purposes of looking more physically attractive.[351]

Despite rather dramatic changes of women's roles in society shown over the years, the roles of their physical attractiveness have remained quite constant. Ten years after the research findings discussed in the prior paragraph came forth, an investigation into the relationship between women's upward social mobility, marriage, education, and physical attractiveness interviewed more than 6,000 women (African American and white).[712] These updated survey data, with their collection controlled to allow for direct comparison with earlier research, found that both physical attractiveness and education are statistically significant for upward mobility in attaining status through marriage, regardless whether the women are African American or white. Data interactions between variables revealed that physical attractiveness and mobility for white women were strongest for women with lower education versus higher education. Conversely, data interactions revealed that for African American women, physical attractiveness and education were stronger for those with higher education compared to those with lower education.

Females, Social Mobility

For females, physical attractiveness relates significantly with their upward social mobility.[200, 679, 712] Casual observation of male and female couples, more readily apparent in some parts of the United States and the world than other parts, strongly illustrates this relationship, which is consistent with research into this sphere of life over time, cultures, and countries. From early scholarly studies up to the very latest studies, physical attractiveness provides females with upward social mobility. Earlier scientific investigations explicitly into this aspect of physical attractiveness phenomenon examined the social rank of the husband in comparison to the woman's premarital social level.[200, 679, 712] The data confirmed that the more physically attractive the woman, the more upwardly mobile she is, as measured by her husband's social class and her premarital social class. In addition, the likelihood of marriage to a man of higher social class is statistically significantly dependent, according to these data, on the woman's physical attractiveness, but independent of the woman's educational achievements.

Across Cultures

In an investigation across cultures, one international study investigated marriage partners among people in the United States (970 in total), Russia (327 in total), and Japan (222 total). These data showed that men care more than women about their partners' physical attractiveness while women care more about their partners' status and other characteristics not directly related to physical attractiveness.[287] Another international investigation into mate preferences of male and female advertisers in Hungary examined personal advertisements.[57] The study looked explicitly at mate preferences concerning physical attractiveness for both males and females interested in short-term dating and long-term mating. Other variables studied were age, family commitment, financial situation, marital status, personal traits, preexisting children, and socioeconomic status. The sample of subjects was personal advertisements (1,000 in total with 500 placed by males and 500 placed by females) published in two national daily newspapers. Data analysis used multiple matrixes, not especially pertinent to discuss here. Among the results, the data documented that males strongly prefer mates of high physical attractiveness and females most prefer mates with significant financial resources and high status. The researchers conclude that both males and females convey rather standard exchange trade-off strategies in their mate preferences. Males with greater financial resources and social status make greater demands for mates with higher physical attractiveness. Females with higher physical attractiveness make greater demands for mates with greater financial resources and social status.

Another internationally oriented study asked subjects in North America (648 college students) and in the People's Republic of China (735 college students) to complete a questionnaire about their preferences for a mate's characteristics.[705] Among the many findings of this study, the most pertinent to physical attractiveness phenomenon is that in both cultures, North America and China, compared to females, males place significantly greater value on physical attractiveness for a mate, whereas females place greater value on earning potential, social status, and wealth as important characteristics for their mate. Other gender differences exposed in these data were consistent with the emphasis on more traditional gender roles in China than in North America. The strongest cultural differences revealed are higher preferences for a mate who "wants children" among American subjects compared to the Chinese subjects, whereas, compared to the American subjects, the Chinese subjects express greater value for a mate who is "creative and artistic" and a "good housekeeper."

A study performed in Germany further pursued the question of gender differences for preferred characteristics among males and females in mate selection.[75] The title of this scientific journal article—"Rich Man and Beautiful Woman? Two Studies on Sex Differences in Mate Preference"—states well the results from the data collection and analysis. The first research project performed a content analysis with personal advertisements (200 in total, with 100 placed by males and 100 placed by females). It found that income and status were more important to females for their mates than to males for their mates, whereas physical attractiveness was more important to males for their mates than to females for their mates. The second research project, described as a direct participation study, asked subjects (202 in total) at a university in Germany to rank a list of sixteen characteristics in terms of relative importance for a potential mate. Among these data was the finding that, again, importance of a mate with high physical attractiveness was significantly more important for males than for females.

Necessity and Luxury

A recent series of three studies with innovative procedures investigated the long-established exchange differences for males and females concerning physical attractiveness of themselves and their mates.[408] These studies, conducted in the United States, refined findings and focuses of prior studies by differentiating between necessities and luxuries. Two of the studies gave budgets to subjects with which to purchase characteristics to design their ideal long-term mates (rather than relatively brief dating relationships) and the third study used a mate-screening paradigm to record the sequence in which subjects inquired about a potential mate's characteristics. The collective data from these three studies uncovered that males and females both ascertain whether potential mates possess sufficient levels of necessities before other characteristics, defined in this study as luxuries, are checked out or ascertained. With that knowledge established, males considered high physical attractiveness of a mate to be a necessity and not a luxury, whereas females considered status and resources as necessities for their mates.

Short-term, Long-term

Another related dimension of investigation has been gender differences when considering physical attractiveness and other characteristics in a mate or partner for the short-term (i.e., "dating someone more than once without an expectation of a short-term or long-term relationship").[665] This is also true for the long-term (i.e., "dating someone for a long time with the possibility, but not certainty, of marriage"). Among the many findings that reveal similarities as well as some dissimilarities, those of particular pertinence are below:

- The preferred characteristics of each gender emphasized different perspectives about the same evolutionary explanation that focuses on reproductive value. For males, the reproductive value of a mate as a driving force in their mate preferences equated most with their interest in the mate's physical attractiveness. For females, the reproductive value of a mate was also a driving force in their mate preferences, but it equated most with the mate's financial earning/income capacity.
- Males and females are more discerning when selecting mates/partners for the long-term compared to the short-term. Males and females differ in their desired characteristics for short-term relationship partners and long-term relationship partners. Overall, males and females exhibit the desire for a long-term mate to have interest in having children, while the desire for a short-term partner emphasizes a mate who has an exciting personality.

Learned Behavior

Learned behavior as a dimension of cognition plays a formidable role in physical attractiveness phenomenon. Women might innately prefer the best-looking men, but yield to social pressure and exigencies to rate economic status and stability higher in their preference for mates.[205] This trade-off has been determined to be an exigency for women, whereas studies of human sexuality conclude repeatedly that men compared to women place more emphasis on physical attractiveness of potential mates not only in short-term relationships but also in long-term relationships. The scholarly implication for choice of mates is that women exchange their own physical attractiveness for non-appearance considerations of mates. Certainly, more blatantly obvious in some parts of the United States and in some parts of the world, nonprofessionals' observations readily bear out this exchange to be factual albeit revolting to the ideals of some people. A research project conducted in 2001 scientifically explored this dimension of mate selection by women in the United States and found significant evidence of the continuing pattern.[728] The data confirmed that even today, women in the United States trade off physical attractiveness, their own and that of their mates/potential mates, for other resources in their mate selection decisions. Those research data also explored the question whether women pursued less physically attractive men as permanent mates with regard to the prospect of cheating by one's mate. Results found that women believe men of higher physical attractiveness are more likely to cheat or leave a long-term relationship and at the same time "showed no aversion" toward men of higher physical attractiveness as a potential long-term mate. These data found that men believe women of higher physical attractiveness are no more likely to cheat in a long-term relationship compared to women of lower physical attractiveness.

Explanation via Theory

One explanation offered by evolutionary theory about the gender differences above rests on "mate value," which is the total value signaled by a person's features most pertinent to the potential contribution to a mate's likelihood of successful reproduction. In this explanation, a woman's value as a mate, her mate value, pivots on physical attractiveness of her appearance that translates into innate reproductive drives. Mate value in this context for a man as a mate, pivots on his financial resources and status that translate into ability to provide best for his mate's reproductive well-being. However repugnant this theoretical explanation about physical attractiveness might be, casual observation and anecdotal testimony supports it. Testimony from Cindy Jackson, a woman approaching 50 years of age, internationally renown for her unique experiences with cosmetic surgery and someone who considers herself a true feminist for taking control of her life, wrote in her 2002 autobiography, "Most of us are still not aware of the extent to which men are influenced by the way a woman looks. And, politically correct or not, it's still a man's world— [at least] for the time being."[316] That same page quotes Teresa Wiltz, author of a *Chicago Tribune* article, to have written, "Society's obsession with beauty is the beast you can't ignore. Whether you have it in abundance or it forever eludes you, you can't deny its power."

Context

People intertwine their preferences for a spousal partner, with psychological and sociological factors. These factors include character traits such as dependency and dominance within both individuals of spousal partner relationships. These intrinsic traits contribute to a person's composition that affects preferences for spousal partner relationships. Surprisingly, however, a potential mate's physical attractiveness exerts values, even when viewed along with intrinsic character traits explained. When searching for a mate who possesses certain intrinsic character traits, his or her physical attractiveness influences judgment about those intrinsic traits both before knowing the traits and after. Consciously or subconsciously, learned or inherited, an observer does not or cannot dismiss context on these intrinsic traits (i.e., physical attractiveness and physical attractiveness phenomenon) no matter how great a desire to do so.

A part of context when dealing with physical attractiveness is that the same observer may see the same stimulus person at different times and rate the individual differently at each time, even when the appearance of the stimulus person has not changed. People cannot escape the influence of context upon either their intrinsic or extrinsic traits. Context considerations that can change evaluations about a person's physical attractiveness and, thus, change preferences for that person are speculated to consist of a long and growing list, with many documented cases. These include physical attractiveness of other individuals associated with a stimulus person, the last person(s) seen before an observer sees a stimulus person, the music playing in the room, quality of air in the environment, and even the amount of time remaining to begin the meeting-mating process in pursuit of a spousal partner.

Gender Differences

Differences between males and females are highly attended to among scholars, scientists, and many others, with bountiful documentations disseminated through everything from popular media to scholarly scientific journals. Among the equalities, inequalities, constants, changes, and political agendas the relationship between physical attractiveness and romantic attraction has proven largely unwavering, both within and between the genders. Overall, physical attractiveness is still more consequential for evaluation of females than it is for evaluation of males.[44, 45] Greater emphasis on feminine physical attractiveness compared to masculine physical attractiveness continues. It is a fact illustrated throughout visual media and appearance/physical attractiveness industries such as cosmetics, fashion, and clothes that permeate much of United States culture, western European culture, and the majority of cultures and subcultures in countries around the world.

While females traditionally are more concerned with their own physical attractiveness than males are concerned with their own physical attractiveness,[722] the trend is changing ever so slowly. According to the author of *Appearance Obsession: Learning to Love the Way You Look*,[326] research published in 1986 revealed only 18 percent of males were concerned about their physical attractiveness, and even they expressed lack of effort to improve it. By 1993, actual sales numbers showed men spending 300 to 400 million U. S. dollars on body building steroids and substantially more than that amount on hair replacement products. The author of *Appearance Obsession*[326] further reported, a study in 1993 with 306 male subjects, that found men check their looks in mirrors as often as women do, and men spend similar amounts of money each month on clothes as women. These equalizing patterns have continued today with differences now not so much of a qualitative order as a magnitude order: Women still spend more money, but men are becoming increasingly engrossed with their own physical attractiveness.

Association, Platonic

Incontrovertible evidence details that people accord rewards to individuals based on their level of physical attractiveness and even to individuals based on the level of physical attractiveness of those with whom they associate. People accord additional interpersonal and intrapersonal compliments to both males and females who associate with partners of higher physical attractiveness, spousal and otherwise. The attributions to these persons are regularly more positive internal traits like greater confidence, sociability, and likeability.[642, 673]

Physical attractiveness of a partner in a platonic friendship as well as romantic relationship can overpower status or prestige of either person within that partnership. Furthermore, a person with high physical attractiveness can overcome or raise low prestige and status of the person while low physical attractiveness can also overcome or lower a person's otherwise high prestige and status. An experiment paired the same female with male stimulus persons either high or low in physical attractiveness.[638] The male stimulus person also underwent vocation manipulation as either a medical student or sales clerk. After viewing the paired female and male stimulus person (in a photograph), along with information about his status/prestige via vocation manipulation, subjects (88 in total, 44 males and 44 females) evaluated the female. Females evaluated most positively were those paired with a male stimulus person of higher physical attractiveness. These more positive evaluations included higher ratings of her physical attractiveness, intelligence, self-confidence, friendliness, talent, likeability, and excitement. The authors stated that manipulation of the status variable did not affect as many attributes as did the physical attractiveness manipulation, and that this experiment's physical attractiveness manipulation caused greater effect on female subjects than on male subjects.

Similar to the effects revealed above for male partners' physical attractiveness upon perceptions and evaluations about females, physical attractiveness of female partners affects perceptions and evaluations of males. An experiment investigating the effects upon a male as a function of a female partner of higher or lower physical attractiveness produced significantly more positive evaluations of males when paired with females of higher rather than lower physical attractiveness.[446] Subjects (males and females) rated males higher in physical attractiveness as well as more positive on non-appearance attributes when stimulus materials paired the evaluated males with females higher in physical attractiveness. Again, manipulation of a partner's intelligence had less impact than manipulation of a partner's physical attractiveness.

Association, Spousal Partners

Effects caused by association with persons of higher and lower physical attractiveness extend beyond platonic relationships into romantic or spousal partner associations. Two experiments with different methodologies to assess the impact of a romantic partner whose physical attractiveness is either high or low uncovered similar findings.[642] The first experiment paired a male stimulus person described as either boyfriend (i.e., intimate relationship) or simply a male friend with a female of higher or lower physical attractiveness. After presentation with one experimental treatment condition, subjects (56 in total, 28 male and 28 female) evaluated the male stimulus persons. Pairings of romantic/intimate association, compared to association as friends, accentuated both the positive and the negative impact of a partner's physical attractiveness. Subjects evaluated the male stimulus person least favorably when paired as a boyfriend with a female stimulus person of lower physical attractiveness and most favorably when paired as a boyfriend with a female stimulus person of higher physical attractiveness.

The second experiment was similar to the first but instead of using ratings by others, asked subjects (40 males) to participate in a role-playing situation that asked them to evaluate how others would perceive them based on their paired partner. The procedure paired each subject with a female described as a girlfriend (i.e., intimate relationship) or simply a female friend of each male subject. Appearance of females was either higher or lower physical attractiveness, and was never discussed with the subjects. Consistent with results from the first experiment, physical attractiveness accentuated impact due to a romantic association. Without explicit mention of the female partner's physical attractiveness, subjects said that people would perceive them most favorably when assigned to the experiment condition of romantic female partner of higher physical attractiveness. Subjects said that people would perceive them least favorably when paired romantically with a female of lower physical attractiveness. These male subjects believed that a physically attractive female partner would increase ratings of the subject's own physical attractiveness, as well as enhancing perceptions of his own intelligence, friendliness, confidence, talents, and appeal as an exciting person.

The greater emphasis that males place on a partner's physical attractiveness is consistent over time. It confirms research indicating a higher correlation between dating popularity and physical attractiveness for females. However, the lack of such statistically significant correlations for physical attractiveness for males[61, 317] is not simply "natural." Sociobiologists explain that "sexual selection favors males who attend to a female's physical attractiveness, and females who attend to a male's material resources,"[317] but this effect is in flux. Witness the increased number of professional women, greater competitiveness for attractive men (the crudely so-called boy toy phenomenon), and the social factor of accommodating a more family-oriented masculine identity. The association factor may be the most important contributing factor to the seeming change in sex-effect trends. Males still consider physical attractiveness of their partners more important than females consider it for their partners,[141, 418] and females still consider financial security above physical attractiveness.[418] However, changes in men's attitudes and activities generally correspond with changes in women's ability to be the one who chooses, which is largely the result of women's increasing financial independence.

Furthermore, lower physical attractiveness for males has effects very similar to lower physical attractiveness for females, demonstrating that physical attractiveness might be more constant than assumed. Baldness, for example, correlates at a statistically significant level with perceptions of being less confident, less interesting and even less friendly, with greater hair loss compounding the correlation.[109, 418, 537, 538] Shortness (lack of stature) yields negative effects both romantically and economically, while empirical data show that sleek, muscular bodies are highly correlated with physically attractiveness and the perception of masculinity,[418] implying that the opposite conditions yield corresponding negative effects.

Research has directly addressed the sex differences with regard to the role that physical attractiveness plays in determining heterosexual attraction. Subjects (177 males and 177 females) asked to judge the importance of physical attractiveness in interpersonal situations show that male subjects consider physical attractiveness significantly more important than female subjects do.[462] However, surveys conducted independently have concluded that women are also significantly and increasingly interested in the physical attractiveness of men. In the 3,370 women's personal advertisements in *Los Angeles Magazine*, from January 1982 through 1989, about one-third specified physical characteristics, including "must have hair," "trim," "fit," and, less euphemistically, "no beer guts," with the oft-repeated code VGL—very good looking.[418]

Some have lauded Internet technology as a means to reduce the power of physical attractiveness in the dating-mating process that leads from meeting to dating to spousal partnership. One study of 568 participants from randomly selected Internet newsgroups reported committed long-term relationships lasting two years in 57 percent of cases, with the research suggesting that physical attractiveness, as a gateway factor, might be of lesser importance arising from an online acquaintanceship.[136, 444] However, online dating companies such as Yahoo! Personals and Match.com routinely declare the opposite, that is, that a picture will generate eight times the response of advertisements without one. Ultimately, bottom-line analysis and conclusion do not support the notion of a decreasing significance for the role of a person's physical attractiveness in considering a potential spousal partner met online. Despite logical and maybe wishful thinking that knowing a person's intrinsic traits before seeing the person diminishes the importance of that person's extrinsic physical attractiveness once seen, physical attractiveness in each of stage of meeting-dating-mating is ever increasing in significance through today's modern technology and social mores.

Three Sequential Stages

Categorizing the meeting-dating-mating process that leads to spousal partners into three sequential stages is helpful. This three-stage categorization is particularly helpful to probe research pertinent to the context that each stage poses and imposes for the role of physical attractiveness within romantic attraction beyond platonic friendship. Although characteristics such as the length of each stage vary for individual partner circumstances, it is accurate to say that every spousal partner relationship involves these stages and this sequence. At each stage, of course, one or both individuals might decide for myriad reasons not to advance into the next stage, but the implications for the role of physical attractiveness remain, regardless. The first of these three stages is the time prior to and including the first meeting. The second stage is the period of becoming acquainted, characterized by dating and courting. Third stage is the period of marriage or equivalent committed relationship.

Contrary to various ideals, research shows convincingly that the role of physical attractiveness in the sequential three-stage process remains significant throughout the stages. While "first impressions" might presumably dominate early encounters—and conventional wisdom might predict a limiting effect on latter interactions—research findings do not support pedestrian notions generally held that physical attractiveness subsides in importance during the romantic progression. Instead, research reveals enduring effects of surprising force. Furthermore, preconceptions that limit many reactions within the "first impression" category are often clearly physical attractiveness stereotypes. Thus, physical attractiveness retains its importance as a primary determinant of mutual romantic attraction, regardless of means to become acquainted, lapse of time involved, number of meetings, and even of competing negative information.

FIRST STAGE: PRIOR TO, AND AT, FIRST MEETING

The importance of the initial encounter cannot be overemphasized because there must always be a first encounter for later encounters to follow. Components that determine the first encounter then become important by their own power to increase and decrease the probability of such meetings. Physical attractiveness phenomenon commands that physical attractiveness is a personal characteristic that is operating even before the first meeting occurs. One research project to assess the role of physical attractiveness within romantic attraction asked subjects (316 in total, 148 females and 168 males) about their preferences for marital partners.[501] Unlike additional research germane to this first stage of the meeting-dating-mating process that occurs before the first actual meeting, this project did not manipulate characteristics of certain stimulus or target persons in order to assess the impact upon subjects. Very importantly, results from this project add to the robustness of data found consistently through a variety of research designs. For a marriage partner, males and females both preferred, by a significant margin, people of higher physical attractiveness rather than their counterparts of lower physical attractiveness for a marriage partner.

Other research has gone beyond only asking preference in general without reference to a specific individual. One research project arranged a limited amount of interaction time between subjects and stimulus persons and then assessed preference at that point of interaction.[153] Stimulus persons of higher and lower physical attractiveness interacted with subjects (40 males and 40 females) in a waiting room for five minutes, after which the preference to date was assessed. The stimulus persons behaved in a standardized manner with all interactions recorded and later analyzed. Actual behavior of subjects did not vary significantly in the presence of the stimulus persons, who did vary in physical attractiveness. However, subjects later expressed greatest preference for potential dates with the stimulus persons of higher physical attractiveness. This research project concluded that because actual behavior presented by stimulus persons did not vary and yet subjects' preferences did vary, physical attractiveness plays a role within romantic attraction even before meeting for the first time, and even after knowing at least some information about the person beyond his or her physical attractiveness.

Preferences and Desires

Definite correlations function between physical attractiveness and predisposition to initiate a meeting between two potential suitors. Subjects (48 males) in one study indicated their desire to date a stimulus female person, but, unknown to them, the experiment research conditions manipulated physical attractiveness, attitude similarity, intelligence, and population.[67] These males expressed substantially greater desire to both date and be friends with a female stimulus person who was higher in physical attractiveness than was her counterpart. Extending this desire, males in another research project exhibited significantly greater likelihood to ask a female for a date when she was of higher physical attractiveness versus lower.[555] Subjects (60 males and 60 females), when assessed through an experiment using a bogus tape recording and snapshot to manipulate the stimulus person's physical attractiveness and social status, further revealed significantly greater desire to date a potential partner who was not only of higher physical attractiveness but also was attributed a likely more favorable personality.[671]

Matches and Mis-Matches

Ideal desires for a spousal partner may differ from less-than-ideal desires; in other words, realistic desires expressed in actual intentions for a spousal partner. The difference is between irrational fantasies that ignore improbabilities of mismatched spousal partners and rational ideas that concede higher probabilities of matched spousal partners. Early research in the explicit study of physical attractiveness phenomenon revealed indications that males in some scenarios prefer a female stimulus person of less than the highest level of physical attractiveness. These preferences are likely a product of an internal calculation (conscious or subconscious) of probabilities about likelihood of acceptance or success based on the female's physical attractiveness.

Field research, rather than highly controlled laboratory research, conducted in four bars/nightclubs frequented by single men and women was used to investigate social strategy explicit to ideal aspiration desires versus realistic matching desires, also known as matching hypothesis.[242] According to an ideal aspiration hypothesis, the women of higher physical attractiveness would receive more frequent approaches by men in a singles bar than would women who were less physically attractive. Alternatively, according to a realistic matching hypothesis, men in the nightclub would more frequently approach the women of less-than-highest physical attractiveness. This second hypothesis assumes the males in the nightclub emulate a normal bell-shaped distribution of physical attractiveness, in which only a small portion are higher in physical attractiveness and the majority are average or below-average in physical attractiveness. Collected data supported a realistic matching strategy, and not an idealistic aspiration hypothesis. The women observed reflected a wide range of levels of physical attractiveness, and men did approach significantly less frequently those women whose appearances were lower in physical attractiveness than counterparts of higher physical attractiveness.

Research has identified a rather well-established matching strategy for physical attractiveness among opposite-sex couples in the meeting-dating-mating process leading to spousal partner relationships.[487, 563, 575] An extension of that spousal partner/romantic attraction research examined if matching occurs within nonromantic attraction, such as among platonic friends.[112] To disguise the physical attractiveness variable of interest, researchers asked subjects their willingness to participate in a psychological project dealing with written communication, and then asked these subjects to ask friends to participate. The researchers then randomly selected subjects (24 males and 24 females) from a much larger population of volunteers. When they arrived, the selected subjects along with their friends were asked to rate their degree of friendship and to pose for a full-length, front-view, smiling photograph. Another group of subjects (male and female) who did not know the research purpose or the people in the photographs, worked independently with a 7-point scale to rate ninety-six photographs of stimulus persons, randomized for each rater. Data analysis showed statistically, with considerable inter-judge reliability, there was a significant relationship between physical attractiveness and extent of liking between the non-intimate, same-sex friends. Furthermore, a series of chi-square tests showed significant similarity of physical attractiveness between close same-sex friends for both males and females. The authors concluded their results presented a valuable extension of related research reporting similar results with opposite-sex dyads in romantic attraction relationships.

Male Perspective

Males are less accurate than females in assessing their own physical attractiveness, but not absolutely. Testing the question about ideal and real desires, male subjects (72 in total) participated in an experiment in which target females/potential dates represented three levels of physical attractiveness and two levels of acceptance or rejection.[311] These males selected the more physically attractive female when assured of acceptance but not otherwise. When asked about the likelihood of female acceptance, the males estimated those females of higher physical attractiveness to be less likely to accept them as a date. Furthermore, the males' self-ratings of physical attractiveness revealed a consistent, evaluative, thought pattern of matching versus mismatching for them. Males self-rated as low in physical attractiveness estimated their chances to be low with a female of high physical attractiveness.

Female Perspective

Females are substantially more accurate, or realistic, when it comes to questions about one's own physical attractiveness and physical attractiveness phenomenon, but it is largely relative rather than absolute. Females do mirror males when it comes to the question about ideal and real desires. Self-ratings by females about their own physical attractiveness relate significantly with their perceived desirability of a potential male date. More so than males, females (138 subjects in this research project) exhibit a significantly inverse relationship in that the perceived desirability of a male date decreases as the self-ratings of a female's own physical attractiveness increases.[266]

A complement to the finding reported in the prior paragraph is the discovery that the self-rated physical attractiveness of a female, combined with her self-calculated probability of acceptance for a date with a target male who is substantially higher in physical attractiveness than she is, determines her interest in that target male. Females' rationale about their probabilities for a particular spousal partner who possesses a certain level of physical attractiveness is analogous, albeit more accurate, to the thinking indicated by males about their chances for a particular spousal partner.[632] A series of three experiments concluded that females use both physical attractiveness (their own and that of target persons) and probability of acceptance in indicating their desire to seek a date with a male target person. Overall, without factoring other considerations into the process, females indicate significantly higher desire to date a potential target male who is higher in physical attractiveness versus lower.

Race and Ethnicity

Even though interactions, perceptions, and tolerances have changed dramatically toward greater acceptance and equality for all people in the United States during the past thirty years or so, already by the 1970s, research showed physical attractiveness phenomenon transcended race. Shown empirically then in the arena of spousal partners, today it is, without a doubt as shown by anecdotal observation, the state of affairs throughout society. Individuals of higher physical attractiveness from a non-majority racial group, more readily transcend societal barriers, ceilings, and socioeconomic ranks than their counterparts of the same race who possess lower physical attractiveness.

Even with different definitions and inherited characteristics concerning determinants of physical attractiveness, agreement is significant among races when speaking about who is high and who is low in physical attractiveness. It is reasonable to hypothesize that the relative importance of physical attractiveness over race, as well as over social class, discussed in the prior paragraph, has increased. Today, its relative importance is likely even greater due in part to lessening discriminatory perceptions and improved tolerance of racial differences in the spirit of encouraging racial diversity. Quite early in the research endeavors to explicitly explore physical attractiveness phenomenon, an experiment introduced race as a rival characteristic to test the relative importance of physical attractiveness in the desirability of dating partners/potential dating partners.[21] It investigated whether physical attractiveness or race had a greater impact on dating choices made by white subjects. Subjects were white (43 male and 35 female university students), and the stimulus persons were either black or white with either high or low physical attractiveness. Results in this test, very likely contrary to what conventional wisdom might have projected, revealed that physical attractiveness rivaled race in determining dating desirability. Largely consistent with overall patterns of physical attractiveness phenomenon, male subjects assigned more weight to physical attractiveness of stimulus persons than race of stimulus persons, whereas females subjects in this situation assigned less weight to physical attractiveness than to race. At the same time, subjects in this experiment were not willing to accept an actual date with the subjects whose race was different from theirs.

Exceeding Socioeconomics

Physical attractiveness of individuals is a powerful means by which people transcend social classes and socioeconomic levels more than is generally acknowledged. Individuals who are born and raised in lower financial, educational, and socioeconomic levels of classes but who possess higher physical attractiveness are more likely to break social barriers and ceilings than counterparts also born and raised in the same lower circumstances but whose appearance is lower in physical attractiveness. Such ascension is not a matter of certainty, but despite how distasteful or objectionable it is, it certainly is a matter of probability in significant favor of those higher in physical attractiveness. The explanation might rest on interdependencies between physical attractiveness, self-confidence, and basics of physical attractiveness phenomenon as pertinent to theories of social reward exchanges.

Research specific to physical attractiveness phenomenon certainly offers definite explanation for meeting-dating-mating preferences. Subjects (100 males and females) viewed a videotaped interaction between couples described as boyfriend-girlfriend. Unknown to the research subjects, researchers varied the physical attractiveness and intelligence of the female partners.[446] One dependent variable was the evaluation of the male partner. Although intelligence manipulations affected a few perceived attributes of the male partner, higher physical attractiveness of his female partner significantly affected favorably all ten dependent measures about the male. Extrapolating, these findings offer explanation that if mere association of a romantic partner affects perceptions of individuals, these perceptions likely influence the role that physical attractiveness plays in the first stage of the meeting-dating-mating process even before moving into the second stage of romantic interactions.

Research discussed in the prior paragraph offers support for theoretical explanation based on social rewards for exchanges between partners, consistent with prediction and explanation by physical attractiveness phenomenon and related values placed on physical attractiveness. While that research focuses more so on males regarding physical attractiveness for their female partners, other research complements these findings with data that reveal the parallel pattern of rewards for females regarding physical attractiveness of their male partners. Research investigating this question conducted an experiment with subjects (36 male and 36 females) interacting in opposite-sex and same-sex social exchanges.[435] These data showed that both men and women of higher physical attractiveness provide greater rewards to their partners in social exchanges regardless if the interaction is platonic or otherwise. This effect in these data occurred significantly more within opposite-sex as opposed to same-sex exchanges. The researchers, based on subsequent testing accordingly focused, concluded that issues of erotic pleasure underlies the reason for this pattern of different social rewards among the dyads of different gender composition. They propose the reason for these greater social awards is that higher physical attractiveness of the other person in these dyads equates with underlying thoughts of greater erotic pleasures.

Intricacies

Effects of physical attractiveness among males and females in a meeting-dating-mating context are not always straightforward within physical attractiveness phenomenon. Subjects (144 females) asked to evaluate paired male and female stimulus persons (presented via photographs) of high and low physical attractiveness revealed that a male of high physical attractiveness was perceived most favorably when paired with a female of high physical attractiveness.[281] In the same direction, subjects rated a male of low physical attractiveness more favorably, including more physically attractive, when paired with a female of high physical attractiveness compared to low. The female subjects rated female stimulus persons of high physical attractiveness as most-liked, and perceived them to possess the most favorable personal characteristics as a good person when associated with a male of low physical attractiveness. Table 7-1[281] illustrates this contrast.

Table 7-1. Ratings by Females of Males and Females Paired with Opposite-Sex Partners of High and Low Physical Attractiveness

	Male of High Physical Attractiveness	Male of Low Physical Attractiveness
Female Partner of High Physical Attractiveness	Females evaluated males in this experimental condition most favorable and highest in physical attractiveness.	Females evaluated females in this experimental condition as most-liked and perceived them to possess the most favorable personal characteristics as a good person.
Female Partner of Low Physical Attractiveness	No significant results were reported.	Females evaluated males in this experimental condition least favorable and lowest in physical attractiveness.

The original researchers propose preferential advantages as an explanation for this difference in the data. These female judges may have perceived that females of high physical attractiveness exploit their inherited beauty with male partners of high physical attractiveness. In contrast, the highly physically attractive females paired with a male partner of low physical attractiveness are good persons with favorable personal characteristics for performing a sort of charitable deed. Unfortunately, this original research project did not fully manipulate the gender of judges in order to gain a more complete understanding about intricacies within this dimension of male and female interactions. For example, research conducted more recently, which documents reactions and perceptions by females toward females who vary in physical attractiveness, might offer an alternate explanation in terms of an underlying envy or jealousy.

In some ways near to the above research project in design and findings, but not the same, is the effect of same-sex platonic partners and partners by proximity who are nearby strangers of varying levels of physical attractiveness. To expand upon opposite-sex findings regarding effects of a partner's physical attractiveness, a research project manipulated four experimental conditions for situation pairings for individuals of the same sex.[347] These association pairings included either friendships or unassociated relationships described as merely in the presence of the stimulus person. After exposure to one of four experimental conditions, subjects (159 in total) evaluated stimulus persons (males and females) paired with a same-sex stimulus person of either low or high physical attractiveness. Statistical data analysis revealed significant interaction between type of association and level of physical attractiveness. In the unassociated experimental condition, subjects rated the stimulus person as more positive when paired with a same-sex partner of low physical attractiveness. However, in the associated condition, the stimulus person received more positively ratings when paired with a same-sex partner of high physical attractiveness.

SECOND STAGE: GETTING ACQUAINTED AND DATING

Early physical attractiveness research explicit to the meeting-dating-mating process of spousal partners contributed most often to the dating stage. Collectively, that research confirms that this sphere of life is not exempt from the impact of physical attractiveness phenomenon. One reason that higher and lower physical attractiveness is correspondingly beneficial and detrimental to a person's meeting-dating-mating situation might be because of the quantity of opportunities to date. People of higher physical attractiveness, males and females, have more social contact that translates into more dating opportunities than do their counterparts of lower physical attractiveness.[367] One research project found that the physical attractiveness of females and the amount of social contact with the opposite sex correlated significantly ($r = .45$), while the correlation for males was not significant ($r = .08$). The number of social contacts with the opposite sex among males in this study was not statistically different for those whose appearances were high and low in physical attractiveness. The authors concluded that males of low physical attractiveness are able to compensate with non-appearance considerations more so than females, but since physical attractiveness is a much greater factor for females' appeal to the opposite sex than it is for males, corresponding non-appearance compensations are not feasible. The collective research about physical attractiveness phenomenon might also explain differences due in part to differences in motivation, confidence, and actions exhibited within individuals of higher and lower physical attractiveness.

Differences in social contacts that provide opportunities that can lead to dating, but which precede actual dating, convert accordingly in favor of people whose appearances are higher in physical attractiveness. Field research that monitored dating activity of subjects (college males and females) during an entire year revealed that effects of physical attractiveness phenomenon operate strongly in the dating stage of interpersonal interactions.[61] That research shows higher physical attractiveness to correlate positively for both males and females, with substantially higher correlation values for females ($r = .61$). The lower correlation values for males ($r = .25$) underscore that, even though a male's physical attractiveness is important in dating, males of lower physical attractiveness have greater opportunity in this dimension of life than females of lower physical attractiveness. Although the gap might lessen and even possibly disappear as males and females approach equality throughout their lives and in the future, opportunities at this time to compensate through non-appearance factors are greater for males of lower physical attractiveness than for females of lower physical attractiveness.

Convergence of Data

The diversity of design, procedures, techniques, topics, and people serving as participants or subjects in research into physical attractiveness phenomenon contributes immensely to the strength of research data, findings, conclusions, applications, and validity to extrapolate and generalize. In addition to data collected through research methodologies based on procedures for experiments, less-obtrusive research techniques have probed and confirmed physical attractiveness phenomenon in natural dating relationships.

The data converges to form a robust collection of consistent findings. For example, analysis of collected survey data revealed a positive correlation (r = .61) between physical attractiveness of females and the number of dates they had during the past year.[61] Those of higher physical attractiveness did have differences in their actual dating practices and experiences than those of lower physical attractiveness. Another study, not focused on a single year, found that women of higher physical attractiveness date more, have more friends, are in love more, and have more sexual experiences compared to women of average or lower physical attractiveness.[336]

Physical attractiveness phenomenon in actual relationships is not limited to females, as replicated in research with both genders. Regardless of gender, physical attractiveness correlates with the frequency of dates.[241] Within dating, physical attractiveness correlates positively with experiences, including sexual experiences, for, again, both males and females.[157] These experiences extend down to young adulthood into adolescence. A longitudinal study on sexual attitudes (focused on data from 91 middle-class adolescents) found that those lower in physical attractiveness were less likely to have a steady dating partner than their counterparts of higher physical attractiveness.[131]

Imbalanced Partners

In a dating relationship, levels of and differences in levels of physical attractiveness of partners appear to affect behavior of each individual. As exhibited throughout physical attractiveness phenomenon, the dating partner with an appearance higher in physical attractiveness tends to have the upper hand, so to speak, in other non-appearance areas of their relationship when level of physical attractiveness is imbalanced between the two partners. Measures of physical attractiveness, romantic love, and dominance obtained from dating couples (123 couples total) revealed that relative differences in physical attractiveness produce significant effects within the relationship of couples.[151] Collected data revealed that the person who considers the other person more physically attractive tended to express greater love for that partner than that person expressed in return. This person also indicated greater submission to a partner who was relatively higher in physical attractiveness as opposed to lower.

Actual differences yield the same effects as perceived differences. Instead of dealing with perceptions of partners, other research has considered the impact of actual discrepancies of physical attractiveness within couples. That research reveals that dating couples who begin their relationship shortly after meeting tend to have small discrepancies of physical attractiveness.[213] Those dating relationships that begin later or more slowly after initial meeting have greater discrepancies of physical attractiveness between the partners. These findings came from data based on couples (49 couples total) described either as "dating steady" or "in love." *Fast pace* was defined as couples who began dating within three months of meeting, and *slower pace* was defined as couples who began dating after knowing each other for at least eight months.

Evidence of correlations between dating progression, or lack thereof, and physical attractiveness of partners lend credence to hypotheses of causality. Research into interpersonal dating problems ranging from jealousy to eventual breakups found significant patterns concerning physical attractiveness of individual partners. Among the subjects (123 couples total) assessed and described in terms of the stage of their relationship: (a) casual dating, (b) serious dating, (c) cohabiting, and (d) engaged to be married.[735] Particularly for couples in the first two stages—casual dating and serious dating—the partner with relatively higher physical attractiveness had more opposite-sex friends and tended to worry less about his or her partner's potential involvement with another person. This issue of worry is consistent with findings from a different study that examined potential connections between jealousy and physical attractiveness. It found a positive correlation between expressed jealousy and physical attractiveness of persons tangentially associated with an existing relationship.[639]

Jealousy is, unfortunately, an emotion that arises from time to time in some dating relationships, and more times than coincidence might dictate it can correlate with the influence that physical attractiveness can exert during dating. Research into dating asked subjects (61 couples total) about their: (a) commitment to their partner, (b) amount of time spent with their partner, (c) amount of time spent arguing, (d) length of relationship with their partner, (e) partner's physical attractiveness, and (f) desire to maintain the relationship with their partner.[366] The most important factor for commitment level was amount of time spent together, and perceived physical attractiveness of partners was the second most important factor. The directional interdependencies of the variables investigated complicate these findings. Amount of time spent together may cause a commitment level, while commitment level may cause the amount of time spent together. Likewise, perceived physical attractiveness (as compared to actual physical attractiveness) may cause a commitment level, and commitment level may cause perceived physical attractiveness.

Endings

The dating stage eventually ends, sometimes when individuals move in the same direction into a much longer-term relationship as spousal partners, or sometimes when they move in separate directions with one or both individuals deciding to part ways from the other. Research confirms that in some instances where one or both individuals decide to part ways, physical attractiveness exerts a significant role in the breakup. The research project discussed above, which surveyed 123 couples, conducted a follow-up study nine months later with the couples described earlier as either casually dating or seriously dating.[735] This follow-up revealed physical attractiveness was predictive of dating progress. Those couples with greatest imbalance in physical attractiveness tended to break-up at a higher rate than did couples with fewer imbalances in the physical attractiveness of each individual.

Another exploration to shed light on the role of physical attractiveness in dating break-ups constituted a two-year longitudinal study to examine factors that predict dating partners who do not progress to be long-term committed spousal partners.[298] Among these subjects (composed of college students), desire to breakup was seldom mutual; female partners were more likely to perceive premarital problems, and female partners were more likely to initiate breakups. Collected research data identified that imbalance of physical attractiveness between the partners was a significant factor, along with numerous other factors, contributing to breakups of dating partners.

Varying Interactions

Although interactions vary in type and length of time within research investigating dating, findings about physical attractiveness prove steadfast throughout. Variations in length of time studied, range from minutes to hours to months without yielding variations in the findings about the importance of physical attractiveness at the dating stage of interpersonal interactions.

Length of Time

While some research has explored the connection between dating and physical attractiveness by questioning individuals with no time of interaction (i.e., before ever meeting); other research questioned subjects after interacting literally a few minutes to become acquainted.[37] Researchers paired subjects (61 males and 61 females) with a partner of the opposite sex for a few minutes to interact and to become acquainted. Afterwards, they rated their own physical attractiveness and that of their partner. Subjects also estimated how their partner would rate the subject's own physical attractiveness. Unknown to the participants, the research question of interest regarded how the physical attractiveness rating of a person (subject) by a potential dating partner with whom the person had interacted for a few minutes would affect desire of the first person to date the potential partner. To investigate this research question, researchers later gave subjects bogus rating values that supposedly were the partner's rating of the subject's physical attractiveness. Researchers then asked subjects to indicate their liking and desire to date the other person as a potential partner. Subjects stated greatest liking for and most desire to date potential partners whose physical attractiveness ratings of the person (subject) exceeded, or at least equaled, the subjects' own self-rating of physical attractiveness.

The first study explicit to physical attractiveness phenomenon and dating employed an interaction time of several hours.[725] The type of interaction was a dance that used a computer procedure to pair individuals/subjects into couples. Afterwards, the participants completed comprehensive questionnaires. Regardless of one's own appearance, the partner's physical attractiveness was the most important determinant of whether the subject liked the partner and expressed interest for additional interaction. Another study several years later also used a computer-dating service procedure.[156, 157] Subjects (150 in total) again expressed that the most significant predictor of meeting-dating-mating attraction was each of their respective rating of the partner's physical attractiveness.

Number of Times

In addition to varying the length of time for interactions regarding dating and physical attractiveness phenomenon, research has varied the number of times that interactions occur in a dating context. Using a computer pairing process similar to that used above in the research project held at a dance, another research project restricted to one encounter the number of interactions for the computer paired partners, with no limit on interaction time.[434] As with data collected through other research procedures, this project concluded from data after this one encounter that the only reliable predictor of dating desirability was the perceived physical attractiveness of partners.

Further exploration of this topic—especially in light of findings about desirability after one interaction—hypothesized that increasing the number of interactions at the dating stage of a relationship might decrease the role of physical attractiveness. A reasonable speculation is that personality information that surfaces after the first encounter might assume a dominant role in attraction at the dating stage of a relationship. This means that non-visual information would cancel or override the effects of physical attractiveness experienced after the initial encounter. However, the research concluded that data from couples (26 in total) who had a series of five encounters showed that, even though personality plays a role in attraction at the dating stage, the physical attractiveness variable has a continuing and non-diminishing effect on attraction in the context of dating.

Time of Measure

Physical attractiveness maintains its role in dating as measured two to four weeks after an initial brief interaction.[354] Through a unique, highly controlled research design, researchers paired subjects (males) with stimulus persons (females) of high or low physical attractiveness and then separated the individuals after an initial brief interaction. Following a lapse of two to four weeks after the initial interaction, researchers questioned subjects about themselves and their brief interaction partners. More male subjects (unknowingly paired earlier with a partner of high physical attractiveness) reported they remembered more details about appearance, thought more often about their partner in the interim, and had a continuing feeling that they liked her than did the other subjects (unknowingly paired earlier with a partner of low physical attractiveness).

Findings from many other research projects conducted early in the study of physical attractiveness phenomenon support this pattern for physical attractiveness and dating throughout the later stages of dating partners and even into the stage of committed long-term spousal/marriage partners.[61, 84, 105, 156, 311, 487, 637] Research documents that such feelings of attraction in the dating stage, and even in far more advanced stages of the meeting-dating-mating dimension of life, stem from significant links between the physical attractiveness of one's partner/potential partner and assessed sensations of love[151, 558] and sex appeal.[117]

THIRD STAGE: LONG-TERM SPOUSAL PARTNER COMMITMENT

When people move into the third stage of the meeting-dating-mating dimension of life, which is a long-term spousal partner commitment, physical attractiveness phenomenon does not cease to be a factor for them. Research data confirm that the importance of physical attractiveness exhibited earlier and elsewhere in their lives continues similarly throughout stages of long-term commitment to a spousal partner. This continuation is not surprising given that individuals who rate themselves higher in physical attractiveness tend to view the entire dating-mating interaction aspect of life more positively, and, probably not coincidentally, they tend to possess greater confidence to attain their wishes than their counterparts of lower physical attractiveness.[554]

Actions might speak louder than words, or maybe actions simply demonstrate overtly what individuals feel covertly. Just as individuals of higher physical attractiveness approach the dating-mating experience more positively than do individuals of lower physical attractiveness, once they are in a long-term spousal partner commitment, those individuals of higher physical attractiveness also approach public situations with their partner more positively. Moreover, if public intimacy displayed by married couples is in some way a valid gauge of satisfaction with the marriage, then a positive relationship exists between physical attractiveness and marriage satisfaction.[277] An unobtrusive research methodology used to observe subjects (558 married couples) in a field setting found that the more physically attractive the couple, the more likely they were to exhibit intimacy in public.

Satisfaction Spanning the Years

Physical attractiveness phenomenon is robust, even enduring, within marriage. This is true regardless of the marriage length. The importance of physical attractiveness does not fade as people move from meeting and dating stages to the marriage stage. Analogous to the two earlier stages, physical attractiveness phenomenon continues to pervade interpersonal interactions throughout the third stage of meeting-dating-mating dimensions of life. Based on the research data collected for a doctoral dissertation the author wrote, "it can be concluded that physical attractiveness is important to the marriage relationship, at least for the first fifteen years."[732]

Findings about the affect of physical attractiveness upon marriage satisfaction hold steady for different measures of physical attractiveness. Although observers of a person's physical attractiveness reveal significant agreement, physical attractiveness is still an esthetic with no absolute standard that definitively defines high and low levels. This consideration is particularly vital in marriage research because familiarity with a person influences evaluation about that person's physical attractiveness. Researchers worked with subjects (22 middle aged married couples married an average of 15.4 years) to assess physical attractiveness through three independent measures: judges who did not know the stimulus persons, self-ratings by each stimulus person/subject, and ratings by the spouses.[487] Researchers administered the Locke-Wallace Marriage Adjustment Scale to measure marriage satisfaction and reasonably concluded that the data revealed physical attractiveness to be an important aspect of marriage satisfaction among these subjects. For these subjects, another finding was that the physical attractiveness of the individuals comprising each couple was very similar (i.e., matched).

Congruency of self-judgment about physical attractiveness and judgment by the spouse differs between the genders and may underlie or at least align with marital satisfaction. Research data from couples defined as married long-term (about five years) or married short-term (about one year) found that wives, regardless if married long or short-term, express significant concern about whether their husbands agree with the wife's self-ratings of physical attractiveness.[38] Husbands, by contrast, regardless if married long-term or short-term, did not express similar concern about perceptions held by the wives about the husband's self-ratings of physical attractiveness. Review of research literature, combined with data collected directly from married couples for a doctoral dissertation, offers meaning about the consequences contained in these congruency measures between self-ratings and ratings by spousal partners.

It found that emphasizing a partner's physical attractiveness is associated with marital satisfaction. Individuals who emphasize physical attractiveness of their spouse to a greater extent possess greater marital satisfaction than those who give less emphasis to physical attractiveness of their spouse.[732]

Satisfaction Spanning the Ages

Overwhelmingly, years of marriage and ages of marriage partners are interdependent. Exceptions occur due to societal shifts and, on rare occasions, elderly people are newlyweds, but generally within an entire population older people are those married longer. As with the number of years of marriage discussed above, physical attractiveness is a valuable ingredient among marriage partners regardless of age: young, middle age, or elderly. Beyond issues and differences concerning matching levels of physical attractiveness between male and female marriage partners, the genders differ with regard to the link between physical attractiveness and satisfaction within their marriages. These variations in satisfaction are not surprising given the greater emphasis for physical attractiveness of females in nearly every population.

Ultimately, satisfaction in marriage is a fact of life that aligns with physical attractiveness phenomenon for all ages of people; and it is a fact that discomforts people who hold wishful thoughts to the contrary. A previously mentioned research project investigating marriage satisfaction studied couples composed of middle aged males and middle aged females (all of whom were married an average of 15.4 years), and found differences in satisfaction based on, or at the least aligned with, their partner's physical attractiveness.[487] These data for married males in middle age uncovered significant correlation between marital satisfaction and perception that the wife was substantially higher in physical attractiveness than the husband was, but these data for females in middle age did not expose a corresponding pattern. Complementing these findings, as previously stated, the data showed the individuals within each couple to be similar (i.e., matched) in their level of physical attractiveness.

Research with couples composed of partners at older ages, beyond middle aged, produces comparable findings. These subjects (32 middle-class couples) ranged in age from 64 to 86 years old.[563] Among these older individuals, with a research procedure similar to that used above to examine middle aged couples,[487] the results revealed that physical attractiveness correlated with marriage adjustment among these elderly couples, who, furthermore the data revealed, were matched closely for levels of physical attractiveness. As with other research, these data revealed a gender difference. The husbands' satisfaction with married life was more highly correlated with his partner's physical attractiveness than was the wives' satisfaction with married life correlated with her partner's physical attractiveness.

Research about physical attractiveness and marriage satisfaction has spanned the entire age continuum. In fact, one project gave a survey about the body to a massive number of couples representative of all ages.[60] Subjects completed a 109-item survey that included questions investigating the relationship between physical attractiveness and marriage satisfaction. Explicitly controlling for gender and age distributions to equate with the United States population distribution, the researchers randomly selected 2,000 questionnaires from a pool of completed questionnaires submitted by more than 62,000 respondents assumed to be readers of the *Psychology Today* magazine. Among the findings from this very large collection of data, marriages with all ages of partners (as well as spanning all number of years in duration) appeared less stable when the physical attractiveness of partners was not similar and more stable when the partners were at similar levels of physical attractiveness.

Matching Hypothesis

Matching strategies, or outcomes, emerge consistently and frequently from the data collected in studies of marriage and physical attractiveness phenomenon. Described as people aligning with other people whose level of physical attractiveness is similar to their own physical attractiveness,[63] the matching hypothesis within physical attractiveness phenomenon functions at the mating stage as well as the stages of meeting and dating. Regardless of underlying cognitions aligned with perspectives, expectations, preferences, and desires, people ultimately align with partners who exemplify quite well the matching hypothesis within physical attractiveness phenomenon; that is, of course, in the meeting-dating-mating context in which substantial imbalances of financial resources, status, and physical attractiveness of individuals are not involved.

Research data confirm what may be somewhat intuitive, or otherwise cognitively comforting, concerning a matching strategy or outcome executed by married people or those involved in other analogous long-term spousal partner commitment. While research data reveal that people at the meeting and dating stages seek partners at levels similar to their own levels of physical attractiveness, further research data reveal significant similarity of physical attractiveness exists between partners within marriage, regardless of ages of individuals or duration of relationships. As referenced above, this matching situation has been revealed while working with couples married short-term (defined as one year), long-term (defined as five years),[38] or even working with couples whose marriages averaged 15.4 years in duration.[487] Likewise, as referenced above, data from married couples revealed the same matching effect for people described as middle aged[487] and older (64 to 86 years old).[563]

Lasting Force

Research has well established that despite conventional wisdom and wishful thoughts, the value of physical attractiveness continues well beyond the initial encounter of males and females leading to long-term committed spousal partners. The impact of physical attractiveness profoundly governs first impressions leading to long-term relationships, let alone the determination of whether the necessary meetings even occur to provide opportunity for a first impression. With those barriers and blockades maneuvered in the context of physical attractiveness phenomenon, the impact of physical attractiveness extends throughout the long-term relationship beyond the interactions that serve as a prologue. When photographs of marriage partners (36 in total) were intermixed, subjects (20 males and 20 females) were asked to sort the individual photographs into nine levels of physical attractiveness.[637] These data uncovered a positive correlation between physical attractiveness of husbands and wives. Marriage partners appeared to make their selections more often than not based on a matching or realistic strategy compared to some aspiration or other strategy.

The collective research literature supports well the existence of this matching effect for physical attractiveness in serious dating and marriage.[115, 486, 672]

Extrapolation from research data about the personality characteristics of marriage partners foretells the physical attractiveness characteristics and, as expected, similarity is the rule. Research conducted as early as the 1930s identified personality similarity at levels significantly greater than chance among marriage partners.[618, 622] This similarity parallels the similarity, or matching, identified in a number of studies with a number of research designs for physical attractiveness in marriages, even after substantial durations of marriage. One research project selected two dissimilar samples of married couples and discovered similar findings that supported the matching hypothesis, and documented it to be stable within and across generations.[575] Subjects between 19 and 31 years old who were recently married formed the first sample, and older married couples, not recently married, between 34 to 64 years of age, made up the second sample. Both samples were Americans of European ancestry, consisting of 55 couples from mainland United States and 72 couples from Hawaii.

Complexities

Evidence of the matching hypothesis might seem initially to conflict with evidence that males place greater importance on their partners' physical attractiveness than do females. Despite well-documented differences in value placed on a partners' physical attractiveness by males compared to females, execution of matching strategies at the long-term commitment stage of spousal partners is more the rule. First, it is true that males do place more importance on their partner's physical attractiveness than do females. Second, it is true that males, at least idealistically and certainly more overtly than females, do prefer the best-looking females to females of less physical attractiveness. However, evidence in support of the matching hypothesis shows that these ideal preferences among males commonly appear to convert, likely through a cognitive process by which people consciously or subconsciously calculate expected outcomes for interacting with persons along the physical attractiveness continuum. It is reasonable to deduce that this cognition considers experiences and now assumes probabilities for rejection by females higher in physical attractiveness compared to females lower in physical attractiveness. As a result, males presumably convert their idealistic (low probability) preferences into more realistic (higher probability) choices. Outcomes are then consistent with the matching hypothesis through which the level of physical attractiveness of men and women in long-term spousal partner commitments tends to resemble their own level of physical attractiveness significantly more often than chance occurrence.

Actual physical attractiveness of marriage partners illustrates well the matching hypothesis at work, but perceived physical attractiveness between the partners is not always straightforward. One research project found females overstate the match, or similarity, of their marriage partner's physical attractiveness, and males understate the match by exaggerating the physical attractiveness of his spouse.[685] Males, well known to place greater importance on physical attractiveness of their partners, might be attempting to resolve their cognitive dissonance for "settling" with a marriage partner with less-than-preferred physical attractiveness. These males also might be attempting to enhance their own perceived value by being with a partner of greater value. Furthermore, these males might be actually exhibiting a rather complicated form of matching hypothesis. The explanation might be that these males, as they genuinely overrate their own physical attractiveness, now attempt to proclaim physical attractiveness of their spouse to be higher than reality, in a manner that inflates the physical attractiveness of his female spouse so it becomes equal to his own.

Endings

In the case of couples that do not last, physical attractiveness plays a role throughout dating and marriage up to the end, be it a formal ending of legal divorce or some other ending. Research in this area deals with both extramarital affairs[283] and divorces.[82] Research focused on extramarital affairs and physical attractiveness grew up from similar procedural research by an investigator who had found people developed different impressions of spouses in extramarital affairs if love was absent or present in the affair and if children were absent or present in the marriage.[282, 284]

Researchers investigating physical attractiveness and extramarital affairs concluded that "…when individuals have affairs, their physical attractiveness affects not only how they are perceived but also the perception of their spouses and the other parties to the affairs."[283] To determine this influence of physical attractiveness on people's impression of spouses connected to an extramarital affair, researchers presented subjects (128 unmarried individuals, 64 males and 64 females) with one of four vignettes describing a male and female married couple. One-half of the vignettes described a husband having an affair outside of marriage and the other half described a wife having an affair outside of marriage. Researchers manipulated the physical attractiveness variable by describing the cheating spouse "as much more attractive than the other spouse in half the conditions [vignettes] and much less attractive in the other half."

Overall, the statistical main effects show, as might be expected, impressions were less favorable for a cheating spouse compared to non-cheating. More focused statistical interaction effects show a significant influence of physical attractiveness on the impressions of a spouse. When the cheating spouse (regardless of whether the vignette referenced this person as the wife or the husband) was lower in physical attractiveness compared to higher, he or she was rated significantly less interesting, less sexually exciting, and less sensual. In impressions of the other person involved in the affair with the cheating spouse, when the cheating spouse was higher in physical attractiveness compared to lower, male subjects rated the other woman in the affair as less good and less sensitive and, surprisingly, the other man in the affair as more good and more sensitive. Comparably, when the cheating spouse was lower in physical attractiveness (regardless if wife or husband), female subjects rated the other person in the affair as less sensitive and less good than when the cheating spouse was higher in physical attractiveness.

Research that focused on divorce and physical attractiveness began with subjects (279 individuals, 118 males and 161 females) reading a two-page profile that described divorcing couples. These profiles described a marriage of five years with no children that was ending due to either incompatibility, adultery by the husband, or adultery by the wife. Measures assessed the subjects' perceptions about the divorcing partners while in the marriage and after the marriage ended. In the marriage, spousal partners whose physical attractiveness was portrayed as higher than their partners' were seen "as significantly more poised, interesting, sociable, independent, warm, exciting, and sexually warm than the unattractive spouse."[82] Subjects perceived the spouse of higher physical attractiveness in the divorcing couples, particularly if it was the wife, as (a) having greater opportunity and temptation for extramarital affairs, (b) not as likely to divorce a second time, and (c) more vain than her counterpart of lower physical attractiveness. The data revealed that subjects did not perceive a spouse of higher physical attractiveness to be more responsible for the divorce, and the subjects did not recommend different financial settlements according to physical attractiveness of the spouses. However, the physical attractiveness of spouses and ex-spouses did significantly affect subjects' perceptions of spouses in their post-divorce stage of life. Subjects perceived the divorced spouse portrayed to have higher physical attractiveness than that of his or her spouse, to have an easier time finding a new spouse (especially for the divorced wives), and more likely to remarry, regardless if the person was the ex-wife or the ex-husband.

SUMMARY

Akin to interpersonal interactions between strangers and platonic friends, a person's physical attractiveness via physical attractiveness phenomenon exerts a powerful influence, albeit distasteful to some people, in relationships oriented toward loving, committed spousal partnerships. Meeting-dating-mating outcomes, whether successful or unsuccessful but which are intended to lead to long-term committed spousal partners, depend on many factors, especially physical attractiveness. Contrary to conventional wisdom and wishful thoughts, physical attractiveness is a key factor with influence that spans each stage of the meeting-dating-mating process. Physical attractiveness even exerts its influence before the first stage, before the first meeting ever occurs between eventual potential spousal partners.

Chapter 8

Today's Generations Tomorrow

[N]o excuse is needed for treating this subject [physical attractiveness] in some detail...What it all turns upon is nothing less than the composition of the next generation...It is not the weal or woe of any one individual, but that of the human race to come, which is here at stake.

British naturalist and theorist
Charles Darwin in the 1800s quoting German
Philosopher Arthur Schopenhauer, concerning
the importance to understand and conduct
scientific research about physical attractiveness.[164]

The bottom line on this vast research enterprise is that looks matter significantly whether considering how mothers treat their babies; one's job prospects, friendship and mateship opportunities, or salary; and how one is viewed by others. [Physically] attractive people get more attention and other investment from others, are viewed more positively in general. Perhaps the most robust and replicable finding in all of social psychology is that looks really matter.

Summary conclusion expressed by two authors, one
American and one European, in a scientific article published
in the scholarly journal *Evolution and Human Behavior*.[695]

INTRODUCTION

The first perspective above concerns importance to understand and to conduct scientific research about physical attractiveness with rather explicit relevance to the role of physical attractiveness in conceiving children. More importantly, children of course form all generations and, thus, the role of physical attractiveness in turn provides a foundation, or framework, pertinent to the documented specifics stated in the second perspective. Within this context, it becomes important to understand perceptions, beliefs, and experiences of younger generations today because those will be the perceptions, beliefs, and experiences of older generations tomorrow.

Juxtaposing the two above perspectives provides convincing insight about tomorrow's role of physical attractiveness phenomenon for generations to come. Certainly, for the generation of today's children and unarguably for sequential generations, physical attractiveness phenomenon starts its impact early in life and then contributes to its continuous promulgation into future generations. Research documents considerable impact of physical attractiveness throughout childhood, continuing to young adulthood and then beyond, all setting the stage or ensuring the stage for continuation of physical attractiveness phenomenon throughout future generations. Consider for a moment that no aspect of child development is more vital for long-term success in life than intelligence. Of course, interpersonal communication-interaction skills, as well as physical health, are also important for success. Although children inherit their intelligence and interconnected abilities, environments in which children grow contribute significantly.

With rare exception, professionals agree that children internalize environments to a substantial extent. These children of course grow into young adults, carrying their internalizations with them, including sometimes a negative consequent of higher physical attractiveness. A research project involving 203 young women in Canada found that people possessing "objective physical beauty" (defined by others' ratings rather than self-ratings) based on facial physical attractiveness had higher "self-report measures of perfectionism, neuroticism, and weight preoccupation."[167] However, not all children are passive recipients of differences perceived about them based on their physical attractiveness. Children of different levels of physical attractiveness appear also to possess actual differences within themselves, beyond the differences perceived about them. In fact, the role of physical attractiveness in shaping future generations may be multifaceted whereby children of higher physical attractiveness may not only be perceived and treated more favorably, but their style of attempting to persuade others may be more effective as well as different from children of lower physical attractiveness.

Actual Difference

Research to explore physical attractiveness phenomenon and children has on occasion stepped away from experiments and surveys and employed unobtrusive procedures to collect data through observations in natural settings. Unobtrusive observations of natural play have revealed differences between children with differences in physical attractiveness. Unobtrusive recording of behavior of subjects composed of children (males and females, ages 3 and 5 years old) in one study revealed children of higher physical attractiveness were less active and played more often with feminine toys than their counterparts.[379] The five-year-old children of lower physical attractiveness in this study exhibited more aggressive behaviors such as hitting peers more frequently, than did the children of higher physical attractiveness. These behaviors observed in natural play lend at least indirect credence to ideas that persuasion or influence strategies and achievements differ between children of different levels of physical attractiveness.

Direct evidence gained from research explicitly addressing physical attractiveness of children and the strategies they employ with the intent to persuade others reveals that people, in this case children, of lower and higher physical attractiveness employ different influence strategies and experience different levels of success in their persuasion attempts. In an experiment to collect information about persuasion attempts, researchers asked subjects (75 fifth and sixth graders, 10 to 12 years of age) to persuade another child of similar grade and age to eat a bad-tasting cracker.[183] The research procedure encouraged motivation of subjects through a small monetary payment for successful outcomes; measured physical attractiveness of subjects with peer consensus based on photographs; and paired partners with subjects of either high or low physical attractiveness unknown to each other.

Results from this research project reinforce other findings about intrapersonal realities emanating from persons with different levels of physical attractiveness. First, with no outside coaching or instruction about how to go about persuading their partner to eat the bad-tasting cracker, the subjects of different levels of physical attractiveness exhibited different persuasion strategies. Second, subjects of different levels of physical attractiveness accomplished different levels of persuasion success. Overall, children of higher physical attractiveness most successfully influenced behavior of their partners in this experiment, particularly when paired with opposite-sex partners. Within this overall effect, female persuaders were more successful when paired with male receivers than were male persuaders paired with female receivers. These children attempting to persuade partners exhibited the following specific strategies in direct relation to the physical attractiveness variable:

- Male children of higher physical attractiveness were assertive but not aggressive (according to the researchers) and attempted more to coax in the form of reassurance and pleading, compared to the males of lower physical attractiveness as well as to both types of females. These males were least successful with male receivers due to a style (according to the researchers) that evoked ambivalent reactions within receivers that reduced compliance.

- Male children of lower physical attractiveness used more direct, aggressive, and commanding behaviors in the form of physical threats when attempting to persuade in this experiment, compared to males of higher physical attractiveness as well as both types of females. This finding substantiates data from an earlier study by the same first author that found aggressive behavior to be more characteristic of children of lower physical attractiveness than higher physical attractiveness.[181]

- Female children of higher physical attractiveness were the most successful at persuading their opposite-sex partners in this experiment, compared to females of lower physical attractiveness as well as both types of males. These females, at the same time, exhibited the least persistence, the least force, and the fewest number of influence attempts.

- Female children of lower physical attractiveness were more assertive but less successful at persuading their partners when compared to females of higher physical attractiveness. These females of lower physical attractiveness were not significantly different from the males of lower physical attractiveness in their success with the same-sex and opposite-sex partners.

Perceived Difference

The above documented difference for persuasive style seems inborn, but earlier environments complete with earlier perceptions and experiences may have shaped it. In fact, the environment of a child at all ages impacts abilities perceived about that child by others, and through dynamics of self-fulfilling prophecy, also known as the Pygmalion Effect, impacts the child's actual abilities. Physical attractiveness is a prominent force with heavy impact in every child's environment, documented to include perceptions of abilities emerging from hospital nurses, parents, peers of schoolchildren, and teachers at all levels of experience. Likewise, a child's physical attractiveness likely influences intelligence during his or her developing years, which according to physical attractiveness phenomenon research begins at birth and continues throughout elementary school. In this context, the earliest ages investigated have been premature infants.[142] That research asked nurses who regularly attend to needs of premature infants to rate intellectual abilities of infants. Subsequent data revealed significant correlation ($r = .90$) between physical attractiveness of a premature infant and evaluations about likely intelligence.

Central for the thesis of this book, the physical attractiveness of even infants exposes them to bias as a function of their physical attractiveness, defined most appropriately as cuteness at this young age. Research uniformly confirms that infants receive differential treatment consistent with physical attractiveness phenomenon with benefits to those whose appearance is higher in physical attractiveness and detriments to those whose appearance is lower in physical attractiveness.[573] Older children, who are either higher or lower in physical attractiveness, experience the same pattern of benefits or detriments as children of younger ages.[9, 137, 343] In turn, research reports this same pattern between a child's physical attractiveness and the evaluation of his or her social status and behavior.[9, 11, 719] Even parents tend to exhibit different expectations of their own children depending on their child's physical attractiveness. Without calling explicit attention to research interest in physical attractiveness, researchers find that parents expect their more physically attractive children to be more popular, more likely to succeed, and to experience greater personal and social successes.[12]

While almost all the documented impacts of physical attractiveness phenomenon flow in the direction from others toward and into children, research shows that preferences and actions based on physical attractiveness of other people also flow from children who make corresponding inferences and decisions. Very young children, even newborns during their first few months of life, exhibit different choices in alignment with values normally associated with different levels of physical attractiveness. When measured by the interaction of infants with adult caretakers, more physically attractive faces maintain attention longer and more intently compared to physically unattractive faces.[396, 567] These choices consistent with the generally documented physical attractiveness phenomenon values occur uniformly among babies, and they operate without cultural values put forth in beauty magazines or instilled by other media exposures often thought to convey certain values. This lends credence to notions and theories that physical attractiveness phenomenon causes natural or inherited cognitive decision-making.

INFANTS AND PRESCHOOLERS

Research documents rather unequivocally the differential treatment for children during early formative years based on their physical attractiveness. Often unknowing it and/or denying it, adults express preferential evaluations and perform preferential actions toward children whose appearance is higher in physical attractiveness, or cuteness. This situation is revealed in studies with infants four and eight months old,[297] three to thirteen months old,[294] and three months old.[294] These empirical data are not surprising, and are in fact understandable, given the perspective of ethological theory concerning caretaking dynamics,[197, 415] which is consistent with these empirical data and can be interpreted to predict that adults will give preferential treatment to infants of higher physical attractiveness and contrasting treatment to infants of lower physical attractiveness. This situation then leads to postulating questions concerning whether a child's level of physical attractiveness aligns or does not align with child abuse. Of course, an equally immediate quest that arises is the quest to discover what determines physical attractiveness in order to identify, minimize, and eventually eliminate the disparate negative treatment.

To understand the impact of appearance of children in terms of physical attractiveness phenomenon, research efforts strive to identify specific dimensions of each physical attractiveness component and the means of determining the evaluation of that component. These efforts began in earnest in the 1970s by attempting to identify actual dimensions of physical attractiveness, or cuteness, in the case of infants. For stimulus persons, one study used photographs of fifty infants, with ten infants for each of five ages: three months, five months, seven months, eleven months, and thirteen months.[296] After judging the level of physical attractiveness defined as cuteness at this age for each infant, the researchers measured fourteen facial features and concluded that quantitative measurements can predict perceived physical attractiveness of an infant. Those infants perceived as most cute are those most likely to have a large forehead, large eyes, and large pupils with short and narrow features.

Ethological theory proposed in the 1940s by Konrad Lorenz provides an unplanned framework for research and knowledge pertinent to how physical attractiveness phenomenon applies to very young children.[415] This theory generally hypothesizes that identifiable characteristics of human infants elicit certain caretaking behaviors in human adults. One study in physical attractiveness phenomenon examined adult preferences as a function of forehead height and forehead curvature of infants.[308] The manipulations involved four variations normally displayed in profiles of infants, to which subjects' data indicated distinct preferences for profiles described as infantile shape as opposed to adult shape. These results are consistent with the work of another researcher who found that the infant head shape viewed most physically attractive is the one most characteristic of younger infants.[22]

Another investigation into physical attractiveness concerning infants focused on the pupil size of their eyes.[352] Stimulus persons were infants (represented by photographs of their faces). Subjects were supermarket shoppers (ten females) shown four photographs of an infant and asked to select the most physically attractive infant. Researchers did not tell subjects that the only difference among the four photos was the size of the infant's pupils— set at four levels. To assure uniformity between stimulus persons, investigators altered the pupils of the photographed infants by mechanical means and then reproduced the photos described as natural in appearance for each of the four experimental conditions: dilated pupils highlighted, dilated pupils not highlighted, constricted pupils highlighted, and constricted pupils not highlighted. Again, without identifying interest in the research variable of pupil size, resulting data revealed that the infants judged most physically attractive were those with constricted pupils highlighted.

SCHOOLCHILDREN

The impact of physical attractiveness phenomenon extends beyond a child's infancy. It occurs throughout the whole and very important school environment, from the direction of teachers, parents, and other children. This impact of physical attractiveness upon children is particularly noteworthy because time spent in school is one of the most influential periods in life; school experiences commonly remain with individuals throughout their lives. During this time, individuals learn social messages in addition to formal academic information. One social message presented convincingly, albeit probably not consciously, is that people in authority treat persons of different levels of physical attractiveness differently. Physical attractiveness research provides compelling data that, throughout the educational milieu, those higher in physical attractiveness generally elicit expectations that are more positive and receive preferential treatment over those of lower physical attractiveness.

Teachers are certainly pivotal in the lives of students. Research most directly pertinent to physical attractiveness and education attends to teachers' perceptions, teachers' expectations, and teachers' treatment of children with regard to their educational abilities. Perceptions underlie conscious and subconscious actions, and perceptions held by teachers are a critical topic that has received the majority of research on the role of physical attractiveness within educational environments. Another category of research goes beyond perceptions to investigate actual realities. Still another set of studies, albeit scant in number, explores whether actual educational performance differs according to physical attractiveness of children. In addition, other research, also scant, addresses perceptions held by schoolchildren about their teachers based on differences in physical attractiveness of teachers.

Preschool

Within a few years after infancy, children move into preschool environments replete with physical attractiveness phenomenon. In a study that controlled or concealed interest in physical attractiveness extremely well, preschool teachers were interviewed with regard to initial teacher expectations for students.[7] Variables studied included physical attractiveness, sex, and race of preschool children. Those preschoolers receiving less positive ratings were, respectively, boys, children of lower physical attractiveness, and black students compared to girls, children of higher physical attractiveness, and white students. These data revealed that preschool teachers believed either consciously or subconsciously, that children of higher physical attractiveness, compared to those of lower, were significantly higher in intellectual ability, greater in academic achievement, more socially outgoing, and possess greater athletic ability.

The author concluded that a preschool child's physical attractiveness has a strong influence on the initial expectations of preschool teachers. He suggested that even trained professionals expected to treat children without regard to appearance, still stereotype children as young as three and four in correlation with their physical attractiveness. The article ends with an alarming note about growing research that states "stereotyping leads to the internalization of the stereotyped personality image by the target person."[7] A similar study published several years later reported similar findings for preschool children aged three, four, and five years old.[666] Preschool teachers who perceived children higher in physical attractiveness perceived them as more attentive, friendly, and relaxed compared to their counterparts perceived lower in physical attractiveness.

Regardless of whether judges are teachers or parents, expectations of preschool children are consistent with physical attractiveness phenomenon. Two related studies used preschool children (39 boys and 35 girls) as stimulus persons and mothers (55 total), fathers (36 total), and teachers (20 total) of these preschool children as subjects.[10] The researchers conducted a series of experimental tasks to assess expectations about behavior held by mothers, fathers, and teachers of these children. Parents and teachers consistently expressed expectations congruent with physical attractiveness phenomenon: the children expected to behave more positively were those whose appearance was higher in physical attractiveness. The published research report noted that parents and teachers serve as strong socialization agents for physical attractiveness phenomenon.

Beyond Preschool

Research investigating stimulus persons within educational contexts beyond preschool report results comparable with those reported about much younger schoolchildren. These research efforts show peer perceptions, interpersonal relations, and liking are all influenced by physical attractiveness phenomenon among children,[180, 181] college students,[182, 645] and for both middle aged and older teachers.[12]

One of the more disturbing findings is that teacher expectations vary according to differences in student physical attractiveness while teacher behavior affects student behavior. This combination raises universal pedagogical concern when considered in light of physical attractiveness of students in their respective classrooms. The research has addressed this interaction through scrutiny of records for measures of school achievement. It seems apparent that a dynamic of self-fulfilling prophecy occurs in view of the significant correlation exposed between school performance measures and student physical attractiveness. This correlation is not surprising, since teaching embraces setting expectations. If teachers knowingly or unknowingly set expectations higher and lower for students according to their level of physical attractiveness, then the dynamics of self-fulfilling prophecy are logical. In other words, students expected to perform better by their teachers will ultimately do so, and students expected to perform less well will do so, regardless if educational system expectations concern classroom behaviors, interpersonal interactions, or development of intelligence.

One two-stage study produced mixed results.[137] The first stage was an experiment to investigate teacher expectations based on student physical attractiveness. It found that the higher the child's physical attractiveness, the greater the perceived educational achievement for IQ, parent interest, peer relations, and self-concept. The second stage was not an experiment but did attempt to investigate student educational performance as correlated with student physical attractiveness. While much of this second stage research procedure was consistent with good scientific design, a critical flaw was lack of any measure for physical attractiveness of stimulus persons.

Stimulus persons were second graders (39 total), fourth graders (45 total), and sixth graders (48 total). Teachers (14 in total), who taught the same grade levels at other schools, looked at group photographs of each class to judge the physical attractiveness of these subjects. Data collected from this second stage was not valid because level of physical attractiveness for the students was never actually determined. Statistical analysis invalidated measures to assess physical attractiveness by disclosing a lack of adequate statistical agreement between the judges. The problem was that the judges did not agree, as evidenced by inter-judge correlation values of around $r = .32$, ranging from a low of $r = .23$ for second graders to a high of $r = .40$ for fourth graders. For that reason, the author wrote, "there is relatively little consensus among teachers on judgment of individual [physical] attractiveness."[137] The lack of adequate agreement (i.e., measure reliability) cannot justify reasonable interpretation of the second stage data to offer insight about a relationship between student physical attractiveness and school performance.

Two later studies indicating good levels of validity and reliability detected a significant relationship between physical attractiveness and school performance.[485, 608] These studies used the same two types of school performance indicators to check for impact of physical attractiveness: school grades and standardized achievement test scores. Two types of measures provide excellent balance of data because standardized achievement test scores provide high objectivity due to no personal interaction between test taker and test scorer. Further, school grades provide an element of potential subjectivity due to classroom interactions between students and the teacher who assigns their grades. Stimulus persons in the first of these two studies were third and fifth grade students (440 in total, all Caucasians), whose physical attractiveness was determined through evaluations of photographs by graduate students (7 in total) majoring in special education. Data revealed that standardized achievement scores were somewhat higher for students rated higher in physical attractiveness whereas the school grades (i.e., report cards) were significantly higher for students higher in physical attractiveness.

Stimulus persons in the second of these two studies were high school students (24 males, 17 females), and the research explored the variables of sex and physical attractiveness in relation to school performance.[485] To determine physical attractiveness, college students (20 undergraduates) judged the photographed stimulus persons. Analysis of variance revealed significant main effects due to physical attractiveness and sex for the dependent variables of academic achievement and sociability, specifically, the school performance measure of grade point averages correlated significantly with student's physical attractiveness. The authors concluded that both academic performance and student's physical attractiveness affect teacher evaluations with the implication that physical attractiveness of students appears to impact actual evaluations by their teachers in the same way as it impacts expectations held by teachers.

REVERSING DIRECTIONS

While most physical attractiveness phenomenon research in school environments explores attitudes, expectations, and behaviors *toward* students, some research reverses direction to explore evaluations and actions *from* students. Empirical data reveal effects of physical attractiveness for children are largely reciprocal. Without reference to physical attractiveness, the teachers who students consistently evaluate more favorably on a variety of competency variables are those teachers endowed with higher physical attractiveness, as seen in at least four early research studies to investigate teachers' physical attractiveness and their evaluations by students. Research into the impact of physical attractiveness on teachers through the minds and eyes of students offers an additional dimension that complements the robustness of experimental procedures and variety of subjects. Three studies used a range of elementary students to evaluate elementary school teachers, and a fourth study used college students to evaluate professors.

Elementary Students

Evaluations by elementary school students have spanned different ages and grades in research investigating physical attractiveness of teachers. In one experiment that confirmed the impact of a teacher's physical attractiveness, subjects were nine years of age (60 in total) and thirteen years of age (60 in total).[127] After viewing a videotape of a teacher, researchers asked subjects asked to provide numerous evaluations. Subjects did so with higher evaluations given to teachers whose appearances happened to be higher in physical attractiveness. This pattern emerged for all three ratings assessed: competency of teacher, ability to stimulate students, and ability to motivate students.

Expanded knowledge about effects of teacher physical attractiveness upon evaluations expressed by schoolchildren came from research focused on the variables of teachers' sex and age.[315] This research asked subjects (144 third grade students) to complete a twenty-one-item questionnaire referencing a teacher whose photograph, unknown to the subjects, varied in age and gender. Subsequent data unveiled that physical attractiveness significantly influenced students' evaluations of teachers while age and sex of the teachers did not. Evaluations were more positive for teachers whose appearances happened to be higher in physical attractiveness and more negative for teachers of lower physical attractiveness. Subjects evaluated those teachers of higher physical attractiveness as most likely to be superior teachers and ones likely to be more fun, more interesting, more likely to play games with their students, and with whom these subjects would likely experience more comfort as their students. Surprisingly, there were no interaction effects between the teachers' sex, age, and physical attractiveness variables. Differences in the students' evaluations of teachers were a function of the single visual cue provided by physical attractiveness.

Evaluations by students of teachers align with physical attractiveness phenomenon, as shown by known determinants through which physical attractiveness decreases as age of stimulus persons increases. An experiment controlling for the age, sex, and race of teachers, as well as their teacher's physical attractiveness, asked subjects (150 students at different grade levels) to evaluate seven dimensions of teacher performance.[243] The physical attractiveness variable produced a significant main effect that meant students evaluated teachers of higher physical attractiveness significantly more positively on all performance measures, and this effect occurred among students at all education levels. Upon closer investigation, the data contained interactions between teachers' sex and physical attractiveness in a manner that those teachers receiving the lowest evaluations were teachers of lower physical attractiveness who were either middle-aged females or older males. Furthermore, regardless of student level, younger teachers received higher evaluations than older teachers did for each performance measure.

University Students

Physical attractiveness of college and university professors appears to impact actual measures routinely administered as indicators of teaching quality. Many professors hold unproven ideas (and hopes) that physical attractiveness phenomenon somehow exempts colleges and universities. These ideas are illusionary according to respective research data that disclose professors who rate higher in physical attractiveness score significantly more favorably in separate student evaluation data for ratings of teaching quality measures. Research conducted in 2003 reported findings that university students evaluate professors of higher physical attractiveness significantly more positively on non-appearance factors considered necessary for successful education, learning, and teaching than counterpart professors of lower physical attractiveness.[269] This research, led by a professor of economics at the University of Texas who is a long-time research associate with the National Bureau of Economic Research, asked subjects (university students) to rate physical attractiveness of stimulus persons (94 professors represented by individual photographs). Data revealed that the physical attractiveness level of professors correlated with independent student evaluations commonly used as measures of teaching quality and with criteria for decisions about career promotions and annual salary raises. Interactions within the data found high and low physical attractiveness to be respectively a stronger benefit and stronger detriment for male professors. This difference showed physical attractiveness level affected teaching evaluations for male professors 300 percent more than it affected female professors.

The Chronicle of Higher Education published an article about the findings of this research with numerous interview comments from professors at different colleges and universities across the United States.[471] It is valuable to state the plurality here because people often think that, although physical attractiveness phenomenon functions in general populations, it might not function among the institutions of higher education. However, statements by these professors strongly corroborate the impact of physical attractiveness in their lives and experiences to be the same as documented for general populations around the world and for subgroups within these populations:

- A professor of psychology expressed great surprise about "the finding that the teaching ratings for men were more affected by their looks."
- Expressing supportive anecdotal perspective, a professor of astronomy and astrophysics "…notes that teaching, like acting, is a kind of performance art in which looks play a part."

- Likewise, a professor of psychology stated, "It's sad that [looks] make such a difference, and I'm sure there are many people who are going to read this and say, "Well, they don't matter to me." But they matter to large numbers of other people…"

- True to the denial aspect characteristic of physical attractiveness phenomenon, a professor of environmental studies defiantly stated, "I care more about my teaching… I think my appearance is irrelevant."

- In contrast to the above professor, consider the first-hand, real-world experience of a professor of psychology who was earlier overweight and stated, "But after I went on a crash diet, my faculty evaluations went up…I wanted to laugh. I'm the same person, yet suddenly I'm a genius?"

- Observing how people judge the work of others whose appearance is higher and lower in physical attractiveness, a professor of broadcast journalism put forth, "Looks shouldn't count, but clearly they do. That means ugly professors have to really, really know what they're talking about if they want to get good evaluations, as horrible as that sounds. They have to work harder."

- Offering constructive suggestions in light of the reality of physical attractiveness phenomenon, a professor of psychology observed, "…there's not a lot professors can do about the looks they were born with, so most of them should focus on improving the things they can control—like dress, grooming, and, above all, their teaching."

- Acknowledging the influence on career choices exerted by various professions, occupations, and employment areas that seem to attract and screen out individuals of high and low physical attractiveness, a professor of astronomy and astrophysics asserted: "The good news is that looks are just one of many factors that affect student evaluations. In addition, the bar for beauty is probably low for academics (beautiful professors are rare…) so clearing it may be easier."

- Then there is the self-doubt that a person's high physical attractiveness can cause, as articulated by a professor of anthropology: "Given this information, I'm wondering if I'm better looking than I thought I was because my evaluations have been so good."

- Based on these findings, a professor of English with explicit prior feedback about his own high physical attractiveness mused with self-doubt, wondering if he is as good a teacher as thought previously: "I work very hard at my teaching, and I am a little disturbed at the possibility that students are evaluating my courses based on such a superficial criterion."

Research conducted in 1979, twenty-five years earlier than the study referenced in the two prior paragraphs, found, for all practical purposes, identical proof of physical attractiveness phenomenon in this dimension of educational settings. College students, as well as elementary students, exhibit the same pattern of evaluations about characteristics possessed by their professors according to their physical attractiveness.[412] This research presented subjects (120 university students, 60 males and 60 females) with a stimulus person (photograph) described as a psychology college professor, asked the subjects to view the person/photograph, and to express their evaluations using a standard questionnaire. Unknown to the subjects, physical attractiveness (high, low) and gender (male, female) varied for the stimulus persons.

Significant statistical effects revealed university students evaluate professors of higher physical attractiveness with significantly higher ratings for warmth, sensitivity, superiority, communication ability, and knowledge of subject material. The true magnitude of these findings is tremendous given that the research procedure was not of actual student-professor dyads, but university students evaluating university professors based only on visual information about the professors provided via photograph. These effects due to physical attractiveness of professors were the same across professor gender and subject gender. Additional findings included a preference of both sexes of subjects for male professors versus female professors, and a same-sex effect for male subjects expressing highest ratings of competency for male professors.

TEACHERS

When speaking about schools, teachers are central to the life, learning, and overall educational experience of students. Teachers carry special influence and responsibility for unbiased treatment of all students regardless of a student's physical attractiveness. Teachers are, of course, human and physical attractiveness phenomenon impacts all humans around the world—which is a potent combination. It is for these reasons then that understanding the role of physical attractiveness within teachers and the teaching profession takes on increased value. As already pointed out in research cited above, infants and preschool children, even before beginning the progression through their school years, have experienced physical attractiveness phenomenon based on their own physical attractiveness. Schoolteachers who almost certainly, knowingly or unknowingly, hold perspectives congruent with physical attractiveness phenomenon, also hold huge positions of influence to either confirm or disconfirm the very early, respective, life experiences of their students.

Teachers, not unlike most everyone else in the general population, are predisposed to see a person's appearance through so-called rose-colored glasses in favor of higher physical attractiveness. In one study, subjects (144 female elementary teachers) were presented with a scenario describing misbehavior committed by a child, depicted in a photograph as a male or female child of high or low physical attractiveness.[592] Researchers then asked the subjects to evaluate the student's blame, personality, and punishment for the misdeed. These teachers attributed personalities to be more favorable for students when the appearance of the misbehaving students was higher in physical attractiveness. In the same way, the teachers saw the misdeed as less undesirable when presumably performed by a student whose appearance was higher in physical attractiveness compared to lower, which then likely colored assumptions of blame and feelings of punishment. A separate study with similar procedures focused on student teachers and found comparable data in favor of higher physical attractiveness when presented with combinations of student misbehavior and student physical attractiveness.[429]

Student Teachers

People assume that more experienced teachers are more objective than less experienced teachers. It follows that student teachers might be less objective and accordingly more influenced by student factors such as physical attractiveness. However, predictions that increased levels of education and experience increase objectivity of teachers with regard to physical attractiveness of their students are clearly unfounded as disproved empirically.

One study to test this potential relationship assessed the amount of influence that student physical attractiveness imposes on teachers possessing varying lengths of training and experience.[139] Researchers collected educational and social ability measures by presenting student teachers with a standard report card to which a photograph was attached that represented a student of either high or low physical attractiveness. The subjects were student teachers (687 in total, with 357 females and 330 males) of whom 16 percent were in their second year, 17 percent in the third year, 43 percent in the fourth year, and 23 percent in the fifth year of teaching. Contrary to researchers' expectations, the data revealed that student teachers who are more advanced in their education are just as easily persuaded that they can make meaningful evaluations of students on the basis of superficial information as student teachers who are less advanced in their education.[139]

Evaluations by student teachers about potential students were statistically significant for every measure of educational and social potentials. Without exception, the student teachers perceived and subsequently evaluated more favorably those students higher in physical attractiveness than students lower in physical attractiveness. The dependent variables were (a) the students' IQ, (b) their social relationships with peers, (c) their parents' attitude toward their work, (d) the amount of probable lifetime educational achievement, and (e) their self-concept. Parallel research again used student teachers (141 in total) as subjects, this time to evaluate perceived social and academic attributes of seventh-grade boys.[704] Although these data did not reveal a significant difference for academic attributes, it did reveal student teachers evaluating students of higher physical attractiveness as significantly higher on every social attribute measure in comparison to the less physically attractive students.

Experienced Teachers

Two researchers suggested that physical attractiveness of students may affect expectations of student teachers more than experienced teachers.[704] While intuitively appealing, this notion has neither theoretical nor empirical support. Quite to the contrary, existing findings from empirical research document that teachers, regardless of education or experience, hold expectations about students in agreement with physical attractiveness phenomenon. Research with substantial numbers of teachers in a substantial variety of research designs has reported repeatedly that teachers hold expectations more favorable for students higher in physical attractiveness. These expectations most likely arise from the standard educational process whereby the first and second types of information received by teachers are a child's school record via formal documents and the child's physical appearance upon first seeing them.

Accordingly, an early research project presented school records along with photographs of students to working teachers (404 in total).[138] Stimulus persons were fifth graders, male and female, low or high in physical attractiveness. Responses by the teachers identified significantly higher evaluations of more physically attractive students compared to their counterparts. These evaluation differences dealt with the (a) child's intelligence, (b) parent's interest in the child's education, (c) child's likely eventual educational attainment, and (d) popularity of the student with peers.

Other research has explored teacher expectations while increasing the type of information usually provided about students.[9] Subjects were public school teachers (490 in total, 180 males and 310 females) in eight different school systems, all with at least four-year college degrees and an average of five and one-half years teaching experience. Gerald R. Adams was the first author of this study, and, characteristic of his extensive, distinguished, research record, this project applied strict scientific standards to its procedure. Researchers gave subjects cumulative student folders resembling official school folders with identical information that described a student of slightly above-average academic performance, a report card for kindergarten through second grade, and medical data describing a healthy child. Variable information in the folders was (a) home background representing middle or lower socioeconomic level, (b) negative or positive comment of general ability, and (c) photograph of a boy or a girl either high or low in physical attractiveness. An enclosed evaluation form asked the subjects/teachers to evaluate five items about the student: creative ability level, intellectual ability level, ultimate educational training likely to attain, educational placement, and quality of teacher-student interactions.

Physical attractiveness of students generated significant impacts on teachers' expectations. Teachers also indicated differing expectations due to a child's sex, family's socioeconomic background, and reported general ability. Higher physical attractiveness of students equated with higher teacher's expectations of creativity, intelligence, educational level, and ultimate educational attainment. Despite these recorded expectations, teachers stated that physical attractiveness of students would not affect their teacher-student interactions, consistent with the lack of awareness or denial that is characteristic of physical attractiveness phenomenon. These authors[9] concluded that their findings corroborate those of earlier researchers[138] who have reported finding that teacher expectations vary due to student physical attractiveness. The stated implication was that physical attractiveness phenomenon exists to such a degree as to affect differences in expectations that, in turn, translate into differences in behaviors and interactions between teachers and students. Likewise, empirical data published eight years earlier not only reported compatible interaction differences, but also showed data that extended beyond expectations to include the finding that teachers are more receptive to ideas from students of higher physical attractiveness.[428]

Other supporting research findings go even further than the studies summarized above. In a study of teachers' expectations for future social development and future academic performance, the authors reported their collected data revealed systematic favorable-unfavorable differences held by teachers.[602] These differences followed the typical physical attractiveness phenomenon pattern whereby teachers, without acknowledging the student's appearance, believed those of higher physical attractiveness would in the future realize better social development and academic performance than those of lower physical attractiveness. Furthermore, this pattern among teachers is replete with high inter-judge reliability, which means a statistically significant and consistent perspective exists among teachers.[174] At the same time, while research data overwhelmingly support findings from the studies above, some studies offer less persuasive data. However, even these studies that have used elementary students as stimulus persons still report that teacher expectations and actions might favor students who possess higher physical attractiveness.[12, 211, 217, 218]

Given the strong evidence of physical attractiveness phenomenon within educational contexts, it is reasonable to postulate that actions, let alone beliefs and expectations, do actually occur in interactions between students and teachers based on a student's physical attractiveness. It is not surprising that people in the teaching profession might deny the potency of a student's physical attractiveness upon the teacher's evaluation of his or her students. Teachers who did otherwise would violate social norms and bring social disapproval upon themselves. This state of affairs is not an indictment of people in the teaching profession because almost all people throughout every population resist acknowledging publicly the negative considerations of physical attractiveness phenomenon. Thus, one would expect this resistance or refusal to acknowledge would extend with even greater vehemence to teachers, aware of their influence on future generations through present-day children.

What is somewhat surprising is that within the documented teacher expectancies, which operate in concern to physical attractiveness of students, practically no corresponding research exists. Although scientific research designed to investigate if and how teacher expectations translate into teacher behavior is difficult, it needs implementation. Despite methodological difficulties in all disciplines to measure actual behavior linked to attitudes, some physical attractiveness phenomenon research has attempted to do so in educational contexts through the assessment of behavioral intent as a commonly recognized surrogate for actual behavior. This approach is scientifically sound according to most theorists and researchers. The linkage commonly thought to exist is that attitudes, in this case equated with expectations, precede or lead to behavioral intentions that, in sequence, precede or lead to actual behaviors.

Three studies conducted in the early 1970s to assess actual teacher behavior regarding physical attractiveness in school environments attempted specifically to overcome research obstacles inherent in dissecting attitude-intent-behavior relationships. Two of these studies relied on completely unobtrusive observational research techniques and, unfortunately, yielded no real information for this topic, ultimately because of their limited scope and confounding problems inherent in their specific methodologies.[8, 594] The third study used post-event analysis to explore effects of student physical attractiveness on actual behaviors of teachers, which in this investigation equated with teacher referrals for psychological assessment and speech, reading, and learning disabilities. Stimulus persons were third-grade students (shown in photographs, 100 in total, with 54 males and 46 females) referred for help. Judges of their physical attractiveness were undergraduate college students (50 in total). Collected data revealed the most referrals for children of higher physical attractiveness, and the research article concluded that children of higher physical attractiveness receive greater attention that provides more judicious notice and response to their problems.[48]

ETHNOCENTRICITY

Physical attractiveness, and particularly physical attractiveness phenomenon, can overpower ethnocentricity in more situations than probably presumed by most people. Support for this conclusion comes from research focused on this question and based on data from Caucasian individuals, African American individuals, and Hispanic/Latino individuals. One study with Hispanic and Caucasian stimulus persons who were not schoolchildren investigated variables within a work setting.[469] Among the extensive and interactive results, physical attractiveness appeared to be a more important influential factor than ethnicity for preference to work with peers representing different ethnic groups. The higher the physical attractiveness of Hispanic or white stimulus persons in that research project, the more peers expressed greater acceptability of the person as a work partner, regardless if the subject was Hispanic or white. The world in which physical attractiveness is more important than race or ethnicity in interpersonal interactions is evident early in the lives of individuals for all people, as early as childhood.

Stimulus persons in two related studies were children (second graders, shown in slides) described as African American (identified as black in the original published article), Anglo, or Mexican American. Subjects were adult males and females (university students, 131 in total) of different ethnicity who rated physical attractiveness of the stimulus persons.[381, 659] Data disclosed that stimulus persons rated highest in physical attractiveness were, as a group, Anglo, regardless of the ethnicity of subjects/raters. If the subjects/raters were black or Anglo, stimulus persons rated highest in physical attractiveness were Anglo, even when compared with black stimulus persons of parallel levels of physical attractiveness. Likewise, if subjects were Mexican American, stimulus persons rated highest in physical attractiveness were Anglo for group data for all stimulus persons at the same high level of physical attractiveness. When all the stimulus persons were at the same lower levels of physical attractiveness, Mexican American subjects in this study expressed tendencies toward ethnocentricity with a pattern of higher ratings for Mexican American stimulus persons compared to black and Caucasian stimulus persons at the same level of physical attractiveness.

Research focused on race, and physical attractiveness has served to broaden the data that have long substantiated the breadth and depth of physical attractiveness phenomenon. Not surprising to those of us studying physical attractiveness over the long-term, a study focused on African American children (identified as black children in the actual article published in 1982) concluded physical attractiveness significantly influences African American children.[585] This project was highly controlled, beginning with stimulus persons (African American children) selected in consideration of how they would represent different levels of physical attractiveness; furthermore, African American adults rated actual physical attractiveness of the stimulus persons (12 in total represented by individual photographs). Researchers then presented the rated stimulus persons via photographs to subjects (120 total African American children) divided into groups of 40 five-year-olds, 40 seven-year-olds, and

40 nine-year-olds. Subjects completed a questionnaire to assess preference for affiliation and liking, and revealed, first, high agreement between physical attractiveness ratings by the African American adults and African American children. Second, children preferred most to interact with and to be friends with stimulus children of higher physical attractiveness irrespective of the person's difference or sameness of race.

Other cross-cultural examinations with subjects comprising African American and Caucasian young adults have found physical attractiveness phenomenon to be significantly more similar than dissimilar between the two racial populations, regardless of ages of subjects. These research projects have used experimental procedures rather common for this type of research to attribute psychological characteristics as a function of physical attractiveness,[234] even through draw-a-person projective procedures that are more common to psychoanalytic techniques and therapies.[438]

MISBEHAVIOR

People judge and react more favorably to misbehavior by children of higher physical attractiveness than the same misbehavior by children of lower physical attractiveness, regardless of a child's ethnicity or race. One study described stimulus persons to have committed a misdeed/misbehavior in school. These stimulus persons were children, either African American or white, and either high or low in physical attractiveness.[429] Subjects (60 total student teachers and 137 total practicing teachers) representing diverse education and ages evaluated these stimulus persons. Resultant data uncovered significant differences in evaluations of children representing different levels of physical attractiveness but no such differences according to race of children. These subjects evaluated more negatively the children of higher physical attractiveness, rather than lower physical attractiveness. Although these data may initially appear contradictory to physical attractiveness phenomenon, the researchers interpreted these data to support physical attractiveness phenomenon. They explained that teachers hold higher expectations and subsequently give greater attention to children of higher physical attractiveness, regardless of race or ethnicity of the judges or the judged. Further interpretation is that, even concerning equal misbehavior, teachers are more apt to notice more and to respond more strongly to children of higher physical attractiveness who misbehave than children of lower physical attractiveness, regardless of race of the children.

Without consideration of race or ethnic differences, another research project similarly concluded that children who commit identical misbehavior but who differ in physical attractiveness elicit different responses from adults.[179] To arrive at this conclusion, the research procedure provided subjects (adult females) with a written description of a child's offensive behavior to which was attached a photograph of the so-called offending child who was either high or low in physical attractiveness. Subjects considered the misbehavior to be more serious and more likely a part of the child's permanent character when attributed to a child of low physical attractiveness; whereas, when attributed to a child of high physical attractiveness, subjects viewed the same misbehavior as less serious, probably transitory, and likely atypical of the child. Subjects also asked to contemplate future behavior predicted the child of lower physical attractiveness would continue to display behavior that is negative and would commit offensive misbehaviors more frequently.

A similar but substantially enhanced research project by the same author yielded similar results.[177] This time, the research examined the child's gender in addition to the physical attractiveness variable, and gauged actual responses by adults rather than perceptions. Instead of manipulation of misbehavior as an independent variable, another change in the research was manipulation of mistakes made by a child performing a picture-matching task. The subjects (52 white females and 44 white males) administered punishment based on the incorrect responses of each child. Based on data for variable punishment that took away one to five pennies from the child for each error, a reasonable conclusion based on the data is that subjects were more lenient when punishing a child of higher physical attractiveness than lower.

Involuntary responses by adults parallel their voluntary responses to children whose appearances differ in physical attractiveness. Two experiments investigating involuntary behavior of subjects (adults) in response to a child's physical attractiveness arranged for a stimulus person (child) unknown to be working for the researchers to provoke subjects.[58] To assess potential involuntary responses displayed in the form of displaced aggression, subjects were required to discipline the child after being provoked. The first experiment paired subjects (56 adult females) with a 10-year-old girl of either high or low physical attractiveness. Resultant data showed subjects to vent more aggression on the girl of low physical attractiveness by administering greater punishment compared to the same circumstance with a girl of high physical attractiveness. The second experiment paired subjects (40 in total) with a 10-year-old boy of either high or low physical attractiveness either with a noticeable stutter or with normal speech. These manipulated variables both elicited involuntary aggression. The boy who stuttered and the boy with low physical attractiveness received more severe discipline than their counterparts did. These patterns of biased punishment correspond with data from a series of studies on teachers' responses to transgressions of students as a function of physical attractiveness.[430]

SELF-FULFILLING PROPHECY

A realistic fear radiating from the collective research above is that children live up or down to expectations and treatments by teachers in particular and adults overall. No one, and especially educators and those in positions to set policy, should disregard this issue. Logic, theory, and empirical data establish that children, who are in school as students, do internalize expectations of their teachers through dynamics described as self-fulfilling prophecy. Also known as the Pygmalion effect, this is an especially portentous hazard concerning physical attractiveness phenomenon. What occurs is that interpersonal realities (expectations and treatments between a person and other people) convert to intrapersonal realities (corresponding truths within a person).

In and out of school, the pattern is the same for children as a function of their physical attractiveness. The more and the less favorable expectations held by adults about a particular child combined with corresponding treatments administered toward a child translate into the corresponding development of behaviors and traits of the child. In the same way, children who receive more attention transform into better children in terms of behavior and mentality, and children of higher physical attractiveness do receive more positive attention (i.e., benefits) while children of lower physical attractiveness receive less attention (i.e., detriments). Ultimately, people throughout life, including children during their most formative years, benefit from their appearance if it is higher in physical attractiveness and experience detriments if it is lower in physical attractiveness.

Contrasting Environments

If you believe, as most professionals in developmental psychology believe, that people develop as a function of their environment, then it is important to realize and to take action regarding the fact those children of different levels of physical attractiveness grow up in accordingly different environments. From birth, the environment treats the children differently based on their level of physical attractiveness. Even before being released from the hospital, while still in the nursery after birth, babies of higher physical attractiveness, defined at this age as more cute, are spoken to more, touched more, and held more than babies of lower physical attractiveness (i.e., less cute). If you ask people, they will deny it. However, if you place them in an experimental design, a candid camera setting so to speak, you will see that parents, visitors, and hospital staff speak more to, touch more, and hold more, babies who are more cute compared to those less cute.

In May, 2005, the popular media dealt well with scholarly research findings when the *New York Times* published an article titled "Ugly Children May Get Parental Short Shrift."[39] That article reported findings of researchers in Canada at the University of Alberta. It begins, "Parents would certainly deny it, but Canadian researchers have made a startling assertion: Parents take better care of pretty children than they do ugly ones." Hidden observers who followed the highest scientific research standards collected data in fourteen supermarkets regarding more than 400 parent-child interactions. Male and female parents exhibited more care of their children in this setting when the child was of higher physical attractiveness. Researchers recorded many different types of measures with consistent results. An example: The percent of children that mothers strapped into a protective cart seat was four times greater for children of higher physical attractiveness compared to lower physical attractiveness (13.3 percent versus 4.0 percent). For fathers, the difference was infinitely greater for children of higher versus lower physical attractiveness (12.5 percent versus 0.0 percent).

Differential expectations held by adults can be as dangerous or as damaging to a child. Unlike differential actions, expectations seeded in the child's mind likely translate into self-fulfilling prophecies. Consider when teachers expect children of higher and lower physical attractiveness to be more or less intelligent, more or less behaved, and more or less popular with other kids. Self-fulfilling prophecy driven by differences in physical attractiveness among schoolchildren then translates into dynamics and consequences for children that are not limited to the formal educational process. Other researchers provide interested readers with a thorough coverage of the entire spectrum of physical attractiveness research pertaining to children, especially as applicable to child development.[295, 380]

The environment is quite contrasting for children of lower and higher physical attractiveness. It is a pleasant, forgiving, supportive world for the latter and the opposite for the former. This fact might suppose that children of higher physical attractiveness could be more maladjusted compared to children of lower physical attractiveness because of differences in pampering, favoring, and spoiling. Research data disclose that the reverse is true. Children lower in physical attractiveness are the ones whose personal life adjustments are less positive and less effective, documented in research published as early as the 1950s.[102] Research continues today with evidence throughout societies in general and throughout pertinent social sciences in particular.

Physical attractiveness phenomenon is replete with cautionary ramifications for people lower and higher in physical attractiveness in connection with internalizing one's physical attractiveness. This cautionary note, while valid and potentially alarming for all people throughout their lives, is particularly alarming in connection with educational institutions around the world. These institutions interact with individuals during their most formative childhood years, within highly influential environments that contain figures of formal authority in terms of teachers and informal judges of approval in terms of peers. Substantial theory, logic, and empirical data show that expectations produce self-fulfilling prophecies. In that order, if teachers expect different behavior from students of different levels of physical attractiveness, the students' sense these messages, consciously or subconsciously, internally process the subtle and not-so-subtle cues, and accordingly develop in confirmation of the expectations. As throughout physical attractiveness phenomenon, the result is favorable for those children of higher physical attractiveness and unfavorable for those of lower physical attractiveness.

Expectations by Teachers

An abundance of scientific research authenticates that different levels of physical attractiveness evoke consistent patterns of different responses from strangers and non-strangers alike. Within that published research, data lend credibility to theories and hypotheses that individuals internalize these responses, which translate into significant influences within the subsequent cognitive development of these individuals.[5, 7, 13] In a more broad view, social psychological research offers early data that bear witness to a causal relationship between expectations of others and ultimate corresponding behaviors by the targeted person.[28, 158, 761] Research into teacher expectations offers further data that substantiate a relationship between teachers' expectations and subsequent behavior by students, as put forth in an early definitive book in 1968.[601] This federation of research is not unanimous, but scholars highly respected in this research field have identified, through extensive summaries of research conducted in laboratories and natural settings, evidence that strongly corroborates student-teacher relationships leading to self-fulfilling prophecy.[9, 86, 599, 600]

Among the many articles and authors examining the correlation between expectations of teachers and performance of students, a major *Psychology Today* article in 1973 summarized the research investigating the relationship between student performance and teacher expectation.[598] That article indicates well that teachers' expectations are powerful determinants of students' learning, performance, development, and achievement. While these particular studies do not focus on physical attractiveness phenomenon, they do convincingly report that conscious and subconscious treatment of a child influences the child's later IQ measures, sports accomplishments, mathematics skills, and academic performances, all of which provide affirming evidence about physical attractiveness phenomenon. Later, more recent, thought and research have borne out findings of earlier studies. Based on the evidence, one researcher has concluded that teacher expectations and assumptions regarding a child's potential have a tangible effect on student achievement and research, which "clearly establishes that teacher expectations do play a significant role in determining how well and how much students learn."[41]

Logic together with empirical data provide convincing, combined, support for theories that suggest the tendencies of students to internalize projections of teachers about their students' abilities, which then generally predicts outcome of students' education. Tendencies of students to perform and develop "rise or fall to the level of expectation of their teachers… When teachers believe in students, students believe in themselves. When those you respect think you can, you think you can."[579] For that reason, students perceived to lack in ability, motivation, and expected not to make significant progress, have tendencies to adopt, internalize, and adjust down to these perceptions through the realization that their teachers consider them "incapable of handling demanding work."[419] As stated by another researcher, "teachers' expectations for students—whether high or low—can become a self-fulfilling prophecy. [That is,] students tend to give to teachers as much or as little as teachers expect of them, [which concerning physical attractiveness then underscores the need to fully carry out] a characteristic shared by most highly effective teachers [which] is their adherence to uniformly high expectations."[419] Therefore, a mandate of teachers and those who teach teachers should be to bring awareness of physical attractiveness phenomenon to the forefront of education processes. This mandate would encourage all teachers to explicitly "refuse to alter their attitudes or expectations for their students—regardless of the students' [appearance or physical attractiveness,] race or ethnicity, life experiences and interests, and family wealth or stability."[508]

Positive Linearity

Intrapersonal realities overwhelming reflect positive linearity with physical attractiveness. Positive linearity reflects a straight ascending line relationship in which increasingly higher physical attractiveness translates rather simply into increasingly more favorable benefits. In contrast, a curvilinear relationship would translate more complexly, without a straight ascending line between detriments and benefits aligned with lower and higher physical attractiveness. A curvilinear relationship could reflect a U-shape with greatest benefits for both lower and higher levels of physical attractiveness and least benefits/greatest detriments for middle-range physical attractiveness. Alternatively, a curvilinear relationship could reflect an inverted U-shape with greatest detriments for both lower and higher levels of physical attractiveness and greatest benefits/least detriments for middle-range physical attractiveness.

Evidence is rather ample that the self-fulfilling prophecy functions in a positive linear relationship between physical attractiveness and intrapersonal realities. One research project that sheds light in this area investigated actual differences rather than only expected differences as a function of physical attractiveness. It used children as stimulus persons (56 male fourth graders and 48 male sixth graders) and asked adults (97 in total) to judge each child's physical attractiveness based on photographs taken with a standard pose to minimize potential extraneous effects.[402] Researchers analyzed each child's physical attractiveness in relation to actual academic performance as measured by grade point averages and about social interactions and interpersonal adjustment as measured respectively by responses from peers and observations by teachers. The results disclosed that a child's physical attractiveness correlated positively with actual academic performance as well as with actual social interactions and actual interpersonal adjustment. Another investigation, this one conducted in Germany, utilized formal measures of sociometric status to determine group entropy and individual popularity.[623] Correlation analyses of the data discovered a monotonic increasing relationship between physical attractiveness and sociometric status and popularity of individuals.

What happens as children age? Empirical evidence in addition to anecdotal observations and self-testimonies verify that childhood internalizations equated with physical attractiveness remain throughout a child's lifetime. Through use of unobtrusive measures to study natural interaction patterns, researchers followed up a meeting of young adults (university freshman of traditional college student ages) intended to facilitate same-sex social contacts.[367] Independent judges to whom the stimulus persons (60 males and 60 females) were unknown judged their physical attractiveness. Data collected subsequent to this meeting were predictably consistent with physical attractiveness phenomenon. Those stimulus persons of lower physical attractiveness (most likely in this study, lower-moderate in physical attractiveness) categorized the meeting more often as a rejection by the person with whom they met. Compare this to the stimulus persons of higher physical attractiveness, who categorized the meeting more often as an acceptance by the person with whom they met. Somewhat complicating these data was the indication that stimulus persons who were least physically attractive categorized the meeting most frequently as "unknown" in terms of rejection or acceptance by the other person with whom they met. Given that rejection by a another person is often difficult to accept by oneself let alone admit to a third person, these unknown responses by the least physically attractive stimulus persons might well have been the least painful plausible categorizations for them to express.

Immediate Display

To illustrate additional, long-term internalizations of self-fulfilling prophecy experienced by children, it can be helpful to review research findings focused on the demonstration of more immediate internalization. An example is a research project that analyzed telephone tape recordings in an intricate experimental design that used adult subjects (51 males, 51 females) paired in interactive dyads.[647] Researchers led the male subjects to believe that the female subjects to whom they were speaking in telephone conversations were either high or low in physical attractiveness, but the females were not aware of the designation or that physical attractiveness was even of experimental interest. Separate judges, uninformed about the experimental manipulations and interests, conducted subsequent analyses of tape-recorded telephone conversations. The data revealed that even though the female subjects were unaware of the assumptions held by the male subjects, and even though these assumptions were inaccurate, the female stimulus persons behaved in a manner consistent with physical attractiveness phenomenon. Those female subjects assumed as high in physical attractiveness presented friendlier, more likable, and more socially desirable behavior/conversation than those female subjects assumed as lower in physical attractiveness. *The New York Times* published an article that paraphrased one of the researchers as saying "people will adjust their personalities to meet the expectations of others."[55]

Two separate but interrelated studies conducted by the same first author employed a diary technique to assess actual social interaction as it might be linked to physical attractiveness.[587, 588] As the following details bear out, these research projects found physical attractiveness of participants does influence social relationships. Individuals do actually have different interaction behaviors and experiences in quantity and quality that include more favorable social interactions for those of higher compared to lower physical attractiveness. However, researchers disguised their interest in the physical attractiveness variable by telling subjects who volunteered to participate that it was "a research project on social interactions." Unknown to the subjects, independent judges at another university to whom the subjects were strangers rated their physical attractiveness.

In the first study, subjects (beginning university students, 35 males and 35 females) were required to tabulate every interaction of ten minutes or longer during an eight-month period of their first year in college.[587] With primary interest centered on the effect of physical attractiveness on quantity and quality of social interactions, the research discovered:

- Physical attractiveness significantly affected quantity of social interactions for males and not for females.
- For males of higher physical attractiveness, quantity of social interactions related positively for opposite-sex encounters and related negatively for same-sex encounters.
- Details of the data revealed that males of higher physical attractiveness had more mutually initiated opposite-sex social interactions.
- Males of higher physical attractiveness and females of higher physical attractiveness spent greater quantities of time in conversation and activities with each other than did any other subjects representing the various gender-appearance variables.
- The importance of physical attractiveness to the subjects increased as the interaction time increased, which is contrary to common thought that importance of a person's physical appearance might decrease during duration of an association. This study reported "that satisfaction showed a tendency to be increasingly positively correlated with [physical] attractiveness over time."[587]

In the second study, subjects (43 males and 53 females, university students who were young adults of ages typical for traditional seniors/fourth-year college students) were required to tabulate every interaction of ten minutes or longer within time spans of seven to eighteen days during November of that year.[588] Given the gender differences revealed in the first study, the research project posited a "marketplace economy effect" to explain the different social interactions reported above for males and females. The explanation rests on the ability for first-year university female students to be more selective in their opposite-sex interactions because they more commonly interact with males at all four years of university education, unlike first-year university male students who typically do not. Within the data collected through this investigation, the results matched the first study as well as discovered:

- Males of higher physical attractiveness experienced a greater quantity of social interactions than did their female counterparts. The researchers explain the disparity due to differences in difference in aggressiveness, whereby males of higher physical attractiveness were more aggressive than their counterpart females of higher physical attractiveness. The more physically attractive males were more assertive, less fearful of women, and accordingly, were more likely to approach women. Concurrently, the more physically attractive females were less assertive, more distrustful of the opposite sex, and more likely to wait for others to approach them.

- Females of higher physical attractiveness described their social interactions to be more favorable in quality and greater in quantity compared to females of lower physical attractiveness. The researchers wrote that females of higher physical attractiveness experienced "more satisfying, pleasant, intimate, and disclosing" social interactions than their counterpart females of lower physical attractiveness.[588]

SUMMARY

Children are always the next generation and, of course, the children's children are the next generation's next generation. Although values of a society change, change is incredibly slow and often painfully slow. Given the research knowledge discussed in this chapter, today we can expect the role of physical attractiveness to continue its importance for many generations to come. Certainly casual observation of teenagers today gives every indication that physical attractiveness phenomenon is alive and surely will be transmitted by these individuals for generations to come after them.

With so much time and importance universally associated with a person's school environment and school years, it is not easy to understand why relatively little research addresses actual teacher behavior as a function of student physical attractiveness. Of course, critical masses of research do document pertinent perceptions and expectations. However, these findings serve to amplify the puzzling current limits of research about actual teacher behavior. These findings also, and maybe even more importantly, amplify the current scant research and actions to minimize teachers' related behaviors, expectations, and perceptions.

The level of significance certainly cannot be the reason of the relative scarcity of research exploring questions about behavior of teachers and adults overall in response to the physical attractiveness of children of school age. It is quite the opposite since the questions and answers are essential in significance. One possible reason, therefore, centers on methodological obstacles and related restraints imposed by ethics of research communities. To obtain the all-important causal data for this topic requires formal experiments, but many of the manipulations necessary to produce actual behavior are ethically unacceptable. Codes of ethics as well as legal restrictions rule out procedures that intentionally cause mental or physical harm in pursuit of research about actual behaviors. Alternatively, surrogate behaviors and measures do allow experimental design procedures to go beyond expectations into simulated teacher-student behavioral interactions. Unobtrusive observational procedures present another alternative through which researchers observe actual harmful behaviors in naturalistic settings but do not create them. Analyses after an event has occurred provide still another type of procedures that, while yielding only correlation data, can be a valuable beginning from which to make reasonable and potentially insightful inferences about actual behavior.[47]

Regardless of methodological obstacles, the lack of research attention on the topic of actual teacher behavior is deplorable for individual children today and, ultimately, for the human race for generations to come. Despite the difficulties and imperfections, it is vital to make research attempts because surely, less-than-perfect information is better than no information. Possibly the delay in this particular research is analogous to the delay in which scientific inquiry seemed adverse or at least hesitant to begin exploration of the overall physical attractiveness variable. For example, a prominent professor at Stanford University wrote in the late 1960s, when scientific research into physical attractiveness phenomenon was just getting under way: "Social science is fearful to confirm preferential treatment based on physical attractiveness and...to do so is to acknowledge that amid our democratic philosophies there operates a very undemocratic practice of birthrights."[27]

Thirty years later, research published in the late 1990s, corroborated the discomforting fact that genetic factors (i.e., nature rather than nurture) account substantially, by as much as about 50 percent, for similarities between parents and children.[278] The fact that disposition (i.e., endearing behavior) is likewise transmitted from parent to child genetically cannot be comforting with respect to differentiation/discrimination issues emitting from physical attractiveness. The thought that the innate physical attractiveness of young schoolchildren determines their treatment by teachers is frightening. It is more frightening to think that many people appear to presume explicitly or implicitly that if people ignore a problem of many types, then either the problem does not exist or it will disappear. The only way to initially minimize and eventually eliminate the inequities of physical attractiveness phenomenon is to first identify them, recognize and acknowledge them, and then take actions accordingly.

Perhaps the most meaningful research conducted in the near future will involve how children, despite any limitations of their backgrounds and social and genetic factors, create a sense of autonomy to rise above stereotypical outcomes and to influence others to do likewise. Studies in physical body deformity conform to physical attractiveness phenomenon overall, yet many studies of individually disabled persons reveal how they have helped transform their environment instead of having their environment define and determine them. For the time being, additional research is necessary to complete the impressive research conducted thus far in regard to the patterns within physical attractiveness phenomenon that develop in infancy, persist throughout life, and look to impact generations to come.

Chapter 9

Future Trajectory

It is everlastingly true that on the whole the best guide to the future is to be found in a proper understanding of the lessons of the past.
> Warren G. Harding (1865-1923), elected in 1920 as United States president.[452]

And you, madam, are ugly. But I shall be sober in the morning.
> Attributed to Winston Churchill in reply to Member of Parliament Bessie Braddock, who told him he was drunk.[450]
> Winston Churchill (1874-1965) was prime minister of the United Kingdom (1940-1945, 1951-1955) and is widely regarded as the greatest British leader of the 20th century.[450]

To live is to choose and you should choose what is attainable.
> Kurt Tucholsky (1890–1935), German philosopher[158]

Technology's progress will soon accelerate—exponentially.
> The Wall Street Journal book review[589] about The Singularity Is Near: When Humans Transcend Biology[376] concerning future technological progress.

INTRODUCTION

When you and I awake tomorrow morning and every morning after, our physical attractiveness may not or, more likely, may have changed from today. However, the future trajectory of physical attractiveness phenomenon will most assuredly not have changed. Physical attractiveness phenomenon will be abundantly the same tomorrow as today, and will continue to have a prominent impact on and in the life of every person across the United States and around the world. Within this context, physical attractiveness when defined in terms of trends, fashions, and styles will very, of course, from day to day, but this fact of physical attractiveness phenomenon will be the same tomorrow as today. With an impressive review of research projects and theoretical interpretations, prominent international researchers (at the Ludwig-Boltzman-Institute for Urban Ethology in Austria, the Universite

Pierre et Marie Curie Laboratoire de Parasitologie Evolutive in France, and the University of New Mexico in the United States) concluded in 2003:

> Although beauty standards may vary between cultures and between times, we show in this review that the underlying selection pressures, which shaped the standards, are the same. Moreover, we show that it is not the content of the standards that show evidence of convergence—it is the rules or how we construe beauty ideals that have universalities across cultures [i.e., physical attractiveness phenomenon].[251]

Physical attractiveness phenomenon today frequently poses a quandary. It has permeated life to become a seemingly ever-expanding, never-ending plight that causes good for some people and, in some circumstances, causes the converse for other people. Physical attractiveness phenomenon is not new, even though the current state of affairs makes readily observable, and sometimes painfully so, an assortment of inventive manifestations heavily dependent on modern day advances in media and technology. As reported throughout this book, research conducted in many disciplines document the incessant power, pervasiveness, and other characteristics of physical attractiveness from the start of the human race through today and, with certainty, into the future. The evidence meticulously amassed in contemporary times, has above all made it legitimate to articulate that physical attractiveness always has been and always will be an entity with the potential for two edges. It can be supremely good, but it can be—sometimes and for some people—tremendously bad.

A futuristic society in which physical attractiveness holds a dominating role is no longer fast approaching, but is already upon us and, actually, thoroughly entrenched within us. Recent behaviors of humans around us, combined with technological advancements, increasingly provide witness to the prominence of physical attractiveness throughout an individual's life. However, an article titled "America's Obsession with Beautiful People," published in a 1982 issue of *U. S. News & World Report*, stated that it is evident that "from the moment of birth, good looking people enjoy big advantages, while less attractive individuals are penalized."[709]

The powerful and persuasive phenomenon of physical attractiveness, with benefits and detriments awarded accordingly to individuals of higher and lower physical attractiveness, is escalating. Gender, age, or level of physical attractiveness does not restrict the logical, albeit possibly distasteful, escalation of this phenomenon-driven obsession. Witness the opening report of a national television news program broadcast at the start of the current century, in the year 2000:

> Teenagers undergoing plastic surgery, a bodybuilding routine that dominates one man's waking hours, a fear of gaining weight that leads to a girl's heart attack and blindness, and an obsession with nose size that keeps another man from leading a normal life: In one form or another, all of these people are pursuing physical perfection.[125]

A year later, in 2001, the same national television news program opened its broadcast again with a similar message of escalating obsessions driven by physical attractiveness phenomenon:

Despite leading the industrialized world in obesity, America is obsessed with being thin… And women are not the only ones going to extremes to attain the ideal look; more and more men are being diagnosed with eating disorders such as bulimia and anorexia…in search for the perfect look.[126]

The domineering role wielded upon us by physical attractiveness is not new. Physical attractiveness phenomenon has dispensed the power and pervasiveness of physical attractiveness since the origin of humans. It will not diminish, but instead will continue and even increase among the living and yet to be living. Interesting and, in hindsight very foretelling, I wrote in my first book published in 1985 with rather precise and surprising accuracy about events that have occurred recently, and which are occurring today, regarding the impact of technology, biology, and societal mindset on unborn children, and even those children yet to be conceived:

> Despite societal concerns and ramifications, the importance of an individual's physical attractiveness is likely to continue to increase in magnitude. In fact, it is now reasonable to speculate that the physical attractiveness of even the unborn, and the unconceived, could be of significant consequence in a culture controlled by the physical attractiveness phenomena.[535]

Appearance, and particularly physical attractiveness, can assume rather gigantic proportions in a person's mind and even in the collective conscience of a population, to the demise of those either consumed through their own volition or imposed on them by others. It is apparent today that physical attractiveness can become an issue so important in one's own eyes that a person succumbs to cognitive issues affecting behavior. These behaviors include shame causing a person to withdraw totally from society,[382] violent delinquency in school,[29] medical problems of depression and suicide,[477, 650] and psychological troubles of delusions and imagined ugliness.[111, 565, 566] Responsively, or maybe concomitantly, a wide gamut of products, services, surgeries, and therapies around the world offer options and solutions to address these and other considerations about physical attractiveness connected with physical attractiveness phenomenon.

How and when physical attractiveness phenomenon began is largely irrelevant today. References to the importance of physical attractiveness are apparent in early historical archives discovered by anthropologists and other researchers throughout recorded history. Preferences and definitions have evolved, but the value of physical attractiveness has remained persistently exalted, to the point of diminishing returns. What is essential is the fact that physical attractiveness phenomenon is age-old and customary. Its firm grounding and acceptance suggests absolutely no future developments would diminish the valuable treasure consciously or subconsciously linked to physical attractiveness. The reality is that technology continuously and forever advances, and contributes accordingly to perpetual physical attractiveness phenomenon among all people. In unison, sociology and psychology progressively approve of today's and tomorrow's "better biology" (that is not always better) to achieve greater physical attractiveness through technological preeminence.

IMPACT LIFELONG

Evidence that physical attractiveness phenomenon grips people around the world is readily observable. It is nonsensical to argue otherwise, despite the persistence of people who might fail to see this reality or because of any other reason refuse to acknowledge it. Diet books top the best-sellers lists. Talk shows continuously host beauty experts, representatives from health spas and exercise studios. Expenditures continuously escalate on foods (for example, with low calories and with other compositions and substances) intended to, or, at least primarily marketed with the message to, affect physical attractiveness via appearance. Cosmetic surgeries are increasing geometrically in frequency for each of the past few years. Such listings are reality, readily apparent around the world; all driven by individuals hopeful to enhance their physical attractiveness. Restraints imposed in earlier times were limits of medical and media technology, human biology, and societal attitudes, but whatever those boundaries were yesterday, people today are pushing the boundaries farther and farther beyond the imaginations of just a few years past in pursuit of increased physical attractiveness. On top of this context that has been increasing geometrically, projections about technology are that future technological progress will increase exponentially at speeds and levels faster and farther than people can now comprehend.[376]

Technology and Biology, Surgeries and Non-Surgeries

Today the extremes are so great that entire books address specific body components of physical attractiveness such as thin thighs, beautiful bottoms, and flat stomachs. Many thriving businesses and medical practices that serve general populations around the world, along with the workers within these enterprises, earn their living incomes by facilitating pursuits of higher physical attractiveness that focus on body subcomponents. These subcomponent determinants of physical attractiveness range from smallest of body parts such as esthetically appealing fingernails to every subcomponent of the head such as esthetically appealing hair, ears, teeth, complexion, etc.

One direction to look, to see the future of physical attractiveness and physical attractiveness phenomenon, might be toward the Hollywood elite. Their purchases and practices frequently portend comparable purchases and practices among general populations. In this regard, credible mass media reported in 2005 that twenty-four year old celebrity Paris Hilton had begun to routinely obtain exclusive eyelash extensions.[626] Unlike times past when false eyelashes consisted of a single adhesive to each eye area in pursuit of greater physical attractiveness, these eyelash extensions, like expensive natural hair extensions interwoven with a person's natural head hair, comprise many intricately woven eyelash hairs. In addition to her routine of hair extensions, these eyelash extensions, that last about six weeks, is just one of Ms. Hilton's regular actions in pursuit of greater physical attractiveness.

Technology, biology, surgeries, and non-surgeries, extend far beyond cosmetic applications that might offer temporary options for pursuits of physical attractiveness in contemporary times. A highly respected mainstream American magazine, *U. S. News & World Report*, dedicated a 2004 cover story to physical attractiveness phenomenon with the title "Makeover Nation: Why America's Obsession with Plastic Surgery Is Going Dangerously

Out of Control."[640] That article reported "prime-time television enlightens viewers on the mechanics" of cosmetic surgery with a splash of related programs, from *Extreme Makeovers* to *I Want a Famous Face* to *The Swan*, all showing dramatic before-and-after appearances, in which the after, improved physical attractiveness, is then adored, as rightfully it should be in light of physical attractiveness phenomenon.

Recent years have witnessed a huge escalation in surgeries to increase one's physical attractiveness. With new technologies that increasingly allow a person's biology to accommodate these changes, "more than 8.7 million people [in the United States] underwent cosmetic surgery in 2003, up 33 percent from the year before, according to the American Society of Plastic Surgeons."[640] Despite readily available failure statistics and evidence testifying to risks, regrets, and unfavorable outcomes, "in 2003 [American] consumers paid $9.4 billion for cosmetic procedures, equal to about one third of the [entire] budget of the National Institutes of Health."[640] Cosmetic surgeries are probably more popular in Florida than other states, but since mid-2003 in that one state alone, "at least six patients have died after [surgical] procedures, including a 51-year-old man who had a combined face-lift and chin implant" in pursuit of increased physical attractiveness.[185] Yet, "at least a 20 percent increase" is projected for the coming year by the American Society for Aesthetic Plastic Surgery for body lift or body contouring surgeries to re-shape bodies in search of "cosmetic enhancement."

Coexisting among options in pursuit of greater physical attractiveness is interest in quick, effortless, painless solutions. Despite unproven effectiveness and uncertainty about long-term safety, people market, buy, and ingest pills in their pursuits to lighten skin, tan skin, smooth wrinkles, enlarge breasts, build muscles, etc. A 2005 article published in *The Wall Street Journal* quoted a former beauty editor to say, "We're such a beauty-obsessed society. People are interested, and more will try these [pills in hopes to enhance physical attractiveness]…people are always searching for quick fix alternatives to cosmetic surgery." That article goes on to state, "According to market research company Euromonitor International, ingestible beauty supplements have more than doubled in sales over five years."[129]

Physical attractiveness phenomenon research has long shown that people individually, and collectively as a society, judge younger ages, real or perceived, particularly for women, higher in physical attractiveness. Accordingly, "the quest for youth—or, at least, the appearance of it—is age old."[49] Cosmetic surgery statistics indicate that people today proverbially beg, borrow, and steal to afford cosmetic surgery in pursuits to enhance their physical attractiveness. Television network news reported in 2004 that "not seen among the 8.7 million Americans who last year received cosmetic surgery, up a whopping 33 percent increase in one year, is the financial hardship often caused with at least 40 percent now financing their elective cosmetic surgeries."[1] Hope Donahue, who came from a very financially upscale family, writes in her 2004 autobiography about a five-year period in her life, from ages 22 to 27, when she sold favorite possessions and accumulated $20,000 in debt for cosmetic surgeries that included augmentation of her breasts and lips and enhancement of her eyes and cheekbones.[184]

While cosmetic surgeries are skyrocketing, products, services, efforts, and finances for non-surgical enhancements (frequently en route to later surgery) are skyrocketing. Among the escalation in recent years for non-surgical options to improve physical attractiveness by warding off appearances of aging are growing lists of injectable cosmetics like Botox, Restylane, and collagen, as well as intense, laser-pulse, light treatments, creams, and skin potions of all sorts. According to the American Society of Plastic Surgeons, "6.9 million such procedures were performed [in 2003]—up 41 percent from the year before."[49]

"Younger people are not immune. While nearly half of those who underwent minimally invasive procedures [in 2004] were between 35 and 50 years old, almost 20 percent were between 19 and 34," according to a *Newsweek* article.[49] That article quotes the coauthor of *Midlife Crisis at 30* to have said, "When people in their 20s and early 30s are running off to have Botox, there's a real problem. We place far, far too much emphasis on youth and beauty." Even though the truth might be distasteful to some, the article accurately states, "but research shows that more attractive people get better jobs and salaries, and more respect from peers." That magazine article quotes a psychology professor in the School of Medicine at the University of Pennsylvania, who expresses the reality well:

> We have evidence showing that, whether we like it or not, appearance *does* matter. [People of higher physical attractiveness] get preferential treatment in a variety of situations across a life span. And we know that especially for women, we equate beauty with youthfulness. So trying to present yourself as looking as young as possible might actually make practical sense.[49]

Are these efforts and expenses worthwhile? As much as many of us wish the opposite, the answer seems to be strongly yes. While improvements in state of mind are not easily measured and quantified for people of higher and lower physical attractiveness, research has quantified differences in employment or financial status. To begin, more than 2,000 years later, the idiom "Personal beauty is a greater recommendation than any letter of reference," often attributed to Greek philosopher Aristotle[574] who lived from 384-322 B.C., is still pertinent, at least in modern-day employment and compensation. A broadly disseminated interview article with the author of this book presents a perspective consistent with this proclamation. WebMD published that article in 2000.[371] It includes the explicit message, analogous to that stated by Aristotle, that physical attractiveness and physical attractiveness phenomenon are essential considerations for the long-term unemployed attempting to transition back into employment. WebMD published that article a second time in 2001[370] followed with a medically updated version in 2003,[369] and MedicineNet.com published an editorially reviewed version of it in 2005.[490]

Specific statistics for hiring and earning rates corroborate discussions linking employment and physical attractiveness phenomenon. Researchers at London's Guildhall University found that among 11,000 people surveyed in 2000, "[physically] unattractive people earn substantially less than their colleagues. The penalty for [physical] unattractiveness is around -15 percent [minus fifteen percent] for men and -11 percent [minus eleven percent] for women."[276] Researchers at the University of Texas and at Michigan State University found people of less than average or moderate physical attractiveness earn 5 to 10 percent less than counterparts of moderate physical attractiveness earn. In turn, those of moderate physical attractiveness earn 3 to 8 percent less than people of high physical attractiveness.[416] Although meanings or symbolism of what constitutes higher and lower physical attractiveness can vary by culture, differences in favor of higher physical attractiveness and against lower physical attractiveness ultimately function consistently across cultures. "In capitalist cultures that value individuality, [physically] attractive people are seen as assertive and strong, while in some more collectivistic Asian cultures [physically] attractive people are seen as being more sensitive and understanding."[740]

Interview articles widely disseminated through mass media regularly and frequently express a link between physical attractiveness and employment benefits. Mass media articles that include interviews with the author of this book connecting physical attractiveness phenomenon and corresponding benefits and detriments in employment range from *The Today Show on NBC*, broadcast nationally in the United States in 2005,[145] to the evening primetime television news program *Dateline NBC* in 2004.[567] With global dissemination of information, the Microsoft Internet Explorer homepage that opens to computer users worldwide has in partnership with CareerBuilder.com published an article titled "Do Pretty People Earn More?" regularly and frequently during 2004 and 2005. That article emphasizes the connection between employment and physical attractiveness phenomenon, and includes an interview with the author of this book as published in 2005 by CNN.com.[416, 417]

Economists conducted a study in 2005 at the Federal Reserve Bank of St. Louis in the United States and corroborated a principle finding about physical attractiveness phenomenon: higher physical attractiveness translates into higher pay.[203] (As a footnote, this bank is one of twelve regional banks that make up the Federal Reserve System, also known as the central bank, that formulates U. S. monetary policy and U. S. federal government regulation of financial institutions and payment services.) The April 2005 edition of the quarterly periodical of the United States central bank (*The Regional Economist*) published the analysis, which among the findings included:

- Economists at the University of Texas at Austin (Daniel Hamermesh) and Michigan State University (Jeff Biddle) found, compared to persons of average physical attractiveness, a "beauty premium" whereby persons of higher physical attractiveness earned 5 percent more and a "plainness penalty" whereby the person of lower physical attractiveness earned 9 percent less.[268] Despite conventional wisdom that this physical attractiveness factor might apply only to certain jobs or industries, this research showed the differences across diverse occupations, not limited to any one type of position or industry.

- Separate from the above research, these same two economists found the same sort of beauty premium for attorneys, ranging from 10 percent to 12 percent for those rated higher in physical attractiveness.65 Furthermore, lawyers rated higher in physical attractiveness most often entered private practice versus public practice. In this comparison, "Fifteen years after graduating, the beauty premium for private lawyers was three times that for public lawyers."[203]

- Economists Susan Averett and Sanders Korenman found that obese women earned 17 percent less than women of average weight did; this pattern also occurred among men but with much less differential.36 Their research published in 1996 studied two age groups, 16 to 24 years old and 23 to 31 years, in the 1980s. The benefits and detriments for weight and wages varies between demographics, but the pattern for people of heavier weights receiving lower salaries is most consistent for white women.[119]

- In terms of height, economists Nicola Persico, Andrew Postlewaite, and Dan Silverman found higher salaries are paid to taller people at rates ranging from 1.8 percent to 2.6 percent for every additional inch.[561]

The collective effect of the dynamics and consequences found above predict another broader finding reported in research by four Dutch and American economists.[621] Published by the National Bureau of Economic Research in Cambridge, Massachusetts, this research concluded, "Companies who hire beautiful people go on to make a pretty penny." They based their conclusion on the physical attractiveness ratings of 1,282 executives compared with sales revenues and profitability at their respective companies. The researchers found that companies with executives of higher physical attractiveness were "in most circumstances associated with higher revenues." Furthermore, they reported, "The productivity increase, while it's real, is because of co-workers' and customers' behaviors…it doesn't matter whether it's advertising or steel manufacturing, or radio," the relationship with physical attractiveness was found to be the same.

Increasingly in the United States and around the world, more options and the increasing use of options in pursuit of higher physical attractiveness will continue, begetting greater-than-ever eminence for the already lofty significance of a person's physical attractiveness. In 2004, an article published in *The Wall Street Journal* article titled "Beauty Takes on a New Form—Pills," explained, "Americans readily pay for beauty in a jar. Now, it's also being served up in a pill bottle."[612] Most certainly, physical attractiveness phenomenon's already high prominence will proceed even more comprehensively throughout the population, all the while magnified with wide-ranging technological advances combined with coverage and amplification through the mass media. Individuals and populations will exaggerate the already grand reality of physical attractiveness, both the negative and positive facets of lower and higher physical attractiveness. Making the liabilities and assets of appearance more visible to all people will translate into more extreme, even desperate hunts to attain higher levels of physical attractiveness. In addition to cosmetic surgeries and other medical procedures and yet to be developed technologies, conventional methods to enhance a person's physical attractiveness (e.g., diets, body shaping, clothes, and cosmetics) will continuously multiply along with corresponding exploitations that yield both good and bad effects.

Whatever styles, trends, and modifications define physical attractiveness in the future, the pursuit of solutions to attain that physical attractiveness will extend beyond conventional methods. As well as surgical procedures, pharmaceutical compounds will almost certainly assume increasing importance to alter the determinant measures of physical attractiveness, such as weight and age. Despite a lack of effectiveness, there are already many remedies for people concerned about cellulite. These remedies include wraps, blows, machines, chemicals, massages, and even a medical suction procedure to remove cellulose surgically. General cosmetic surgery is now commonly accepted and growing in popularity, but, of course, currently only for incremental improvement within what might be described as pursuit of higher levels within the normal physical attractiveness range.

Psychology and Sociology

Answers to questions about reasonable and unreasonable cosmetic surgeries exist with a degree of certainty, or absoluteness, in contexts of technology and biology. However, they do not exist in contexts of psychology and sociology. Medical standards for increasing physical attractiveness might have definitive, albeit shifting, definitions and boundaries, while judgmental standards do not. Like medical technologies, judgmental standards shift for improving a person's physical attractiveness. However, unlike medical technologies that at any one time have absolute limits, judgmental standards are significantly relative and intangible. Individuals vary in their limits based on their psychological composition; the limits for some people are more dynamic than for others. Analogously, cultures vary based on their sociological composition, which for some cultures are more dynamic than for others. Of course, the psychology of an individual concerning pursuits of increasing his or her physical attractiveness is interdependent with the sociology of the person's immediate subculture and larger culture.

To explore shifting standards connected to pursuits of increasing physical attractiveness, longitudinal research—as opposed to observational, survey, and experimental research—is especially effective. Rather than conduct a research project with data collection that spans a matter of hours, days, or weeks, longitudinal research conducted into physical attractiveness phenomenon has elicited data from the same subjects over years, decades, and even scores of decades. Unquestionably, conducting multiple types of research into a topic requires extra resources and commitments than circumstances usually permit, but it provides a battery of investigations that strengthens the collective knowledge about a topic of interest, as has been the case for physical attractiveness. In addition to the critical mass of observations, surveys, and experiments for which data have been collected during an explicitly short time span, a substantial amount of research has collected data spanning a much longer time. The results confirm that mirrors can be evil, so to speak, in terms of a person's interpretation over a lifetime of the image reflected back and its impact on self-perception, sense of worth, health, and satisfaction with regard to our physical attractiveness.

As in most areas of psychology and sociology, and often in fields ranging from medicine to business, perception is more important than reality, even though reality influences perception and vice versa. For physical attractiveness, people more often than not internalize what they see and experience about their appearances when looking in a mirror. Different levels of physical attractiveness are associated with different perceptions, interactions, and outcomes. The question is whether these associations reflect only perceptions or if they represent truth to individuals. The answer is truth. In addition to perceptions, different individuals do experience different outcomes as a function of their physical attractiveness. All the major research designs used to study physical attractiveness phenomenon have identified these differences with supporting empirical data.

One longitudinal study that spanned fifty years provided an interesting variation in the types of research designs employed.[606] Over this exceptionally lengthy time for data collection, this research project found that throughout a person's lifetime, people higher in physical attractiveness remember their earlier years as more satisfying than people lower in physical attractiveness. In 1932, from a group of 212 fifth and sixth graders, researchers selected a sample of 91 subjects (45 males and 46 females) to participate in this research project. During the fifty years of longitudinal study, it was clear from their lives that what others perceive about different outcomes from social interactions are not only perceptions. Individuals, whose levels of physical attractiveness differ, actually experienced these differing perceived interactions within their lives.

Another longitudinal study reported data confirming the findings from the above fifty-yearlong study.[712] This second study also identified gender differences consistent with the rather standard finding of generally greater importance of physical attractiveness for females than males. It was an ambitious study began in 1955 with a national sample of high school sophomores. A follow-up survey in 1970 with 4,151 original participants (then in their thirties) yielded 2,077 respondents who mailed back completed questionnaires. Another follow-up study conducted ten years later further investigated these respondents in an attempt to identify actual long-term consequences of physical attractiveness in adult life. At this point of the study, six research assistants (three males and three females) evaluated each respondent's physical attractiveness based on original high school photographs.

The data collected from this longitudinal study spanning nearly thirty years revealed that individuals who differed in physical attractiveness levels experienced actual differences in real life. Even though judges (to whom the stimulus persons were unknown) measured physical attractiveness of individuals objectively, this study's data cannot reveal how the stimulus persons perceived their own physical attractiveness during life. Nor can these data reveal how that perception by these stimulus persons might have affected the views and behaviors of these individuals as they obtained or did not obtain certain life experiences. For these studied individuals, the level of their physical attractiveness in high school proved significantly related to the level of household income twenty to thirty years later for females, but not for males. The authors stated that "the relationship is clear and nearly linear: the more attractive the female, the higher the household income."[712] This relationship did not prove significantly related to the females' own incomes, but only to their household incomes. According to the researchers, a woman of higher physical attractiveness marries a "higher income-producing husband"[712] than her counterpart of lower physical attractiveness. This research project revealed numerous additional findings:[712]

- Both the males and females of higher physical attractiveness married earlier than their counterparts of lower physical attractiveness did.
- While physical attractiveness of males was not significantly related to whether the person twenty to thirty years later was married or not, the authors concluded that the data for females revealed "the least [physically] attractive are ten times as likely never to have married as the most [physically] attractive."
- "The more [physically] attractive the male is, the less educated his wife is" twenty to thirty years later. But "the more [physically] attractive the woman

was in high school, the more highly educated husband she gets," according to the reality twenty to thirty years later.

Since these data for males are different compared to the data for females, the indicated effects might initially appear contradictory to physical attractiveness phenomenon. For example, these data showed males of lower physical attractiveness to be more educated and to possess higher occupational status, whereas these data did not show a relationship to exist for their physical attractiveness and income. Regardless, males also benefit from an appearance of higher physical attractiveness. Further analysis of the data reveals that those at lower and higher levels of physical attractiveness had similar job status, but this similarity existed despite the fact that standardized tests during adolescent years indicated significantly higher verbal and math scores for those males lower in physical attractiveness. The authors interpreted these data to mean:[712]

- Males with lower physical attractiveness "are socially handicapped in high school, which leads them to concentrate on educational achievement," which results in positions of corresponding prestige but no greater financial earnings compared to males with less educational achievement but with higher physical attractiveness.
- Males with higher physical attractiveness "in spite of their ordinary showing on educational achievement, do nearly as well in job prestige as the most homely men."

IMPACT BEFORE AND AFTER LIFELONG

Physical attractiveness phenomenon of a person extends far beyond any individual person's lifetime, as well as beyond any one generation of people in any part of the world. Technology, combined with changes in societal attitudes, makes physical attractiveness a characteristic considered increasingly at the starting threshold of an individual's life span, even before the person is born. At the ending threshold of an individual's life span, after a person's life has ceased, traditions combined with religious perspectives, makes physical attractiveness again a consideration.

Before Birth, Before Conception

Scientific advances of tomorrow will transcend medical limits of today, permitting still further enhancements of physical attractiveness before birth and even before conception. One certainty is toward advancements that allow greater authorship of a person's presumably natural inherited physical attractiveness. Although still in its early stages, procedures that allow access to the unborn are being developing more and more by our society. Current pregnancy tests permit valuable information about the health of unborn children, and inquiries about the physical attractiveness of unborn children is not far away from somewhat common practice. The use of, and frequency of, surgeries performed on unborn babies were already raising voiced concerns in 2005 as reflected by the title of, for example, the article in one major newspaper: "Despite Doubts, Fetal Surgeries Increase: Doctors Proceed Even When Baby Isn't In Danger."[144] Even more foretelling with rather explicit reference to physical attractiveness and physical attractiveness phenomenon, that article goes on to state:

> Just a few years ago, fetal surgeries were rare…That is quickly changing. Doctors are expanding the type of fetal conditions they are willing to treat. Doctors also are considering surgeries to repair cleft palates and other cosmetic procedures.[144]

Earlier in the reproductive process before a child is even conceived, and farther into the future, plausible projection is that technology and societal attitudes will permit changes to a person's physical attractiveness through genetic engineering. A 2005 book, *The Singularity Is Near: When Humans Transcend Biology*, written by a highly credible prizewinning scientist, puts forth that future technology in general will develop at exponential, currently incomprehensible speeds and levels.[376] That book further proposes a complicated scenario with no correct answer, along with cautionary perspective, about the significance for populations to be cognizant and proactive about potential technological advances that go too far or that go directions with more harm than benefit.

Well before the future submitted in the prior paragraph, even today the world has pertinent, significant technologies that include both external and internal procedures. One external procedure discussed in a 1982 publication concerning diagnostic testing is obstetric ultrasonography, which uses ultrasound waves to evaluate the fetus yielding "a realistic Polaroid picture" that identifies abnormal pregnancies.[511] Also discussed at that time is transabdominal amniocentesis, which allows extraction of fluid from the amniotic cavity to provide valuable information about unborn children. The accuracy and importance that medical science places on this procedure was illustrated in a 1982 textbook that states "if chromosomal or genetic aberrations are suspected, the test should be done early enough (14 to 16 weeks) to easily allow safe abortion.[511] Now, twenty-some years later, we have evolved to using these technologies potentially to decide if abnormality of unborn children might possibly extend to include a lower level of physical attractiveness than desired by society or the parents. Simply consider a cover story published in 2004 in *Newsweek* titled and subtitled "Girl or Boy? Parents Now Have the Power to Choose Gender of Children. But as Technology Answers Prayers, It Also Raises Some Troubling Questions."[337] The article states: "If couples can request a baby boy or girl, what's next on the slippery slope of modern reproductive medicine? Eye color? Height?"[337]

Somewhere in the future, a "logical" extension of this prenatal information could be the parents' request for physical attractiveness with consequent decisions for appropriate action. Such abilities may not be too distant. Our technologies have long permitted visual observations of internal body parts. Laparoscopy was already described in 1982 as a standard (albeit sophisticated) diagnostic procedure through which "the abdominal organs can be visualized by inserting a fiberoptic scope through the abdominal wall."[511] Increasingly more, even before the child is conceived, the near future will allow manipulations of appearance through genetic engineering; although not yet practical at this time of writing, genetic engineering is receiving serious attention by scientific and religious communities. Theoretically possible as demonstrated in laboratories, these prospective applications of genetic engineering are generating discussions, articles, and books about accordant opportunities and ramifications.

Technology has recently evolved to include PGD (preimplantation genetic diagnosis) that tests the gender of embryos created outside the womb can and can "with almost 100 percent certainty" guarantee the gender of a baby. Accordingly, "choosing gender may obliterate one of the fundamental mysteries of procreation, but for people who have grown accustomed to taking 3-D ultrasounds of fetuses, learning a baby's sex within weeks of conception, and scheduling convenient delivery dates, it's simply the next logical step."[337] To accompany this "next logical step" of choosing the gender of a baby, one can expect the additional step of choosing the physical attractiveness of a baby.

Be it a baby's gender or a baby's physical attractiveness, technology is, of course, typically a two-edged sword. Additionally, societal attitudes, moral questions, religious convictions, and political realities, frequently contribute to concerns surrounding technological capabilities and the appropriateness, rightness, and ethics to perform those capabilities. Technology combined with societal attitudes that allow intrusion into the biology of birth and conception practices poses particularly questionable dimensions of ethics concerning the unborn, but also poses opportunities for more humane treatment. Consider an extreme pre-birth decision and practice that continue currently and not rarely, despite public discouragements and denials. In parts of Asia, particularly in parts of India, parts of China, and parts of South Korea, in which sexism in favor of male offspring is so strongly ingrained, due only to their gender, healthy female fetuses very near birth are aborted not infrequently and healthy female babies are put to death not infrequently within moments of their birth.[507, 690] A 2004 article in *Newsweek* subtitled "In parts of Asia, sexism is ingrained and gender selection often means murder," reported that for these parents, who have no benefit of conception technologies yet are affected by the influence of the above sexism:

> ...boys are a treasured commodity in Bihar [India] and if a couple can't choose a child's sex prenatally, they can see a dai [who helps a woman give birth, and who] for 80 cents more, will take a newborn girl, hold her upside down by the waist and give a sharp jerk, snapping the spinal cord. [Because in these cultures] many couples insist that we [who help women give birth] get rid of the baby girl at birth..., the ratio of infant boys to girls is far off balance. Worldwide, 106 boys are born for every 100 girls—but in Korea, it's 110 to 100. Among fourth-born children, it's an astonishing 168 to 100. In China...the last census logged 119 boys per 100 girls, and most Chinese infants up for adoption are female... In wealthy Haryana [India], where clinics flourish, there are 114 boys for every 100 girls. In China's Hyaiyuan County...for every 100 girls born there, there are 120 boys [born].[108]

Into Death

As a person passes into his or her death, customary practices in most cultures mandate clean up, make up, and dress up of the deceased person. Even under circumstances of death, hair, face, and clothes are considerations in pursuit of achieving higher physical attractiveness; accordingly, people alter these determinants of physical attractiveness upon death. A comment frequently expressed by people viewing the deceased person in an open coffin in such countries as the United States, typically as welcomed reassurance and words of comfort to the family and other loved ones is that the deceased "looks good." Likewise, in countries such as the United States, when coffins are not open for viewing, family and loved ones display the person's appearance with a portrait or other pictures of an earlier time. Practically always, these portraits and pictures display the person when he or she was most physically attractive, again eliciting comparable sentiments that the deceased man "was such a good-looking man" or the deceased woman "was such as good-looking." Likewise, the death of a child frequently elicits sentiments surrounding the funeral ceremony that the child "was such a cute little boy" or "was such a cute little girl."

Physical attractiveness is significant during a person's life stages, as well as during the stages before and after life. Even more significant is the fact that people pass physical attractiveness phenomenon on to later generations. Consciously or subconsciously, people promulgate the significance and dynamics of physical attractiveness beyond any one person and any one generation on to those that follow. As this promulgation occurs, the related self-fulfilling prophecy discussed in the prior chapter becomes increasingly consequential. Consider for a moment that no aspect of child development may be more vital for long-term success in life than intelligence. Even though children inherit their intelligence and interconnected abilities, the environments in which children grow contribute significantly. With rare exception, professionals agree that children internalize environments to a substantial extent. At the same time, the empirical data, much as discussed in the prior chapter, reveal that people of all types hold different perceptions and assumptions and bring to bear different treatments to children of different levels of physical attractiveness, including perceptions about intelligence.

The impact of what children of different levels of physical attractiveness internalize from their correspondingly different experiences appears significant enough to affect life itself for these individuals. Researchers at the University of Waterloo in Canada conducted a project with scientifically solid methodology and concluded, "facial [physical] attractiveness is predictive of future longevity."[289] One of the researchers added, "Some people have found the research upsetting. I guess it's just the idea that there are so many benefits to being attractive, which they find kind of unfair."[290] One group of judges rated physical attractiveness of this study's stimulus persons, and, separately, another group rated apparent health. All these judges based their ratings on yearbook photographs of adolescents approximately 17 years of age from a set of 1924–1927 high school yearbooks. Still different judges compared the age of death for these individuals, which averaged 72.50 years for males and 74.57 for females, with the ratings of their physical attractiveness. Statistical analyses of the data revealed significant Pearson Product correlations between all gender dyads for the male and female stimulus persons and the male and female judges.

The published journal article does not report exact mean ages for the stimulus persons at time of their death, but follow-up communications with one of the researchers provided additional detail about age differences at the time of death.[291] Females rated with higher physical attractiveness when approximately 17 years of age lived an average of 76 years, versus 73 years for their counterparts of lower physical attractiveness. Males rated with higher physical attractiveness when approximately 17 years of age lived an average of 76 years, versus 69 years for those rated with lower physical attractiveness. Upon hearing these findings, a student at Howard University commented, "…it seems that being a beautiful baby means much more than landing a Gerber commercial. I've always been the cute one out of my group of friends… It is nice to know that I'm going to get something out of this later."[472]

Life and Death

Physical attractiveness has long been a life-and-death issue in one form or another and this fact is widespread in cultures around the world throughout history. The forms of these issues span a continuum, from obstructed views that partially conceal its impact, to unobstructed views with no concealment. Already in the 1800s, as cited earlier in this book, Charles Darwin wrote that physical attractiveness "is not the weal or woe of any one individual, but that of the human race to come, which is here at stake."[164] That declaration expresses well the unobstructed views displayed by the severe, blatantly brutal, life-and-death actions that can occur. The current chapter of this book (chapter 9) identifies a few specific examples of this reality.

Darwin's words quoted above also express obstructed views that embody much less visceral gate keeping and screening functions of physical attractiveness as discussed previously, in chapter 7 of this book, about meeting-dating-mating research. Of course, as the newly born child progresses through life, physical attractiveness further exerts its influence on the human race to come as wielded through the psychological and sociological dimensions of physical attractiveness phenomenon. Along this life journey, depending on a person's psychology, physical attractiveness, and sociological experiences, a convergence of circumstances in physical attractiveness phenomenon occasionally leads the person to end his or her life and, in still less frequent cases, to end the lives of others around him or her accordingly.

Obstructed Views

Obstructed views involve actions that are somewhat subtle due to their longer-term impact. These actions function more on a macro level that combines lives of individuals into entire populations defined collectively as the human race, thereby tending to obscure the actions. For example, even before possibilities arise to conceive a new life, the individuals who could be parents if paired, confront the gate keeping and screening that are parts of physical attractiveness phenomenon, which nearly always control who does and does not pair with whom. Although the mating-dating-mating material discussed in earlier in this book is particularly relevant to this discussion, it is worthwhile to take at least a momentary glance at related research concerning this intersection of physical attractiveness and its influence beyond the life of any one individual or any one population. Scientific research published in the 1930s put forth that appearance characteristics govern dating; that normally precedes the progression to reproductive possibilities that may or may not include lifelong spousal commitment.[724] In a direct test of this proposition, scientific research published in the 1950s asserted that personality characteristics govern such dating frequency.[72]

Reality is no doubt a combination of appearance factors and personality factors that interdependently and with great complexity drive the dating activity and, subsequently, the reproductive possibilities that may or may not include lifelong spousal commitment. More contemporary research projects have further explored these two opposing theories about appearance and personality.[654] Subjects were young women (undergraduate university students, 323 in total) who responded to 1,500 randomly mailed questionnaires that requested self-rating data for personality, physical attractiveness, dating frequency, and number of men dated. These data firmly supported predictive superiority for physical attractiveness as opposed to personality. In other words, physical attractiveness was significantly more predictive of dating behavior than personality. Similarly, another researcher several years later concluded physical attractiveness was more important in love than any of the personality variables she investigated.[427]

Still other research discovered that individuals self-rated as physically unattractive compared to physically attractive report significantly greater difficulty in interpersonal relationships, judge their social skills as inadequate, and report higher levels of anxiety leading to opposite-sex interactions.[467] Related self-ratings carry special significance in consideration of the physical attractiveness dimension represented by weight, as reported by a 2005 television news program stating that parents have reason to worry. "Recent research on teen suicide reveals that teens who see themselves as either too skinny or too fat were twice as likely to attempt suicide as teens with normal body images."[2]

Unobstructed Views

Unobstructed views involve actions that are direct and explicit between physical attractiveness phenomenon and consequences due to a person's level of physical attractiveness. Whereas psychology, sociology, biology, and evolutionary theories described the situation in the past, physical attractiveness phenomenon has integrated continually with real-world, life-and-death, issues in the past and present, and will no doubt continue this integration in the future. What might look like isolated real-world flare-ups incidental to physical attractiveness phenomenon, accurately describe unobstructed views into the realities of physical attractiveness realities as studied by psychology, sociology, biology, and many other scientific fields. Because these actions function more on a micro level, people try to minimize or even deny their occurrences, which provide dramatic examples of an appalling but real dimension of physical attractiveness phenomenon.

About one-hundred years after Darwin's above statement concerning the influence or even determination of physical attractiveness upon the future of humans, the national American news media covered a murder trial in 1983 about a well-educated, highly respected professional in Chicago, Illinois, named Dr. Daniel McKay.[286] Neighbors described Dr. McKay, a 35-year-old veterinarian with a respected practice, as the "nicest, most gentle person." Police reports presented in court, however, testified that when Dr. McKay was in the hospital delivery room with his wife and saw their newborn child had a cleft palate, he "immediately grabbed the baby and beat the infant's head on the floor until it was dead." Physicians reported that the cleft palate was correctable by surgery to achieve proper function of the oral region. Regardless, Dr. McKay's inability to accept his newborn son with less than desired physical attractiveness produced deathly consequences.

Another case involved slightly different circumstances from above, but chillingly similar ingredients of physical attractiveness phenomenon and related actions of a parent that led to a child's death. In this case, the parent was a mother, the child was unborn, and the action by the parent resulting in the child's death was motivated by the mother's concern about her own physical attractiveness above the life of her child.[607] Court legal documents allege that Melissa Ann Rowland, a 28-year-old pregnant woman in Salt Lake City, Utah, "ignored medical warnings to have a caesarean section to save her twins [and] was charged Thursday with murder after one of the babies was stillborn." Physicians said the baby died two days before delivery but would have survived with the delivery surgery that doctors had urged to the mother. Prosecutors in the case said Ms. Rowland "didn't want the scars that accompany the surgery." A spokesperson for the district attorney's office said, "We are unable to find any reason other than the cosmetic motivations for the mother's decision."[499]

Different cultures in different ways display the same physical attractiveness phenomenon among parents and their children worldwide. Readily observed situations demonstrate a person's physical attractiveness not only determines the person's quality of life but also very blatantly determines life itself for the person. In a chapter that I wrote in 1988 for a book titled *Advances in Clinical Child Psychology*, I referenced a 1984 national television network news report that stated: "death favors children of higher physical attractiveness (i.e., they have a lower chance of death) in the current famine in Ethiopia."[550] In that particular culture, a determinant of higher physical attractiveness is a bald head and, predictably, the news program reported, "parents shave the heads of starving children in hopes they will receive more food."[135] Around that same time, another news report by a national television network described two children, an 8-year-old boy and a 15-year-old girl, in Ecuador who had a facial component judged in that culture to be a determinant of lower physical attractiveness.[616] Consistent with physical attractiveness phenomenon, the news program reported about the boy:

> He won't even go out to school. He has already learned the lesson of the way
> he looks. ...[he] is seen as a disgrace for his family. The other children tease
> him... When strangers come, he runs to his room and hides his face.[616]

About the girl, again consistent with physical attractiveness phenomenon, the news program reported:

> She is ashamed of her face, embarrassed to smile. [The mother explains that
> her daughter] ...doesn't go out anywhere. When there's a party, she says she's
> not going. She hides behind books or a handkerchief. She has too much of a
> complex to stop doing that.[616]

Twenty years after the news reports cited above, a 2004 news magazine article with extensive photographs describes current famine conditions in the western Sudan region of Darfur.[432] The article does not explicitly describe physical attractiveness considerations, as do the news reports above. However, even in this deplorable situation of conflict between military and militia in Sudan, the article pictures children who, by themselves or with assistance from adults, are taking actions to enhance their physical attractiveness via adornments. Further consideration of physical attractiveness phenomenon or, maybe equally descriptive in this case, appearance phenomenon, is a 2004 *Time* magazine quote attributed to government-backed militiamen "who have been raping dark-skinned women as part of a campaign to ethnically cleanse Darfur, Sudan," claiming that, "We want to make a light baby."[699]

CROSS-CULTURALLY, GLOBALLY

Physical attractiveness phenomenon is immense and expansive. People often want to localize or rationalize physical attractiveness, ascribing its phenomenon to the United States or to certain parts or cities of the United States. However, physical attractiveness phenomenon occurs in every community and every population, ranging from the smallest to the largest, across the United States and around the world, regardless of geographical locations, political boundaries, cultures, subcultures, awareness, acceptance, and denial. No matter what the precise manifestations—the parallels and analogies, the power and pervasiveness, or the acknowledgements and denials—the dynamics and consequences are consistently similar, as described, predicted, and explained by physical attractiveness phenomenon. An indicator of the physical attractiveness phenomenon around the world might be a count of the number of cosmetic surgeons in different locations. In 2005, California with a population of 34 million people had 864 cosmetic surgeons according to official government data. In comparison, in 2005, South Korea, with a population of 48 million people, had 960 cosmetic surgeons representing an 85 percent increase since 2000, according to the Korean Society of Aesthetic and Plastic Surgery.[208]

Surgery in pursuit of higher physical attractiveness is escalating worldwide, but certain locations have much longer traditions for assisting people in pursuit of greater physical attractiveness through surgery. Colombia is ranked 21st in the world by the International Association of Aesthetic Plastic Surgery for the number of cosmetic procedures performed.[190] With a population of about forty-two million people,[451] Colombia has nearly five hundred cosmetic surgery clinics.[190] Statistics show that Medellin, a city of three million people, has more than 65 such clinics. Indicators of the future, based on youth of today, reveal analogous patterns around the world. "Indian youngsters are warming up to the idea as cosmetic surgery in India takes off…body [surgeries] in the age group of 17-28 has almost doubled in the past two years. …cosmetic procedures and surgeries by middle class youngsters…is bound to increase by 70-80 percent in the next three years," stated a 2005 published report from New Delhi.[688]

The research pertinent to physical attractiveness phenomenon presented in this book has often mentioned the country in which researchers conducted the study if outside the United States. Collectively, the variety of countries represented substantiate the universality of physical attractiveness phenomenon and, at the same time, the locations cited are intentionally broad because physical attractiveness phenomenon is neither the domain nor disproportionate bane of any particular country. Likewise, physical attractiveness phenomenon spans the diversity of populations within countries even though the extent of diversity varies between countries, and even though every country has diversity in terms of subcultures based on any number of criteria beyond the most frequently considered groups such as race, ethnicity, age, socioeconomic level, and so forth.

The remaining text of this chapter discusses a few more research projects conducted in different countries that explicitly investigate physical attractiveness phenomenon. Although these studies contribute to the global, cross-cultural robustness of data concerning physical attractiveness phenomenon, the researchers did not design them to be comparative investigations with focus to identify cross-cultural differences and similarities in different parts of the world. Nevertheless, these collected data have led to separate discoveries with equivalent results that further corroborate the universality of physical attractiveness phenomenon. Ultimately, the collective research findings provide evidence that substantiates that physical attractiveness phenomenon truly is multicultural, unrestrained by the many factors (e.g., location, age, education, religion, ethnicity, political stance, and so on) that commonly differ between populations and within populations and which form respective groups, cultures, and subcultures.

Scientific research conducted worldwide documents the principal findings consistent with the overwhelming findings of physical attractiveness research conducted in the United States. Published scholarly studies conducted in countries literally around the world collectively offer sufficient quantity and quality to reveal the effects of physical attractiveness are not unique to people in the United States. A principal dimension of physical attractiveness phenomenon, which is the pursuit of increased physical attractiveness, often at extreme lengths, is evident in every country, culture, and time throughout history. Just one example is China, ranging from nineteenth century foot-binding to increase physical attractiveness, accentuated recently in a 2005 novel,[629, 729] to the current escalation of cosmetic surgeries deliberated in a 2005 *Beijing Review* newspaper article descriptively titled "Taking a Risk to be Beautiful."[759] Of course, while foot-binding is a far distant memory, parallels exist today, such as the continuing popularity of stiletto shoes to enhance a woman's physical attractiveness as well as sex appeal.[149, 150] According to John Liggett, who authored *The Human Face* when he was a psychology professor in Wales,[409] people throughout history around the world have pursued painful treatments and options, most frequently focused on their face, to increase their physical attractiveness:

> …all peoples, sophisticated as well as primitive, seem prepared to go through almost unbelievable suffering in the pursuit [of greater physical attractiveness. The benefits ascribed to people of higher physical attractiveness drive the motivations that] …beauty must be pursued at whatever price, because it confers on its possessor profound social influence, power and respect.[409]

Determinants

Determinants of physical attractiveness are many, complicated, dynamic, and much more. Characteristics range from compensatory to non-compensatory as well as physical and non-physical, but the whole person is the ultimate determinant rather than any one of the myriad of separate components that compose an individual. Physiology can further perplex determinants of physical attractiveness. Researchers in Japan discovered that self-perceived heart rate is, at times, even a determinant of rating the physical attractiveness of another person.[312] In this study, the research procedure presented subjects (males) with slides of nude stimulus persons (females) and manipulated physiological information by providing subjects with misleading feedback about their own heart rate while viewing the stimulus persons. Regardless of the subjects' actual heart rate responses to stimulus persons, when they were provided false information about increases in their heart rate, they then rated the photographed stimulus persons significantly higher in physical attractiveness than when the information stated either no rate change or a decrease in heart rate. An important note here is that erotic appeal, or sexiness, can represent a potentially confounding factor in this study because erotic appeal and physical attractiveness are not necessarily synonymous constructs.[520, 528]

Still another sphere of physical attractiveness determinants incorporates intangible deeds of stimulus persons or, even more obfuscating, the lack of a specific intangible deed. Consider this study in which researchers told subjects (160 male and female university students) in India that a crime victim, with physical attractiveness described as either high or low, retaliated or did not retaliate against an aggressor (male stimulus person) with physical attractiveness described as either high or low in physical attractiveness.[339] The resulting data disclosed significant effects due to physical attractiveness, even though this project employed verbal designation of the level of physical attractiveness rather than visual representations of different levels of physical attractiveness, the more typical procedure. The victims rated highest in physical attractiveness were those who did not retaliate, whereas victims related lower in physical attractiveness were those who retaliated. Ratings by these subjects underscore the higher values consistently placed on higher physical attractiveness, as suggested by these data that divulged consistently less negative views as the aggressor's physical attractiveness increased.

While research into determinants of physical attractiveness includes aspects as identified above concerning physiology of judges and the lack of particular behavior by the judged, most research about determinants involves aspects that are more tangible. As discussed earlier in this book, a study conducted in England about body types as determinants of physical attractiveness masked the faces of stimulus persons and found quite neutral feelings about mesomorphs (average/medium body build), positive feelings for endomorphs (large/overweight compared to average, sometimes accompanied by muscular build), and negative opinions of ectomorphs (small/thin compared to average).[664] Another study also discussed earlier about body type as a determinant of physical attractiveness was a direct cross-cultural comparative investigation between people in the United States and Israel.[239] In terms of physical attractiveness phenomenon, a series of analysis of variance tests performed on the data discovered no significant effects due to cross-cultural differences. Among the extensive interactions that occurred among practically all combinations of manipulated variables—abdomen, shoulder, neck, head, and body shape—abdomen wielded a consistently powerful impact whereby subjects without fail evaluated physical attractiveness lower for stimulus persons with a protruding abdomen compared to persons without a protruding abdomen.

Ability Enhanced

Higher physical attractiveness accentuates a person's (evaluated/perceived) ability or competence, according to research conducted in the United States and elsewhere. Subjects (female high school students, 90 in total) in Belgium evaluated creativity of writing accompanied by a photo of the person credited to have written the work.[393] The assumed writer was one of five stimulus persons (male college students,) representing different levels of physical attractiveness. Subjects evaluated the writing as more creative when the assumed writer/stimulus person was higher in physical attractiveness compared to lower.

Another research investigation about the influence of higher or lower physical attractiveness upon the evaluation of ability and work also utilized writing as the work evaluated.[97] Researchers presented subjects (48 teachers and 24 students) in England with essays identical in content and different in format—typed, handwritten well, or handwritten poorly. A photograph attached to each essay visually communicated the supposed author of the work (i.e., the stimulus persons) who was a male or female of high or low physical attractiveness. Physical attractiveness of presumed authors influenced evaluations by both teachers and students serving as subjects. Overall, subjects evaluated essay quality more favorably when written by a presumed author of higher compared to lower physical attractiveness. Interaction effects in the data revealed that subjects evaluated most favorably the essays attributed to a female of high physical attractiveness. The research manipulation of physical attractiveness in this project did not reveal significant differences for male authors/stimulus persons.

Strangers Interacting

As noted, research in multiple countries shows that individuals will provide more help and do more work when requested, passively or actively, by individuals of higher compared to lower physical attractiveness. At the same time, those of higher physical attractiveness also can elicit more behaviors such as favorable responses to friendly gestures. The situation seems to be that people of higher physical attractiveness possess greater social powers that may or may not be interdependent with the well-documented perceptions and expectations in their favor. To test this hypothesis or notion, researchers explicitly designed a comparative cross-cultural study to assess differences in the responses of children to a smiling or non-smiling stranger.[19] Subjects were elementary school students in Israel (485 total second- and third-graders) and elementary school students in the United States (377 total second- and third-graders). Two findings concluded by these researchers (which, incidentally, both carry potent meaning for the stranger-child abduction problem that occurs worldwide) were:

- Strangers of higher physical attractiveness who smile at targeted others receive more smiling behavior in return than do counterpart strangers of lower physical attractiveness. The data underlying this finding were collected using adult strangers who smiled or did not smile at targeted children.

- Strangers higher and lower in physical attractiveness elicit a response pattern the same in different cultures/countries. Researchers collected the respective data for this finding from two countries and involved adult strangers who smiled or did not smile at targeted children.

Collected data document well that the physical attractiveness of help seekers is not a neutral factor for the quality and quantity given by help providers. On the flip side, the physical attractiveness of help providers also is not a neutral factor; it affects whether or not help seekers will ask for their assistance. Researchers in Israel found that subjects seek more assistance from help providers lower in physical attractiveness, especially when help seekers and help providers are the same sex.[488] These researchers interpreted this apparent reversal of physical attractiveness phenomenon as due to the social distance that individuals of moderate or lower physical attractiveness feel toward individuals of higher physical attractiveness, especially in situations that might amplify feelings of weakness and inferiority such as seeking help. Gender, particularly opposite gender dyads, produced significant interaction effects in the data. Male subjects sought more help from female providers of lower physical attractiveness, whereas female subjects sought less help from male providers of lower physical attractiveness.

Legal Proceedings

Substantial research concerns physical attractiveness and its importance within the legal system, as identified in my 1985 book titled *The Physical Attractiveness Phenomena* (see "Crime and Courts" in chapter 3, beginning on page 60 of that book).[535] Physical attractiveness is clearly not neutral in the legal systems of countries throughout the world as well as in the United States; nor is it neutral in any particular type of legal proceedings ranging from civil (non-criminal) cases to criminal cases. Of course, much of the knowledge and perspective about this topic is proprietary to practicing legal professionals, whether working in prosecution or defense of accused individuals, portraying clients and victims, or screening and selecting jurors.

Research investigating obedience to authority provides some fundamental insight about why physical attractiveness might be noteworthy in legal proceedings, particularly as it concerns accused individuals. One early study examined perception and prediction of obedience to authority as a function of physical attractiveness and gender of stimulus persons. It utilized 240 subjects (120 males and 120 females) in two experiments with Milgram's obedience paradigm.[460] The researchers concluded subjects perceived individuals of higher physical attractiveness as more caring, more responsible, more independent, and, distinctly pertinent to legal proceedings, more internally motivated and more resistant to control by others. The implication is that people are likely to believe that individuals of higher physical attractiveness are less likely to commit negative, harmful behaviors; subsequently, they may be less likely to be assigned guilt and punishment when accused of crime.

The ramifications of disparate legal actions based on differences in physical attractiveness are disturbing. One of the bedrocks of democratic cultures is equal and fair treatment for all people, highlighted in a legal system that proclaims the law to presume every person innocent until proven guilty. However, once in the courtroom, the legal system puts the physical attractiveness variable on view, intentionally or unintentionally, when all people who will judge the accused person's innocence and guilt have the opportunity to see the person's physical attractiveness. Defense attorneys certainly recognize the capacity of physical attractiveness as they advise their clients to maximize their appearance through grooming, posture, behavior, and dress. Real-world experience has no doubt established that these subtle and legal maneuvers do influence juries and increase the likelihood of favorable treatment for the defendant of higher physical attractiveness. Both for legal crimes and social offenses, research shows jurors treat defendants of higher physical attractiveness more leniently,[321] including less harsh punishments.[27, 114, 116, 196, 228] Even in civil cases, simulated court settings reveal jurors give plaintiffs of higher physical attractiveness more favorable judgments including larger monetary awards.[660]

Legal proceedings present one of the few irregular scenarios associated with physical attractiveness phenomenon. While the overwhelmingly common pattern of benefits and detriments aligns with higher and lower physical attractiveness, researchers have found the reverse in certain select legal instances. Research conducted in Germany found, as expected according to the most part of physical attractiveness phenomenon, that when a simulated traffic offense of questionable intention that resulted in a street accident occurred, offenders of higher physical attractiveness received more lenient punishments than offenders of lower physical attractiveness.[568] However, interaction effects occurred within the physical attractiveness data for this research that used subjects (44 males and 44 females) in an experimental design to investigate length of imprisonment recommended. If the accident did not cause a death, subjects gave defendants of higher physical attractiveness more favorable treatment, but if the accident caused a fatality, the reverse occurred whereby subjects gave defendants of lower physical attractiveness more favorable treatment.

Despite ideals for objectivity and judgments based only on defined facts, judgments clearly appear also to be impacted by the physical attractiveness of defendants, victims, jurors, and even opposing attorneys. An opinion survey of potential jury members reveals another illustration of contradiction between what people say and what people do concerning physical attractiveness. People certainly believe in ideals of objectivity for legal proceedings: 79 percent of respondents in this survey said jurors' decisions should be influenced by character and history of defendants and 93 percent said physical attractiveness of defendants should not influence jurors' decisions.[196] To investigate further these data, an experiment conducted in a simulated court setting presented the legal case summaries of defendants along with a photograph of the presumed defendants who were either high or low in physical attractiveness. In direct contrast to attitudes and behavioral intentions expressed in the survey data, the experimental data exposed significant influence of defendants' physical attractiveness upon actual behavior by potential jurors. Those defendants of higher physical attractiveness received statistically different evaluations of less certainty of guilt and less severity of recommended punishment. Regardless of explanation, the fact remains that preferential treatment occurred in this investigation of legal processes. Every reasonable speculation in light of physical attractiveness phenomenon is that it occurs in actual legal proceedings, too.

Friends and Strangers

Nonromantic interactions characterized by interpersonal exchanges between friends and strangers occur frequently, and certainly more frequently than romantic exchanges. Some people might suspect physical attractiveness influences less the exchanges between friends and strangers than romantic interactions, but research in diverse cultures in the United States and beyond does not support this suspicion. One research project varied physical attractiveness of stimulus persons by manipulating the appearance of their face so the skin looked more or less healthy.[77] This study, conducted in Germany, used photographs in an experiment designed to eliminate or minimize potential factors other than the face in the stimulus persons' physical attractiveness and, specifically, potential factors other than the more or less healthy appearance of the face skin. The experimental treatment employed a natural photograph showing a person with face skin of low physical attractiveness in contrast to a retouched photograph showing the same person with face skin of high physical attractiveness. Data revealed subjects judged those stimulus persons of higher physical attractiveness as more appealing and they expressed a preferred smaller social distance compared to the data about stimulus persons of lower physical attractiveness.

Another study conducted with subjects (236 males and 255 females) in Germany administered a sociometric questionnaire to students in rural schools.[375] Statements imbedded within the questionnaire asked subjects to list three peers who represented positive characteristics and three peers who represented negative characteristics. The resulting data were rather uniformly consistent with physical attractiveness phenomenon; the nonromantic peers identified to represent positive characteristics were students who happened to be also higher in physical attractiveness and the nonromantic peers identified to represent negative characteristic were students who were also lower in physical attractiveness.

Meeting-Dating-Mating

Romantic attractions concerning long-term spousal commitments in the context of meeting-dating-mating outcomes are undoubtedly a dimension of physical attractiveness phenomenon most open to speculation by the nonscientific population. American research on reciprocal interpersonal interactions within physical attractiveness phenomenon focused on meeting-dating-mating interactions early in the development of physical attractiveness research, and it documented robustly that physical attractiveness in romantic attraction is constant across countries and cultures. One study, an observational research design approximating techniques characteristic of content analysis research, examined romantic attraction in India.[128] This research conducted in 1974 randomly selected personal marriage advertisements for advertisers (200 males and 200 females) in a major Indian newspaper and found that the advertisers were generally middle class, highly educated, and of relatively high social status. To determine the importance of physical attractiveness in courtship leading to marriage, the researchers searched for statements specifying physical attractiveness and other words and terms meaning physical attractiveness in the advertisements. For males seeking female partners, 91 percent of advertisements referred to physical attractiveness, compared to 10 percent of advertisements for females seeking male partners. Given the substantial references to physical attractiveness, despite a strong tradition throughout this country/population against such preferences related to appearance, the authors concluded that physical attractiveness plays an important role in courtship and marriage in India. Similarly, *The Wall Street Journal* published an article in 1983 that reported even in cultures with a tradition of arranged marriages, such as Japan in this case, "the men are all looking for good-looking women" as marriage partners.[394]

Intrapersonal Reality

This cross-cultural section references some early research conducted in different parts of the world that contribute to verifying the global nature of physical attractiveness phenomenon. The research projects by and large document interpersonal realities concerning the effect of physical attractiveness between individuals, which then complements research referenced from many countries cited earlier in this book. In addition, these research projects help to verify intrapersonal realities within individuals due to effects of physical attractiveness phenomenon.

Maybe through self-fulfilling prophecy or some mixture of nature and nurture, actual personalities, rather than only perceived personalities, differ between individuals of different levels of physical attractiveness. Investigating relationships between physical attractiveness and actual personalities, subjects (high school students in Germany, 115 males and 92 females) self-rated their physical attractiveness while researchers independently assessed their personalities with standard testing measures and protocols.[716] Researchers found that subjects who rated themselves higher in physical attractiveness exhibited better social adjustment and had fewer problems related to personality characteristics than did those rated lower in physical attractiveness. Congruently, research with subjects in Japan (796 Japanese secondary students and college students, evenly divided between males and females), discovered those who held less favorable views of their physical attractiveness also possessed actual lower self-esteem.[398]

FORMAL RESISTANCE

Opposition to the role that physical attractiveness exerts within our society is mostly hypocritical. Much of the outward opposition is fleeting and faux resistance expressed by individuals who "say one thing and do another" and who exemplify the proverbial wisdom that "actions speak louder than words." These people, despite what they say verbally, as well as maybe what they wish to be true, still strongly adhere, consciously or subconsciously, to physical attractiveness phenomenon. At the same time, individuals, endeavors, and organizations of all types and sizes are helping individuals who are disadvantaged by physical attractiveness phenomenon, and are helping resist physical attractiveness phenomenon along the lines of the slogan that, "if you cannot do everything, then do not do nothing." Actions underway, albeit diminutive in their beginning stages, include legal options and support options in formal resistance to physical attractiveness phenomenon. Both these options provide avenues to empower greater and more apparent help and opposition to physical attractiveness phenomenon than might exist currently.

Legal Options

Legal options include efforts to generate government legislation and efforts to file individual lawsuits. Some pertinent legislation has occurred, albeit infrequently, in a few municipalities in the United States. Laws have passed in Santa Cruz, California to make employment decisions illegal if based on height, weight, or physical characteristics, and employment decisions based on height or weight are illegal in the state of Michigan and the city of San Francisco.[715] Although the goals are worthy, the impact is very slow to come and not enough to be meaningful for significant numbers of people.

Possibly an interesting inconsistency within the legal arena is "Washington, D.C. [which] outlaws employment discrimination based on personal appearance."[715] Perhaps, that legislation was facilitated by the near certainty that physical attractiveness phenomenon and the physical appearance of every elected official in Washington played a role in their election, and will again in their campaign efforts if they decide to make a bid for re-election. Moreover, physical attractiveness phenomenon seems to have exerted its influence at the very top of the legal system. A case in point is when, against strong political-philosophical odds, the U. S. Senate confirmed John Roberts in 2005 to serve as chief justice of the United States Supreme Court. Some political analysts in the media and academia attributed his high physical attractiveness to have significantly helped his persuasiveness that led to his successful confirmation. When discussion focuses on the physical appearance of John Roberts, it always explicitly or implicitly identifies determinants commonly identified with physical attractiveness phenomenon—handsomeness, relatively youthful looks, tallness, and impressive clothes.[714]

Formal resistance against discrimination in the workplace concerning physical attractiveness is ongoing and is not new. In 1976, *U. S. News & World Report* published an article titled "Now, a Drive to End Discrimination Against 'Ugly' People."[711] Then, again, in 1983 the same highly-respected newsmagazine published an article of similar sentiment titled "Bias Against Ugly People."[710] Beyond attempts to create government policies that address related legalities, legal actions are typically individual court cases against employers. However, legal opinion is that, "Employers are free to be unfair, says Bill O'Brien, a Minneapolis-based employment lawyer. Other than some protected classes, there isn't a great deal employees can do about it."[715]

To remedy discrimination based on physical attractiveness through legal means is not impossible, but it is extremely difficult. The difficulty is due partly to the inability to construct a standard definition of the physical attractiveness variable. Therefore, plaintiffs concerning employment discrimination most frequently articulate interrelated surrogate measures such as weight, height, and a list of protected-class demographic variables. One such lawsuit that received substantial mass media attention was filed in 2003 against the upscale retailer Abercrombie & Fitch.[113] Plaintiffs initially claimed employment discrimination based on physical attractiveness, but later shifted the claim to the protected-class demographics of race and ethnicity.

The Abercrombie & Fitch lawsuit illustrates the murkiness that complicates efforts to challenge discrimination based on the level of a person's physical attractiveness. First, it is not (yet) illegal to discriminate in employment on physical attractiveness, even though former managers at Abercrombie & Fitch as well as legal experts and media commentators acknowledge the retailer takes explicit actions to hire good-looking people, and once hired, gives them more compensation than people who are less good looking. Second, the distinction as well as ability in the mind of many people to differentiate people based on their physical attractiveness is blurry at best. Consider a few statements and perspectives specific to this lawsuit against this retail company as reported in a CBS Television network news program:[124]

- Two former managers at Abercrombie & Fitch report the company was "after a certain look [of physical attractiveness] for their sales force, and the less a salesperson had of this look, the less they worked."

- One former manager states: "I was sick of getting my schedule back every week with lines through names. I can't look the people that work for me, that want to be there, in the eye and lie to them and say we don't have hours [for you to work] when, really, it's because they weren't pretty enough."

- Another former manager identified to have worked earlier as a model states he "had a similar experience" concerning his superiors scheduling hours differently for his employees of higher and lower physical attractiveness. For himself, the news program reports, "he says his look [of high physical attractiveness] is what got him a job…it was 90 percent of it and your interaction with other people was 10 percent."

- A lawyer and radio talk show host who is African American defends the company's hiring practices based on physical attractiveness. He "likens [physically] unattractive people's failure to be hired by Abercrombie & Fitch to white people failing to be hired for on-air work by Black Entertainment Television: "There is a no-fly zone over certain people and certain industries that discriminate all the time." According to him, the Abercrombie & Fitch situation "is about a business deciding, pursuant to its own best interests, rightly or wrongly, that a particular type of salesperson is more likely to generate more dollars."

- The company denies any discrimination based on race or gender in their hiring practices, substantiated by the two former managers above when they say, "…what they saw was 'lookism' rather than racism. Applications from minorities were handled the same as a white person's. File it away in the yes pile to call back or in the no pile. The no pile was for applications of people whose looks [levels of physical attractiveness] she [the manager] knew wouldn't pass muster."

A newspaper article published by the *New York Times* News Service amplifies the CBS Television network news program above.[259] First, it quotes a former assistant store manager for Abercrombie & Fitch (separate from the two above managers cited) who states, "If someone came in with a pretty face, we were told to approach them and ask them if they wanted a job. [Central corporate management] thought if we had the best-looking college kids working in our store, everyone will want to shop there." Second, it reports the following:

- "Abercrombie's aggressive approach to building a pretty and handsome sales force, an effort that company officials proudly acknowledge, is a leading example of what many industry experts and sociologists describe as a steadily growing trend in American retailing."
- "Hiring for looks [of high physical attractiveness] is old news in some industries. But many companies have taken that approach to sophisticated new heights in recent years, hiring workers to project an image. In doing so, some of those companies have been skirting the edges of antidiscrimination laws and provoking a wave of private and government lawsuits."
- "Hiring [only physically] attractive people is not necessarily illegal, but discriminating on the bias of age, sex or ethnicity is. That is where things can get confusing and contentious."
- According to the director of the Los Angeles office of the Equal Employment Opportunity Commission, "If you're hiring by looks [of high physical attractiveness], then you can run into problems of race discrimination, national origin discrimination, gender discrimination, age discrimination and even disability discrimination." Accordingly, the Commission office "has accused several companies of practicing race and age discrimination by favoring good-looking...people in their hiring," who were "good-looking young white people."

Support Options

Some efforts in resistance to physical attractiveness phenomenon have transformed into various support options unrelated to lawsuits filed by individuals, with more likely to develop in the future. Support options are individuals and groups who provide assistance pertinent to physical attractiveness phenomenon for individuals and groups of individuals. These include organized groups, entities, and associations, to contend with and to help with selected aspects of physical attractiveness phenomenon.

Support groups typically offer assistance and advocacy focusing on one or more tangible surrogate dimensions known to be determinants of physical attractiveness. These dimensions typically are some that lend themselves most readily to objective or quantitative measures. Intentions of these efforts and groups are admirable while operating with less than desired financial resources and organizational structure, all combined with a huge challenge in the context of the solidly ingrained, societal momentum that not only maintains but also promulgates the physical attractiveness phenomenon. Two, not necessarily representative groups, that have sustained (and with whom I first communicated by personal letter in 1983) include the National Association to Aid Fat Americans, Inc.[207] and Little People of America, Inc.[273] Certainly, not all concerns and issues connected to a person being overweight or of short stature are associated with appearance or physical attractiveness, but some considerations aligned with physical attractiveness phenomenon are particularly pertinent, meaningful, and well within the scope of such organizations.

Many admirable, long-term, well-established groups and individuals with varying degrees of finances, organization, and recognition have missions and scopes with varying degrees of overlap or pertinence to physical attractiveness phenomenon. As with many organizations and entities, their missions and scopes may not be initially apparent concerning physical attractiveness phenomenon. Within these organizations and among these individuals can be offices, entities, and interests that align to varying extents with considerations pertinent to physical attractiveness phenomenon and a person's appearance/physical attractiveness. Any one comprehensive listing of such organizations, individuals, entities, and programs would be long and require expensive continuous updating, especially if the many tangential professionals, government agencies, and other organizations were to be included. However, some individuals close to this topic, government agencies, and library personnel can be good starting points for information that identify support options available to assist and advocate concerns about physical attractiveness phenomenon, as well as provide the interested persons with a start to understanding and utilizing resources available.

Advocacy and Assistance

Merging into the future from the present will challenge many individuals and populations in relation to physical attractiveness phenomenon. Individuals, groups, entities, and associations can facilitate future, as well as current, challenges to resist and to contend with dimensions of physical attractiveness phenomenon. Many groups and individuals offer assistance and advocacy, and some focus on one or more tangible surrogate dimensions known to be determinants of physical attractiveness. These dimensions typically lend themselves most readily to objective or quantitative measures, but not entirely. Even though individuals and populations will experience challenges due to the solidly ingrained, societal momentum that maintains and promulgates physical attractiveness phenomenon, people can flourish with pertinent knowledge as they choose to oppose and challenge, choose to cooperate and cope, or choose some combination of these actions.

Among the options to facilitate successful opposition, coping, and flourishing, I propose the further development of the Appearance Phenomenon Institute. Before introducing this Institute in the following section, permit me here to say that a multitude of options is available to address concerns and issues connected to a person's appearance, or physical attractiveness. Some of those are not-for-profit entities, and others are for-profit entities. Within them are ways for interested readers to start to understand, utilize, and/or financially support alternatives available to assist challenges and advocacies regarding physical attractiveness phenomenon. In addition, in every community or adjacent district, county, and state in the United States and around the world there is likely the potential assistance of one sort or another. A person can find expertise, interests, services, and products concerning physical attractiveness phenomenon among respective professionals and entities of all types. For example (in alphabetical order): attorneys, businesses, charities, child protective offices, corporations, dentists, elected government officials, government agencies and offices, philanthropic individuals, philanthropic foundations, physicians, psychiatrists, psychologists, school counselors, social workers, university professors, university researchers, and so forth. Also, while difficult to identify formally, individual professionals of all types of specialties and sub-specialties, as well as everyday individuals, who are good hearted, well meaning, and who care about physical attractiveness phenomenon along with its impact on individuals and groups of individuals.

Advisory

In all matters of life, change is constant. Research progresses, products and technologies advance, attitudes evolve, laws become legislated, and people move. Likewise, contact information of course changes on occasion for individuals and organizations. Accordingly, depending when an interested reader may wish to communicate with one or more individuals or organizations, it may be necessary to identify alternate contact information. The Internet is a useful tool in this regard.

In matters pertaining to physical attractiveness and physical attractiveness phenomenon, people need to choose, decide, and act wisely. Regardless if their interest is to understand, utilize, or provide financial support, *Caveat Emptor*, the Latin phrase often used in legal proceedings for "let the buyer beware," applies to options available pertaining to physical attractiveness. As people make decisions and choices concerning physical attractiveness, they need to be informed and aware of what is attainable and what is not attainable. Given the realities within populations around the world, as well as across the United States, people, entities, and products that compose physical attractiveness phenomenon reflect the competent and incompetent, the ethical and unethical, and the honest and dishonest.

Appearance Phenomenon Institute

The Appearance Phenomenon Institute focuses on physical attractiveness phenomenon. It recognizes that appearance of a person impacts every individual—from birth to death—and that, physical attractiveness is inextricably interrelated with, and largely inseparable from, appearance. It functions presently in early phases of development. Its complete formal title is the Appearance Phenomenon Institute (API) for Research, Advocacy, and Assistance, commonly referenced in shortened form as Appearance Phenomenon Institute, API, or Institute depending on context. API's founder and current director, Gordon L. Patzer, holds Ph.D., MBA, MS, and BA degrees. He has published numerous books, many scholarly journal articles, been cited in hundreds of publications written by other scholarly researchers, and national and international mass media have recognized his expertise and long-term work concerning physical attractiveness phenomenon.

A written administrative document of description and proposal, approximately fifty pages in length, describes the Appearance Phenomenon Institute presently and as planned when fully developed. It presents statements about mission, vision, core values, strategies, functions, activities, finances, and overseers, as well as information about the director and founder. As API becomes increasingly more developed, an objective is accordingly to serve all people interested in physical attractiveness phenomenon. Central to this service is the intention to provide help to understand, access, and utilize support (including financial support); to assist, challenge, and advocate in favor of desirable aspects and against undesirable aspects of physical attractiveness phenomenon.

The Appearance Phenomenon Institute intends ultimately to provide help concerning physical attractiveness phenomenon for entities of all types, including individuals, groups, not-for-profit organizations, businesses, causes, and government agencies. When more fully developed, API will be multidisciplinary, cross-cultural, and not-for-profit with a potentially wide range of funding sources, which is the same as now in its present early stages of development, the Institute. Upon adequate funding, API will provide financial assistance to interested students, scholars, and other researchers to study physical attractiveness and physical attractiveness phenomenon. This financial assistance will be primarily for scientific research projects based in universities, regardless of academic discipline. Physical attractiveness phenomenon is worldwide and, accordingly, the interests and perspectives of API always will be global.

Analogous with all living entities, the Appearance Phenomenon Institute will change. Changes will comprise foreseen and unforeseen developments, advancements, and continuous improvements. They will come from the founder, director, and other people and organizations that support the mission, vision, and functions of API. Some changes will take place in anticipation of factors both controllable and uncontrollable for API, while other changes will be in response to such factors. Locations, addresses, and telephone numbers also change over time for most all people and entities. As well as direct communications with API's director, the Internet is a useful tool regarding all changes.

The mission of the Appearance Phenomenon Institute for Research, Advocacy, and Assistance (API) is three-dimensional:

- To advance understanding about appearance, particularly physical attractiveness.
- To increase awareness of appearance phenomenon, particularly physical attractiveness phenomenon.
- To improve assistance for people disadvantaged by appearance phenomenon, particularly physical attractiveness phenomenon.

To accomplish its mission, the Appearance Phenomenon Institute emphasizes (1) scientific research to advance understanding, (2) diverse means to increase awareness, and (3) partnerships with not-for-profit organizations, government agencies, for-profit companies/businesses, and individuals, to improve assistance for people disadvantaged by their appearance, appearance phenomenon and particularly by their physical attractiveness and physical attractiveness phenomenon.

MERGING THE CURRENT INTO THE FUTURE

The Times They Are A-Changin' proclaimed singer-songwriter Bob Dylan from his frequently cited song released in 1964,[193] one year before the first scientific research article explicit to physical attractiveness phenomenon was published in 1965 by the *Journal of*

Personality and Social Psychology.[464] Changing times for physical attractiveness phenomenon means those future times, worldwide, will assuredly match past times replete with abundant sameness concerning physical attractiveness phenomenon and differences expected concerning physical attractiveness. In other words, transitory fashions and fads will change for defining physical attractiveness, but physical attractiveness phenomenon will remain the same. Physical attractiveness will continue to serve as an informational cue from which people infer extensive information that triggers assumptions, expectations, attitudes, and behaviors that cause pervasive and powerful consequences/effects. The effects will continue to favor overwhelmingly people with appearances higher in physical attractiveness and disfavor people with appearances lower in physical attractiveness.

Differences between past and future will be limited, but similarities will be imposing. One very substantial positive difference will be that greater knowledge will exist tomorrow than today about the entire topics of physical attractiveness and physical attractiveness phenomenon. This knowledge will continue to come from all parts of the world, from researchers of great diversity who include cross-cultural and cross-discipline perspectives using varied research methodologies, with all adding to the discovery of findings that address micro questions and macro questions. Together these robust research efforts and findings will help to advance our already robust understanding. Researchers concerned with continuously evolving topics and questions about physical attractiveness phenomenon will continuously provide answers to macro questions emphasizing psychology and sociology in their broadest definitions.

Similarly, researchers will continue to find answers to micro questions for the continuously evolving topics and questions. Consider the recent work produced by a research team composed of one professor in the Netherlands and another in the United States.[717] Their findings documented that pairing negative and positive words with human faces of higher physical attractiveness significantly facilitates the cognitive processing task of categorizing these words. Another cross-cultural team documented that sperm from males of higher and lower physical attractiveness, when analyzed according to World Health Organization guidelines, correlated significantly and positively with sperm morphology, motility, and a Sperm Index.[649] Subjects and stimulus persons were all in Spain, while the cross-disciplinary research team came from departments of functional biology and physical anthropology in Spain, chemistry and biology in the country of Colombia, and in the United States from the Harvard Medical School.

A difference, albeit moderate, might be some increase in the awareness and open confirmation of physical attractiveness phenomenon among the non-research population. However, the greatest but still limited differences between past and future will be concentrated on apparent, or readily seen, dimensions of physical attractiveness, particularly in how these dimensions take shape, metamorphose, and otherwise change to meet internal drives within people for novelty and to accommodate changes in technology and societal attitudes. In other words, fashions defining physical attractiveness will change, but the much larger universe of physical attractiveness phenomenon will not change.

One need simply look at recent media to see the rather explicit description of physical attractiveness phenomenon along with its promulgation. Consider the following several examples promulgating physical attractiveness phenomenon through messages that span present-day populations, from national-international presidential politics, to movies and television, to sports and comics:

- "In Politics, as in Life, Good Looks are an Advantage," stated the headline published in the front section of the Sunday, July 11, 2004, issue of *The New York Times* for an article concerning the increased likelihood that voters would elect a certain person to lead the United States. The article criticized the value or importance equated with the high physical attractiveness possessed by one of the major candidates in the 2004 United States November presidential election, and claimed that the leader of unarguably the most powerful nation in the international arena today would be elected because of looks.[668]

- "In 'Entourage,' Mark Wahlberg Exposes the Ugly Life of a Posse," stated the headline published on the front page of the "Arts & Leisure" section of the same (July 11, 2004) issue of The New York Times as cited above. This article described the negative and detrimental relationships, "[f]or these friends, having their most parasitic moments replayed for a national audience…" in an upcoming television series.[445] The article explains this to be a national broadcast scheduled initially across the United States, and almost certain international release soon to follow. According to the article, the program equates ugliness or lower physical attractiveness with disfavor, unpleasantness, and evil, and ultimately conveys that ugly people, those of lower physical attractiveness, are of less value and that people should avoid them.

- "They have some beautiful women combined with some pretty great tennis" stated the former world champion of men's tennis, John McEnroe, in an interview published in Time magazine on July 12, 2004.[611] As noted in this article, he is now an internationally respected authority in sports broadcasting about tennis and, respectively, holds the number one commentary role for BBC (British Broadcasting Corporation) sports, which carries great significance given the worldwide reach and respect of BBC television. Mr. McEnroe's apparently well-received statement, made in his role as a recognized world authority on this sport, not only explicitly references physical attractiveness and athletic ability, but also even states the former (beauty/physical attractiveness) first. His statement was in response to an interviewer's question asking, "Why do the women seem to be ahead of the men right now?" in tennis audience spectatorship.

- Employees in the comic "Dilbert" work to make products to sell to customers "so our executives can afford trophy wives" stated the box-scene in this syndicated Sunday newspaper comic from 2004 in newspapers across the United States and beyond.[14] Given that "Dilbert" is a particularly popular comic that newspapers publish in either their comics or business section, it likely has a disproportionate influence as a reflector and shaper of societal values. Thus, in this particular edition, it promulgates notions that people (women/wives in this situation) are more valued/more costly when their physical attractiveness is high, so much so that the phrase "trophy wife" is used to indicate that higher physical attractiveness can be exchanged for a partner with much greater wealth and prestige than lower physical attractiveness.

- Physically "unattractive women are only good for easy sex," is the message, and nearly verbatim words, sung out clearly and repetitively by superstar rap artist Nelly (Cornell Haynes Jr.), who in 2004 began to perform his song titled "Tip Drill," according to an article published by the *Chicago Tribune*.[748] Not always obvious on the surface, a significant portion of songs within most genres, spanning trendiest hits to time-honored conventional standards and performed by singers at all levels of popularity, reinforce physical attractiveness phenomenon. While these lyrics pertain most often to females, males are not excluded. Through these means of delivery, listeners and viewers receive these messages with, in effect, no questioning. A consequence is that physical attractiveness phenomenon ingrains further into every person's mind and, especially notable, into the minds of today's young people; who are future adults who will pass these perspectives onto their own children with continuing promulgation.

Our future world will almost certainly extend the past and present universe of physical attractiveness phenomenon with no significant changes, although connected aspects will travel along albeit with their own definite changes. As referenced earlier in this book, genders are increasingly equalizing on many dimensions of life, though the changes are slower or faster than some people prefer. Some people view the changes desirable, but other people find the changes undesirable. An illustrative example is the trophy wife, or, increasingly, the trophy spousal partner. While social mores are changing visibly concerning genders of meeting-dating-mating partnerships, the impact of physical attractiveness phenomenon for these partnerships is amazingly stable. Even moderately astute observation of reality readily confirms the exchanges of disparate levels of physical attractiveness in meeting-dating-mating spousal partnerships occur more frequently than chance or natural matching would identify. Furthermore, these unequal exchanges around physical attractiveness are extending without change into the future from the past and present, despite the changes occurring overtly with aspects (e.g., gender combinations) connected to or affected by physical attractiveness phenomenon.

This age-old exchange pattern around physical attractiveness continues today and assuredly will continue tomorrow for traditionally recognized male and female partnerships, and its apparentness will be increasingly evident at every stage and form. It starts with interest even before seeing, speaking, or meeting, traverses through attraction and courting/dating, and continues through a publicly recognized commitment for faithfulness that either leads to the long-standing, worldwide tradition of marriage or more recent practices of cohabitations and civil unions of all dyad combinations of males and females. Consider for the moment an excerpt from the mass media magazine article that *Newsweek* published July 12, 2004, as its cover story about changing roles (personally, professionally, financially, and socially) of women, with emphasis in this article on the United States:

> And like their fathers before them, powerful women are learning to savor the attentions of a companion who is physically attractive but not as rich, successful—or old—as they are.[20]

CONCLUSION

As in the past and present, physical attractiveness phenomenon in the future will continue to connect physical attractiveness with an extraordinary structure of hidden values, far deeper than skin deep and far more than meets the eye. In universal and sometimes complicated patterns, higher physical attractiveness will continue to be beneficial and lower physical attractiveness will continue to be detrimental to those individuals whose appearances differ correspondingly. People of both genders and of all ages will continue to pursue higher and higher levels of physical attractiveness, often with unaffordable and negative consequences.

Many dimensions will continue to define appearance in the future, and physical attractiveness will maintain its predominance to impact every individual throughout every community, across the United States and around the world. Physical attractiveness will hold its position as it triggers, exerts, and controls a phenomenon that is powerful and pervasive despite the fact that people seldom see it, seldom recognize it, and very frequently deny it. Inherent in situation, mainstream society will continue, albeit not always recognized, to reinforce and promulgate physical attractiveness phenomenon. One illustration is an enduringly popular rock song, first released in 1978 by Bob Seger, containing lyrics that unknowingly describe, endorse, and encourage the power of physical attractiveness found repeatedly in physical attractiveness phenomenon research. Inspired by international supermodel Cheryl Tiegs, the lyrics state well the power, appeal, and value exerted by people whose appearance represents higher physical attractiveness:[630] "She had been born with a face that would let her get her way. He saw that face and he lost all control."

Said another way, higher physical attractiveness always has and always will provide the holder with greater choice and opportunity, in countries and communities around the world. In 2005, a United Kingdom newspaper in Scotland published an article that reported:

> Looks do matter when it comes to climbing the career ladder. That's the verdict of Scots women, despite decades of struggling to be accepted for their brains rather than their beauty. According to the *Female Body Survey of Great Britain 2005*, commissioned by *Top Sante* magazine, more than half of all women in Scotland said that, if they [were more physically attractive, body and face], they would change their career. ...No wonder more and more ordinary women now see cosmetic surgery as the key to changing their lives, be it their career, partner, or general lifestyle.[159]

What has transpired in the past and present will continue in the future. A modification is the growing importance of a male's physical attractiveness that is moving increasingly in the direction toward levels of importance of a female's physical attractiveness. The newspaper article and data cited immediately above are today and increasingly into the future applicable to men as well as women, regardless of location, socioeconomics, or demographics. In conclusion, rather than diminishing the impact of physical attractiveness, the future will be emboldened and, perchance, even ablaze with intensification of hidden, and not so hidden, values of physical attractiveness, for men and women, boys and girls, and, all, with the power and paradox of physical attractiveness phenomenon.

References

1. ABC Television Network News. "Financing of Cosmetic Surgery, Special Report." In *ABC Nightly News with Peter Jennings*. New York: ABC Television Network News, 2004, July 30.
2. ————. "Teens Feel Pressure to Diet From Parents." In *Good Morning America*. New York: ABC Television Network News, 2005, July 6.
3. Abelson, R. P., Frey, K. P., and Gregg, A. P. *Experiments with People: Revelations from Social Psychology*. Mahwah, N.J.: Lawrence Erlbaum, 2004.
4. Adams, G. R. "Physical Attractiveness." In *In the Eye of the Beholder: Contemporary Issues in Stereotyping*, edited by A. G. Miller. New York: Praeger, 1982.
5. ————. "Physical Attractiveness Research: Toward a Developmental Social Psychology." *Human Development*, Vol. 20 (1977b): pp. 217-240.
6. ————. "Physical Attractiveness, Personality, and Social Reactions to Peer Pressure." *Journal of Psychology*, Vol. 96 (1977a): pp. 287-296.
7. ————. "Racial Membership and Physical Attractiveness Effects on Preschool Teachers' Expectations." *Child Study Journal*, Vol. 8 (1978): pp. 29-41.
8. Adams, G. R., and Cohen, A. S. "Children's Physical and Interpersonal Characteristics that Effect Student-Teacher Interactions." *Journal of Experimental Education*, Vol. 44 (1974): pp. 1-5.
9. ————. "An Examination of Cumulative Folder Information used by Teachers in Making Differential Judgments of Children's Abilities." *Alberta Journal of Educational Research*, Vol. 22 (1976): pp. 216-225.
10. Adams, G. R., and Crane, P. "An Assessment of Parents' and Teachers' Expectations of Preschool Children's Social Preference for Attractive or Unattractive Children and Adults." *Child Development*, Vol. 51 (1980): pp. 224-231.
11. Adams, G. R., and LaVoie, J. C. "The Effect of Student's Sex, Conduct, and Facial Attractiveness on Teacher Expectancy." *Education*, Vol. 95 (1974): pp. 76-83.
12. ————. "Parental Expectations of Educational and Personal-Social Performance and Childrearing Patterns as a Function of Attractiveness, Sex, and Conduct of the Child." *Child Study Journal*, Vol. 5 (1975): pp. 125-142.
13. Adams, G. R., and Read, D. "Personality and Social Influence Styles of Attractive and Unattractive College Women." *The Journal of Psychology*, Vol. 114 (1983): pp. 151-157.
14. Adams, S. "Dilbert (daily newspaper comic)." *Chicago Tribune*, Vol. 158, No. 191 (2004, July 18): p. 3 (section 9).
15. Agarwal, P., and Prakash, N. "Perceived Physical Attractiveness as Related to Attitudes toward Women's Liberation Movement." *Indian Psychological Review*, Vol. 15 (1977): pp. 31-34.
16. Agocha, V. B., and Cooper, M. L. "Risk Perceptions and Safer-Sex Intentions: Does a Partner's Physical Attractiveness Undermine the Use of Risk-Relevant Information?" *Personality and Social Psychology Bulletin*, Vol. 25 (1999): pp. 746-759.
17. Ahrens, R. "Beitrage zur Entvicklung des Physiognomia—und Mimikerkennes." *Zeitschrift fur Experimentelle und Angewandte Psychologies*, Vol. 2 (1954): pp. 412-454.
18. Alden, S. D., Laxton, R., Patzer, G. L., and Howard, L. "Establishing Cross-Disciplinary Marketing Education." *Journal of Marketing Education*, Vol. 13, No. 2 (1991): pp. 25-30.
19. Alexander, I. E., and Babad, E. Y. "Returning the Smile of the Stranger: Within-Culture and Cross-Culture Comparisons of Israeli and American Children." *Genetic Psychology Monographs*, Vol. 103 (1981): pp. 31-77.
20. Ali, L., and Miller, L. "The Secret Lives of Wives." *Newsweek*, Vol. 144, No. 2 (2004, July 12): pp. 46-54.

21. Allen, B. P. "Race and Physical Attractiveness as Criteria for White Subjects' Dating Choices." *Social Behavior and Personality*, Vol. 4 (1976): pp. 289-296.

22. Alley, T. R. "Head Shape and the Perception of Cuteness." *Developmental Psychology*, Vol. 17 (1981): pp. 650-654.

23. American Obesity Association. "Lose 30 Pounds in 30 Days!!!" (2002, July 24): Retrieved July 24, 2002, from http://www.obesity.org/subs/fastfacts/obesity_consumer_protect.shtml

24. Anderson, P. F. "Marketing, Scientific Progress, and Scientific Method." *Journal of Marketing*, Vol. 47 (1983): pp. 18-31.

25. Ang, A. "China Touts Made-To-Order Beauty." *Chicago Tribune*, Vol. 158, No. 348 (2004, December 13): p. 2 (section 1).

26. ———. "Chinese Contestants Prepare for First Pageant for Manmade Beauties." *Associated Press Worldstream* (2004, December 12): Retrieved July 23, 2005, from http://www.highbeam.com/library/doc2000.asp

27. Aronson, E. "Some Antecedents of Interpersonal Attraction." In *Nebraska Symposium on Motivation*, edited by W. J. Arnold and D. Levine. Lincoln, Nebraska: University of Nebraska Press, 1969.

28. Aronson, E., and Carlsmith, J. M. "Performance Expectancy as a Determinant of Actual Performance." *Journal of Abnormal and Social Psychology*, Vol. 65 (1962): pp. 179-182.

29. Arseneault, L., Tremblay, R. E., Boulerice, B., Seguin, J. R., and Saucier, J. F. "Minor Physical Anomalies and Family Adversity as Risk Factors for Violent Delinquency in Adolescence." *American Journal of Psychiatry*, Vol. 157 (2000): pp. 917-923.

30. Asch, S. E. "Effects of Group Pressure upon the Modification and Distortion of Judgments." In *Readings in Social Psychology (Rev. ed)*, edited by G. E. Swanson, T. M. Newcomb and E. L. Hartley, pp. 2-11. New York: Holt, 1952a.

31. ———. *Social Psychology*. New York: Prentice-Hall, 1952b.

32. ———. "Studies of Independence and Conformity: A Minority of One Against a Unanimous Majority." *Psychological Monographs*, Vol. 70, No. 9 (1956): pp. 1-70.

33. Assassa, S. "Beverly Hills MD's New Mini Face-Lift Wipes Away 10 Years." (2005, July 7): Retrieved July 26, 2005, from http://www.highbeam.com/library/doc2000.asp

34. Associated Press. "Obesity Surgery Has Great Risks, Study Says." *Redeye: An Edition of the Chicago Tribune*, Vol. 159, No. 292 (2005, October 19): p. 3.

35. Athanasiou, R., and Greene, P. "Physical Attractiveness and Helping Behavior." *Proceedings of the 81st Annual Convention of the American Psychological Association*, Vol. 8 (1973): pp. 289-290.

36. Averett, S., and Korenman, S. "The Economic Reality of The Beauty Myth." *Journal of Human Resources*, Vol. 31, No. 2 (1996, Spring): pp. 304-330.

37. Bailey, R. C., and Schreiber, T. S. "Congruency of Physical Attractiveness Perceptions and Liking." *Journal of Social Psychology*, Vol. 115 (1981): pp. 285-286.

38. Baily, R. C., and Price, J. P. "Perceived Physical Attractiveness in Married Partners of Long and Short Duration." *Journal of Psychology*, Vol. 99 (1978): pp. 155-161.

39. Bakalar, N. "Ugly Children May Get Parental Short Shrift." *The New York Times*, Vol. 154, No. 53,203 (2005, May 3): p. 7 (section F).

40. Balban, M. "Accuracy in Self Evaluation of Physical Attractiveness as a Function of Self Esteem and Defensiveness." Doctoral dissertation, University of Southern Mississippi, Hattiesburg, Mississippi, 1981.

41. Bamburg, J. *Raising Expectations to Improve Student Learning*. Oak Brook, Illinois: North Central Regional Educational Laboratory, 1994.

42. Banziger, G., and Hooker, L. "The Effects of Attitudes toward Feminism and Perceived Feminism on Physical Attractiveness Ratings." *Sex Roles*, Vol. 5 (1979): pp. 437-442.

43. Bar-Tal, D., and Saxe, L. "Effect of Physical Attractiveness on the Perception of Couples." *Personality and Social Psychology*, Vol. 1 (1974): pp. 30-32.

44. ———. "Perceptions of Similarly and Dissimilarly Attractive Couples and Individuals." *Journal of Personality and Social Psychology*, Vol. 33 (1976a): pp. 772-781.

45. ———. "Physical Attractiveness and It Relationship to Sex-Role Stereotyping." *Sex Roles*, Vol. 2 (1976b): pp. 123-133.

46. Barker, K. "Malls Sprout at Breakneck Pace in India." *Chicago Tribune*, Vol. 158, No. 52 (2005, February 21): p. 4 (section 1).

47. Barocas, R., and Black, H. K. "Referral Rate and Physical Attractiveness in Third-Grade Children." *Perceptual and Motor Skills*, Vol. 39 (1974): pp. 731-734.

48. Barocas, R., and Vance, F. L. "Physical Appearance and Personal Adjustment Counseling." *Journal of Counseling Psychology*, Vol. 21 (1974): pp. 96-100.

49. Barrett, J. "No Time for Wrinkles." *Newsweek*, Vol. 143, No. 21 (2004, May 10): pp. 82-85.

50. Bassili, J. N. "The Attractiveness Stereotype: Goodness or Glamour?" *Basic and Applied Social Psychology*, Vol. 2, No. 4 (1981): pp. 235-252.

51. Beale, J. M., and Keil, F. C. "Categorical Effects in the Perception of Faces." *Cognition*, Vol. 57, No. 3 (1995): pp. 217-239.

52. Beck, S., Ward-Hull, C., and McLear, P. "Variables related to Women's Somatic Preferences of Male and Female Body." *Journal of Personality and Social Psychology*, Vol. 34 (1976): pp. 1200-1210.

53. Bell, P. A., and Baron, R. A. "Environmental Influences on Attraction: Effects of Heat, Attitude Similarity, and Personal Evaluations." *Bulletin of the Psychonomic Society*, Vol. 4 (1974): pp. 479-481.

54. Bendersky, A. "Avril's no punk." *Redeye: An Edition of the Chicago Tribune*, Vol. 157, No. 67 (2004, March 8): p. 44.

55. Bennetts, L. "Beauty is Found to Attract Some Unfair Advantages." *The New York Times* 1978, March 18, 10.

56. Benson, P. L., Karabenick, S. A., and Lerner, R. M. "Pretty Pleases: The Effects of Physical Attractiveness, Race, and Sex on Receiving Help." *Journal of Experimental Social Psychology*, Vol. 12 (1976): pp. 409-415.

57. Bereczkei, T., Voros, S., Gal, A., and Bernath, L. "Resources, Attractiveness, Family Commitment; Reproductive Decisions in Human Mate Choice." *Ethnology*, Vol. 103, No. 8 (1997): pp. 681-699.

58. Berkowitz, W. R. "Perceived Height, Personality, and Friendship Choice." *Psychological Reports*, Vol. 24 (1969): pp. 373-374.

59. Berns, G. S., Chappelowa, J., Zinka, C. F., Pagnonia, G., Martin-Skurskia, M. E., and Richards, J. "Neurobiological Correlates of Social Conformity and Independence During Mental Rotation." *Biological Psychiatry* (2005): Retrieved July 30, 2005, from http://www.sciencedirect.com/science

60. Berscheid, E., and Bohrnstedt, G. "The Happy American Body: A Survey Report." *Psychology Today*, Vol. 7 (1973): pp. 119-131.

61. Berscheid, E., Dion, K. K., Walster, E., and Walster, G. W. "Physical Attractiveness and Dating Choice: A Test of the Matching Hypothesis." *Journal of Experimental Social Psychology*, Vol. 7 (1971): pp. 173-189.

62. Berscheid, E., and Walster, E. "Beauty and the Best." *Psychology Today*, Vol. 5 (1972): pp. 42-46.

63. ———. "Physical Attractiveness." In *Advances in Experimental Social Psychology*, edited by L. Berkowitz. New York: Academic Press, 1974.

64. Berscheid, E., Walster, E., and Bohrnstedt, G. "The Happy American Body: A Survey Report." *Psychology Today*, Vol. 7 (1973): pp. 119-131.

65. Biddle, J. E., and Hamermesh, D. S. "Beauty, Productivity, and Discrimination: Lawyers' Looks and Lucre." *Journal of Labor Economics*, Vol. 16, No. 1 (1998, January): pp. 172-201.

66. Birmingham Post. "Biggest is No Longer Breast for Women." *Birmingham Post* (2005, June 20): Retrieved July 24, 2005, from http://www.highbeam.com/library/doc2000.asp

67. Black, H. K. "Physical Attractiveness and Similarity of Attitude in Interpersonal Attraction." *Psychological Reports*, Vol. 35 (1974): pp. 403-406.

68. Black, S. L., and Biron, C. "Androstenol as a Human Pheromone: No Effect on Perceived Physical Attractiveness." *Behavior and Neural Biology*, Vol. 34 (1982): pp. 326-330.

69. Blakeslee, S. "What Other People Say May Change What You See." *The New York Times*, Vol. 154, No. 53,258 (2005, June 28): p. D3.

70. Bloch, R., and Richins, M. "You Look "Mahvelous": The Pursuit of Beauty and the Marketing Concept." *Psychology and Marketing*, Vol. 9, No. 1 (1992): pp. 3-15.

71. Blood, G. W., Mahan, B. W., and Hyman, M. "Judging Personality and Appearance from Voice Disorders." *Journal of Communication Disorders*, Vol. 12 (1979): pp. 63-68.

72. Blood, R. O. "A Retest of Waller's Rating Complex." *Marriage and Family Living*, Vol. 17 (1955): pp. 41-47.

73. ———. "Uniformities and Diversities in Campus Dating Preferences." *Journal of Marriage and Family Living*, Vol. 18 (1956): pp. 37-45.

74. Bond, R., and Smith, P. B. "Culture and Conformity: A Meta-Analysis of Studies using Asch's (1952b, 1956) Line Judgment Task." *Psychological Bulletin*, Vol. 119, No. 1 (1996): pp. 111-137.

75. Borkenau, P. "Rich Man and Beautiful Woman? Two Studies on Sex Differences in Mate Preferences." *Zeitschrift fur Sozial Psychologie*, Vol. 42, No. 5 (1993): pp. 289-297.

76. Bornstein, R. F. "Exposure and Effect—Overview and Meta-Analysis of Research." *Psychological Bulletin*, Vol. 106 (1989): pp. 265-289.

77. Bosse, K. "Social Situation of Persons with Dermatoses as a Phenomenon of Interpersonal Perception." *Zeitschrift fur Psychosomatische Medizin und Psychoanalyse*, Vol. 22 (1976): pp. 3-61.

78. Bower, T. G. R. *A Primer of Infant Development*. San Francisco: Freeman, 1977.

79. Branch, S., and Ball, D. "Using Reality to Sell: Dove Campaign Hopes to Redefine Notions of Beauty." *Chicago Tribune*, Vol. 159, No. 173 (2005, June 22): p. 3 (section 8).

80. Brenner, D., and Hinsdale, G. "Body Build Stereotypes and Self-Identification in Three Age Groups of Females." *Adolescence*, Vol. 13 (1978): pp. 551-562.

81. Bridges, J. S. "Sex-Typed May be Beautiful but Androgynous is Good." *Psychological Reports*, Vol. 48 (1981): pp. 267-272.

82. Brigham, J. C. "Limiting Conditions of the "Physical Attractiveness Stereotype": Attributions about Divorce." *Journal of Research in Personality*, Vol. 14 (1980): pp. 365-275.

83. Brislin, R. W. *Understanding Culture's Influence on Behavior*. New York: Harcourt, Brace, Janovich, 2000.

84. Brislin, R. W., and Lewis, S. A. "Dating and Physical Attractiveness: Replication." *Psychological Reports*, Vol. 22 (1968): p. 976.

85. Britt, S. H. *Psychological Principles of Marketing and Consumer Behavior*. Lexington, Massachusetts: Lexington Books, 1978.

86. Brophy, J. E., and Good, T. L. *Teacher-Student Relationships: Causes and Consequences*. New York: Holt, Rinehart, & Winston, 1974.

87. Brown, T., and Eng, K. "The Effects of Race, Physical Attractiveness and Value Similarity on Interpersonal Attraction." University of British Columbia (1970): Unpublished manuscript.

88. Bruce, V., and Young, A. W. "Understanding Face Recognition." *British Journal of Psychology* (1986): pp. 305-327.

89. Bruner, J. S., and Goodman, C. C. "Value and Need as Organizing Factors in Perception." *Journal of Abnormal and Social Psychology*, Vol. 42 (1947): pp. 33-44.

90. Brunswik, E. "Perceptual Characteristics of Schematized Human Figures." *Psychological Bulletin*, Vol. 36 (1939): p. 553.

91. Bruyer, R., Laterre, C., Seron, X., Feyereisen, P., Stryptien, E., Pierrard, E., and Rectem, D. "A Case of Prosopagnosia with Some Preserved Covert Remembrance of Familiar Faces." *Brain and Cognition*, Vol. 2 (1983): pp. 257-284.

92. Bryne, D., London, C., and Reeves, K. "The Effects of Physical Attractiveness, Sex, and Attitude Similarity on Interpersonal Attraction." *Journal of Personality*, Vol. 36 (1968): pp. 259-271.

93. Budge, H. S. "Dimensions of Physical Attractiveness: How Others See Us." Doctoral dissertation, University of Utah, Salt Lake City, Utah, 1981.

94. Bull, A. J., Burboge, S. E., Crandall, J. E., Fletcher, C. I., Lloyd, J. T., Rosenberg, R. L., and Rockett, S. L. "Effects of Noise and Intolerance of Ambiguity upon Attraction for Similar and Dissimilar Others." *Journal of Social Psychology*, Vol. 88 (1972): pp. 151-152.

95. Bull, R., and Rumsey, N. *Social Psychology of Facial Appearance*. New York: Springer Verlag, 1988.

96. Bull, R., and Shead, G. "Pupil Dilation, Sex of Stimulus, and Age and Sex of Observer." *Perceptual and Motor Skills*, Vol. 49 (1979): pp. 27-30.

97. Bull, R., and Stevens, J. "The Effects of Attractiveness of Writer and Penmanship on Essay Grades." *Journal of Occupational Psychology*, Vol. 52 (1979): pp. 53-59.

98. Burley, N. "Sex Ratio Manipulation and Selection of Attractiveness." *Science*, Vol. 211 (1981): pp. 721-722.

99. Buss, D. *The Evolution of Desire: Strategies of Human Mating*. New York: Basic Books, 1994.

100. Buss, D. M. *The Evolution of Desire*. New York: Harper Collins Publishers, Inc., 1994.

101. Buss, D. M., and Barnes, M. "Preferences in Human Mate Selection." *Journal of Personality and Social Psychology*, Vol. 50 (1986): pp. 559-570.

102. Buss, D. M., Shackelford, T. K., Kirkpatrick, L. A., and Larsen, R. J. "A Half Century of Mate Preferences: The Cultural Evolution of Values." *Journal of Marriage and the Family*, Vol. 51, No. 4 (2001): pp. 491-503.

103. Byrne, D. *The Attraction Paradigm*. New York: Academic Press, 1971.

104. Byrne, D., and Clore, G. L. "A Reinforcement Model of Evaluative Responses." *Personality: An International Journal*, Vol. 1 (1970): pp. 103-128.

105. Byrne, D., Ervin, C. R., and Lamberth, J. "Continuity between the Experimental Study of Attraction and "Real Life" Computer Dating." *Journal of Personality and Social Psychology*, Vol. 16 (1970): pp. 157-165.

106. Byrne, D., London, C., and Reeves, K. "The Effects of Physical Attractiveness, Sex, and Attitude Similarity on Interpersonal Attraction." *Journal of Personality*, Vol. 36 (1968): pp. 259-271.

107. Campanella, A., Hanoteau, C., Depy, D., Rossion, B., Bruyer, R., Crommerlinck, M., and Guerit, J. M. "Right N170 Modulation in a Face Discrimination Task." *Psychophysiology*, Vol. 37 (2000): pp. 796-806.

108. Carmichael, M. "No Girls, Please." *Newsweek*, Vol. 143, No. 4 (2004, January 26): p. 50.

109. Cash, T. F. "Psychosocial Effects of Male Pattern Balding." *Grant administered by Old Dominion University Foundation, funded by Manning, Selvage, and Lee (for The Upjohn Company)* (1987).

110. Cash, T. F., and Cash, D. W. "Women's Use of Cosmetics: Psychosocial Correlates and Consequences." *International Journal of Cosmetic Science*, Vol. 4 (1982): pp. 1-14.

111. Cash, T. F., Cash, D. W., and Butters, J. "Mirror, Mirror on the Wall...?" *Social Psychology Bulletin*, Vol. 9 (1983): pp. 351-358.

112. Cash, T. F., and Derlega, V. J. "The Matching Hypothesis: Physical Attractiveness among Same-Sex Friends." *Personality and Social Psychology Bulletin*, Vol. 4 (1978): pp. 240-243.

113. Cassidy, S. H. "Gonzalez et al. v. Abercrombie & Fitch." (2003): Lieff Cabraser Heimann & Bernstein, LLP (law firm). Attorney Stephen H. Cassidy, telephone: 415-956-1000, law firm Website: http://www.lieffcabraser.com, law firm e-mail: mail@lchb.com.

114. Cavior, H. E., Hayes, S. C., and Cavior, N. "Facial Attractiveness of Female Offenders: Effects on Institutional Performance." *Criminal Justice and Behavior*, Vol. 1 (1974): pp. 321-331.

115. Cavior, N., and Boblett, P. J. "Physical Attractiveness of Dating versus Married Couples." *Proceedings of the 80th Annual Convention of the American Psychological Association*, Vol. 7 (1972): pp. 175-176.

116. Cavior, N., and Howard, L. R. "Facial Attractiveness and Juvenile Delinquency Among Black and White Offenders." *Journal of Abnormal Child Psychology*, Vol. 1 (1973): pp. 202-213.

117. Cavior, N., Jacobs, A., and Jacobs, M. "The Stability and Correlation of Physical Attractiveness and Sex Appeal Ratings." West Virginia University, Morgantown, West Virginia (1974): Unpublished manuscript.

118. Cavior, N., Miller, K., and Cohen, S. H. "Physical Attractiveness, Attitude Similarity, and Length of Acquaintance as Contributors to Interpersonal Attraction among Adolescents." *Social Behavior and Personality*, Vol. 3 (1975): pp. 133-141.

119. Cawley, J. "The Impact of Obesity on Wages." *Journal of Human Resources*, Vol. 39, No. 2 (2004, Spring): pp. 451-474.

120. CBS Television Network News. "Did You Know?" In *CBSNews.com: Inside Scoop*. New York: CBS Television Network News, 2003, December 12.

121. ————. "Did You Know?" In *CBSNews.com: Inside Scoop*. New York: CBS Television Network News, 2003, November 19.

122. ————. "Did You Know?" In *CBSNews.com: Inside Scoop*. New York: CBS Television Network News, 2004, August 23.

123. ————. "(An Interview With) Goldie Hawn." In *60 Minutes*. New York: CBS Television Network News, 2005, May 1.

124. ————. "The Look of Abercrombie & Fitch." In *60 Minutes*. New York: CBS Television Network News, 2003, December 7.

125. ————. "Price of Perfection." In *48 Hours*. New York: CBS Television Network News, 2000, June 8.

126. ————. "Slim Chance." In *48 Hours*. New York: CBS Television Network News, 2001, March 14.

127. Chaikin, A. L., Gillen, B., Derlega, V. J., Heinen, J. R. K., and Wilson, M. "Students' Reactions to Teachers' Physical Attractiveness and Nonverbal Behavior: Two Exploratory Studies." *Psychology in Schools*, Vol. 15 (1978): pp. 588-595.

128. Chakrabarti, T. "Attitudes Reflected in Matrimonial Advertisements." *Australian and New Zealand Journal of Sociology*, Vol. 10 (1974): pp. 142-143.

129. Chao, L. "Beauty: Searching for a Quick Fix." *The Wall Street Journal*, Vol. 246, No. 75 (2005, October 11): p. D6.

130. Chenetz, R. "Face Value." *Dateline NBC* (2004, January 11).

131. Chess, S., Alexander, T., and Cameron, M. "Sexual Attitudes and Behavior Patterns in a Middle-Class Adolescent Population." *American Journal of Orthopsychiatry*, Vol. 46, No. 690-701 (1976).

132. Chicago Tribune. "The Dance of Seduction." *Chicago Tribune*, Vol. 157, No. 42 (2004, February 11): p. 1 (Section 8).

133. ———. "Skin-Deep a No-Win on HDTV." *Chicago Tribune*, Vol. 158, No. 238 (2004, August 23): p. 20 (section 21).

134. Choo, T. "Communicator Credibility and Communication Discrepancy as Determinants of Opinion Change." *Journal of Social Psychology*, Vol. 64 (1976): pp. 1-20.

135. Chung, C. "Special Segment: Famine in Ethiopia." In *NBC Nightly News with Connie Chung*. New York: NBC Television Network, 1984, December 1.

136. Clay, R. A. "Linking Up Online: Is the Internet Enhancing Interpersonal Connections or Leading to Greater Social Isolation." *Monitor on Psychology*, Vol. 31, No. 4 (2000): Retrieved July 22, 2005, from http://www.apa.org/monitor/apr2000/linking.html

137. Clifford, M. M. "Physical Attractiveness and Academic Performance." *Child Study Journal*, Vol. 5 (1975): pp. 201-209.

138. Clifford, M. M., and Walster, E. "The Effect of Physical Attractiveness on Teacher Expectations." *Sociology of Education*, Vol. 46 (1973): pp. 248-258.

139. Clifton, R. A., and Baksh, I. J. "Physical Attractiveness, Year of University, and the Expectations of Student-Teachers." *Canadian Journal of Education*, Vol. 3 (1978): pp. 37-46.

140. Coin, C., and Tiberghien, R. "Encoding Activity and Face Recognition." *Memory*, Vol. 5 (1997): pp. 545-568.

141. Coombs, R. H., and Kenkel, W. F. "Sex Differences in Dating Aspirations and Satisfaction with Computer-Selected Partners." *Journal of Marriage and the Family*, Vol. 28 (1966): pp. 62-66.

142. Corter, C., Trehub, S., Bonkydis, C., Ford, L., Celhoffer, L., and Minde, K. "Nurses' Judgments of the Attractiveness of Premature Infants." University of Toronto, Ontario, Canada (1975): Unpublished manuscript.

143. Coslin, P. G., and Winnykamen, F. "A Contribution to the Study of the Genesis of Stereotypes: Attribution of Negative or Positive Aspects as a Function of Dress and Ethnic Appearance." *Psychologie Francaise*, Vol. 26 (1981): pp. 39-48.

144. Costello, D. "Despite Doubts, Fetal Surgeries Increase: Doctors Proceed Even When Baby Isn't In Danger." *Chicago Tribune*, Vol. 159, No. 285 (2005, October 12): p. 7 (section 8).

145. Couric, K., Lauer, M., and Roker, A. "Looks and the Workplace." In *Today Show*. New York: NBC Television Network, 2005, July 25.

146. Covey, S. *The 7 Habits of Highly Effective Teens: The Ultimate Teenage Success Guide*. New York: Fireside Books, Simon & Schuster Inc., 1998.

147. Cowley, G. "The Biology of Beauty." *Newsweek*, Vol. 127, No. 3 (1996, June 3): pp. 61-69.

148. ———. "Health for Life: The Biggest Prize of All." *Newsweek*, Vol. 141, No. 24 (2003, June 16): p. 46.

149. Cox, C. *Stiletto*. New York: Harper Design International, 2004.

150. Critchell, S. "Stilettos Hurt, Yet They Endure." *Chicago Sun-Times*, Vol. 57, No. 294 (2004, January 13): p. 45.

151. Critelli, J. W. "Physical Attractiveness in Dating Couples." Paper presented at the Annual Conference of the Midwestern Psychological Association, Chicago, Illinois 1975.

152. Cross, J. F., Cross, J., and Daly, J. "Sex, Race, Age, and Beauty as Factors in Recognition of Faces." *Perception and Psychophysics*, Vol. 10 (1971): pp. 393-396.

153. Crouse, B. B., and Mehrabian, A. "Affiliation of Opposite-Sexed Strangers." *Journal of Research in Personality*, Vol. 11, No. 1 (1977): pp. 38-47.

154. Cunningham, M. R., Roberts, A. R., Barbee, A. P., Druen, P. B., and Wu, C. H. "Their Ideas of Beauty are, on the Whole, the Same as Ours: Consistency and Variability in the Cross-Cultural Perception of Female Physical Attractiveness." *Journal of Personality and Social Psychology*, Vol. 68 (1995): pp. 261-279.

155. Cunnington, C. W. *Why Women Wear Clothes*. London, England: Faber & Faber, 1941.

156. Curran, J. P. "Correlates of Physical Attractiveness and Interpersonal Attraction in the Dating Situation." *Social Behavior and Personality*, Vol. 1 (1973): pp. 153-157.

157. Curran, J. P., and Lippold, S. "The Effects of Physical Attraction and Attitude Similarity on Attraction in Dating Dyads." *Journal of Personality*, Vol. 43 (1975): pp. 528-538.

158. Dailey, C. A. "The Effects of Premature Conclusion upon the Acquisition of Understanding of a Person." *Journal of Psychology*, Vol. 33 (1952): pp. 133-152.

159. Daily Record. "Most Scots Women Think They Would Climb the Career Ladder Quicker If They Had A Better Body and Were More Attractive." *Daily Record (Glasgow, Scotland)* (2005, August 2): pp. Retrieved October 29, 2005, from http://www.highbeam.com/library/doc2000.asp.

160. Dannenmaier, W. D., and Thumin, F. J. "Authority Status as a Factor in Perceptual Distortion of Size." *Journal of Social Psychology*, Vol. 63 (1964): pp. 361-365.

161. Darvick, D. "Service With a Smile, And Plenty of Metal." *Newsweek*, Vol. 144, No. 2 (2004, July 12): p. 20.

162. Darwin, C. *Descent of Man and Selections in Relation to Sex*. London: John Murray, 1871.

163. ———. *The Expression of the Emotions in Man and Animals*. London: Murray, 1872.

164. ———. "The Origin of Species by Means of Natural Selection. The Descent of Man and Selection in Relation of Sex (1871)." In *Great Books of the Western World (Vol. 49)*, edited by R. M. Hutchins. Chicago, IL: Encyclopedia Britannica, 1952.

165. Dasgupta, N., and Greenwald, A. G. "On the Malleability of Automatic Attitudes: Combating Automatic Prejudice with Images of Admired and Disliked Individuals." *Journal of Personality and Social Psychology*, Vol. 81 (2001): pp. 800-814.

166. DataFace. "Physical Attractiveness of the Face and the Attractiveness Halo." *DataFace* (2004): Retrieved August 3, 2004, from http://www.face-and-emotion.com/dataface/facets/attractiveness.jsp

167. Davis, C., Claridge, G., and Fox, J. "Not Just a Pretty Face: Physical Attractiveness and Perfectionism in the Risk for Eating Disorders." *International Journal of Eating Disorders*, Vol. 27, No. 1 (2000): pp. 67-73.

168. Davis, C. H., and Patzer, G. L. "Ethics: An Integral Aspect of All Business Disciplines." In *Midwest Society for Case Research: 1992 Proceedings*, edited by J. Wedell, pp. 11-15. Chicago, Illinois: Midwest Business Administration Association, 1992.

169. Davis, G., Ellis, H., and Shepard, J. "Cue Saliency in Faces as Assessed by the "Photofit" Technique." *Perception*, Vol. 6 (1977): pp. 263-269.

170. Deam, J. "Where is Miss America Going? No One Knows." *Chicago Tribune*, Vol. 159, No. 292 (2005, October 19): p. 7 (section 8).

171. DeBruine, L. M. "Resemblance to Self Increases the Appeal of Child Faces to Both Men and Women." *Evolution and Human Behavior*, Vol. 25, No. 3 (2004): pp. 142-154.

172. Deen, E. "Letters: Ouch. A Piercing Rebuttal." *Newsweek*, Vol. CXLIV, No. 4 (2004, July 26): p. 18.

173. Dellande, S., Gilly, M. C., and Graham, J. L. "Gaining Compliance and Losing Weight: The Role of the Service Provider in Health Care Services." *Journal of Marketing*, Vol. 68, No. 3 (2004): pp. 78-91.

174. DeMeis, D. K., and Turner, R. R. "Effects of Students' Race, Physical Attractiveness, and Dialect on Teachers' Evaluations." *Contemporary Educational Psychology*, Vol. 3 (1978): pp. 77-86.

175. Deutsch, C. H. "Cosmetics Break the Skin Barrier: Sophisticated Science Being Used to Deliver Creams Behind the Lines." *The New York Times*, Vol. 154, No. 53,088 (2005, January 8): pp. 1, 3 (section C).

176. Didie, E. R., and Sarwer, D. B. "Factors That Influence the Decision to Undergo Cosmetic Breast Augmentation Surgery." *Journal of Women's Health*, Vol. 12, No. 3 (2003): pp. 241-253.

177. Dion, K. K. "Children's Physical Attractiveness and Sex as Determinants of Adult Punitiveness." *Developmental Psychology*, Vol. 10 (1974): pp. 772-778.

178. ———. "The Incentive Value of Physical Attractiveness for Young Children." *Personality and Social Psychology Bulletin*, Vol. 3 (1977): pp. 67-70.

179. ———. "Physical Attractiveness and Evaluations of Children's Transgressions." *Journal of Personality and Social Psychology*, Vol. 24 (1972): pp. 207-213.

180. ———. "Young Children's Stereotyping of Facial Attractiveness." *Developmental Psychology*, Vol. 9 (1973): pp. 183-188.

181. Dion, K. K., and Berscheid, E. "Physical Attractiveness and Peer Perception Among Children." *Sociometry*, Vol. 14 (1974): pp. 97-108.

182. Dion, K. K., Berscheid, E., and Walster, E. "What is Beautiful is Good." *Journal of Personality and Social Psychology*, Vol. 24 (1972): pp. 285-290.

183. Dion, K. K., and Stein, S. "Physical Attractiveness and Interpersonal Influence." *Journal of Experimental Social Psychology*, Vol. 14 (1978): pp. 97-108.

184. Donahue, H. *Beautiful Stranger: A Memoir of an Obsession with Perfection.* New York: Gotham Books, 2004.

185. Donahue, W. "When Inner Beauty Simply Isn't Enough." *Chicago Tribune*, Vol. 158, No. 30 (2005, January 30): p. 1 (section 13).

186. Douglas, S. P., and Solomon, M. R. "Clothing the Female Executive: Fashion or Fortune." In *1983 American Marketing Association Educators' Conference Proceedings*, edited by P. E. Murphy and G. R. Laczniak. Chicago, Illinois, 1983.

187. Downs, A. C., and Walz, P. J. "Sex Differences in Preschoolers' Perceptions of Young, Middle-Aged, and Elderly Adults." Paper presented at the Annual Meeting of the Western Psychological Association, Honolulu, Hawaii 1980.

188. Downs, A. C., and Wright, A. D. "Differential Conceptions of Attractiveness: Subjective and Objective Ratings." *Psychological Reports*, Vol. 50 (1982): p. 282.

189. Dubois, S., Rossion, B., Schiltz, C., Bodart, J. M., Michel, C., Bruyer, R., and Crommelinck, M. "Effect of Familiarity on the Processing of Human Faces." *Neuroimage*, Vol. 9 (1999): pp. 278-289.

190. Dudley, S. "Saying No to Voluptuous Models in Colombia." *Chicago Tribune*, Vol. 159, No. 243 (2005, August 31): p. 7 (section 8).

191. Dukes, W. F., and Bevan, W. "Size Estimation and Monetary Value: A Correlation." *Journal of Psychology*, Vol. 34 (1952): pp. 43-53.

192. Durvasula, S., Lysonski, S., and Watson, J. "Does Vanity Describe Other Cultures? A Cross-Cultural Examination of the Vanity Scale." *Journal of Consumer Affairs*, Vol. 35, No. 1 (2001): pp. 180-199.

193. Dylan, B. "The Times They Are A-Changin' (song title)." In *The Times They Are A-Changin' (album title).* New York: Sony Music Entertainment, Inc., 1964.

194. E-Harmony.com. "More Marriages per Match than Any Online Dating Service (advertisement)." *U. S. News & World Report*, Vol. 136, No. 7 (2004, March 1): p. 59.

195. Eagly, A. H., Ashmore, R. D., Makhijani, M. G., and Longo, L. C. "What is Beautiful is Good, But...: A Meta-Analytic Review of Research on the Physical Attractiveness Stereotype." *Psychological Bulletin*, Vol. 110 (1991): pp. 109-128.

196. Efran, M. G. "The Effect of Physical Appearance on the Judgment of Guilt, Interpersonal Attraction, and Severity of Recommended Punishment in a Simulated Jury Task." *Journal of Research in Personality*, Vol. 8 (1974): pp. 45-54.

197. Eibl-Eibesfeldt, I. *Ethology, The Biology of Behavior.* New York: Hold, Rinehart, & Winston, 1970.

198. Ekman, G. H. *Darwin and Facial Expression.* New York: Academic Press, 1973.

199. Elder, G. H. "Achievement Motivation and Intelligence in Occupational Mobility: A Longitudinal Analysis." *Sociometry*, Vol. 31 (1968): pp. 327-354.

200. ———. "Appearance and Education in Marriage Mobility." *American Sociological Review*, Vol. 34 (1969): pp. 519-533.

201. Ellis, H. *Studies in the Psychology of Sex (Vol. 4).* Philadelphia, Pennsylvania: F. A. Davis, 1926.

202. Engel, J. F., Wales, H. G., and Warshaw, M. R. *Promotional Strategy.* Homewood, Illinois: Richard D. Irwin, 1971.

203. Engemann, K. M., and Owyang, M. T. "So Much for That Merit Raise: The Link between Wages and Appearance." *The Regional Economist* (2005, April 12): Retrieved July 29, 2005, from http://www.stlouisfed.org/publications/re/2005/b/pages/appearances.html

204. Epstein, Y. M., and Karlin, R. A. "Effects of Acute Experimental Crowding." *Journal of Applied Social Psychology*, Vol. 5 (1975): pp. 34-53.

205. Etcoff, N. *Survival of the Prettiest: The Science of Beauty.* New York: Anchor Books, 1999.

206. Exline, R. V. "Visual Interaction—The Glances of Power and Preference." In *Nebraska Symposium on Motivation*, edited by J. K. Cole (Ed.). Lincoln, Nebraska: University of Nebraska Press, 1971.

207. Fabrey, W. J. "Personal communication/letter from Chairman, National Association to Aid Fat Americans, Inc." (1983, April 10).

208. Fairclough, G. "Korea's Makover From Dull to Hip Changes Face of Asia." *The Wall Street Journal*, Vol. 246, No. 83 (2005, October 20): pp. A1, A8.

209. Fantz, R. L. "Pattern Discrimination and Selective Attention as Determinants of Perceptual Development from Birth." In *Perceptual Development in Children*, edited by A. H. Kidd and J. L. Rivoire. New York: International Universities Press, 1966.

210. Fast, J. *Body Language*. New York: Pocket Books, 1970.

211. Feeg, V. D., and Peters, D. L. "Children's Physical Appearance and Adult Expectations." Paper presented at the National Association for the Education of Young Children, Atlanta, Georgia 1979.

212. Feingold, A. "Good-Looking People Are Not What We Think." *Psychological Bulletin*, Vol. 111 (1992): pp. 304-341.

213. ———. "Physical Attractiveness and Romantic Evolvement." *Psychological Reports*, Vol. 50 (1982a): p. 802.

214. Feinman, S., and Gill, G. W. "Females' Response to Males' Beardedness." *Perceptual and Motor Skills*, Vol. 44 (1977): pp. 533-534.

215. ———. "Sex Differences in Physical Attractiveness Preferences." *Journal of Social Psychology*, Vol. 105 (1978): pp. 43-52.

216. Feleky, A. M. "The Expression of the Emotions." *Psychological Review*, Vol. 21 (1914): pp. 33-41.

217. Felson, R. B. "Physical Attractiveness, Grade and Teachers' Attributions of Ability." *Representative Research in Social Psychology*, Vol. 11 (1980): pp. 64-71.

218. Felson, R. B., and Bohrnstedt, G. W. "Are the Good Beautiful or the Beautiful Good? The Relationship between Children's Perceptions of Ability and Perceptions of Physical Attractiveness." *Social Psychology Quarterly*, Vol. 42 (1979): pp. 386-392.

219. Fiser, I., and Fiserova, O. "Beauty and Cosmetics in Ancient India." *New Orient*, Vol. 5 (1969): pp. 92-94.

220. Fleishman, J. J., Buckley, M. L., Klosinsky, M. J., Smith, N., and Tuck, B. "Judged Attractiveness in Recognition Memory of Faces." *Perceptual and Motor Skills*, Vol. 43 (1976): pp. 709-710.

221. Flynn, E. "Beauty: Babes Spot Babes." *Newsweek*, Vol. 144, No. 12 (2004, September 20): p. 10.

222. Ford, C. S., and Beach, F. A. *Patterns of Sexual Behavior*. New York: Harper, 1951.

223. Freedman, D. "The Survival Value of the Beard." *Psychology Today*, Vol. 3 (1969): pp. 36-39.

224. Freedman, J. L., Levy, A. S., Buchanan, R. W., and Price, J. "Crowding and Human Aggressiveness." *Journal of Experimental Social Psychology*, Vol. 8 (1972): pp. 528-548.

225. Freud, S. *The Future Prospects of Psychoanalytic Theory. Collected Papers (Vol. 2)*. New York: Basic Books, 1959.

226. Friday, N. *The Power of Beauty*. New York: HarperCollins, 1996.

227. ———. *Women on Top: How Real Life Has Changed Women's Sexual Fantasies*. New York: Pocket Books, 1992.

228. Friend, R. M., and Vinson, M. "Leaning Over Backwards: Jurors' Responses to Defendants' Attractiveness." *Journal of Communication*, Vol. 24 (1974): pp. 1124-1129.

229. Frith, M. "Fat and Happy? That's Not What Women Say." *The Independent (London, England)* (2005, June 30): Retrieved July 24, 2005, from http://www.highbeam.com/library/doc2000.asp

230. Fugita, S. S., Agle, T. A., Newman, I., and Walfish, N. "Attractiveness, Self-Concept, and a Methodological Note about Gaze Behavior." *Personality and Social Psychology Bulletin*, Vol. 3 (1977): pp. 240-243.

231. Gangestad, S. W., Thornhill, R., and Yeo, R. A. "Facial Attractiveness, Developmental Stability, and Fluctuating Asymmetry." *Ethology and Sociobiology*, Vol. 15 (1994): pp. 73-85.

232. Garner, D. M. "The 1997 Body Image Survey Results." *Psychology Today*, Vol. 30, No. 1 (1997): pp. 30-84.

233. Gartman, K. A. "Letters: Ouch. A Piercing Rebuttal." *Newsweek*, Vol. 144, No. 4 (2004, July 26): p. 18.

234. Garwood, S. G., Cox, L., Kaplan, V., Wasserman, N., and Sulzer, J. L. "Beauty is Only "Name" Deep: The Effect of First-Name on Ratings of Physical Attraction." *Journal of Applied Social Psychology*, Vol. 10 (1980): pp. 431-435.

235. Gazlay, K. "Dusty Springfield, Pop Singer Whose Heydey was '60s, 59." *Orange County Register (California)*, Vol. 95, No. 63 (1999, March 4): pp. M-5.

236. Gillen, B. "Physical Attractiveness: A Determinant of Two Types of Goodness." *Personality and Social Psychology Bulletin*, Vol. 7 (1981): pp. 277-281.

237. Gillen, B., and Sherman, R. C. "Physical Attractiveness and Sex as Determinants of Trait Attributions." *Multivariate Behavioral Research*, Vol. 15, No. 423-437 (1980).

238. Gilley, M. "The Girls All Get Prettier at Closing Time (song title)." In *Live at Gilley's (album title)*. Los Angeles, California: Q Records, 1978.

239. Gitter, A. G., Lomranz, J., and Saxe, L. "Factors Affecting Perceived Attractiveness of Physiques by American and Israeli Students." *Journal of Social Psychology*, Vol. 118 (1982): pp. 167-175.

240. Gladwell, M. *Blink: The Power of Thinking Without Thinking*. New York: Little, Brown & Company, 2005.

241. Glasgow, R. E., and Arkowitz, H. "The Behavioral Assessment of Male and Female Social Competence in Dyadic Heterosexual Interactions." *Behavior Therapy*, Vol. 6 (1975): pp. 488-498.

242. Glenwick, D. S., Jason, L. A., and Elman, D. "Physical Attractiveness and Social Contact in the Singles Bar." *Journal of Social Psychology*, Vol. 105 (1978): pp. 311-312.

243. Goebel, B. L., and Cashen, V. M. "Age, Sex, and Attractiveness as Factors in Student Ratings of Teachers: A Developmental Study." *Journal of Educational Psychology*, Vol. 71 (1979): pp. 646-653.

244. Goffaux, V., Jemel, B., Jacques, C., Rossion, B., and Schyns, P. G. "Event-Related Potential Evidence for Task Modulations on Face Perceptual Processing at Different Spatial Scales." *Cognitive Science*, Vol. 27, No. 2 (2003): pp. 313-325.

245. Goffman, E. *Stigma: Notes on the Management of Spoiled Identity*. Englewood Cliffs, NJ: Prentice-Hall, 1963.

246. Goldstein, A. G., and Papageorge, J. "Judgments of Facial Attractiveness in the Absence of Eye Movements." *Bulletin of the Psychonomic Society*, Vol. 15 (1980): pp. 269-270.

247. Goodheart, A. "Change of Heart: Civil Rights Today." *AARP: The Magazine*, Vol. 47, No. 3B (2004, May): pp. 44-47, 98.

248. Graham, D., and Perry, R. P. "Limitations in Generalizability of the Physical Attractiveness Stereotype: The Self-Esteem Exception." *Canadian Journal of Behavioural Science*, Vol. 8 (1976): pp. 263-274.

249. Graham, J. A., and Jouhar, A. J. "The Effects of Cosmetics on Person Perception." *International Journal of Cosmetic Science*, Vol. 3 (1981): pp. 199-210.

250. Grammer, K. *Signale der Liebe: Die Biologischen Gesetze der Partnerschaft*. Berlin: Hoffman and Campe, 1993.

251. Grammer, K., Fink, B., Moller, A. P., and Thornhill, R. "Darwinian Aesthetics: Sexual Selection and the Biology of Beauty." *Biological Reviews*, Vol. 78, No. 3 (2003): pp. 385-407.

252. Grammer, K., and Thornhill, R. "Human (Homo sapiens) Facial Attractiveness and Sexual Selection: The Role of Symmetry and Averageness." *Journal of Comparative Psychology*, Vol. 108, No. 3 (1994): pp. 233-242.

253. ———. "Human Facial Attractiveness and Sexual Selection: The Role of Symmetry and Averageness." *Journal of Comparative Psychology*, Vol. 108 (1994): pp. 233-242.

254. Grant, M. J., Button, C. M., Hannah, T. E., and Ross, A. S. "Uncovering the Multidimensional Nature of Stereotype Inferences: A Within-Participants Study of Gender, Age, and Physical Attractiveness." *Current Research in Social Psychology*, Vol. 8, No. 2 (2002): pp. 19-38.

255. Grauerholz, L., and Baker-Sperry, L. "The Pervasiveness and Persistence of the Feminine Beauty Ideal in Children's Fairy Tales." *Gender & Society*, Vol. 17, No. 5 (2003).

256. Graziano, W. G., Brothen, T., and Berscheid, E. "Height and Attraction: Do Men and Women See Eye to Eye?" *Journal of Personality*, Vol. 46 (1978): pp. 128-145.

257. Grealy, L. *Autobiography of a Face*. New York: Houghton Mifflin Company, 1994.

258. Greene, J. "Microsoft: The Mouse That Glowed." *BusinessWeek* (2004, July 19): p. 16.

259. Greenhouse, S. "Businesses Hiring for Looks Running into Anti-Bias Laws." *New York Times News Service/The Sun (Southern California Newspaper)*, Vol. 111, No. 194 (2003, July 13): p. A7.

260. Griffitt, W., and Veitch, R. "Hot and Crowded: Influences of Population Density and Temperature on Interpersonal Affective Behavior." *Journal of Personality and Social Psychology*, Vol. 17 (1979): pp. 92-98.

261. Grogan, L. "State of Beauty." *The Palm Beach Post* (2005, June 16): Retrieved July 24, 2005, from http://www.highbeam.com/library/doc2000.asp

262. Gross, A. E., and Crofton, C. "What is Good is Beautiful." *Sociometry*, Vol. 40 (1977): pp. 85-90.

263. Gupta, S. "What's New in Cosmetic R&D?" *Happi.com* (2003, March): Retrieved August 18, 2005, from http://www.happi.com/current/March2033.htm

264. Haddock, V. "Here's Lookin' at You, Kid; In the Mayoral Race, the Hunk Factor is No Junk, say the Experts." *San Francisco Chronicle*, Vol. 139, No. 341 (2003, December 7): p. D1.

265. Hadjistavropoulous, T., and Genest, M. "The Underestimation of the Role of Physical Attractiveness in Dating Preferences: Ignorance or Taboo?" *Canadian Journal of Behavioural Science*, Vol. 26 (1993): pp. 298-318.

266. Hagiwara, S. "Visual versus Verbal Information in Impression Formation." *Journal of Personality and Social Psychology*, Vol. 32 (1975): pp. 692-698.

267. Halberstadt, J., and Rhodes, G. "It's Not Just Average Faces that are Attractive: Computer-Manipulated Averageness Makes Birds, Fish, and Automobiles Attractive." *Psychonomic Bulletin & Review*, Vol. 10, No. 1 (2003): pp. 149-156.

268. Hamermesh, D. S., and Biddle, J. E. "Beauty and the Labor Market." *American Economic Review*, Vol. 84, No. 5 (1994, December): pp. 1,174-171,194.

269. Hamermesh, D. S., and Parker, A. M. *Beauty in the Classroom: Professors' Pulchritude and Putative Pedagogical Productivity (NBER Paper No. W9853)*: National Bureau of Economic Research, University of Texas, Austin, Texas, 2003.

270. Hamid, P. N. "Changes in Person Perception as a Function of Dress." *Perceptual and Motor Skills*, Vol. 2926 (1969): pp. 191-194.

271. ———. "Style of Dress as a Perceptual Cue in Impression Formation." *Perceptual and Motor Skills*, Vol. 26 (1968): pp. 904-906.

272. Hannix, M. "Health Watch: It's Good for You, No, It's Bad for You." *U. S. News & World Report*, Vol. 139, No. 3 (2005, July 25): p. 56.

273. Hansen, M. E. "Personal Communication/Letter from District Director, Little People of America, Inc." (1983, August 1).

274. Hanson, E. J., Pollard, G. D., and Williams, C. M. "Persuasion Tactics Used by College Age Females on College Age Males." Paper presented at the National Communication Association, Seattle, Washington, 12-08 2000.

275. Hardy, A. D., Sutherland, H. H., and Vaishnav, R. "A Study of the Composition of Some Eye Cosmetics (Kohls) Used in the United Arab Emirates." *Journal of Ethnopharmacology*, Vol. 80, No. 2-3 (2002): pp. 137-145.

276. Harper, B. "Does Appearance Matter in the Labour Market?" *London Guildhall University—News and Events* (2000, November 22): Retrieved July 14, 2005, from http://www.shortsupport.org/news/0301.html

277. Harrell, W. A. "Physical Attractiveness and Public Intimacy of Married Couples: An Observational Study." *Social Behavior and Personality*, Vol. 7 (1979): pp. 65-75.

278. Harris, J. R. *The Nurture Assumption: Why Children Turn Out the Way They Do*. New York: The Free Press / Simon and Schuster, 1998.

279. Hartley, G. F. "The Effect of Subject's Weight (Normal vs. Obese) on Judgments of Physical Attractiveness, Liking and Performance." Master of Arts thesis, Loyola College, Baltimore, Maryland, 1986.

280. Hartnett, J., Bailey, K. G., and Hartley, C. S. "Body Height, Position, and Sex as Determinants of Personal Space." *Journal of Psychology*, Vol. 87 (1974): pp. 129-136.

281. Hartnett, J., and Elder, D. "The Princess and the Nice Frog: Study in Person Perception." *Perceptual and Motor Skills*, Vol. 37 (1973): pp. 863-866.

282. Hartnett, J. J., Mahoney, J. M., and Berstein, A. "The Errant Spouse: A Study in Person Perception." *Perceptual and Motor Skills*, Vol. 45 (1977): pp. 747-750.

283. Hartnett, J. J., and Secord, G. "Physical Attraction and Its Effects on the Perception of Extramarital Affairs." *Perceptual and Motor Skills*, Vol. 56 (1983): p. 310.

284. Hartnett, J. J., and Wollman, N. "Extra-Marital Affairs: A Study in Person Perception." *Perceptual and Motor Skills*, Vol. 48 (1979): p. 1306.

285. Harvey, F. "Does the New Security Work? Our Unique Physical Characteristics Will Soon Be Used To Verify Our Identity." *Financial Times*, No. 35,357 (2004, January 22): p. 8.

286. Harvey, P. "Paul Harvey News (radio broadcast)." Chicago 1983, June 29.

287. Hatfield, E., and Sprecher, S. "Men's and Women's Preferences in Marital Partners in the United States, Russia, and Japan." *Journal of Cross-Cultural Psychology*, Vol. 44, No. 3 (1995): pp. 728-750.

288. Haxby, J. V., Hoffman, E. A., and Gobbini, M. I. "The Distributed Human Neural System for Face Perception." *Trends in Cognitive Science*, Vol. 4 (2000): pp. 223-233.

289. Henderson, J. J. A., and Anglin, J. M. "Facial Attractiveness Predicts Longevity." *Evolution and Human Behavior*, Vol. 24, No. 5 (2003): pp. 351-356.

290. Hendrick, B. "No Fair: Good Looks and Longevity Too." *Chicago Tribune*, Vol. 158, No. 340 (2004, December 5): p. 9 (section 13).

291. ———. "Ugly Truth: Life Span, Looks May be Linked." *The Atlanta Journal-Constitution* (2004, November 24): Retrieved July 16, 2005, from http://www.ajc.com/health

292. Hess, E. H. "Attitude and Pupil Size." *Scientific American*, Vol. 212 (1965): pp. 46-54.

293. Hicks, R. A., Pellegrini, R. J., and Tomlinson, N. "Attributions of Female College Students to Male Photographs as a Function of Attractiveness and Pupil Size." *Perceptual and Motor Skills*, Vol. 47 (1978): pp. 1265-1266.

294. Hildebrandt, K. A. "Parents' Perceptions of Infant's Physical Attractiveness." Paper presented at the International Conference on Infant Studies, New Haven, Connecticut 1980, April.

295. ———. "The Role of Physical Appearance in Infant and Child Development." In *Theory and Research in Behavioral Pediatrics (Vol. 1)*, edited by B. Fitzgerald, M. Lester and M. W. Yogman. New York: Plenum Press, 1982.

296. Hildebrandt, K. A., and Fitzgerald, H. E. "Adults' Perceptions of Infant Sex and Cuteness." *Sex Roles*, Vol. 5 (1979): pp. 471-481.

297. ———. "Adults' Responses to Infants Varying in Perceived Cuteness." *Behavioral Processes*, Vol. 3 (1978): pp. 159-172.

298. Hill, C. T., Rubin, Z., and Peplau, L. A. "Breakups Before Marriage: The End of 103 Affairs." *Journal of Social Issues*, Vol. 32 (1976): pp. 147-168.

299. Hindo, B. "Having it All, Women's Pace: Steady But Slow." *BusinessWeek* (2004, April 12): p. 14.

300. Hochberg, J. E. *Perception*. Englewood Cliffs, New Jersey: Prentice-Hall, 1964.

301. Hopkins, K. A. "Why Do Babies Find Faces Attractive?" *Australian Journal of Early Childhood*, Vol. 5 (1980): pp. 25-28.

302. Horvath, T. "Correlates of Physical Beauty in Men and Women." *Social Behavior and Personality*, Vol. 7 (1979): pp. 145-151.

303. ———. "Physical Attractiveness: The Influence of Selected Torso Parameters." *Archives of Sexual Behavior*, Vol. 10 (1981): pp. 21-24.

304. Hoss, R., A., and Langlois, J. H. *Infants Prefer Attractive Faces*. Edited by O. Pascalis and A. Slater, *Development of Face Processing in Infancy and Early Childhood: Current Perspectives*. Hauppauge, NY, USA: Nova Science Publishers, Inc., 2003.

305. Hoult, R. "Experimental Measurement of Clothing as a Factor in Some Social Ratings of Selected American Men." *American Sociological Review*, Vol. 19 (1954): pp. 324-328.

306. Hovland, C. I., Janis, I. L., and Kelley, H. H. *Communication and Persuasion*. New Haven, Connecticut: Yale University Press, 1953.

307. Hovland, C. I., and Weiss, W. "The Influence of Source Credibility on Communicator Effectiveness." *Public Opinion Quarterly*, Vol. 15 (1951): pp. 635-650.

308. Huckstedt, B. "Experimentelle Untersuchungen zum Kindchenschema." *Zeitschrift fur Experimentelle und Angewandte Psychologie*, Vol. 12 (1965): pp. 421-450.

309. Hulse, F. S. "Selection for Skin Color Among Japanese." *American Journal of Physical Anthropology*, Vol. 27 (1967): pp. 143-156.

310. Hume, D. K., and Montgomerie, R. "Facial Attractiveness Signals Different Aspects of Quality in Men and Women." *Evolution and Human Behavior*, Vol. 22 (2001): pp. 93-112.

311. Huston, T. L. "Ambiguity of Acceptance, Social Desirability, and Dating Choice." *Journal of Experimental Social Psychology*, Vol. 9 (1973): pp. 32-42.

312. Inamori, Y. "Effects of False Heart Feedback on Cognitive Appraisal and Physiological Responses to Emotional Stimuli." *Japanese Psychological Research*, Vol. 21 (1979): pp. 153-157.

313. Insko, C. A., Thompson, V. D., Strobe, W., Shaud, K. F., Pinner, B. E., and Layton, B. D. "Implied Evaluation and the Similarity-Attraction Effect." *Journal of Personality and Social Psychology*, Vol. 25 (1973): pp. 297-308.

314. Ioannidis, J. P. A. "Contradicted and Initially Stronger Effects in Highly Cited Clinical Research." *Journal of the American Medical Association*, Vol. 294, No. 2 (2005, July 13): pp. 218-228.

315. Irilli, J. P. "Students' Expectations: Ratings of Teacher Performance as Biased by Teachers' Physical Attractiveness." Paper presented at the Annual Meeting of the American Educational Research Association, Toronto, Ontario, Canada 1978.

316. Jackson, C. *Living Doll: Cindy Jackson*. London, England: Metro Publishing Ltd., 2002.

317. Jackson, L. A. *Physical Appearance and Gender: Sociobiological and Sociocultural Perspectives*. New York: University of New York Press, 1992.

318. Jackson, L. A., and Ervin, K. S. "Height Stereotypes of Women and Men: The Liabilities of Shortness for Both Sexes." *Journal of Social Psychology*, Vol. 41, No. 2 (1992): pp. 433-445.

319. Jackson, L. A., Hunter, J. E., and Hodge, C. N. "Physical Attractiveness and Intellectual Competence: A Meta-Analytic Review." *Social Psychology Quarterly*, Vol. 58 (1995): pp. 108-122.

320. Jacobi, L., and Cash, T. F. "In Pursuit of the Perfect Appearance: Discrepancies Among Self- and Ideal-Percepts of Multiple Physical Attributes." *Journal of Applied Social Psychology*, Vol. 24 (1994): pp. 379-396.

321. Jacobson, S. K., and Berger, C. R. "Communication and Justice: Defendant Attributes and Their Effect on the Severity of His Sentence." *Speech Monographs*, Vol. 41 (1974): pp. 282-286.

322. JapanToday. " 'White' Look Back In Among Japanese Women." *Japan Today Features* (2004, February 3): Retrieved February 2, 2004, from http://www.japantoday.com/gidx/news64970.html

323. Jeffes, S. *Appearance Is Everything.* Pittsburgh, Pennsylvania: Sterling House Publisher, 1998.

324. Johnson, C. M., and Alsarraf, R. *The Aging Face: A Systematic Approach.* Saint Louis, Missouri: W. B. Saunders Co., 2002.

325. Johnson, R. W. "Perceived Physical Attractiveness of Supporters of Canada's Political Parties: Stereotype or In-Group Bias." *Canadian Journal of the Behavioural Sciences*, Vol. 13 (1981): pp. 320-325.

326. Johnston, J. E. *Appearance Obsession: Learning to Love the Way You Look.* Deerfield Beach, Florida: Health Communications, Inc., 1994.

327. Johnston, V. S. "Female Facial Beauty: The Fertility Hypothesis." *Pragmatics & Cognition (Facial Information Processing, Special Issue)*, Vol. 8, No. 1 (2002): pp. 107-122.

328. Johnston, V. S., Hagel, R., Franklin, M., Fink, B., and Grammer, K. "Male Facial Attractiveness Evidence for Hormone-Mediated Adaptive Design." *Evolution and Human Behavior*, Vol. 22 (2001): pp. 251-267.

329. Jones, B. T., Jones, B. C., Thomas, A. P., and Piper, J. "Alcohol Consumption Increases Attractiveness Ratings of Opposite-Sex Faces: A Possible Third Route to Risky Sex." *Addiction*, Vol. 98, No. 8 (2003, August): pp. 1,069-061,075.

330. Jones, D. "An Evolutionary Perspective on Physical Attractiveness." *Evolutionary Anthropology*, Vol. 5 (1996b): pp. 97-109.

331. ———. *Physical Attractiveness and the Theory of Sexual Selection.* Ann Arbor, Michigan: Museum of Anthropology, University of Michigan, 1996a.

332. Jones, D., and Hill, K. "Correlates of Facial Attractiveness in Five Populations." *Human Nature*, Vol. 4 (1993): pp. 271-296.

333. Jones, W. T., Sontag, F., Beckner, M. O., and Fogelin, R. J. *Approaches to Ethics.* 3rd ed. New York: McGraw-Hill, 1977.

334. Jourard, S. M., and Secord, P. F. "Body Size and Body-Cathexis." *Journal of Consulting Psychology*, Vol. 18 (1954): p. 184.

335. Judge, T. A., and Cable, D. M. "The Effect of Physical Height on Workplace Success and Income: Preliminary Test of a Theoretical Model." *Journal of Applied Psychology*, Vol. 89, No. 3 (2004): pp. 428-441.

336. Kaats, G. R., and Davis, K. E. "The Dynamics of Sexual Behavior of College Students." *Journal of Marriage and the Family*, Vol. 32 (1970): pp. 390-399.

337. Kalb, C. "Brave New Babies." *Newsweek*, Vol. 143, No. 4 (2004, January 26): pp. 44-52.

338. Kalis, L. "Cord Control." *The Wall Street Journal*, Vol. 241, No. 66 (2003, April 4): p. W10.

339. Kanekar, S., Mazumdar, D., and Kolsawalla, M. B. "Perception of an Aggressor and His Victim as a Function of Physical Attractiveness and Retaliation." *Journal of Social Psychology*, Vol. 113 (1981): pp. 289-290.

340. Kanwisher, N., McDermott, J., and Chun, M. "The Fusiform Face Area: A Module in Human Extrastriate Cortex Specialized for Face Perception." *Journal of Neuroscience*, Vol. 17 (1997): pp. 4302-4311.

341. Kaplan, R. M. "Is Beauty Talent? Sex Interaction in the Attractiveness Halo Effect." *Sex Roles*, Vol. 4 (1978): pp. 195-204.

342. Keating, C. F., Mazur, A., and Segall, M. H. "Facial Gestures which Influence the Perception of Status." *Sociometry*, Vol. 40 (1977): pp. 374-378.

343. Kehle, T. J., Bramble, W. J., and Mason, J. "Teachers' Expectations: Ratings of Student Performance as Biased by Study Characteristics." *Journal of Experimental Education*, Vol. 43 (1974): pp. 54-60.

344. Kenny, C. T., and Fletcher, D. "Effects of Beardedness on Person Perception." *Perceptual and Motor Skills*, Vol. 37 (1973): pp. 413-414.

345. Kenrick, D. T., and Gutierres, S. E. "Contrast Effects and Judgments of Physical Attractiveness: When Beauty Becomes a Social Problem." *Journal of Personality and Social Psychology*, Vol. 38 (1980): pp. 131-140.

346. Kerber, K. W., and Coles, M. G. "The Role of Perceived Physiological Activity in Affective Judgments." *Journal of Experimental Social Psychology*, Vol. 14 (1978): pp. 419-433.

347. Kernis, M. H., and Wheeler, L. "Beautiful Friends and Ugly Strangers: Radiation and Contrast Effects in Perceptions of Same-Sex Pairs." *Personality and Social Psychology Bulletin*, Vol. 7 (1981).

348. Kerr, N. L., and Kurtz, S. T. "Reliability of "The Eye of The Beholder:" Effects of Sex of the Beholder and Sex of the Beheld." *Bulletin of the Psychonomic Society*, Vol. 12 (1978): pp. 179-181.

349. Key, E. "Beauty for Everyone." In *Encarta Book of Quotations*: Microsoft Corporation, 2000.

350. Keyes, R. *The Height of your Life*. Boston, Massachusetts: Little, Brown and Company, 1980.

351. Khan, S. "Survey Finds That Reunions Are a Prime Reason People Revamp Their Looks." *PR Newswire* (2005, June 29): Retrieved July 1, 2005, from http://www.highbeam.com/library

352. Kirkland, J., and Smith, J. "Preferences for Infant Pictures with Modified Eye-Pupils." *Journal of Biological Psychology*, Vol. 20 (1978): pp. 33-34.

353. Kleck, R. E., Richardson, S. A., and Ronald, L. "Physical Appearance Cues and Interpersonal Attraction in Children." *Child Development*, Vol. 43 (1974): pp. 305-310.

354. Kleck, R. E., and Rubenstein, C. "Physical Attractiveness, Perceived Attitude Similarity, and Interpersonal Attraction in an Opposite-Sex Encounter." *Journal of Personality and Social Psychology*, Vol. 31 (1975): pp. 107-114.

355. Kleinke, C. L., and Kahn, M. L. "Perceptions of Self-Disclosers: Effects of Sex and Physical Attractiveness." *Journal of Personality*, Vol. 48 (1980): pp. 190-205.

356. Kleinke, C. L., and Staneski, R. A. "First Impressions of Female Bust Size." *Journal of Social Psychology*, Vol. 110 (1980): pp. 123-134.

357. Kleinke, C. L., Staneski, R. A., and Berger, D. E. "Evaluation of an Interviewer as a Function of Interviewer Gaze, Reinforcement of Subject Gaze, and Interviewer Attractiveness." *Journal of Personality and Social Psychology*, Vol. 31 (1975): pp. 115-122.

358. Knickmeyer, E. "For Tribe, Male Beauty is 'Our Heritage'." *Chicago Tribune*, Vol. 157, No. 356 (2003, December 22): p. 4 (section 1).

359. Knight Rider Tribune News Service. "Ink Job: Fewer Employers See that Tattoo as a Taboo." *Redeye: An Edition of the Chicago Tribune*, Vol. 157, No. 22 (2004, January 22): pp. 10-11.

360. Kobrin, S. "Asian-Americans see Negative Side of Eyelid Surgery." *Chicago Tribune*, Vol. 158, No. 238 (2004, August 23): p. 20 (section 21).

361. Konner, M. "Mind of a Man: Bridging Our Differences." *Newsweek*, Vol. 141, No. 24 (2003, June 16): pp. 74-77.

362. Koopman, P. A., and Ames, E. W. "Infants' Preferences for Facial Arrangements: A Failure to Replicate." *Child Development*, Vol. 39 (1968): pp. 481-487.

363. Korabik, K. "Changes in Physical Attractiveness and Interpersonal Attraction." *Basic and Applied Social Psychology*, Vol. 2, No. 59-65 (1981).

364. Korthase, K. M., and Trenholme, I. "Perceived Age and Perceived Physical Attractiveness." *Perceptual and Motor Skills*, Vol. 54 (1982): pp. 1251-1258.

365. Koulack, D., and Tuthill, J. A. "Height Perception: A Function of Social Distance." *Canadian Journal of the Behavioural Sciences*, Vol. 4 (1972): pp. 50-53.

366. Kramer, R. M. "Some Determinants of Commitment Levels in Premarital Relationships." Paper presented at the Annual Convention of the Rocky Mountain Psychological Association, Denver, Colorado 1978.

367. Krebs, D., and Adinolfi, A. A. "Physical Attractiveness, Social Relations, and Personality Style." *Journal of Personality and Social Psychology*, Vol. 31 (1975): pp. 245-253.

368. Kretschmer, E. *Physique and Character*. New York: Harcourt, Brace, 1925.

369. Krieger, E. "Magic in a Makeover." *WebMD* (2003, April 24): Retrieved August 14, 2005, from http://my.webmd.com/content/article/2065/72778.htm

370. ———. "Magic in a Makeover." *WebMD* (2001, October 17): Retrieved August 14, 2005, from http://my.webmd.com/content/article/2011/1674_51074.htm

371. ———. "Magic in a Makeover." *WebMD* (2000, October 30): Retrieved October 15, 2004, from http://my.webmd.com/search/search_results/?filter=mywebmd_all_filter&query=October+2000&go.x=2018&go.y=2019

372. Kruse, M. I., and Fromme, K. "Influence of Physical Attractiveness and Alcohol on Men's Perceptions of Potential Sexual Partners and Sexual Behavior Intentions." *Experimental and Clinical Psychopharmacology*, Vol. 13, No. 2 (2005): pp. 146-156.

373. Kuffel, F. *Passing for Thin: Losing Half My Weight and Finding My Self.* New York: Broadway Books, 2004.

374. Kuno, N. "Skin-Beautifying Agent, Anti-Aging for the Skin, Whitening Agent and External Agent for the Skin." *United States Patent Application 20020176903* (2002): Retrieved August 18, 2005, from http://appft2001.uspto.gov/netacgi

375. Kury, H., and Bauerle, S. "The Personality Structure of Popular and Unpopular School Children." *Psychologie in Erziehung und Unterricht*, Vol. 24 (1977): pp. 244-247.

376. Kurzweil, R. *The Singularity Is Near: When Humans Transcend Biology.* New York: Viking Adult, 2005.

377. Kyodo World News Service. "China Holds 1st Plastic Surgery Pageant." *Kyodo World News Service* (2004, December 12): Retrieved July 26, 2005, from http://www.highbeam.com/library/doc2000.asp

378. Langlois, J., and Roggman, L. A. "Attractive Faces Are Only Average." *Psychological Science*, Vol. 1 (1990): pp. 115-121.

379. Langlois, J. H., and Downs, A. C. "Peer Relations as a Function of Physical Attractiveness: The Eye of the Beholder or Behavioral Reality?" *Child Development*, Vol. 50, No. 409-418 (1979).

380. Langlois, J. H., and Stephan, C. W. "Beauty and the Beast: The Role of Physical Attractiveness in the Development of Peer Relations and Social Behavior." In *Developmental Social Psychology: Theory and Research*, edited by S. S. Brehm, S. M. Kassin and F. X. Gibbons. New York: Oxford University Press, 1981.

381. ———. "The Effects of Physical Attractiveness and Ethnicity on Children's Behavioral Attributions and Peer Preferences." *Child Development*, Vol. 4 (1977): pp. 1694-1698.

382. Lansky, M. R., and Morrison, A., P. *The Widening Scope of Shame.* Hillsdale, NJ: The Analytic Press, Inc., 1997.

383. Larkin, E. "Golden Globe Nominees and Winners 2004." (2004, January 26): Retrieved July 24, 2005, from http://primetimetv.about.com/library/blgoldenglobes2004_nominees.htm

384. Larrance, D. T., and Zuckerman, M. "Facial Attractiveness and Vocal Likeability as Determinants of Nonverbal Sending Skills." *Journal of Personality*, Vol. 49 (1981): pp. 349-362.

385. Lasswell, H. D. "The Structure and Function of Communications in Society." In *The Communication of Ideas*, edited by L. Bryson (Ed.). New York: Harper & Row, 1948.

386. Lauerman, C. "Show Me the Makeover: Is a Media Barrage Feeding Women's Anxiety About Their Looks? Some Plastic Surgeons and Therapists Think So." *Chicago Tribune*, Vol. 158, No. 196 (2004): pp. 1, 7 (section 8).

387. Laurence, C. "Latest US Fad Sees Cosmetic Surgery Patients 'Going Public' to Show Off Their Enhancements." *The Sunday Telegraph* (2003, November 23).

388. Lawrence, S. "Older Woman / Younger Man Relationships." *WebMD* (2003, December 29): Retrieved August 14, 2005, from http://www.msnbc.msn.com/id/3679116/

389. Lawson, C., and Taber, A. "Shrug It Off." *Men's Health*, Vol. 17, No. 8 (2002, October): pp. 116-122.

390. Lee, J. "Leave Your Hat On, But Lose the Jeans." *Newsweek*, Vol. 142, No. 24 (2003, December 15): p. 22.

391. Lee, L. "Love Those Boomers: Their New Attitudes and Lifestyles Are a Marketer's Dream." *BusinessWeek*, No. 3956 (2005, October 24): pp. 94-102.

392. Lee, S. "School Daze (movie title)." Los Angeles: Columbia Tristar, 1988.

393. Lefebvre, L. M., and McNeel, S. P. "Attractiveness, Cost and Dependency in the Exchange of Unlike Behaviors." *European Journal of Social Psychology*, Vol. 3 (1973): pp. 9-26.

394. Lehner, U. C. "For Better or Worse, Arranged Marriages Still Thrive in Japan." *The Wall Street Journal*, Vol. 202, No. 20 (1983, July 29): pp. A1, A12.

395. Leigh, S. "Our Most Popular Resolution." *Today's Chicago Woman*, Vol. 22, No. 4 (2004): p. 5.

396. Lemley, B. "Isn't She Lovely?" *Discover*, Vol. 21, No. 2 (2000): pp. 42-49.

397. Lerner, R. M., and Gellert, E. "Body Build Identification, Preference, and Aversion in Children." *Developmental Psychology*, Vol. 1 (1969): pp. 456-462.

398. Lerner, R. M., Iwawaki, S., Chihara, T., and Sorell, G. T. "Self-Concept, Self-Esteem, and Body Attitudes among Japanese Male and Female Adolescents." *Child Development*, Vol. 41 (1980): pp. 847-855.

399. Lerner, R. M., and Karabenick, S. A. "Physical Attractiveness, Body Attitudes, and Self-Concept in Late Adolescents." *Journal of Youth and Adolescence*, Vol. 3 (1974): pp. 307-316.

400. Lerner, R. M., Karabenick, S. A., and Stuart, J. L. "Relations Among Physical Attractiveness, Body Attitudes, and Self-Concept in Male and Female College Students." *Journal of Psychology*, Vol. 83 (1973): pp. 119-129.

401. Lerner, R. M., and Korn, S. J. "The Development of Body Build Stereotypes in Males." *Child Development*, Vol. 43 (1972): pp. 908-920.

402. Lerner, R. M., and Lerner, J. V. "Effects of Age, Sex, and Physical Attractiveness on Child-Peer Relations, Academic Performance, and Elementary School Adjustment." *Developmental Psychology*, Vol. 13 (1977): pp. 585-590.

403. Lerner, R. M., and Moore, T. "Sex and Status Effects on Perception of Physical Attractiveness." *Psychological Reports*, Vol. 34 (1974): pp. 1047-1050.

404. Lerner, R. M., and Schroeder, C. "Physique Identification, Preference, and Aversion in Kindergarten Children." *Developmental Psychology*, Vol. 5 (1971): p. 538.

405. Lev, M. A. "East Meets West at the Mall." *Chicago Tribune*, Vol. 158, No. 189 (2004, July 7): p. 1 (section 1).

406. Levine, D. "Race as a Visual Feature: Using Visual Search and Perceptual Discrimination Tasks to Understand Face Categories and the Cross-Race Recognition Deficit." *Journal of Experimental Psychology*, Vol. 129 (2000): pp. 559-573.

407. Levine, M. "Cup & Gown." *Levine Breaking News E-Lert* (2004, June 14): Retrieved June 14, 2004, from http://www.guerrillapr.net/elert.html

408. Li, N. P., Bailey, J. M., Kenrick, D. T., and Linsenmeier, J. A. "The Necessities and Luxuries of Mate Preferences: Testing the Tradeoffs." *Journal of Personality and Social Psychology*, Vol. 82, No. 6 (2002): pp. 947-955.

409. Liggett, J. *The Human Face*. New York: Stein and Day, 1974.

410. Light, L. L., Hollander, S., and Kayra-Stuart, F. "Why Attractive People are Harder to Remember." *Personality and Social Psychology Bulletin*, Vol. 7 (1981): pp. 269-276.

411. Linder, D. E., and Crane, K. A. "Reactance Theory Analysis of Predecisional Cognitive Processes." *Journal of Personality and Social Psychology*, Vol. 15 (1970): pp. 258-264.

412. Lombardo, J. P., and Tocci, M. E. "Attribution of Positive and Negative Characteristics of Instructors as a Function of Attractiveness and Sex of Subject." *Perceptual and Motor Skills*, Vol. 48 (1979): pp. 491-494.

413. Lombroso, C. *The Man of Genius*. London: Scott, 1891.

414. Lorenc, Z. P., and Hall, T. "Less Really Is More." *Newsweek*, Vol. 144, No. 3 (2005, January 17): p. 55.

415. Lorenz, K. "Die Angeborenen Formen Moglicher Erfahrung." *Zeitschrift Tierpsychologie*, Vol. 5 (1943): pp. 235-209.

416. ———. "Do Pretty People Earn More?" *CNN.com / CareerBuilder.com* (2005, July 8): Retrieved July 8, 2005, from http:www.cnn.com/2005/US/Careers/2007/2008/looks

417. ———. "Do Pretty People Earn More?" *CNN.com / CareerBuilder.com* (2005, July 11): Retrieved July 12, 2005, from http:www.cnn.com/2005/US/Careers/2007/2008/looks

418. Luciano, L. *Looking Good: Male Body Image in Modern America*. New York: Hill and Wang, 2001.

419. Lumsden, L. "Expectations for Students (ED 409 609)." *ERIC Digest*, No. 116 (1997).

420. Lyman, B., Hatlelid, D., and Macurdy, C. "Stimulus-Person Cues in First-Impression Attraction." *Perceptual and Motor Skills*, Vol. 52 (1981): pp. 59-66.

421. Mahoney, E. R. "Body-Cathexis and Self-Esteem: The Importance of Subjective Importance." *Journal of Psychology*, Vol. 88 (1974): pp. 27-30.

422. Mahoney, E. R., and Finch, M. D. "Body Cathexis and Self-Esteem." *Journal of Social Psychology*, Vol. 99 (1976a): pp. 251-258.

423. ———. "The Dimensionality of Body-Cathexis." *Journal of Psychology*, Vol. 92 (1976b): pp. 277-279.

424. Mahoney, S. D. "The Effects of Physical Appearance and Behavior upon Ratings of Social Attractiveness." Paper presented at the Annual Convention of the Rocky Mountain Psychological Association, Denver, Colorado 1978.

425. Manning, J. T., Trivers, R. L., Singh, D., and Thornhill, R. "The Mystery of Female Beauty." *Nature*, Vol. 399 (1999): pp. 214-215.

426. Manz, W., and Lueck, H. "Influence of Wearing Glasses on Personality Ratings: Cross-Sectional Validation of an Old Experiment." *Perceptual and Motor Skills*, Vol. 27 (1968): p. 7704.

427. Maroldo, G. K. "Shyness and Love on a College Campus." *Perceptual and Motor Skills*, Vol. 55 (1982): pp. 819-824.

428. Martinek, T. J. "Physical Attractiveness: Effects on Teacher Expectations and Dyadic Interactions in Elementary Age Children." *Journal of Sport Psychology*, Vol. 3 (1981): pp. 196-205.

429. Marwit, K. L., Marwit, S. J., and Walker, E. "Effects of Student Race and Physical Attractiveness on Teachers' Judgments of Transgressions." *Journal of Educational Psychology*, Vol. 70 (1978): pp. 911-915.

430. Marwit, S. J. "Students' Race, Physical Attractiveness and Teachers' Judgments of Transgressions: Follow-Up and Clarification." *Psychological Reports*, Vol. 50 (1982): p. 242.

431. Mashman, R. C. "The Effect of Physical Attractiveness on the Perception of Attitude Similarity." *Journal of Social Psychology*, Vol. 106 (1978): pp. 103-110.

432. Masland, T. "Living and the Dead." *Newsweek*, Vol. 144, No. 1 (2004, July 5): pp. 38-41.

433. Maslow, A. H. *Motivation and Personality*. New York: Harper & Row, 1954.

434. Mathes, E. W. "The Effects of Physical Attractiveness and Anxiety on Heterosexual Attraction Over a Series of Five Encounters." *Journal of Marriage and the Family*, Vol. 37 (1975): pp. 769-773.

435. Mathes, E. W., and Edwards, L. L. "Physical Attractiveness as an Input in Social Exchanges." *Journal of Psychology*, Vol. 98, No. 267-275 (1978).

436. Mathews, J. "The Election: It's Inching Down on Us." *Washington Post*, Vol. 127, No. 24 (2003, December 29): pp. C-01.

437. May, J. L., and Hamilton, P. A. "Effects of Musically Evoked Affect on Women's Interpersonal Attraction Toward and Perceptual Judgments of Physical Attractiveness of Men." *Motivation and Emotion*, Vol. 4 (1980): pp. 217-228.

438. McCullers, J. C., and Staat, J. "Draw an Ugly Man: An Inquiry into the Dimensions of Physical Attractiveness." *Journal of Personality and Social Psychology*, Vol. 1 (1974): pp. 33-35.

439. McCullough, E. A., Miller, M. F., and Ford, I. M. "Sexually Attractive Clothing: Attitudes and Usage." *Home Economics Research Journal*, Vol. 6 (1977): pp. 164-170.

440. McGuire, W. J. "Nature of Attitudes and Attitude Change." In *Handbook of Social Psychology*, edited by G. Lindzey and E. Aronson. Reading, Massachusetts: Addison-Wesley, 1969.

441. McKelvie, S. J. "The Effects of Verbal Labelling on Recognition Memory for Schematic Faces." *Quarterly Journal of Experimental Psychology*, Vol. 28 (1976): pp. 459-474.

442. ———. "Sex Differences in Facial Memory." In *Practical Aspects of Memory*, edited by M. M. Gruneberg, P. E. Morris and R. N. Sykes. New York: Academic Press, 1978.

443. ———. "Sex Differences in Memory for Faces." *The Journal of Psychology*, Vol. 107 (1981): pp. 109-125.

444. McKenna, K. Y. A., and Bargh, J. A. "Plan 9 from Cyberspace: The Implications of the Internet for Personality and Social Psychology." *Personality and Social Psychology*, Vol. 4, No. 1 (2000): pp. 57-75.

445. McKinley, J. "With Friends Like These: In "Entourage," Mark Wahlbert Exposes the Ugly Life of a Posse." *The New York Times*, Vol. 153, No. 52,907 (2004, July 11): pp. 1, 21 (section 22).

446. Meiners, M. L., and Sheposh, J. P. "Beauty or Brains: Which Image for Your Mate?" *Personality and Social Psychology Bulletin*, Vol. 3 (1977): pp. 262-265.

447. Melamed, L., and Moss, M. K. "The Effect of Context on Ratings of Attractiveness of Photographs." *Journal of Psychology*, Vol. 90 (1975): pp. 129-136.

448. Merritt, J., and Lavelle, L. "Tomorrow's B-School? It Might be a D-School." *BusinessWeek*, No. 3945 (2005, August 1): pp. 80-81.

449. Microsoft Corporation. "Avedon, Richard." *Microsoft Encarta Reference Library 2005* (2005): Retrieved August 18, 2005, from Encarta Reference Library Premium 2005 DVD—Quotations.

450. ———. "Churchill, Sir Winston Leonard Spencer." *Microsoft Encarta Reference Library 2005* (2005): Retrieved August 18, 2005, from Encarta Reference Library Premium 2005 DVD—Article.

451. ———. "Colombia." *Microsoft Encarta Reference Library 2005* (2005): Retrieved November 27, 2005, from Encarta Reference Library Premium 2005 DVD—Colombia

452. ————. "Harding, Warren G." *Microsoft Encarta Reference Library 2005* (2005): Retrieved August 28, 2005, from Encarta Reference Library Premium 2005 DVD—Quotations.

453. ————. "Lincoln, Abraham." *Microsoft Encarta Reference Library 2005* (2005): Retrieved August 18, 2005, from Encarta Reference Library Premium 2005 DVD—Quotations.

454. ————. "Madame de Sevigne." *Microsoft Encarta Reference Library 2005* (2005): Retrieved August 18, 2005, from Encarta Reference Library Premium 2005 DVD—Quotations.

455. ————. "Pope, Alexander." *Microsoft Encarta Reference Library 2005* (2005): Retrieved August 18, 2005, from Encarta Reference Library Premium 2005 DVD—Quotations.

456. ————. "T. H. Huxley." *Microsoft Encarta Reference Library 2005* (2005): Retrieved August 18, 2005, from Encarta Reference Library Premium 2005 DVD—Quotations.

457. ————. "Tolstoy, Leo Nikolayevich." *Microsoft Encarta Reference Library 2005* (2005): Retrieved August 18, 2005, from Encarta Reference Library Premium 2005 DVD—Quotations.

458. ————. "Tucholsky, Kurt " *Microsoft Encarta Reference Library 2005* (2005): Retrieved August 18, 2005, from Encarta Reference Library Premium 2005 DVD—Quotations.

459. Miller, A. G. "Role of Physical Attractiveness in Impression Formation." *Psychonomic Science*, Vol. 19 (1970): pp. 241-243.

460. Miller, A. G., Gillen, B., Schenker, C., and Radlove, S. "The Prediction and Perception of Obedience to Authority." *Journal of Personality*, Vol. 42 (1974): pp. 23-42.

461. Miller, G. R., and Basehart, J. "Source Trustworthiness, Opinionated Statements, and Response to Persuasive Communication." *Speech Monographs*, Vol. 36 (1969): pp. 1-7.

462. Miller, H. L., and Rivenbark, W. "Sexual Differences in Physical Attractiveness as a Determinant of Heterosexual Likings." *Psychological Reports*, Vol. 27 (1970): pp. 701-702.

463. Miller, M. C. "Mind of a Man: Stop Pretending Nothing's Wrong." *Newsweek Magazine*, Vol. 141, No. 24 (2003, June 16): pp. 71-72.

464. Mills, J., and Aronson, E. "Opinion Change as a Function of the Communicator's Attractiveness and Desire to Influence." *Journal of Personality and Social Psychology*, Vol. 1 (1965): pp. 173-177.

465. Mims, P. R., Hartnett, J. J., and Nay, W. R. "Interpersonal Attraction and Help Volunteering as a Function of Physical Attractiveness." *Journal of Psychology*, Vol. 89 (1975): pp. 125-131.

466. Mischel, W. "On the Interface of Cognition and Personality: Beyond the Person-Situation Debate." *American Psychologist*, Vol. 34 (1979): pp. 740-754.

467. Mitchell, K. R., and Orr, F. E. "Heterosexual Social Competence, Anxiety, and Self-Judged Physical Attractiveness." *Perceptual and Motor Skills*, Vol. 43 (1976): pp. 553-554.

468. Miyamoto, S. F., and Dornbusch, S. M. "A Test of Interactionist Hypotheses of Self-Conception." *The American Journal of Sociology*, Vol. 61 (1956): pp. 399-403.

469. Mohajer, F., and Steinfatt, T. M. "Communication and Interracial Conflict: The Role of Disagreement, Prejudice, and Physical Attraction on the Choice of Mixed Race, Mixed Sex Work-Partners." Paper presented at the Annual Meeting of the Western Speech Communication Association, Denver, Colorado 1982.

470. Moller, A. P., and Thornhill, R. "Bilateral Symmetry and Sexual Selection: A Meta-Analysis." *American Naturalist*, Vol. 151 (1997): pp. 174-192.

471. Montell, G. "Do Good Looks Equal Good Evaluations?" *The Chronicle of Higher Education: Chronicle Careers* (2003, October 15): Retrieved July 20, 2005, from http://chronicle.com/jobs/2003/2010/2003101501c.htm

472. Moore, M. "Some People Have Looks to Die For." *The Hilltop (Howard University student newspaper)* (2005, January 18): Retrieved July 16, 2005, from http://www.thehilltoponline.com/media/paper2590/news/2005/2001/2018/LifeStyle/Some-People.Have.Looks.To.Die.For-834359.shtml

473. Moran, J. D. *Young Children's Conception of Physical Attractiveness as Evidenced in Human Figure Drawings (ED 196 538), ERIC Report, No. MF01-PC01*: ERIC: The Educational Resources Information Center, 1976.

474. Morse, S. J., Gruzen, J., and . "The Eye of the Beholder: A Neglected Variable in the Study of Physical Attractiveness." *Journal of Personality*, Vol. 44 (1976): pp. 209-225.

475. Morse, S. J., Reis, H. T., Gruzen, J., and Wolff, E. "The "Eye of the Beholder": Determinants of Physical Attractiveness Judgments in the U. S. and South Africa." *Journal of Personality*, Vol. 42 (1974): pp. 528-542.

476. Morselli, E. "Sulla Dismorfofobia e Sulla Tafefobia." *Bolletinno dellla R Accademia di Genova*, Vol. 6 (1891): pp. 110-119.

477. Moscicki, E. K. "Epidemiology of Suicide." In *The Harvard Medical School Guide to Suicide Assessment and Intervention*, edited by D. G. Jacobs. San Francisco: Jossey-Bass, 1999.

478. Moses, Y., Edelman, S., and Ullman, S. "Generalization to Novel Images in Upright and Inverted Faces." *Perception*, Vol. 25 (1996): pp. 443-461.

479. Moss, L. "Women Considering Cosmetic Surgery to Further Careers." *Western Mail (Cardiff, Wales)* (2005, August 2): Retrieved October 29, 2005, from http://www.highbeam.com/library/doc2000.asp

480. Moss, M. K., and Page, R. A. "Reinforcement and Helping Behavior." *Journal of Applied Social Psychology*, Vol. 2 (1972): pp. 360-371.

481. Mouchetant-Rostaing, Y., Giard, M. H., Bentin, S., Aguera, P. E., and Pernier, J. "Neurophysiological Correlates of Face Sex Processing in Humans." *European Journal of Neuroscience*, Vol. 12 (2000): pp. 303-310.

482. MSNBC News. "Countdown for September 19, 2003." In *Countdown with Keith Olbermann*. New York: MSNBC News, 2003, September 19.

483. Mumrikova, G. "Culinary Beautification." *WHERE* (2003, April): pp. 27-31.

484. Munn, L. "The Effect of a Knowledge of the Situation Upon Judgment of Emotion from Facial Expression." *Journal of Abnormal and Social Psychology*, Vol. 35 (1940): pp. 324-338.

485. Murphy, M. J., Nelson, D. A., and Cheap, T. L. "Rated and Actual Performance of High School Students as a Function of Sex and Attractiveness." *Psychological Reports*, Vol. 48 (1981): pp. 103-106.

486. Murstein, B. I. "Physical Attractiveness and Marital Choice." *Journal of Personality and Social Psychology*, Vol. 22 (1972): pp. 8-12.

487. Murstein, B. I., and Christy, P. "Physical Attractiveness and Marriage Adjustment in Middle-Aged Couples." *Journal of Personality and Social Psychology*, Vol. 34 (1976): pp. 537-542.

488. Nadler, A., Shapira, R., and Ben-Itzhak, S. "Good Looks May Help: Effects of Helper's Physical Attractiveness and Sex of Helper on Males' and Females' Help-Seeking Behavior." *Journal of Personality and Social Psychology*, Vol. 42 (1982): pp. 90-99.

489. Nahmad, V. "Gift Kits Aid Recovery from Breast Surgery." *Chicago Tribune*, Vol. 158, No. 12 (2005, January 12): p. 3 (section 8).

490. Nazario, B. "Magic in a Makeover." *WebMD* (2005, January 31): Retrieved August 14, 2005, from http://www.medicinenet.com/script/main/art.asp?articlekey=52139

491. NBC Television Network News. "America's Obesity." In *NBC Nightly News with Tom Brokaw*. New York: NBC Television Network News, 2004, January 18.

492. Neave, N., Laing, S., Fink, B., and Manning, J. T. "Second to Fourth Digit Ratio, Testosterone and Perceived Male Dominance." *Proceedings of the Royal Society of London: Biological Sciences*, Vol. 270, No. 1,529 (2003): pp. 2167-2172.

493. Neave, N., and Wolfson, S. "Testosterone, Territoriality, and the 'Home Advantage'" *Physiology & Behaviour*, Vol. 78 (2003): pp. 269-275.

494. Netemeyerm, R. S., Burton, S., and Lichtenstein, R. "Trait Aspects of Vanity: Measurement and Relevance to Consumer Behavior." *Journal of Consumer Research*, Vol. 21, No. 4 (1995): pp. 612-625.

495. Newman, R. "Short People (song title)." In *Little Criminals (album title)*. Los Angeles, California: Warner Brothers Records, 1977.

496. Newsweek. "Perspectives." *Newsweek*, Vol. 145, No. 11 (2005, March 14): p. 2.

497. ————. "Perspectives." *Newsweek*, Vol. 144, No. 23 (2004, December 6): p. 21.

498. Newsweek Magazine Staff. "Perspectives." *Newsweek*, Vol. 113, No. 6 (2004, February 9): p. 23.

499. Newsweek Staff. "Perspectives." *Newsweek*, Vol. 143, No. 12 (2004, March 22): p. 21.

500. Neziroglu, F. "Body Dysmorphic Disorder: A Common But Underdiagnosed Clinical Entity." *Psychiatric Times*, Vol. 15, No. 1 (1998): Retrieved August 16, 2005, from http://www.psychiatrictimes.com/p980111.html

501. Nida, S. A., and Williams, J. E. "Sex-Stereotyped Traits, Physical Attractiveness, and Interpersonal Attraction." *Psychological Reports*, Vol. 41 (1977): pp. 1311-1322.

502. Nielsen, J. P., and Kernaleguen, A. "Influence of Clothing and Physical Attractiveness in Person Perception." *Perceptual and Motor Skills*, Vol. 42 (1976): pp. 775-780.

503. Nussbaum, B. "The Best Product Design: Annual Design Awards 2005." *BusinessWeek*, No. 3941 (2005, July 4): pp. 62-72.

504. ————. "The Best Product Designs of the Year: Winners 2004." *BusinessWeek* (2004, July 5): pp. 60-68.

505. ————. "Get Creative." *BusinessWeek*, No. 3945 (2005, August 1): pp. 60-67.

506. Oates, J. C. "Do You Love Me? Ann Patchett Recalls her Relationship with Lucy Grealy, Who Wrote *Autobiography of a Face*." *The New York Times*, Vol. 153, No. 52,851 (2004, May 16): p. 8 (The New York Times Book Review section)

507. Omestad, T. "A Nation of Lost Boys." *U. S. News & World Report*, Vol. 137, No. 4 (2004, August 9): p. 12.

508. Omotani, B. J., and Omotani, L. "Expect the Best: How Your Teachers Can Help All Children Learn." *The Executive Educator*, Vol. 18, No. 8 (1996): pp. 27, 31.

509. Orstein, R. E. *The Psychology of Consciousness*. San Francisco, California: Freeman, 1972.

510. Orwell, G. *Nineteen Eighty-Four*. New York: McGraw-Hill, 1949.

511. Pagana, K. D., and Pagana, T. J. *Diagnostic Testing & Nursing Implications : A Case Study Approach*. St. Louis, Missouri: Mosby, 1982.

512. Page, R. A., and Balloun, J. L. "The Effect of Voice Volume on the Perception of Personality." *Journal of Social Psychology*, Vol. 105 (1978): pp. 65-72.

513. Page, S. "Election-Predicting Tools Point Both Ways." *USA Today*, Vol. 22, No. 200 (2004, June 24): p. 2A.

514. Panferov, V. N. "The Perception and Interpretation of Personal Appearance." *Voprosy Psikhologii*, Vol. March-April, No. 2 (1974): pp. 59-64.

515. Parkin, A. J., and Hayward, C. "The Influence of Trait and Physical-Feature-Based Orienting Strategies on Aspects of Facial Memory." *British Journal of Psychology*, Vol. 74 (1983): pp. 71-82.

516. Patchett, A. *Truth & Beauty: A Friendship*. New York: HarperCollins Publishers, 2004.

517. Patzer, G. L. "Advertising Research: Theoretical Models, Mechanical Aids, and General Principles." In *1981 Proceedings: Southwestern Marketing Association*, edited by R. H. Ross, F. B. Kraft and C. H. Davis, pp. 102-105. Wichita, Kansas: The Southwestern Marketing Association, 1981.

518. ————. "Affirmative Action vs Client Wishes." In *Arthur Anderson & Company Business Ethics Program*, pp. Mktg-01 section, pp.01-04. Chicago, Illinois: Arthur Anderson & Co., Mktg-01: Minicase, 1992.

519. ————. "Another Type of Discrimination." In *Arthur Anderson & Company Business Ethics Program*, pp. Mktg-09 section, pp.01-05. Chicago, Illinois: Arthur Anderson & Co., Mktg-09: Minicase, 1992.

520. ————. "A Comparison of Advertisement Effects: Sexy Female Communicator versus Non-Sexy Female Communicator." In *Advances in Consumer Research, Association for Consumer Research, Vol. 7*, edited by J. Olson, pp. 359-364. Ann Arbor, Michigan, 1979b.

521. ————. "Determinants of Judgments of Physical Attractiveness and the Attribution of Sexual Attitudes to Strangers." Master of Science (MS) thesis, Pittsburg State University, Pittsburg, Kansas, 1975.

522. ————. "The Effectiveness of Female Nudity in Advertising." In *1982 Conference Proceedings: Western Marketing Educators' Association*, edited by S. Achtenhagen, pp. 83-84. Los Angeles, California: (This paper received special recognition as the reviewers' number one ranking.), 1982.

523. ————. "Effects of Sexual Attitudes and Physical Attractiveness on Heterosexual Attraction." Bachelor of Arts (BA) Senior Project, Minnesota State University Moorhead, 1973.

524. ————. "Ethics in Marketing Strategy that Exploits and Promulgates The Physical Attractiveness Phenomena." In *Marketing: A Return to the Broader Dimensions (American Marketing Association Proceedings: 1988 Educators' Winter Conference)*, edited by S. Shapiro and A. H. Walle, pp. 207-211. Chicago, Illinois, 1988a.

525. ————. *Experiment- Research Methodology in Marketing: Types and Applications*. Westport, Connecticut: Quorum Books, 1996.

526. ————. *Experiment- Research Methodology in Marketing: Types and Applications*. Westport, Connecticut: Quorum Books, 1996.

527. ————. "An Experiment Investigating the Influence of Communicator Physical Attractiveness on Attitudes." In *1983 American Marketing Association Educators' Proceedings*, edited by P. E. Murphy and G. R. Laczniak, pp. 25-29. Chicago, Illinois, 1983b.

528. ————. "An Experimental Investigation of the Relationship between Communicator Facial Physical Attractiveness and Non-Personal Persuasive Communication Effectiveness." Doctor of Philosophy (Ph.D.) dissertation, Virginia Polytechnic Institute and State University, Blacksburg, Virginia, 1980.

529. ———. "Falsification of Data." In *Arthur Anderson & Company Business Ethics Program*, pp. Mktg-10 section, pp. 11-14. Chicago, Illinois: Arthur Anderson & Co., Mktg-10: Minicase, 1992.

530. ———. "Improving Self-Esteem by Improving Physical Attractiveness." *Journal of Esthetic Dentistry*, Vol. 9, No. 1 (1997): pp. 44-46.

531. ———. "Measurement of Physical Attractiveness: Truth-of-Consensus." *Journal of Esthetic Dentistry*, Vol. 6, No. 4 (1994): pp. 185-188.

532. ———. "The Moderate Physical Attractiveness Hypothesis." Virginia Polytechnic Institute and State University, Blacksburg, Virginia (1979a): Unpublished research report.

533. ———. "Multiple Dimensions of Performance for 30-Second and 15-Second Television Commercials." *Journal of Advertising Research*, Vol. 31, No. 4 (1991): pp. 18-25.

534. ———. "The Physical Attractiveness and Persuasive Communication Relationship." Virginia Polytechnic Institute and State University, Blacksburg, Virginia (1978): Unpublished research report.

535. ———. *The Physical Attractiveness Phenomena*. Edited by E. Aronson, *Perspectives in Social Psychology*. New York and London: Plenum Press, 1985.

536. ———. "Product Perception as a Function of Communicator Sex." In *1983 American Marketing Association Educators' Proceedings*, edited by P. E. Murphy and G. R. Laczniak, pp. 41-44. Chicago, Illinois, 1983a.

537. ———. "Psychologic and Sociologic Dimensions of Hair: An Aspect of The Physical Attractiveness Phenomenon." In *Clinics in Dermatology—Androgenetic Alopecia: From Empiricism to Knowledge* edited by R. L. DeVillez, L. M. P. Griggs and B. Freeman, pp. 93-101. New York: Harper & Row, 1988, October-December.

538. ———. "Psychological and Sociological Dimensions of Hair: An Aspect of The Physical Attractiveness Phenomena." Paper presented at the Brook Lodge Medical Symposium on Androgenetic Alopecia (sponsored by The Upjohn Pharmaceutical Company), Kalamazoo, Michigan 1987, February 16-20.

539. ———. "Reality of Physical Attractiveness." *Journal of Esthetic Dentistry*, Vol. 6, No. 1 (1994): pp. 35-38.

540. ———. "Research Claims that Beauty is Wallet-Deep." *Marketing News*, Vol. 19, No. 18 (1985a): p. 4.

541. ———. "Research Claims that Beauty is Wallet-Deep." *Collegiate Edition Marketing News*, Vol. 3, No. 7 (1985b): p. 8.

542. ———. "The Right Stuff: Marketing Research in the Movie Industry." *Ad L.A.*, Vol. September (1989): p. 17.

543. ———. "Self-Esteem and Physical Attractiveness." *Journal of Esthetic Dentistry*, Vol. 7, No. 6 (1995): pp. 274-277.

544. ———. "Source Credibility as a Function of Communicator Physical Attractiveness." *Journal of Business Research*, Vol. 11, No. 2 (1983c): pp. 229-241.

545. ———. "Understanding the Causal Relationship Between Physical Attractiveness and Self-Esteem." *Journal of Esthetic Dentistry*, Vol. 8, No. 3 (1996): pp. 144-147.

546. ———. "Use of The Physical Attractiveness Phenomena in Political Campaigns: A Marketing Strategy and a Social Responsibility." In *Marketing: A Return to the Broader Dimensions (American Marketing Association Proceedings: 1988 Educators' Winter Conference)*, edited by S. Shapiro and A. H. Walle, pp. 212-217. Chicago, Illinois, 1988b.

547. ———. "Use of the Physical Attractiveness Variable in Marketing Management Strategy." Master of Business Administration (MBA) Plan B project, University of Minnesota, Minneapolis, Minnesota, 1976.

548. ———. *Using Secondary Data in Marketing Research: United States and Worldwide*. Westport, Connecticut: Quorum Books, 1995.

549. ———. *Using Secondary Data in Marketing Research: United States and Worldwide*. Westport, Connecticut: Quorum Books, 1995.

550. Patzer, G. L., and Burke, D. M. "Physical Attractiveness and Child Development." In *Advances in Clinical Child Psychology, 11th Annual Volume*, edited by B. B. Lahey and A. E. Kazdin, pp. 325-368. New York: Plenum Press, 1988.

551. Patzer, G. L., and Davis, C. H. "Business Education: Bridging the Ethics Gap Between University Classroom and Corporate Boardroom." In *International Business Practices: Contemporary Readings, 1996 Edition*, edited by S. G. Amin and S. Fullerton, pp. 172-179. London, England: Academy of Business Administration, International Conference, 1996.

552. Patzer, G. L., and Mills, M. E. "Correlates of Patients' Satisfaction with Cosmetic Surgery Outcome." Paper presented at the Second Annual Convention of the American Psychological Society, Dallas, Texas 1990, June 7-10.

553. Patzer, G. L., and Rawwas, M. Y. A. "Marketing the Mental Health Hospital: Identification of Communication Factors." *Journal of Hospital Marketing*, Vol. 8, No. 2 (1994): pp. 43-66.

554. Pellegrini, R. J., Hicks, R. A., and Meyers-Winton, S. "Self-Evaluation of Attractiveness and Perceptions of Mate-Attraction in the Interpersonal Marketplace." *Perceptual and Motor Skills*, Vol. 50 (1980): pp. 812-814.

555. ———. "Situational Affective Arousal and Heterosexual Attraction: Some Effects of Success, Failure, and Physical Attractiveness." *Psychological Record*, Vol. 29 (1979): pp. 453-462.

556. Pennebaker, J. W., Dyer, M. A., Caulkins, R. S., Litowitz, D. L., Ackerman, P. L., Anderson, D. B., and McGraw, K. M. "Don't the Girls get Prettier at Closing Time: A Country and Western Application of Psychology." *Personality and Social Psychology Bulletin*, Vol. 5 (1979): pp. 122-125.

557. Penton-Voak, I. S., and Perrett, D. J. "Female Preference for Male Faces Change Cyclically: Further Evidence." *Evolution and Human Behavior*, Vol. 21 (2000): pp. 39-48.

558. Peplau, L. A. "Sex, Love, and the Double Standard." Paper presented at the Annual Conference of the American Psychological Association, Washington, D.C. 1976.

559. Perlini, A. H., and Hansen, S. D. "Moderating Effects of Need for Cognition on Attractiveness Stereotyping." *Social Behavior and Personality*, Vol. 49, No. 6 (2001): pp. 313-322.

560. Perrin, F. A. C. "Physical Attractiveness and Repulsiveness." *Journal of Experimental Psychology*, Vol. 4 (1921): pp. 203-217.

561. Persico, N., Postlewaite, A., and Silverman, D. "The Effect of Adolescent Experience on Labor Market Outcomes: The Case of Height." *Journal of Political Economy*, Vol. 112, No. 5 (2004, October): pp. 1019-1053.

562. Peskin, M., and Newell, F. N. "Familiarity Breeds Attraction: Effects of Exposure on the Attractiveness of Typical and Distinctive Faces." *Perception*, Vol. 33, No. 2 (2004): pp. 147-157.

563. Peterson, J. L., and Miller, C. "Physical Attractiveness and Marriage Adjustment in Older American Couples." *Journal of Psychology*, Vol. 105 (1980): pp. 247-252.

564. Pheterson, M., and Horai, J. "The Effects of Sensation Seeking, Physical Attractiveness of Stimuli, and Exposure Frequency on Liking." *Social Behavior and Personality*, Vol. 4 (1976): pp. 241-247.

565. Phillips, K. A. "Body Dysmorphic Disorder: The Distress of Imagined Ugliness." *American Journal of Psychiatry*, Vol. 148, No. 9 (1991): pp. 1138-1149.

566. Phillips, K. A., McElroy, S. L., Keck, P. E. J., Pope, H. G. J., and Hudson, J. I. "Body Dysmorphic Disorder: 30 Cases of Imagined Ugliness." *American Journal of Psychiatry*, Vol. 150, No. 2 (1993): pp. 302-308.

567. Phillips, S., and Morrison, K. "Face Value." In *Dateline NBC*. New York: NBC Television Network, 2004, January 11.

568. Piehl, J. "Integration of Information in the "Courts:" Influence of Physical Attractiveness on Amount of Punishment for a Traffic Offender." *Psychological Reports*, Vol. 41 (1977): pp. 551-556.

569. Piliavin, I. M., Piliavin, J. A., and Rodin, J. "Costs, Diffusion, and the Stigmatized Victim." *Journal of Personality and Social Psychology*, Vol. 32 (1975): pp. 429-438.

570. Platek, S. M., Raines, D. M., Gallup, G. G., Mohamed, F. B., Thomson, J. W., Myers, T. E., Panyavin, I. S., Levin, S. L., Davis, J. A., Fonteyn, L. C. M., and Arigo, D. R. "Reactions to Children's Faces: Males are More Affected by Resemblance than Females Are, and So Are Their Brains." *Evolution and Human Behavior*, Vol. 25, No. 6 (2004): pp. 394-405.

571. Portnoy, S. "Height as a Personality Variable in a Conformity Situation." Doctoral dissertation, Temple University, Philadelphia, Pennsylvania, 1972.

572. Postrel, V. *The Substance of Style: How the Rise of Aesthetic Value Is Remaking Commerce, Culture, and Consciousness.* New York: HarperCollins, 2003.

573. Power, T. G., Hildebrandt, K. A., and Fitzgerald, H. E. "Adults' Responses to Infants Varying in Facial Expression and Perceived Attractiveness." *Infant Behavior and Development*, Vol. 5 (1982): pp. 33-44.

574. Prashad, S. "Ugly Truth: Beautiful People Earn More." *Toronto Star* (2005, April 8): Retrieved July 22, 2005, from http://www.thestar.com/NASApp/cs/ContentServer

575. Price, R. A., and Vandenberg, S. G. "Matching for Physical Attractiveness in Married Couples." *Personality and Social Psychology Bulletin*, Vol. 5 (1979): pp. 398-400.

576. Princeton Survey Research Associates. "Men's Health, The Man Poll." *Newsweek Magazine*, Vol. 141, No. 24 (2003, June 16): p. 53.

577. Putnam, C. "Ann Patchett's Memoir of her friendship with Lucy Grealy." *Chicago Tribune*, Vol. 158I, No. 172 (2004, June 20): p. 4 (section 14).

578. Quinsey, V. L., Ketsetzis, M., Earls, C., and Karamanoukin, A. "Viewing Time as a Measure of Sexual Interest." *Ethology and Sociobiology*, Vol. 17 (1996): pp. 341-354.

579. Raffini, J. *Winners Without Losers: Structures and Strategies for Increasing Student Motivation To Learn.* Needham Heights, Massachusetts: Allyn and Bacon, 1993.

580. Ramachandran, N. "Career Spotlight: Tattoos are Showing Up All Over." *U. S. News & World Report* (2005, July 5): Retrieved July 6, 2005, from http://www.usnews.com/usnews/biztech/articles/o50702/50702career.htm

581. Rand, C. S., and Hall, H. A. "Sex Differences in the Accuracy of Self-Perceived Attractiveness." *Social Psychology Quarterly*, Vol. 46 (1983): pp. 359-363.

582. Rawwas, M. Y. A., Patzer, G. L., and Klassen, M. L. "Consumer Ethics in Cross-Cultural Settings: Entrepreneurial Implications." *European Journal of Marketing*, Vol. 29, No. 7 (1995): pp. 62-78.

583. Rawwas, M. Y. A., Patzer, G. L., and Vitell, S. J. "A Cross-Cultural Investigation of the Ethical Values of Consumers: The Potential Effect of War and Civil Disruption." *Journal of Business Ethics*, Vol. 17 (1998): pp. 435-448.

584. Reagan, C. E. *Ethics for Scientific Researchers.* Springfield, IL: Charles C. Thomas, 1969.

585. Reaves, J. Y., and Friedman, P. "The Relationship of Physical Attractiveness and Similarity of Preferences of Peer Affiliation among Black Children." *Journal of Negro Education*, Vol. 51 (1982): pp. 101-110.

586. Reilly, S., and Snider, J. "Interracial Marriages Increasing." *USA Today*, Vol. 22, No. 79 (2004, January 6): p. 1A.

587. Reis, H., Nazlek, J., and Wheeler, L. "Physical Attractiveness in Social Interaction." *Journal of Personality and Social Psychology*, Vol. 38 (1980): pp. 604-617.

588. Reis, H., Wheeler, L., Spiegle, N., Kernis, M. H., and Nezlek, J. P., M. "Physical Attractiveness in Social Interaction: II. Why Does Appearance Affect Social Experience?" *Journal of Personality and Social Psychology*, Vol. 43 (1982): pp. 979-996.

589. Reynolds, G. H. "Here It Comes." *The Wall Street Journal*, Vol. 246, No. 67 (2005, October 1): p. A8.

590. Rhodes, G., Halberstadt, J., and Brajkovich, G. "Generalization of Mere Exposure Effects in Social Stimuli." *Social Cognition*, Vol. 19 (2001): pp. 57-70.

591. Rhodes, G., Simmons, L. W., and Peters, M. "Attractiveness and Sexual Behavior: Does Attractiveness Enhance Mating Success?" *Evolution and Human Behavior*, Vol. 26, No. 2 (2005): pp. 186-201.

592. Rich, J. "Effects of Children's Physical Attractiveness on Teachers' Evaluations." *Journal of Educational Psychology*, Vol. 67 (1975): pp. 599-609.

593. Richards, I. A. *Coleridge on Imagination.* London: Jonathan Cape, 1934.

594. Rist, R. C. "Student Social Class and Teacher Expectations: The Self-Fulfilling Prophecy in Ghetto Education." *Harvard Educational Review*, Vol. 40 (1970): pp. 411-415.

595. Roan, S. "Breasts, Redefined." *Los Angeles Times*, Vol. 124, No. 191 (2005, June 13): pp. F1, F10.

596. Roff, M., and Brody, D. S. "Appearance and Choice Status during Adolescence." *Journal of Psychology*, Vol. 36 (1953): pp. 347-356.

597. Rosen, G. M., and Ross, A. O. "Relationships of Body Image to Self-Concept." *Journal of Consulting and Clinical Psychology*, Vol. 32 (1968): p. 100.

598. Rosenthal, R. "The Pygmalion Effect Lives." *Psychology Today*, Vol. 7 (1973): pp. 56-63.

599. ———. "Teacher Expectations and Pupil Learning." In *Teachers and the Learning Process*, edited by R. D. Strom (Ed.). Englewood Cliffs, New Jersey: Prentice-Hall, 1971a.

600. ———. "Teacher Expectations and Their Effects upon Children." In *Psychology and Educational Practice*, edited by G. S. Lesser (Ed.). Glenview, Illinois: Scott, Foresman, 1971b.

601. Rosenthal, R., and Jacobson, L. *Pygmalion in the Classroom.* New York: Holt, Rinehart, & Winston, 1968.

602. Ross, M. B., and Salvia, J. "Attractiveness as a Biasing Factor in Teacher Judgments." *American Journal of Mental Deficiency*, Vol. 80 (1975): pp. 96-98.

603. Rotton, J., Barry, T., Frey, J., and Soler, E. "Air Pollution and Interpersonal Attraction." *Journal of Applied Social Psychology*, Vol. 8 (1978): pp. 57-71.

604. Rubenstein, C. "The Face." *Psychology Today* (1983, January): pp. 48-55.

605. Rubin, R. "Second Company Gets OK to Sell Silicone-Gel Breast Implants." *USA Today*, Vol. 24, No. 6 (2005, September 22): p. 9D.

606. Runyan, W. M. "The Life Satisfaction Chart: Perceptions of the Course of Subjective Experience." *Internal Journal of Aging and Human Development*, Vol. 11 (1980): pp. 45-64.

607. Sage, A. "Woman Charged With Murder of Unborn Baby." *AP (Associated Press)* (2004, March 3): Retrieved August 8, 2005, from http://www.highbeam.com/library/doc2000.asp

608. Salvia, J., Algozzine, R., and Sheare, J. B. "Attractiveness and School Achievement." *Journal of School Psychology*, Vol. 15 (1977): pp. 60-67.

609. Samuels, A. "Celebs Ease Black Women's Taboos Against Cosmetic Surgery." *Daily Herald (Chicago)*, Vol. 132, No. 271 (2004, July 12): p. 1 (section 3).

610. Santayana, G. *The Sense of Beauty*. New York: Scribners, 1936.

611. Saporito, B. "Interview: 10 Questions for John McEnroe." *Time*, Vol. 164, No. 2 (2004, July 12): p. 8.

612. Saranow, J. "Beauty Takes On a New Form—Pills." *The Wall Street Journal*, Vol. 243, No. 62 (2004, March 30): p. D10.

613. ———. "The Power Chin: From Faux Clefts to Implants, Procedures for Men Surge; The Risks of Nerve Damage." *The Wall Street Journal*, Vol. 243, No. 116 (2004, June 15): pp. D1, D4.

614. Saranow, J., and Efrati, A. "FDA Approves a New Facial Filler." *The Wall Street Journal*, Vol. 244, No. 24 (2004, August 4): p. D12.

615. Sardis, K. "Loose Talk: What the Stars Said This Week." *Us Weekly* (2004, September 13): p. 6.

616. Sawyer, D. "A Different Kind of Diplomat." In *60 Minutes*. New York: CBS Television Network News, 1986, March 2.

617. Scheib, J., Gangestad, S. W., and Thornhill, R. "Facial Attractiveness, Symmetry and Cues of Good Genes." *Proceedings of the Royal Society of London: Biological Sciences*, Vol. 266 (1999): pp. 1913-1917.

618. Schiller, B. "A Quantitative Analysis of Marriage Selection in a Small Group." *Journal of Social Psychology*, Vol. 3 (1932): pp. 297-319.

619. Schmich, M. "College Reunion Rekindles a Self that is Ageless." *Chicago Tribune*, Vol. 158, No. 124 (2005, May 4): p. 1 (section 2).

620. Schoedel, J., Frederickson, W. A., and Knight, J. M. "An Extrapolation of the Physical Attractiveness and Sex Variables within the Byrne Attraction Paradigm." *Memory and Cognition*, Vol. 3 (1975): pp. 527-530.

621. Schoenberger, C. R. "Study Says the Handsome Turn Handsome Profits for Their Firms." *The Wall Street Journal*, Vol. 138, No. 30 (1997, August 12): p. B1.

622. Schooley, M. "Personality Resemblances Among Married Couples." *Journal of Abnormal and Social Psychology*, Vol. 31 (1936): pp. 340-347.

623. Schunk, M., and Selg, H. "Sociometric Status and the Dimensions Attractiveness, Academic Performance and Aggressiveness in Classrooms (Correlations and Group Entropy)." *Psychologie in Erzienhung und Unterricht*, Vol. 26 (1979): pp. 267-275.

624. Schweinberger, S. R., Burton, A. M., and Kelly, S. W. "Asymmetric Dependencies in Perceiving Identity and Emotion: Experiments with Morphed Faces." *Perception and Psychophysics*, Vol. 61 (1999): pp. 1102-1115.

625. Scodel, A. "Heterosexual Somatic Preference and Fantasy Dependence." *Journal of Consulting Psychology*, Vol. 21 (1957): pp. 371-374.

626. Scott, W. "Personality Parade." *Parade: Supplement Magazine of the Chicago Tribune*, Vol. 159, No. 261 (2005, September 18): p. 2.

627. Seamon, J. G., Stolz, J. A., Bass, D. H., and Chatinover, A. I. "Recognition of Facial Features in Immediate Memory." *Bulletin of the Psychonomic Society*, Vol. 12 (1978): pp. 231-234.

628. Secord, P. F., and Jourard, S. M. "The Appraisal of Body-Cathexis: Body-Cathexis and the Self." *Journal of Consulting Psychology*, Vol. 17 (1953): pp. 343-347.

629. See, L. *Snow Flower and the Secret Fan*. New York: Random House, 2005.

630. Seger, B. "Hollywood Nights (song title)." In *Stranger in Town (album title)*. New York: Capitol Records, Inc., 1978.

631. Selvin, M. "Innovations, Reinventing the Brassiere: Companies Engineering New Foundations." *Chicago Tribune*, Vol. 159, No. 318 (2005, November 14): pp. 1, 4 (section 4).

632. Shanteau, J., and Nagy, G. F. "Probability of Acceptance in Dating Choice." *Journal of Personality and Social Psychology*, Vol. 37 (1979): pp. 522-533.

633. Shapiro, H. L. "From the Neck Up." *Natural History*, Vol. 56 (1947): pp. 456-465.

634. Shaw, J. "Reaction to Victims and Defendants of Varying Degrees of Attractiveness." *Psychonomic Science*, Vol. 27 (1972): pp. 229-230.

635. Sheldon, W. H. *The Varieties of Human Physique: An Introduction to Constitutional Psychology*. New York: Harper, 1940.

636. Shepard, S. B. "In Praise of Design." *BusinessWeek* (2004, July 5): p. 1.

637. Shepherd, J. W., and Ellis, H. D. "Physical Attractiveness and Selection of Marriage Partners." *Psychological Reports*, Vol. 30 (1972): p. 1004.

638. Sheposh, J. P. "The Radiating Effects of Status and Attractiveness of a Male Upon Evaluations of His Female Partner." Paper presented at the Annual Conference of the Western Psychological Association, Seattle, Washington 1976.

639. Shettel-Neuber, J., Bryson, J. B., and Young, L. E. "Physical Attractiveness of the "Other Person" and Jealousy." *Personality and Social Psychology Bulletin*, Vol. 4 (1978): pp. 612-615.

640. Shute, N. "Cover Story: Makeover Nation." *U. S. News & World Report*, Vol. 136, No. 19 (2004, May 31): pp. 52-63.

641. Sigall, H., and Aronson, E. "Liking for an Evaluator as a Function of Her Physical Attractiveness and Nature of the Evaluation." *Journal of Experimental Social Psychology*, Vol. 5 (1969): pp. 93-100.

642. Sigall, H., and Landy, D. "Radiating Beauty: Effects of Having a Physically Attractive Partner on Person Perception." *Journal of Personality and Social Psychology*, Vol. 28 (1973): pp. 218-224.

643. Sigall, H., Page, R., and Brown, A. "The Effects of Physical Attraction and Evaluation on Effort Expenditure and Work Output." *Representative Research in Social Psychology*, Vol. 2 (1971): pp. 19-25.

644. Silverman, S. S. *Clothing and Appearance, their Psychological Implications for Teenage Girls*. New York: Bureau of Publications (No. 912), Teachers College, Columbia University, 1945.

645. Singer, J. E. "The Use of Manipulative Strategies: Machiavellianism and Attractiveness." *Sociometry*, Vol. 27 (1964): pp. 128-150.

646. Smits, G. J., and Cherhoniak, I. M. "Physical Attractiveness and Friendliness in Interpersonal Attraction." *Psychological Reports*, Vol. 39 (1976): pp. 171-174.

647. Snyder, M., Tanke, E. D., and Berscheid, E. "Social Perception and Interpersonal Behavior: On the Self-Fulfilling Nature of Social Stereotypes." *Journal of Personality and Social Psychology*, Vol. 35 (1977): pp. 656-666.

648. Social Psychology Network. "Professional Profile: Elliot Aronson." *Social Psychology Network* (2004, May 17): Retrieved November 27, 2005, from http://aronson.socialpsychology.org

649. Soler, C., Nunez, M., Gutierrez, R., Nunez, J., Medina, P., Sancho, M., Alvarez, J., and Nunez, A. "Facial Attractiveness in Men provides Clues to Semen Quality." *Evolution and Human Behavior*, Vol. 24, No. 2 (2003, May): pp. 199-207.

650. Soloff, P. H., Lynch, K. G., Kelly, T. M., Malone, K. M., and Mann, J. J. "Characteristics of Suicide Attempts of Patients with Major Depressive Episode and Borderline Personality Disorder: A Comparative Study." *American Journal of Psychiatry*, Vol. 157, No. 4 (2000): pp. 601-608.

651. Sommer, R. *Personal Space*. Englewood Cliffs, New Jersey: Prentice-Hall, 1969.

652. Sorokin, P. *Social and Cultural Mobility*. Glencoe, Illinois: Free Press, 1927.

653. Spitz, R. A., and Wolf, K. M. "The Smiling Response: A Contribution to the Ontogenesis of Social Relations." *Genetic Psychology Monographs*, Vol. 34 (1946): pp. 57-125.

654. Spreadbury, C. L., and Reeves, J. B. "Physical Attractiveness, Dating Behavior, and Implications for Women." *Personnel and Guidance Journal*, Vol. 57 (1979): pp. 338-340.

655. Sprecher, S., and Regan, P. C. "Liking Some Things (in Some People) More than Others: Partner Preferences in Romantic Relationships and Friendships." *Journal of Social and Personal Relationships*, Vol. 50, No. 6 (2002): pp. 463-481.

656. Springen, K. "Injections: The 'Youth Corridor' Is the New Forehead." *Newsweek*, Vol. 145, No. 26 (2005, June 27): p. 11.

657. Staffieri, J. R. "Body Build and Behavioral Expectancies in Young Females." *Developmental Psychology*, Vol. 6 (1972): pp. 125-127.

658. ———. "A Study of Social Stereotype of Body Image in Children." *Journal of Personality and Social Psychology*, Vol. 6 (1967): pp. 101-104.

659. Stephan, C. W., and Langlois, J. H. "Physical Attractiveness and Ethnicity: Implications for Stereotyping and Social Development." *Journal of Genetic Psychology*, Vol. 137 (1980): pp. 303-304.

660. Stephan, C. W., and Tully, J. C. "The Influence of Physical Attractiveness of a Plaintiff on the Decisions of Simulated Jurors." *Journal of Social Psychology*, Vol. 101 (1977): pp. 149-150.

661. Steptoe, S. "Interview: 10 Questions for Gloria Steinem." *Time*, Vol. 163, No. 14 (2004, April 5): p. 8.

662. Sternglanz, S. H., Gray, J. L., and Murakami, M. "Adult Preferences for Infantile Facial Features: An Ethological Approach." *Animal Behaviour*, Vol. 25 (1977): pp. 108-115.

663. Sternlicht, M. "Perceptions of Ugliness in the Mentally Retarded." *Journal of Psychology*, Vol. 99 (1978): pp. 139-142.

664. Stewart, R. A., Tutton, S. J., and Steele, R. E. "Stereotyping and Personality: I. Sex Differences in Perception of Female Physiques." *Perceptual and Motor Skills*, Vol. 36 (1973): pp. 811-814.

665. Stewart, S., Stinnett, H., and Rosenfeld, L. B. "Sex Differences in Desired Characteristics of Short-Term and Long-Term Relationship Partners." *Journal of Social and Personal Relationships*, Vol. 49, No. 3 (2000): pp. 843-853.

666. Stohl, C. "Perceptions of Social Attractiveness and Communication Style: A Developmental Study of Preschool Children." *Communication Education*, Vol. 30 (1981): pp. 367-376.

667. Stokes, S. J., and Bickman, L. "The Effect of the Physical Attractiveness and Role of the Helper on Help Seeking." *Journal of Applied Social Psychology*, Vol. 4 (1974): pp. 286-294.

668. Stolberg, S. G. "Cute, Sure, but Is He Electable?" *The New York Times*, Vol. 153, No. 52,907 (2004, July 11): pp. 1, 5 (section 1).

669. Strane, K., and Watts, C. "Females Judged by Attractiveness of Partner." *Perceptual and Motor Skills*, Vol. 45 (1977): pp. 225-226.

670. Streisand, B. "Turn Back The Clock." *U. S. News & World Report*, Vol. 139, No. 18 (2005, November 14): pp. 76-78.

671. Stretch, R. H., and Figley, C. R. "Beauty and the Boast: Predictors of Interpersonal Attraction in a Dating Experiment." *Psychology: A Quarterly Journal of Human Behavior*, Vol. 17 (1980): pp. 35-43.

672. Strobe, W., Insko, C. A., Thompson, V. D., and Layton, B. D. "Effects of Physical Attractiveness, Attitude Similarity, and Sex on Various Aspects of Interpersonal Attraction." *Journal of Personality and Social Psychology*, Vol. 18 (1971): pp. 79-91.

673. Strune, K., and Watts, C. "Females Judged by Attractiveness of Partner." *Perceptual and Motor Skills*, Vol. 45 (1977): pp. 225-226.

674. Sugarman, D. B. "Perceiving Physical Attractiveness: The Beauty of Contrast." *Representative Research in Psychology*, Vol. 11 (1980): pp. 106-114.

675. Symons, D. *The Evolution of Human Sexuality*. Oxford: University Press, 1979.

676. Tanke, E. D. "Dimensions of the Physical Attractiveness Stereotype: A Factor/Analytic Study." *Journal of Psychology*, Vol. 110, No. 63-73 (1982).

677. Taruiri, R. "Person Perception." In *Handbook of Social Psychology (Vol. 2)*, edited by G. Lindzey and E. Aronson. Boston, MA: Addison-Wesley, 1954.

678. Taylor, E. "About This Issue." *Chicago Tribune Magazine*, Vol. 158, No. 214 (2004, August 1): p. 2.

679. Taylor, P. A., and Glenn, N. D. "The Utility of Education and Attractiveness for Females' Status Attainment through Marriage." *American Sociological Review*, Vol. 41 (1976): pp. 484-497.

680. Tennis, G. H., and Dabbs, J. M. "Judging Physical Attractiveness: Effects of Judges' Own Attractiveness." *Personality and Social Psychology*, Vol. 1 (1975): pp. 513-516.

681. Terry, R. L. "Further Evidence on Components of Facial Attractiveness." *Perceptual and Motor Skills*, Vol. 45 (1977): p. 130.

682. Terry, R. L., and Brady, C. S. "Effects of Framed Spectacles and Contact Lenses on Self-Ratings of Facial Attractiveness." *Perceptual and Motor Skills*, Vol. 42 (1976): pp. 789-790.

683. Terry, R. L., and Davis, J. S. "Components of Facial Attractiveness." *Perceptual and Motor Skills*, Vol. 42 (1976): p. 198.

684. Terry, R. L., and Kroger, D. L. "Effects of Eye Correctives on Ratings of Attractiveness." *Perceptual and Motor Skills*, Vol. 42 (1976): p. 562.

685. Terry, R. L., and Macklin, E. "Accuracy of Identifying Married Couples on the Basis of Similarity of Attractiveness." *Journal of Psychology*, Vol. 97 (1977): pp. 15-20.

686. Terry, R. L., and Zimmerman, D. J. "Anxiety Induced by Contact Lenses and Framed Spectacles." *Journal of American Optometric Association*, Vol. 41 (1970): pp. 257-259.

687. Tesser, A., and Brodie, M. "A Note on the Evaluation of a Computer Date." *Psychonomic Science*, Vol. 23 (1971): p. 300.

688. The Economic Times. "A Stitch in Time Gets You a Face-Saving Option." *The Economic Times (New Delhi, India)* (2005, August 3): Retrieved November 27, 2005, from http://www.highbeam.com/library/doc2000.asp

689. The University of Pennsylvania Almanac. "Death of Solomon Asch." *The University of Pennsylvania Almanac*, Vol. 42, No. 23 (1996, March 5): Retrieved July 30, 2005, from http://www.upenn.edu/almanac/v2042/n2023/030596.html

690. The Wall Street Journal. "To Have Girls Is Glorious." *The Wall Street Journal*, Vol. 244, No. 34 (2004, August 18): p. A10.

691. Thompson, J. K., Heinberg, L. J., Altabe, M. N., and Tantleff-Dunn, S. *Exacting Beauty: Theory, Assessment, and Treatment of Body Image Disturbance*. Washington, D.C.: American Psychological Association Books, 1999.

692. Thorndike, E. L. *An Introduction to the Theory of Mental and Social Measurements (2nd ed. revised)*. New York: Teachers College, Columbia University, 1919.

693. Thornhill, R., and Gangestad, S. W. "The Evolution of Human Sexuality." *Trends in Ecology and Evolution* (1996): pp. 98-102.

694. ———. "Facial Attractiveness." *Trends in Cognitive Sciences*, Vol. 3, No. 12 (1999): pp. 452-460.

695. Thornhill, R., and Grammer, K. "The Body and Face of Woman: One Ornament that Signals Quality?" *Evolution and Human Behavior*, Vol. 20 (1999): pp. 105-120.

696. Thornhill, R., and Moller, A. P. "Developmental Stability, Disease and Medicine." *Biological Reviews* (1997): pp. 497-548.

697. Thornton, G. R. "The Effect of Wearing Glasses upon Judgments of Personality Traits of Persons Seen Briefly." *Journal of Applied Psychology*, Vol. 28 (1944): pp. 203-207.

698. Time Magazine Staff. "Notebook: Verbatim." *Time*, Vol. 165, No. 11 (2005, March 14): p. 13.

699. ———. "Notebook: Verbatim." *Time*, Vol. 164, No. 2 (2004, July 2): p. 19.

700. ———. "Numbers." *Time*, Vol. 166, No. 18 (2005, October 31): p. 24.

701. ———. "Numbers." *Time*, Vol. 165, No. 10 (2005, March 7): p. 15.

702. ———. "Your Time: Health." *Time*, Vol. 166, No. 7 (2005, August 15): p. 73.

703. Todorov, A., Mandisodza, A. N., Goren, A., and Hall, C. C. "Inferences of Competence from Faces Predict Election Outcomes." *Science*, Vol. 308, No. 5728 (2005, June 10).

704. Tompkins, R. C., and Boor, M. "Effects of Students' Physical Attractiveness and Name Popularity on Student Teachers Perceptions of Social and Academic Attributes." *Journal of Psychology*, Vol. 106 (1980): pp. 37-42.

705. Toro-Morn, M., and Sprecher, S. "A Cross-Cultural Comparison of Mate Preferences among University Students; The United States vs. The People's Republic of China (PRC)." *Journal of Comparative Family Studies*, Vol. 51, No. 6 (2003): pp. 151-170.

706. Tossey, L. D. "How Do Presidential Candidates Measure Up?" In *Maryland Newsline - Politics Special Report: Maryland Votes 2004*. College Park, Maryland: University of Maryland, Philip Merrill College of Journalism, 2004, February 10.

707. Tsiantar, D. "The War on Wrinkles." *Time*, Vol. 165, No. 15 (2005, April 11): pp. A16-A19.

708. U. S. Food and Drug Administration (FDA). "Quackery Targets Teens (FDA Publication No. 90-1147)." *FDA Consumer* (1990, April).

709. U. S. News & World Report. "America's Obsession with Beautiful People." *U. S. News & World Report*, Vol. 92, No. 1 (1982, January 11): pp. 60-61.

710. ———. "Bias Against Ugly People: How They Can Fight It." *U. S. News & World Report*, Vol. 95, No. 22 (1983, November 28): pp. 53-54.

711. ———. "Now, A Drive to End Discrimination Against "Ugly" People." *U. S. News & World Report*, Vol. 81, No. 8 (1976, August 23): p. 50.

712. Udry, J. R., and Eckland, B. K. "The Benefits of Being Beautiful: Differential Payoffs for Men and Women." University of North Carolina, Chapel Hill, North Carolina (1983): Unpublished manuscript.

713. Unger, A. "Galbraith Turning Economics to Show Biz." *Christian Science Monitor* (1977, May 18): p. p. 22.

714. University Wire. "LSU Profs Say Roberts' Physical Appearance Factors Into Nomination." *University Wire (Baton Rouge, Louisiana)* (2005, September 23): Retrieved November 27, 2005, from http://www.highbeam.com/library/doc2000.asp

715. USATODAY.com. "Your Appearance Can Affect Size of Your Paycheck." *USATODAY.Com* (2005, July 19): Retrieved July 21, 2005, from http://www.biz.yahoo.com/usat/050719

716. Vagt, G., and Majert, W. "Relationships Between Physical Attractiveness and Kindness: Testing a Prejudice." *Psychologische Beitrage*, Vol. 21 (1979): pp. 49-61.

717. van Leeuwen, M. L., and Macraw, C. N. "Is Beautiful Always Good? Implicit Benefits of Facial Attractiveness." *Social Cognition*, Vol. 22, No. 6 (2004): pp. 637-649.

718. Varnadore, A. E. "Why Do I Like You? Students' Understanding of the Impact of the Factors That Contribute to Liking." Paper presented at the Annual Meeting of the Southeastern Psychological Association, New Orleans, Louisiana 1994.

719. Vaughn, B. E., and Langlois, J. H. "Physical Attractiveness as a Correlate of Peer Status and Social Competence in Preschool Children." *Developmental Psychology*, Vol. 19 (1983): pp. 561-567.

720. Vigil, J. M., Geary, D. C., and Byrd-Craven, J. "A Life History Assessment of Early Childhood Sexual Abuse in Women." *Developmental Psychology*, Vol. 41, No. 3 (2005): pp. 5653-5561.

721. Wagatsuma, E., and Kleinke, C. L. "Ratings of Facial Beauty by Asian-American and Caucasian Females." *Journal of Social Psychology*, Vol. 109 (1979): pp. 299-300.

722. Wagman, M. "Sex Differences in Types of Daydreams." *Journal of Personality and Social Psychology*, Vol. 7 (1967): pp. 329-332.

723. Walker, C. "Can TV Save the Planet?" *American Demographics*, Vol. 18 (1996, May): pp. 42-49.

724. Waller, W. "The Rating and Dating Complex." *American Sociological Review*, Vol. 2 (1937): pp. 727-737.

725. Walster, E., Aronson, V., Abrahams, D., and Rottman, L. "Importance of Physical Attractiveness in Dating Behavior." *Journal of Personality and Social Psychology*, Vol. 4 (1966): pp. 508-516.

726. Wasson, J. "Pearson Product-Moment Correlation Coefficient." (2005): Retrieved October 23, 2005, from http://www.mnstate.edu/wasson/ed2602pearsoncorr.htm

727. Waters, R. "Beauty and Job Application." *Fairleigh Dickinson University Bulletin* (1980, Spring): p. 11.

728. Waynforth, D. "Mate Choice Trade-Offs and Women's Preference for Physically Attractive Men." *Human Nature*, Vol. 50, No. 3 (2001): pp. 207-219.

729. Weingarten, M. "Women Share a Lifeline in a China of Tortured Beauty." *Los Angeles Times*, Vol. 124, No. 206 (2005, June 28): p. E8.

730. Weise, E. "Beauty products have ugly side, researchers say." *The Arizona Republic*, Vol. 115, No. 38 (2004, June 25): pp. A1, E3.

731. Weiss, J., and Younts, J. "New Research Unmasks the Beauty Ideal." *Allure Magazine: The Allure State of Beauty Study* (2005, May 23): Retrieved July 26, 2005, from http://www.prnewswire.com/cgi-bin/stories.pl

732. Weiszhaar, O. "Sex Drive, Accentuation of Physical Attraction, and Marital Satisfaction." Doctoral dissertation, University of Minnesota, Minneapolis, Minnesota, 1978.

733. West, S. G., and Brown, T. J. "Physical Attractiveness, the Severity of the Emergency and Helping: A Field Experiment and Interpersonal Simulation." *Journal of Experimental Social Psychology*, Vol. 11 (1975): pp. 531-538.

734. Westermarck, E. *The History of Human Marriage*. London: MacMillan, 1921.

735. White, G. L. "Physical Attractiveness and Courtship Progress." *Journal of Personality and Social Psychology*, Vol. 39 (1980): pp. 660-668.

736. Wicklund, R. A. *Freedom and Reactance*. New York: Halsted, 1974.

737. Wiggins, J. S., Wiggins, N., and Conger, J. C. "Correlates of Heterosexual Somatic Preference." *Journal of Personality and Social Psychology*, Vol. 10 (1968): pp. 81-90.

738. Wikipedia Encyclopedia. "List of U. S. Presidents by Height Order." *Wikipedia Encyclopedia* (2005): Retrieved July 23, 2005, from http://en.wikipedia.org/wiki/List_of_U.S._Presidents_by_height_order

739. ———. "Pearson Product-Moment Correlation Coefficient." *Wikipedia Encyclopedia* (2005): Retrieved October 23, 2005, from http://en.wikipedia.org/wiki/Pearson_product-moment_correlation_coefficient

740. ———. "Physical Attractiveness." *Wikipedia Encyclopedia* (2005): Retrieved July 14, 2005, from http://en.wikipedia.org/wiki/physical_attractiveness

741. ———. "Physiognomy." *Wikipedia Encyclopedia* (2005): Retrieved October 18, 2005, from http://en.wikipedia.org/wiki/Physiognomy

742. Wild, H. A., Barrett, S. E., Spence, M. J., O'Toole, A. J., Cheng, Y. D., and Brooke, J. "Recognition and Sex Categorisation of Adults' and Children's Faces." *Journal of Experimental Child Psychology*, Vol. 77 (2000): pp. 269-291.

743. Wilson, D. W. "Helping Behavior and Physical Attractiveness." *Journal of Social Psychology*, Vol. 104 (1978): pp. 313-314.

744. Wilson, P. R. "Perceptual Distortion of Height as a Function of Ascribed Academic Status." *Journal of Social Psychology*, Vol. 74 (1968): pp. 97-102.

745. Wiser, P. "Animal Magnetism: What Fuels the Attraction for These Unlikely Hollywood Hunks?" *Chicago Sun Times*, Vol. 57, No. 130 (2004, July 6): p. 52.

746. Wolff, P. H. "Observations on the Early Development of Smiling." In *Determinants of Infant Behaviour (Vol. 2)*, edited by B. M. Foss. New York: Wiley, 1963.

747. Woll, S. B., and McFall, M. E. "The Effects of False Feedback on Attributed Arousal and Rated Attractiveness in Female Subjects." *Journal of Personality*, Vol. 47 (1979): pp. 214-229.

748. Womack, Y. "The Beat Goes On: Female Hip-Hop Fans Look Past Misogyny." *Chicago Tribune*, Vol. 157, No. 147 (2004, May 26): pp. 1, 7 (section 8).

749. Wulff, J. "Pressure To Be Perfect." *People* (2004, July 26): Retrieved July 13, 2005, from http://www.people.com

750. Yarbus, A. L. *Eye Movements and Vision*. New York: Plenum Press, 1967.

751. Yarmey, A. D. "Age as a Factor in Eyewitness Memory." In *Eyewitness Testimony: Psychological Perspectives*, edited by G. L. Wells and E. L. Loftus, pp. pp. 142-154. New York: Cambridge University Press, 1984.

752. ———. "The Effects of Attractiveness, Feature Saliency and Liking on Memory for Faces." In *Love and Attraction*, edited by M. Cook and G. Wilson. New York: Pergamon Press, 1979.

753. ———. "Eyewitness Identification by Elderly and Young Adults." *Law and Human Behavior*, Vol. 4, No. 4 (1980): pp. 359-371.

754. ———. "Recognition Memory for Familiar Public 'Faces': Effects of Orientation and Delay." *Psychonomic Science*, Vol. 24 (1971): pp. 286-288.

755. ———. "Through the Looking Glass: Sex Differences in Memory for Self Facial Poses." *Journal of Research in Personality*, Vol. 13 (1979): pp. 450-459.

756. Yarmey, A. D., and Jones, H. P. T. "Accuracy of Memory of Male and Female Eyewitnesses to Criminal Assault and Rape." *Bulletin of the Psychonomic Society*, Vol. 2 (1983): pp. 89-92.

757. Yarmey, A. D., Jones, H. P. T., and Rashid, S. "Eyewitness Memory of Elderly and Young Adults." In *Topics in Psychology and Law*, edited by D. J. Miller, D. E. Blackman and A. J. Chapman. Chichester, England: Wiley, 1983.

758. Young-Eisendrath, P. *Women and Desire: Beyond Wanting to Be Wanted*. New York: Harmony Books, 1999.

759. Yuankai, T. "Taking a Risk to be Beautiful." *Beijing Review*, Vol. 48, No. 24 (2005, June 16): p. 22.

760. Zaidel, D., Aarde, S. M., and Baig, K. "Appearance of Symmetry, Beauty, and Health in Human Faces." *Brain and Cognition*, Vol. 57, No. 3 (2005, April): pp. 261-263.

761. Zajonc, R. B. "Attitudinal Effects of Mere Exposure." *Journal of Personality and Social Psychology*, No. 9 (1968): pp. 1-27.

762. Zebrowitz, L. A., and Montepare, J. M. "Appearance DOES Matter." *Science*, Vol. 308, No. 5728 (2005, June 10): p. 1565.

References Addendum

763. Morris, J. S., Friston, K. J., Buchel, C., Frith, C. D., Young, A. W., Calder, A. J., and Dolan, R. J. "A Neuromodulatory Role for the Human Amygdala in Processing Emotional Face Expressions." *Brain*, Vol. 121, No. 1 (1998): pp. 47-57.

764. Rossion, B. "Is Sex Categorization from Faces Really Parallel to Face Recognition?" *Visual Cognition*, Vol. 9, No. 8 (2002): pp. 1003-1020.

765. Rossion, B., Dricot, L., Bodart, J. M., Devolder, A., Crommelinck, M., de Gelder, B., and Zoontjes, R. "Hemispheric Asymmetries for Whole-Based and Part-Based Face Processing in the Fusiform Gyrus." *Journal of Cognitive Neuroscience*, Vol. 12, No. 5 (2000): pp. 793-802.

766. Rossion, B., and Gauthier, I. "How Does the Brain Process Upright and Inverted Faces?" *Behavioral and Cognitive Neuroscience Reviews*, Vol. 1, No. 1 (2002): pp. 62-74.

767. Rossion, B., Gauthier, I., Tarr, M. J., Despland, P., Bruyer, R., Linotte, S., and Crommelinck, M. "The N170 Occipito-Temporal Component Is Delayed and Enhanced to Inverted Faces But Not to Inverted Objects: An Electrophysiological Account of Face-Specific Processes in the Human Brain." *Neuroreport*, Vol. 11, No. 1 (2000): pp. 69-74.

768. Rossion, B., Schiltz, C., Robaye, L., Pirenne, D., and Crommelinck, M. "How Does the Brain Discriminate Familiar and Unfamiliar Faces?" *Journal of Cognitive Neuroscience*, Vol. 13, No. 7 (2001): pp. 1019-1034.

Glossary

Appearance – The way someone or something looks. Appearance possesses many dimensions and communicates even more dimensions: physical attractiveness, age, education, ethnicity, gender, race, socioeconomic level, intelligence, fortune-misfortune, health-illness, respect, authority, expertise, liking, sex appeal, suspicion-trust, friend-enemy-terrorist, and so forth. (See, Physical Attractiveness in this glossary.)

Appearance Phenomenon – The collective realities of appearance. Appearance phenomenon is the environment and apparatus through which appearance transforms into a value that can be a blessing or a curse, an asset or a liability, a benefit or a detriment. Appearance phenomenon accordingly makes holders of different appearances, to be strong or weak, liked or disliked, and desired or undesired. Applied to people, appearance phenomenon surrounds, permeates, and includes all of us. Its impact spans our lives, from birth to death. (See, Physical Attractiveness Phenomenon in this glossary.)

Baby Boomers – Individuals born between 1946 and 1964, often noted as individuals born shortly after the end of World War II. Demographic studies estimate the size of this population in the United States to be about 77 million people.[391]

Causality[526] – A relationship in which a change in one variable causes a change or effect in another variable. The first variable is the independent variable, and it causes an effect on the second variable also known as the dependent variable. Causality is by and large synonymous with cause-and-effect relationship, causal relationship, and the phrase "X causes Y." Causality is a term misused often in everyday conversation and in the news media. Causality is a complex topic within research theory involving different types of causality and, most important, at least three conditions are required to reasonably conclude or infer causality:[526] evidence of association, appropriate timing, and elimination of alternative explanations.

Causal Relationship – see Causality.

Circular Four-Stage Process of Physical Attractiveness Phenomenon – A circular four-stage process that depicts physical attractiveness phenomenon. This process can be depicted through a diagram as introduced in chapter 1 (see page 21, Figure 1-1. Circular Four-Stage Process of Physical Attractiveness Phenomenon). Central to this process, physical attractiveness serves as an informational cue. From this informational cue, people infer extensive information that triggers assumptions, expectations, attitudes, and behaviors that cause pervasive and powerful consequences/effects. The effects overwhelmingly favor people with appearances higher in physical attractiveness and disfavor people with appearances lower in physical attractiveness. These consequences circulate back to influence the informational cue stage of the process.

Confederate – A term used infrequently in research and depending on context is either the same as stimulus persons or, unknown to the research project's subjects, is a person interacting with the subjects who is working with the researchers in undercover or disguised fashion.

Confounding Error[526] – see Extraneous Variable. Specific type of experimental error as named. When it occurs, it aligns with an extraneous variable that the researcher does not control. Often, this lack of control is because the researcher is not aware of the extraneous variable and therefore takes no action to eliminate it or to contend with it. When it occurs, it is potentially detrimental to the accuracy of the collected data and accuracy of related conclusions.

Constant Error[526] – Specific type of experimental error as named that occurs systematically. When it occurs, it is potentially detrimental to the accuracy of the collected data and accuracy of related conclusions.

Control Group[526] – The group of subjects in an experiment who do not receive an experimental treatment, are not exposed to any of the experiment's independent variable values, and are treated in every way possible the same as in the past, which is to, as best as possible, maintain the status quo for these subjects. The purpose of the control group is to serve as a standard against which to compare the effects measured for subjects in the experimental treatment group(s). Experiments should always have at least two groups: an experimental group of subjects who receive an experimental treatment and a control group who receive no experimental treatment; however, many experiments include no control group.

Demand Characteristic(s)[526] – Something in the research procedure, particularly with experiment research designs, that unintentionally provides subjects with information about the study or, more seriously, some way motivates the subjects to respond in a manner they think the researcher desired. When a demand characteristic occurs, it is potentially detrimental to the accuracy of the collected data and accuracy of related conclusions.

Dependent Variable[526] – A variable that is responsive to (i.e., depends on) an independent variable.

Ectomorph – A person's body structure that is thin or lean, including a light body build and/or slight muscular development, especially compared to average.

Endomorph – A person's body structure that is heavy and flabby, including a rounded body build and/or tendency toward fat or becoming fat; sometimes accompanied by muscular build, especially compared to average.

Experiment[526] – A research design/procedure to test a hypothesis that a causal relationship exists between two or more variables (contrasted with a relationship of correlation or association common for surveys). The test focuses on a belief or hypothesis that a change in one variable (independent variable) causes a change or effect in another variable (dependent variable).

Experimental Condition – see Experimental Treatment.

Experimental Control Group – see Control Group

Experimental Error[526] – Any type of error that occurs in an experiment. When it occurs, it is potentially detrimental to the accuracy of the collected data and accuracy of related conclusions.

Experimental Research – see Experiment.

Experimental Research Design – see Experiment.

Experimental Treatment[526] – The independent variable value to which subjects in an experiment are exposed. Experiments with more than one independent variable value have the respective number of experimental treatments. Experimental treatment is term or phrase used synonymously with experimental condition.

External Validity[526] – see Validity. Specific type of validity concerning the extent to which researchers and other people can generalize the measures (i.e., collected data) and findings beyond the subjects, setting, variables, and other aspects of the current research project. When researchers do not achieve external validity in an experiment, it is potentially detrimental to the accuracy of the collected data and accuracy of related conclusions. Its complement is internal validity. Note: external validity and internal validity are not mutually exclusive in that it is usually necessary to forego some reality/natural setting (i.e., external validity) to increase the internal validity of an experiment.

Extraneous Variable[526] – see Confounding Error. An uncontrolled variable that, when present, causes an effect on the dependent variable. This "extra" variable confuses or confounds data about hypothesized relationships between independent and dependent variables. A result when an extraneous variable is present in an experiment is that conclusions made about the effect on the dependent variable(s) caused by the independent variable(s) may not be accurate.

Factorial Experiment[526] – An experiment involving simultaneous study of more than one independent variable. Factor and level are two related terms. Factor is an independent variable in a factorial experiment, and level is a value of an independent variable in a factorial experiment. A benefit or strength of factorial experiment design is that it provides (or permits the provision of) dependent variable data to be collected for every possible combination of independent variables (i.e., factors) and their values (i.e., levels). Note: A 2 x 3 (read "two by three") factorial experiment means two factors (independent variables) with the first factor comprised of two levels (values) and the second factor comprised of three levels.

Field Experiment[526] – An experiment conducted in as natural a setting as possible (contrasted with an experiment conducted in a highly controlled laboratory setting). A field experiment should involve explicit thoughts/actions by the researchers not to make any more changes than essential in the naturalness of an experiment's setting and to be able still to conduct the experiment. The main advantage of a field experiment is its realistic, natural setting with the further advantage of potential for great reliability and external validity. Their potential weakness is internal validity. Its complement and in many ways its opposite is the lab experiment, which is normally conducted in a highly controlled setting that is necessarily a setting largely void of being natural.

Hypothesis[526] – An unproven proposition. In formal research projects, a hypothesis should: (1) state reality that is empirically testable, (2) respond directly to the research question(s), (3) express a precise statement that reflects relationships believed to exist between two or more variables (i.e., between an independent and a dependent variable), and (4) serve as a guide for design of all the other research project components.

Independent Variable[526] – A factor in an experiment that the researcher controls/manipulates in order to measure the effect it causes. It is commonly comprised of two or more values.

Independent Variable Value[526] – see Independent Variable.

Internal Validity[526] – see Validity. Specific type of validity concerning the extent that changes in an independent variable actually cause changes in a dependent variable. When an experiment does not achieve internal validity, it is potentially detrimental to the accuracy of the collected data and accuracy of related conclusions about findings. Its complement is external validity. Note: internal validity and external validity are not mutually exclusive in that it is usually necessary to forego some internal validity to increase the reality/natural setting (i.e., external validity) of an experiment. Common threats to internal validity are history effect, maturation effect, testing effect, instrumentation effect, statistical regression effect, selection effect, and mortality effect.

Interpersonal – Inter can express between, and interpersonal is between individuals such as how physical attractiveness affects the behavior and interactions between people.

Intrapersonal – Intra can express within, and intrapersonal is within an individual such as how physical attractiveness affects the personality and self-esteem within individual persons.

Lab Experiment[526] – An experiment conducted in a setting expressly prepared for the research project. Its main advantage is research control with the further advantage of the potential for great validity, especially internal validity. Its complement is field experiment. Potential weakness of lab experiments is external validity due to their highly controlled settings that are often necessarily void of being natural. Lab experiment is a phrase synonymous with laboratory experiment.

Laboratory Experiment – see Lab Experiment.

Literature Search[549] – see Secondary Data. Literature search is an examination of existing data, knowledge, or material collected, tabulated, or otherwise assembled for purposes not related directly to the current research project. These existing items are frequently the artifacts and outcomes of separate, largely unrelated research projects performed by separate researchers with no consideration for the current research project. Literature searches scrutinize and investigate existing research procedures and findings for information pertinent to a current research project. Credible research projects intended to collect primary data always first conduct a literature search to collect secondary data to provide context, foundation, and familiarity with the topic and existing knowledge.

Longitudinal Research – Research project conducted over an extended period, during which time researchers collect primary data spanning a period of months, years, or even decades. In contrast, a survey or experiment research typically collects primary data over a period of days or weeks.

Mesomorph – A person's body structure that is average or medium, including sometimes sturdy, strong, and sometimes well-developed muscular build.

Meta-Analysis Research – A research project that analyzes results from many other research projects performed independently with focus on a particular topic, essentially a study of studies. Meta-analysis research in some respects is a project that conducts a macro analysis or macro view to arrive at collective results made possible by bringing together and analyzing many microanalyses or micro views represented by a series of individual research projects.

Observation Research – Research projects in which participants are not aware of their participation and accordingly have no overt interaction between participants and researchers.

Obtrusive Research – Research projects in which participants are aware of their participation, such as the overt interaction required in survey research projects and as often required in experiment research projects that involve lab experiments. Its complement is unobtrusive research, also defined in this glossary.

Operational Definition – The actions or operations described to measure or define, the variable(s) of interest to a particular research project, especially useful for research variables without absolute or objective measures. While some variables that interest people can be objectively measured (e.g., height, weight, speed of a car, temperature of air, etc.), many variables that interest people cannot be so objectively measured (e.g., love, hate, depression, political goodwill, etc.). For physical attractiveness, researchers can employ a truth of consensus method whereby people judge the physical attractiveness of a stimulus person, and these collective judgments measure the person's level of physical attractiveness. (See Truth of Consensus, defined in this glossary.)

Operationally Defined – see Operational Definition.

Pearson Product-Moment Correlation Coefficient (lower case "r") – Measure of how well a linear equation describes the relation between two variables X and Y measures on the same object or organism.[739] The Pearson Product Moment Correlation Coefficient is the most widely used measure of correlation or association and the symbol for the correlation coefficient is lower case "r" described as the sum of the product of the z-scores for the two variables divided by the number of scores.[726]

Perceived Physical Attractiveness – see Physical Attractiveness. Perceived physical attractiveness is by and large the same as physical attractiveness because perception is reality in most considerations of physical attractiveness, except when a person's self-rating or a significant other's rating is contrasted with the ratings of a group of judges to whom the stimulus person is unknown. Although physical attractiveness is an esthetic versus an absolute, there is significant agreement in physical attractiveness ratings such that perceived physical attractiveness is, for all practical purposes, actual physical attractiveness.

Physical Attractiveness – How pleasing someone or something looks. Physical attractiveness is inextricably interrelated with, and largely inseparable from, appearance. Physical attractiveness ranges from high to low and serves as a respective informational cue within physical attractiveness phenomenon. In formal research projects, physical attractiveness is the extent to which a stimulus person is pleasing to observe. (This definition in no way intends to supersede other research manipulations of the physical attractiveness variable and is meant only to be an attempt to provide a common standard reference as the term is used in this book.) It might be further noted that operational definitions of physical attractiveness for conducting a particular research project is defined, as stated in this glossary for Truth of Consensus, as respective mean rating values combined with the variances or standard deviations in those rating values.

Physical Attractiveness Phenomenon – The collective realities of appearance as distinguished by, or aligned with, physical attractiveness. Physical attractiveness phenomenon is analogous to appearance phenomenon. For example, physical attractiveness phenomenon is the environment and apparatus that transforms physical attractiveness into a value that can be a blessing or curse, asset or liability, benefit or detriment. It can make the holder strong or weak, liked or disliked, and desired or undesired through which favorable and unfavorable consequences yield collective realities. Applied to people, physical attractiveness phenomenon surrounds, permeates, and includes all of us, and its impact spans our lives, from birth to death. Its impact is pervasive and powerful, while often unrecognized, unknown, or not admitted and denied. Physical attractiveness phenomenon takes place through a circular four-stage process that begins with the use of physical attractiveness as an informational cue.

Primary Data[549] – Data and other pieces of information collected for the purpose of the current particular research project. When different researchers, or even the same researchers, use these data later for another particular project, these primary data become secondary data as used for this separate, second research project. Normally, researchers collect primary data for a particular research project only after collecting and analyzing secondary data. Then, again, towards the end of the research project, researchers interpret the primary data and put forth respective findings with secondary data providing important foundation and context.

r (lower case "r," used in connection with a correlation value) – Lower case "r" is the standard universally-recognized symbol when combined with a statistical test correlation value, to report values calculated on data analyzed with the Pearson Product correlation coefficient statistical technique.[726] Also, see Pearson Product-Moment Correlation Coefficient.

Random Error[526] – Specific type of experimental error as named that occurs by chance. When it occurs, it is potentially detrimental to the accuracy of the collected data and accuracy of related conclusions.

Reliability[526] – Extent to which a measurement is free of error in terms of providing consistent information. Its complement is validity. When a research project, particularly an experiment, does not achieve reliability, it is potentially detrimental to the accuracy of the collected data and accuracy of reported findings and related conclusions.

Respondent[526] – A participant in a survey from whom information is collected. For research data and findings to be credible, these participants in a survey must accurately represent some larger group of people about whom researchers generalize information. Survey respondents know they are participating in a research project, but they frequently do not know in advance nor do they know during their participation what exactly is the purpose or focus of the research. Respondent is the term typically used to reference a participant in a survey, whereas subject is the term typically used to reference a participant in an experiment.

Secondary Data[549] – Data and other pieces of information that were earlier collected first for another research project other than a current particular research project. When researchers use data and findings for a current particular research project that researchers, themselves or more commonly other researchers, had collected from an earlier and separate research project, these data used for this later or second current project are correspondingly secondary data. Researchers typically collect and analyze these secondary data first, before collecting primary data. A literature search provides important secondary data. For most research, secondary data help formulate the research problem and hypotheses for which primary data will then be collected. Towards the end of the current research project, these secondary data again provide valuable foundation and context for researchers to interpret the newly collected primary data en route to deciding findings and making conclusions.

Sexiness[520]– The extent to which the appearance of a stimulus person arouses a sexual or an erotic idea in the observer's mind. This arousal may relate directly to one's own response to a stimulus person or it may be the observer's perceptions of others' response to a stimulus person.

Stimulus Person – The person whose physical attractiveness is rated, typically by subjects in a research project unaware of the experimental conditions under study and sometimes by judges whose ratings are used to establish a person's physical attractiveness to later be used in one or more experimental conditions.

Subject[526] – A participant in an experiment from or about whom information is collected. The intention is that these participants in an experiment will accurately represent some larger group of people about whom researchers will generalize information. Subjects may or may not know they are participants in a research project but they should never know in advance or during their participation the purpose or focus of the research or the independent variable manipulations. Subject is the term typically used to reference a participant in an experiment, whereas respondent is the term typically used to reference a participant in a survey.

Survey[526] – A research design/procedure to test a hypothesis that a relationship, typically a relationship of correlation or association, exists between two variables (contrasted with a causal relationship common for experiments). The test focuses on measuring frequency or extent that one variable is present or not present when another variable is present or not present. Survey is a term also used synonymously to reference a questionnaire completed by respondents.

Survey Research – see Survey.

Survey Research Design – see Survey.

Truth of Consensus – A procedure used in physical attractiveness phenomenon research to measure or determine, in other words to define, a person's physical attractiveness. It requires statistical analysis of mean values of evaluation scores about a stranger's physical attractiveness and variances/standard evaluations of those values, and permits research to establish, manipulate, and study the physical attractiveness variable with scientifically sound validity and reliability, which then permits conclusions based on data that accurately documents and contributes to understanding physical attractiveness phenomenon. Furthermore, it largely is not critical whether a specific characteristic or the overall appearance is the determinant of physical attractiveness. If a substantial number of judges rate a stimulus person as high or low in physical attractiveness, then, for research purposes, this stimulus person represents that respective level of physical attractiveness.

Unobtrusive Research – Research projects in which participants typically are not aware of their participation, such as observation research in contrast to research conducted through surveys or experiments. Its complement is obtrusive research.

Validity[526] – Extent to which a measurement is free of error in terms of providing information intended. When an experiment does not achieve this validity, it is potentially detrimental to the accuracy of the collected data and accuracy of related conclusions. Its complement is reliability, which is also defined in this glossary.

Index

About the Author

Gordon L. Patzer, Ph.D., is respected and recognized internationally for his expertise concerning physical attractiveness phenomenon. Hundreds of researchers and scholars have cited formally his published analyses and perspectives, while scores of reporters for popular mass media have published interview quotes. His commitment to scientifically understand the psychology and sociology of physical attractiveness at levels far more than meets the eye and far beyond skin deep is a long-term quest. The national American primetime television news program *Dateline NBC*, while featuring his expert analyses on-camera for an investigative segment broadcast in 2004, reported that, "Dr. Patzer has spent more than 30 years studying physical attractiveness."

Interviews with Dr. Patzer discussing physical attractiveness phenomenon have been reported by the Associated Press, published by newspapers from west coast USA (*Los Angeles Times*) to east coast USA *(Boston Sunday Herald)* to England *(Sunday Correspondent*, London), magazines (*Harper's Bazaar, ELLE, Working Woman, Self Magazine*, and *Los Angeles Times Magazine*), on radio in large and small American markets, and on the Internet (*WebMD*, MSNBC, CNN.com, online magazines internationally, and blog discussions originating in many countries). *The Today Show on NBC*, a national morning talk-and-news television program, featured him on-camera for a research news segment broadcast in 2005 about employment and pay differences caused by physical attractiveness. Recent endorsement review comments from professionals, available on request, further emphasize his respected and recognized expertise.

Dr. Patzer has succeeded in executive positions in and out of academia. These include more than ten years as a university dean, ten years as a university department chair, and progress up professorial ranks to tenured professor, as well as earning a Ph.D., MBA, MS, and BA. Business employments have focused on organizational strategy for consumer / audience behavior in primetime programming at CBS Television Network and in the movie industry at Saatchi & Saatchi. Earlier, as an entrepreneur, he started two small businesses: a talent booking agency and an employment agency. International travels have spanned Argentina, Australia, Brazil, Canada, China, Czechoslovakia, England, France, Germany, Guatemala, Hong Kong, Ireland, Italy, Japan, Macau, Mexico, New Zealand, Nicaragua, Poland, Russia, San Salvador, Switzerland, and Thailand. Prior to accepting a dean's position at Roosevelt University in Chicago, California State University honored his service while a dean with their lifetime title of Professor Emeritus.